Roberto Posenato · Irene Vanderfeesten
Editors

Advanced Information Systems Engineering Workshops

CAiSE 2026 Workshops
Verona, Italy, June 8–12, 2026
Proceedings

Springer

Editors
Roberto Posenato
University of Verona
Verona, Italy

Irene Vanderfeesten
KU Leuven
Brussels, Belgium

ISSN 1865-1348 ISSN 1865-1356 (electronic)
Lecture Notes in Business Information Processing
ISBN 978-3-032-28159-3 ISBN 978-3-032-28160-9 (eBook)
https://doi.org/10.1007/978-3-032-28160-9

This Springer imprint is published by the registered company Springer Nature Switzerland AG
The registered company address is: Gewerbestrasse 11, 6330 Cham, Switzerland

Preface

The 38th edition of the CAiSE conference, held from 8–12 June 2026 in Verona, Italy, brought together the international Information Systems Engineering community under the theme *"Rethinking Information Systems Engineering in a continuously changing information systems world."* As part of the conference program, the CAiSE workshops were held on 8–9 June, providing a vibrant setting in which researchers, practitioners, and students could explore emerging topics, exchange ideas, present early-stage research, and engage in focused discussions that complemented the main conference.

This proceedings volume brings together the contributions presented across the CAiSE 2026 workshops. Each workshop offered a unique lens on contemporary challenges—from conceptual modeling, requirements engineering, and business process management to data governance, socio-technical systems, and domain-specific applications. The papers collected here reflect the diversity and richness of these themes, showcasing both foundational advances and exploratory work that pushes the boundaries of established research areas.

Eight workshops were part of the CAiSE 2026 program. Of these, only EPAIS 2026 did not contribute papers to this volume:

- **GenSyn 2026 – 2nd Workshop on Generation of Synthetic Datasets for Information Systems.** Focused on methods, tools, and evaluation techniques for generating synthetic datasets to support machine learning, simulation, digital twins, and information systems engineering.
- **MIDas4CS 2026 – 4th Workshop on Modelling and Implementation of Digital Twins for Complex Systems.** Addressed conceptual modeling, architectures, and implementation approaches for Digital Twins in complex socio-technical and cyber-physical environments.
- **LLM–SOA 2026 – 2nd Workshop on Large Language Models for Service-Oriented Architectures and Systems Design.** Explored the role of large language models in software architecture, service discovery, and system design.
- **BC4ISE 2026 – 2nd International Workshop on Blockchain for Information Systems Engineering.** Examined blockchain-enabled information systems, including smart contracts, decentralized governance, interoperability, and trustworthy data management.
- **EASI 2026 – 1st International Workshop on Engineering Autonomous Systems Intelligence.** Investigated the interplay between autonomous systems and information systems, with a focus on AI-enabled autonomy, data governance, and socio-technical integration.
- **CAI 2026 – 2nd Workshop on Compliance in the Era of Artificial Intelligence.** Discussed the challenges and opportunities of AI-driven compliance, including regulatory alignment, risk management, explainability, and responsible AI in organizational processes.

- **HybridAIMS 2026 – 4th Workshop on Hybrid Artificial Intelligence and Enterprise Modelling.** Brought together symbolic AI, machine learning, and enterprise modeling to advance hybrid intelligent systems and neuro-symbolic approaches for organizational decision-making.
- **EPAIS 2026 – Engineering and Operations of Process-Aware Information Systems.** Collaboratively identified key topics for a research roadmap on process-aware information systems (PAIS), addressing open challenges and outlining visions for how to engineer and operate these systems.

All workshops invited research papers for presentation, except EPAIS, which followed a discussion-oriented format.

The workshops attracted a total of:

- **67** submissions,
- of which **25** were accepted as full papers and **8** as short papers.

The selection process was based on reviews from three program committee members per submission, using a single-blind evaluation scheme. In addition to contributed research papers, several workshops also featured keynote presentations and discussion papers, enriching the overall program.

We extend our sincere gratitude to the workshop organizers for their excellent work in shaping the programs, coordinating reviews, and fostering engaging discussions that made these events possible. We also thank the members of the program committees and all reviewers for their timely, thoughtful, and constructive evaluations, as well as the publicity chairs for their efforts in attracting high-quality submissions. Our appreciation further goes to the Workshops Proceedings Chair, Anna Bernasconi, and to Springer for their efficient communication and support throughout the production process. We warmly acknowledge the General Co-chairs, Carlo Combi and Hajo Reijers, as well as the entire CAiSE organization team, for their invaluable support. Finally, we thank all authors for their contributions and for choosing the CAiSE workshops as a venue to share their research with the community.

We hope that this volume will serve not only as a record of the work presented but also as a source of inspiration for future research. The CAiSE workshops continue to demonstrate the value of collaborative exploration and open dialogue, and we are pleased to present these proceedings as a testament to that spirit.

June 2026

Roberto Posenato
Irene Vanderfeesten

Organization

Chairs

Roberto Posenato	University of Verona, Italy
Irene Vanderfeesten	KU Leuven, Belgium

GENSYN

2nd Workshop on Generation of Synthetic Datasets for Information Systems

In the age of advanced information systems, data plays a crucial role in deploying those systems in real-world applications, as well as in empirical evaluations of proposed systems. However, collecting that data in usable benchmarks is often challenging due to privacy concerns, limited sources, and legal or ethical constraints. The advent of generative AI models has revolutionized different fields, as demonstrated by recent events. In particular, the generation of synthetic datasets has become valuable for machine learning-related tasks, even though generating datasets that accurately reflect real-world systems while ensuring data representativeness remains challenging. In particular, synthetic datasets can support and improve data-driven applications, AI and model-based systems, modern, innovation-driving paradigms such as the IoT and Digital Twins, and models for business processes and (co-)simulation.

The *Second Workshop on Generation of Synthetic Datasets for Information Systems (GenSyn)* was held in conjunction with the 38th International Conference on Advanced Information Systems Engineering (CAiSE), in Verona, Italy. The workshop provided a forum to discuss both generative AI and classical techniques for creating synthetic datasets for AI and non-AI information systems, presenting state-of-the-art tools and approaches.

This year, we received six submissions. For each paper, three single-blind reviews were collected. Considering the reviews and the maximum acceptance rate of Springer (which is set around 50%), we accepted three papers, one regular paper and two short ones. All submissions were reviewed by three members of the Program Committee following a single-blind review process, ensuring the quality and relevance of the selected contributions. We sincerely thank all the authors who presented at the GenSyn workshop and the Program Committee members who supported this process.

In "Benchmarking Natural Language Database Conversational Agents", Lenzi et al. propose an automated method for verifying the performance of LLM-based agents on databases before the agent is deployed. The method consists of a procedure for generating a dialogue test dataset (TD) specific to the original dataset and an evaluation agent that, using TD, automatically assesses the performance of the agent using the set of metrics defined in the paper.

In "Synthetic log generation under control-flow conditions using autoregressive models", Kuhn et al. propose a Petri Net Conditioned Synthesizer (PNC-SYN) to generate synthetic logs that are conformant with a given normative Petri net. In particular, the main contribution is a generation mechanism that enforces control-flow conformance by construction while retaining a data-driven component for learning realistic sequential and temporal patterns.

In “Graphtender: An Interactive Generator of Absence-Aware Synthetic Graph Datasets”, Calderon et al. propose Graphtender, a web-based tool that treats node omission as a first-class explanatory variable when synthesizing graph datasets. The use of a structured generation framework ensures that absence-based explanations are systematically embedded in the graphs, enabling the validation of explainability methods that more faithfully capture the dynamics of evolving information systems.

June 2026

Dominik Bork
Claudio Di Sipio
Arianna Fedeli
Riccardo Rubei
Paul Tiwald

Organization

Workshop Chairs

Dominik Bork	TU Wien, Austria
Claudio Di Sipio	Johannes Kepler University Linz, Austria
Arianna Fedeli	Gran Sasso Science Institute, Italy
Riccardo Rubei	Mälardalen University, Sweden
Paul Tiwald	MostlyAI, Austria

Program Committee

Adem Ait Fonollà	University of Luxembourg, Luxembourg
Andrea Maldonado Hernandez	TU Munich, Germany
Boqi Chen	McGill University, Canada
Charlotte Verbruggen	TU Wien, Austria
James Pontes Miranda	CEA-List, France
José Antonio Hernández López	University of Murcia, Spain
Martin Kuhn	DFKI, Germany
Pablo Gomez Abajo	Universidad Autónoma de Madrid, Spain
Stefan Klikovits	Johannes Kepler Universität Linz, Austria

MIDas4CS

4th Workshop on Modelling and Implementation of Digital Twins for Complex Systems

The concept of Digital Twins (DTs) has gained significant traction in recent years, evolving from its origins in the context of Smart Industry (Industry 4.0) into a broad paradigm for representing, analyzing, and managing complex systems. A Digital Twin can be understood as a digital representation of a physical or conceptual counterpart, whose scope may range from individual objects and processes to large-scale socio-technical systems and cyber-physical environments. This counterpart may be tangible or intangible, continuously evolving through data-driven feedback loops between the physical and digital worlds.

Digital Twins offer a wide range of benefits, including real-time monitoring and control, predictive maintenance, scenario analysis, and improved decision-making. More recently, their role has expanded toward enabling explainability, governance, and integration with Artificial Intelligence techniques, including data-driven and hybrid approaches. As such, DTs are increasingly positioned at the intersection of modeling, data management, and intelligent system design.

The *Fourth Workshop on Modelling and Implementation of Digital Twins for Complex Systems (MIDas4CS 2026)* was held in conjunction with the 38th International Conference on Advanced Information Systems Engineering (CAiSE 2026), in Verona, Italy. The workshop provided a forum for researchers and practitioners to explore methods, tools, and applications for modeling and implementing Digital Twins in complex domains.

This year's edition featured five regular papers and one short paper that reflect both foundational and emerging directions in the field.

In "From Associational to Causality-Aware Digital Twins: An Architectural Framework", Raju et al. present a conceptual architecture that extends Digital Twins with causal modeling, prior knowledge integration, and uncertainty quantification. The approach supports capabilities such as intervention analysis and counterfactual reasoning, and is illustrated in domains characterized by high uncertainty, such as healthcare.

In "Event-Driven Digital Twins", Picone et al. present an event-driven architectural approach for Digital Twins based on reactive and asynchronous mechanisms. The architecture supports modular and configurable designs, enabling real-time interactions between physical and digital components. The approach is illustrated through a healthcare emergency management scenario and evaluated using open-source Digital Twin solutions.

In "Digital Twins and World Models: A Systematic Taxonomic Disambiguation", Suri and Arnez propose a taxonomy to distinguish Digital Twins from World Models.

By defining key criteria and comparing the two paradigms across multiple dimensions, the work clarifies their differences and relationships.

In “Digital Process Twin Classification and Software Selection”, Kremer et al. propose an approach that links Digital Process Twin characteristics to required software capabilities. Based on a consolidated metamodel, they introduce a technology radar to support the assessment and selection of suitable tools, bridging conceptual modeling and practical implementation.

In “AI Compliance-Threaded Digital Twins in Critical Infrastructure”, Dzhusupova and van den Brand present a framework that integrates regulatory compliance into the lifecycle of AI-enabled Digital Twins. The approach links obligations from the EU AI Act to different roles across the value chain and embeds compliance-related information within the Digital Twin to support traceability and governance across distributed and multi-organizational settings.

In “A Symbolic Virtual World for Training Agents in Cross-World Exploration”, Sawyerr introduces a symbolic virtual environment designed to support the training and evaluation of agents across multiple scenarios. The approach models cross-world exploration as a meta-decision problem and incorporates configurable regime parameters, while maintaining alignment with real-world environments through adapter-based integration.

Together, these papers highlight the growing maturity of the field while also pointing to open challenges in modeling, interoperability, and trustworthy deployment.

All submissions were reviewed by three members of the Program Committee following a single-blind review process, ensuring the quality and relevance of the selected contributions.

We would like to thank all authors for their valuable submissions and for their interest in the workshop. We are also grateful to the members of the Program Committee for their careful and constructive reviews. Finally, we sincerely thank the CAiSE 2026 workshop chairs and the entire organizing team for their support in making this workshop possible.

We hope that the reader will find this collection of papers insightful and useful for advancing research and practice in the field of Digital Twins for complex systems.

June 2026

Pedro Valderas
Fabrizio Fornari
Luís Ferreira Pires
Marten van Sinderen
João Moreira

Organization

Workshop Chairs

Massimiliano Garda	University of Brescia, Italy
Ada Bagozi	University of Brescia, Italy
Ilche Georgievski	University of Stuttgart, Germany

Advisory Board

Massimo Mecella	University of Rome "La Sapienza", Italy
Monique Snoeck	KU Leuven, Belgium
Barbara Pernici	Politecnico di Milano, Italy
Devis Bianchini	University of Brescia, Italy

Program Committee

Amirali Amiri	TU Wien, Austria
Maurizio Atzori	University of Cagliari, Italy
Nicola Bena	University of Milan, Italy
Marwa Boulakbech	Aix-Marseille University, France
Christian Decker	University of Reutlingen, Germany
Andrea Delgado	Universidad de la República, Uruguay
Joyce El Haddad	Paris Dauphine University - PSL, France
Kyriakos Kritikos	University of the Aegean & ICS-FORTH, Greece
Indika Kumara	Tilburg University - Jheronimus Academy of Data Science, Netherlands
Mingyi Liu	Harbin Institute of Technology, China
Yan Liu	Concordia University, Canada
Lara Mauri	University of Milan, Italy
Michele Melchiori	University of Brescia, Italy
Flavia Monti	University of Rome "La Sapienza", Italy
José Antonio Parejo Maestre	University of Sevilla, Spain
Mohamed Ragab	Birmingham City University, UK
Stephan Reiff-Marganiec	University of Derby, UK
Christian Zirpins	Karlsruhe University of Applied Sciences, Germany

BC4ISE

2nd Workshop on Blockchain for Information Systems Engineering

Blockchain technology supports decentralized, transparent, and immutable transaction execution and storage. The advent of smart contracts has provided the opportunity to manage digital assets and implement business logic on blockchain platforms. Thanks to its characteristics, blockchain enables mutually distrusting parties to share data in a trusted way, without requiring third-party authorities. Its execution environment also offers additional trust guarantees, enhancing auditing and verification activities.

The distinctive nature of blockchain technology and its application in novel Information Systems (IS) raise challenges from different perspectives. From a conceptual perspective, important challenges revolve around requirements engineering, modeling, integration, governance, and system evolution. From a technical perspective, the development of blockchain-based IS raises challenges related to data sharing, data management, system optimization, and the adoption of on- and off-chain solutions.

These opportunities and challenges have generated a strong and continuously growing interest from industry and academia in the engineering of blockchain-based information systems. To help further expand knowledge around this technology and provide relevant answers to blockchain-specific engineering questions, we organized the second edition of the Blockchain for Information Systems Engineering (BC4ISE) workshop.

The workshop was held in conjunction with the 38th International Conference on Advanced Information Systems Engineering (CAiSE 2026), a well-established conference series addressing contemporary information systems engineering topics. We invited researchers working in fields including conceptual modeling, ontology engineering, business process modeling and analysis, and information systems to submit contributions to the workshop. Eleven papers were submitted; one was out of scope, and each of the other ten received two single-blind reviews. Taking into consideration the reviews and Springer's maximum acceptance rate, three full papers and one short paper were accepted and presented.

As chairs of the BC4ISE workshop, we would like to express our gratitude to the chairs of the CAiSE conference, to all the people who contributed to the organization of the workshop, and to the authors for their valuable contributions. We look forward to meeting again at the third edition of BC4ISE in 2027!

June 2026

Alessandro Marcelletti
Sarah Bouraga
Felix Härer

Organization

Workshop Chairs

Alessandro Marcelletti	University of Camerino, Italy
Sarah Bouraga	EM Normandie Business School, France
Felix Härer	FHNW University of Applied Sciences and Arts, Switzerland

Program Committee

Marco Comuzzi	Ulsan National Institute of Science and Technology, South Korea
Claudio Di Ciccio	University of Utrecht, The Netherlands
Nicolas Herbaut	Paris 1 Panthéon-Sorbonne University, France
Tiphaine Henry	Université Paris-Saclay, CEA, France
Julius Köpke	University of Klagenfurt, Austria
Wim Laurier	Saint-Louis University, Brussels, Belgium
Edoardo Marangone	Sapienza University of Rome, Italy
Giovanni Meroni	Technical University of Denmark, Denmark
Andrea Morichetta	University of Camerino, Italy
Georgios Palaiokrassas	Yale University, USA
Barbara Re	University of Camerino, Italy
Francesco Tiezzi	University of Florence, Italy

Organization

Workshop Chairs

Sara Pettinari	Gran Sasso Science Institute, Italy
Iva Vasic	University of Fribourg, Switzerland
Yannis Bertrand	Hasselt University, Belgium

Program Committee

Janik-Vasily Benzin	Technical University of Munich, Germany
Edyta Brzychczy	AGH University of Science and Technology, Poland
Roberto Casadei	University of Bologna, Italy
Ivan Compagnucci	Gran Sasso Science Institute, Italy
Martina De Sanctis	Gran Sasso Science Institute, Italy
Agnes Koschmider	University of Bayreuth, Germany
Andrea Marrella	Sapienza University of Rome, Italy
Marko Milojkovic	University of Niš, Serbia
Darko Mitic	University of Niš, Serbia
Jesus Munoz Cadiz	University of Fribourg, Switzerland
Nenad Petrovic	University of Niš, Serbia
Barbara Re	University of Camerino, Italy
Stefanie Rinderle-Ma	Technical University of Munich, Germany
Lorenzo Rossi	University of Camerino, Italy
Ronny Seiger	University of St. Gallen, Switzerland
Mohsen Shirali	Catholic University of Louvain, Belgium
Francesco Tiezzi	University of Florence, Italy

Additional Reviewer

Arvid Lepsien	Kiel University, Germany

CAI

2nd Workshop on Compliance in the Era of Artificial Intelligence

The 2nd Workshop on Compliance in the Era of Artificial Intelligence (CAI) explored the evolving role of compliance in business processes and information systems. As organizations face stringent regulatory requirements, such as GDPR, SOX, AML, and ISO standards, compliance is increasingly vital to operational strategy, helping organizations to avoid penalties, protect reputations, and remain competitive.

In addition to traditional methods like control definition, risk assessment, compliance monitoring and reporting, CAI focuses on how emerging technologies, particularly Artificial Intelligence (AI) and Large Language Models (LLMs), can transform compliance management. These tools can automate repetitive tasks, process large datasets, enhance risk detection, and ensure real-time alignment with regulations, offering a more efficient and scalable approach.

The second edition of CAI received eight submissions. Each submission underwent a thorough review process by three members of the Program Committee, ensuring high-quality feedback and selection. As a result, two regular and two visionary papers were accepted for inclusion in the proceedings. The papers were presented at the workshop, held in conjunction with the CAiSE 2026 conference in Verona, Italy, and sparked engaging discussions among participants. The four accepted papers encompassed a diverse range of compliance topics.

In *A Neuro-symbolic Framework for Compliance Management with Declarative Models, Varvoutas et al.* present a neuro-symbolic framework for eliciting and refining a normative model from regulatory texts. The resulting model, expressed as a Multi-perspective Dynamic Condition Response graph, can be used to check the compliance of existing cases with applicable law, and compliance violations can be verbalized to different stakeholders using a Large Language Model.

In *From Architecture to Compliance: A Model-Driven Assessment of AI Systems, Ekeh et al.* focus on the challenge of supporting the assessment of compliance coverage in AI systems. To address this challenge, the paper proposes an AI asset system model and an architectural approach which help to identify compliance gaps in AI systems.

In *Trustworthy Robotic Process Automation: Challenges and Emerging Research Directions, Agostinelli et al.* propose a research agenda for trust in Robotic Process Automation (RPA). The paper identifies five key challenges that emerged from a Dagstuhl seminar and include, e.g., the need for calibration between trust and trustworthiness, as well as the need to conduct experimental studies to investigate trust in RPA.

In *Detecting Gender Patterns in Programming Datasets: Towards Compliance and AI Governance, De Luzi et al.* follow a design science research approach to develop a methodological pipeline that reveals structural programming patterns potentially related to gender in educational datasets. This artifact helps to support fairness-aware auditing and compliance in AI-enabled learning systems and was evaluated in a case study based on an introductory programming exam of a university-level Foundations of Computer Science course.

The organizers wish to thank all the authors who submitted papers to CAI 2026, the many participants who contributed to fruitful discussions, and the CAI 2026 Program Committee members for their valuable work in reviewing the submissions. We look forward to future editions of the workshop.

June 2026

Cristina Cabanillas
Andrea Marrella
Monica Palmirani
Manuel Resinas
Karolin Winter

Organization

Workshop Chairs

Cristina Cabanillas	University of Seville, Spain
Andrea Marrella	Sapienza University of Rome, Italy
Monica Palmirani	University of Bologna, Italy
Manuel Resinas	University of Seville, Spain
Karolin Winter	Eindhoven University of Technology, Netherlands

Program Committee

Simone Agostinelli	Universitas Mercatorum, Italy
Francesca De Luzi	Sapienza University of Rome, Italy
Walid Fdhila	University of Vienna, Austria
Pablo Fernandez	University of Seville, Spain
Chiara Di Francescomarino	University of Trento, Italy
Laura Genga	Eindhoven University of Technology, Netherlands
Hugo A. López	University of Copenhagen, Denmark
Raimundas Matulevičius	University of Tartu, Estonia
Marco Montali	Free University of Bozen-Bolzano, Italy
Roberto Nai	University of Turin, Italy
Luise Pufahl	TU Munich, Germany
Jana-Rebecca Rehse	University of Mannheim, Germany
Emilio Sulis	University of Turin, Italy

HybridAIMS

4th Workshop on Hybrid Artificial Intelligence and Enterprise Modelling

Hybrid Artificial Intelligence continues to gain momentum as a research paradigm that bridges sub-symbolic AI—including machine learning, Large Language Models, and Generative AI—with symbolic AI—encompassing ontologies, Knowledge Graphs, rule-based systems, and formal logic. By combining the pattern-recognition capabilities of neural approaches with the reasoning, transparency, and constraint-enforcement strengths of symbolic methods, Hybrid AI offers a principled path toward more robust, explainable, and trustworthy Intelligent Information Systems.

Over the past year, this convergence has accelerated. Large Language Models are increasingly augmented with structured knowledge representations to ground their outputs in verifiable facts and domain-specific rules. At the same time, symbolic frameworks benefit from neural components that make them more adaptive and scalable. These developments raise new research questions around architecture design, evaluation methodology, and governance—particularly in regulated and resource-constrained environments where transparency, sovereignty, and compliance are non-negotiable.

Building such systems remains a deeply interdisciplinary endeavor. It requires expertise spanning sub-symbolic and symbolic AI, software engineering, and—critically—the application domain itself. Involving domain experts from the earliest stages of development improves system quality, yet collaboration across business, domain, IT, and AI stakeholders is often hindered by divergent perspectives, terminologies, and expectations.

Enterprise Modeling (EM) addresses this challenge by providing well-founded theories and graphical notations for the conceptual representation, design, implementation, and analysis of information systems. EM facilitates alignment between the business and technical worlds, improving communication and enabling more informed decision-making among heterogeneous stakeholder groups.

The integration of Hybrid Artificial Intelligence with Enterprise Modeling therefore holds significant promise: it combines the analytical and reasoning power of hybrid AI with the stakeholder-oriented, model-driven rigor of EM, advancing the design and implementation of Intelligent Information Systems that are at once capable, interpretable, and aligned with organizational goals.

HybridAIMS 2026 invited contributions to explore this intersection—from foundational methods and architectures to applications, evaluations, and governance frameworks—as the community works toward intelligent information systems that are technically sound, trustworthy, and practically valuable.

HybridAIMS 2026 received eleven high-quality international submissions. Each paper was subjected to a single-blind review by two to three members of the Program

Committee. The top four manuscripts were accepted for publication as full papers and one as a short paper. All the papers were presented on June 8–9, 2026. Hans-Friedrich Witschel was in charge of the workshop's review process.

We thank the authors for their noteworthy contributions and the members of the Program Committee for their invaluable help in the reviewing and discussion phases. We hope that the reader will benefit from reading these papers to learn more about the latest advances in research about the convergence of Hybrid Artificial Intelligence and Enterprise Modeling.

Full papers. Angelica Berdini *et al.* proposed and evaluated a hybrid AI framework that combines large language models with a scientific knowledge graph to generate more explainable, traceable, and effective biomedical hypotheses for expert analysis.

Eveline Walker *et al.* presented a knowledge graph-grounded low-code system that enables language teachers—without technical expertise—to create and maintain chatbot-ready educational content. It shows that this approach effectively abstracts ontology complexity, allowing teachers to act as citizen developers in building domain-specific educational chatbots.

Aritha Kumarasinghe and Marite Kirikova proposed a multi-step, schema-aware RAG approach that retrieves Enterprise Architecture (ArchiMate) model elements more efficiently for use with large language models. While achieving similar response quality to a baseline method, it significantly reduces token usage by up to sixfold.

Alessandro Berti *et al.* introduced an unsupervised method to derive interpretable execution states from object-centric event logs by encoding event sequences and mapping them to self-organizing maps to detect transitions. It demonstrates how these learned states can be linked to operational regimes (e.g., stock levels) and used to support decision-making through policy matrices.

Short paper. Adam Aron Rynkiewicz *et al.* showed how to enhance semi-automatic extraction of Petri net models from biomedical literature by introducing iterative document-aware extraction and a multi-agent verification framework to improve evidence tracking and reduce unsupported relations. They demonstrated that this approach produces more reliable and traceable outputs for expert curation, trading some recall for higher-quality, evidence-grounded results.

The Keynote. Ivan Donadello, from the Free University of Bozen-Bolzano, delivered a keynote titled "Neuro-symbolic Artificial Intelligence and Process Mining: a Promising Marriage" that explored the intersection of two complementary AI paradigms—sub-symbolic AI (notably neural networks) and symbolic AI (knowledge representation and reasoning)—and how their combination under the Neuro-symbolic AI (NeSy AI) umbrella can address longstanding limitations of each approach in isolation. While neural networks excel at robust learning from noisy data, symbolic systems offer expressivity, semantic grounding, and explainable reasoning; NeSy AI seeks to harness both strengths in a unified framework. The talk surveyed the foundational concepts of NeSy AI and examined its applicability to Process Mining, with a particular focus on Predictive Process Monitoring. Several NeSy frameworks developed for this domain were presented, and promising research directions at the crossroads of NeSy AI and process-oriented data analysis were outlined

The Fireside Chat. The workshop also featured a fireside chat with Alessandro Oltramari, from the Carnegie Bosch Institute (at Carnegie Mellon University, College of Engineering). Drawing on his extensive experience at the intersection of knowledge representation and machine learning, Oltramari shared his personal journey in bringing NeSy AI from academic research into industrial projects at Bosch. The conversation touched on the strategic value of integrating structured knowledge representations with neural models to build more robust and explainable intelligent systems—a paradigm that, as Oltramari illustrated, is already generating tangible results for Bosch across domains such as context-aware decision intelligence, autonomous systems, and smart environments. His reflections offered the audience a rare industry perspective on the practical challenges and opportunities of transitioning NeSy AI from research prototypes to production-grade solutions.

June 2026

Emanuele Laurenzi
Hans-Friedrich Witschel
Óscar Pastor
Peter Haase
Marco Montali

Organization

Workshop Chairs

Emanuele Laurenzi	FHNW - University of Applied Sciences and Arts Northwestern Switzerland
Hans-Friedrich Witschel	FHNW - University of Applied Sciences and Arts Northwestern Switzerland
Óscar Pastor	Polytechnic University of Valencia, Spain
Peter Haase	metaphacts, Germany
Marco Montali	Free University of Bozen-Bolzano, Italy

Program Committee

Kurt Sandkuhl	University of Rostock, Germany
Heiko Maus	Research Center for AI (DFKI), Germany
Frank van Harmelen	Vrije Universiteit Amsterdam, The Netherlands
Giancarlo Guizzardi	University of Twente, The Netherlands
Alessandro Oltramari	Carnegie Mellon University & Bosch Research Technology Center, USA
Pascal Hitzler	Kansas State University, USA
Steven Alter	University of San Francisco, USA
Aurona Gerber	Stellenbosch University, South Africa
Robert Andrei Buchmann	Babeş-Bolyai University of Cluj Napoca, Romania
Henderik A. Proper	TU Wien, Austria
Dominik Bork	TU Wien, Austria
Jānis Grabis	Riga Technical University, Latvia
Raimundas Matulevičius	University of Tartu, Estonia
Knut Hinkelmann	FHNW, Switzerland
Andreas Martin	FHNW, Switzerland
Stefano Borgo	CNR-ISTC, Italy
Maria Luisa Sapino	University of Turin, Italy
Massimo Callisto De Donato	University of Camerino, Italy

Contents

GENSYN

MIDas4CS

LLM-SOA

BC4ISE

HybridAIMS

GENSYN

Benchmarking Natural Language Database Conversational Agents

Tomás P. Lenzi[1], Eduardo R. S. Nascimento[1,3], Matheus O. Silva[3], Grettel M. García[1], Yenier T. Izquierdo[1], Michelle S. P. Facina[2], Isabela G. Siqueira[2], Melissa Lemos[1,3], and Marco A. Casanova[1,3](✉)

[1] Instituto Tecgraf, PUC-Rio, Rio de Janeiro, RJ 22451-900, Brazil
{lenzitomas,rogerrsn,ggarcia,ytorres,melissa}@tecgraf.puc-rio.br, casanova@inf.puc-rio.br

[2] Petrobras, Rio de Janeiro, RJ 20231–030, Brazil
{michelle.facina,isabela.siqueira}@petrobras.com.br

[3] Departamento de Informática, PUC-Rio, Rio de Janeiro, RJ 22451–900, Brazil
matheusolivsilv.ai@gmail.com

Abstract. This paper addresses the problem of testing a natural language database conversational agent for a given database D. The paper first introduces a procedure to create a dialogue test dataset T_D for D, a collection of dialogue performance metrics, and an evaluation agent that simulates a user interacting with the database conversational agent over D, guided by T_D. The procedure that creates the dialogue test datasets simulates a user navigating through the database schema. The paper then describes a set of experiments using four databases, including an industrial database that is in production. The experiments suggest that the dialogue test datasets and the evaluation agent help differentiate the performance of database conversational agents across the databases of interest before deployment.

Keywords: Conversational Text-to-SQL · AI Agents · ReAct · Large Language Models · Relational Databases

1 Introduction

Natural language database conversational agents allow users to interact with databases through dialogues formulated in their language. They typically permit users to formulate a question step-by-step and express a new question by referring to an older one or to a previously defined context. Once the user's question is understood, the interface translates it into an SQL query to retrieve the desired data from the database.

This paper concentrates on a practical problem, namely:

R. Posenato and I. Vanderfeesten (Eds.): CAiSE 2026 Workshops, LNBIP 586, pp. 3–11, 2026.
https://doi.org/10.1007/978-3-032-28160-9_1

The Conversational Test Problem (CTP): Given a database D, how to assess the performance of a natural language database conversational agent over D?

The central contribution of the paper is to address the Conversational Test Problem for a given database D by defining a collection of dialogue performance metrics, a procedure to create a dialogue test dataset T_D specific to D, and an evaluation agent that simulates a user interacting with the database conversational agent over D, guided by the dialogue test dataset T_D.

The paper includes a set of experiments with database conversational agents designed for the Mondial database [5], an industrial database, and the Formula 1 and Super Hero databases from the BIRD benchmark [7], using dialogue test datasets automatically generated for these databases and the evaluation agent.

This paper is organized as follows. Section 2 covers related work. Section 3 introduces a database conversational agent architecture and discusses implementations. Section 4 details the construction of dialogue test datasets. Section 5 focuses on the automated evaluation of database conversational agents. Section 6 describes the experiments. Finally, Sect. 7 contains the conclusions.

2 Related Work

MultiSQL [6] extends previous conversational text-to-SQL benchmarks in three key aspects: diverse SQL operations, schema-integrated context, and extended dialogues. It comprises nearly 800 dialogue groups and over 9,000 interaction turns across 166 complex databases.

PRACTIQ [2] is a practical conversational text-to-SQL dataset, based on Spider, consisting of 2,800 conversations with ambiguous and unanswerable questions.

MMSQL [3] is a comprehensive test suite designed to evaluate LLMs' question classification and SQL generation capabilities by simulating real-world scenarios with diverse question types and multi-turn Q&A interactions.

Lastly, BIRD-INTERACT [4] is a multi-turn benchmark based on fixed, predefined databases.

The above dialogue benchmarks are not designed to test natural language database conversational agents on a given database. Thus, rather than relying on generic benchmarks, this paper introduces a procedure to create a dialogue test dataset T_D specifically for assessing the performance of database conversational agents on a given database D. Therefore, this approach differs from previous benchmarks, which are based on fixed, predefined databases.

The paper defines metrics to assess the performance of database conversational agents and describes an evaluation agent that computes these metrics. The evaluation agent simulates a user dialogue with a database conversational agent for D by reading a dialogue test dataset T_D created for D.

Table 1. Benchmark Statistics.

Database	# Tables	# Cols	# Dialogues	# Interactions	Text-to-SQL Tool
Mondial	46	184	50	149	DFE tool
Industrial	27	585	50	140	KwS-assisted tool
Formula 1	13	94	23	69	Basic tool
Super Hero	10	31	28	84	Basic tool

Table 2. Summary of the results.

Database	Metric	With Memory	Without Memory
Mondial	User Turn Intention Alignment Rate	100.0%	59.7%
	SQL Query Correctness Rate	90.8%	32.6%
	Dialogue Intention Alignment Rate	100.0%	68.0%
	Avg Num Turn Pairs per Interaction	1.01	1.73
Industrial	User Turn Intention Alignment Rate	95.3%	69.0%
	SQL Query Correctness Rate	82.6%	41.3%
	Dialogue Intention Alignment Rate	100.0%	92.0%
	Avg Num Turn Pairs per Interaction	1.06	1.45
Formula 1	User Turn Intention Alignment Rate	98.6%	66.3%
	SQL Query Correctness Rate	77.5%	19.6%
	Dialogue Intention Alignment Rate	100%	78.3%
	Avg Num Turn Pairs per Interaction	1.03	1.33
Super Hero	User Turn Intention Alignment Rate	97.7%	62.4%
	SQL Query Correctness Rate	94.2%	60.2%
	Dialogue Intention Alignment Rate	100.0%	35.7%
	Avg Num Turn Pairs per Interaction	1.02	1.11

ran without memory, thereby failing to maintain dialogue context and, as a consequence, exhibiting severe performance degradation.

7 Conclusions

Given a database D one is interested in and a natural language database conversational agent A that is a candidate to be adopted, the central contribution of this paper is an automated method for verifying the performance of agent A on database D, before the agent is deployed. The method consists of a procedure for generating a dialogue test dataset T_D specific to D and an evaluation agent that, using T_D, automatically assesses the performance of agent A using the set of metrics defined in the paper. The experiments suggested that the dialogue test datasets and the evaluation agent were sufficient to demonstrate differences in performance among the natural language database conversational agents tested, in line with the primary goal of the paper.

As for future work, further experiments will be conducted over other databases that are in production, organized as a database federation, to equip the federation with a natural language conversational agent.

Acknowledgments. This work was partly funded by FAPERJ, grant E-26/204.322/2024; by CNPq grant 305587/2021-8; and by Petrobras/ANP, under a research agreement between CENPES and PUC-Rio.

Disclosure of Interests. The authors have no competing interests to declare that are relevant to the content of this article.

References

1. Coelho, G.M.C., et al.: Improving the accuracy of text-to-sql tools based on large language models for real-world relational databases. In: Database and Expert Systems Applications: 35th International Conference, DEXA 2024, Naples, Italy, 26–28 August 2024, Proceedings, Part I, pp. 93–107. Springer-Verlag, Berlin, Heidelberg (2024). https://doi.org/10.1007/978-3-031-68309-1_8
2. Dong, M., et al.: PRACTIQ: A practical conversational text-to-SQL dataset with ambiguous and unanswerable queries. In: Chiruzzo, L., Ritter, A., Wang, L. (eds.) Proc. 2025 Conf. of the Nations of the Americas Chapter of the Association for Computational Linguistics: Human Language Technologies (Volume 1: Long Papers), pp. 255–273. Association for Computational Linguistics, Albuquerque, New Mexico (2025). https://doi.org/10.18653/v1/2025.naacl-long.13
3. Guo, Z., et al.: Evaluating and enhancing LLMs for multi-turn text-to-SQL with multiple question types (2025). https://arxiv.org/abs/2412.17867
4. Huo, N., et al.: Bird-interact: re-imagining text-to-sql evaluation for large language models via lens of dynamic interactions (2025). https://arxiv.org/abs/2510.05318
5. Izquierdo, Y., et al.: Busca360: a search application in the context of top-side asset integrity management in the oil & gas industry. In: Proc. 39th Brazilian Symposium on Data Bases, pp. 104–116. SBC, Porto Alegre (2024). https://doi.org/10.5753/sbbd.2024.240793
6. Li, C.: MultiSQL: a schema-integrated context-dependent Text2SQL dataset with diverse SQL operations. In: Findings of the Association for Computational Linguistics: ACL 2024, pp. 13857–13867. Association for Computational Linguistics, Bangkok, Thailand (2024). https://doi.org/10.18653/v1/2024.findings-acl.823
7. Li, J.: Can LLM already serve as a database interface? a big bench for large-scale database grounded text-to-SQLs. In: Proc. 37th Int'l. Conf. on Neural Information Processing Systems. NIPS '23, Curran Associates Inc, Red Hook, NY, USA (2023)
8. Nascimento, E.R., et al.: A text-to-sql strategy based on large language models and knowledge graphs for real-world databases. Data Knowl. Eng., 102580 (2026). https://doi.org/10.1016/j.datak.2026.102580
9. Nascimento, E.R., et al.: Text-to-sql meets the real-world. In: Proceedings of the 26th International Conference on Enterprise Information Systems - Volume 1, pp. 61–72 (2024). https://doi.org/10.5220/0012555200003690

10. Silva, M.O.: Automation in the generation and evaluation of dialogues for textto-SQL systems: an agent-based approach. Master's thesis, Department of Informatics, PUC-Rio, Rio de Janeiro, Brazil (2025). https://doi.org/10.17771/PUCRio.acad.74368
11. Zheng, H., Liu, Y., Ge, Y., Awadallah, A.H., Gao, J.: Judging LLM-as-a-judge: Evaluating large language models for summarization evaluation. In: Proceedings of the 61st Annual Meeting of the Association for Computational Linguistics (ACL 2023), pp. 11034–11056. (2023). https://doi.org/10.18653/v1/2023.acl-long.616

Synthetic Log Generation Under Control-Flow Conditions Using Autoregressive Models

Martin Kuhn[1(✉)], Tony Trinh[1], Joscha Grüger[1,2], and Ralph Bergmann[1,2]

[1] German Research Center for Artificial Intelligence (DFKI), Trier, Germany
{martin.kuhn,tony.trinh}@dfki.de, {grueger,bergmann}@uni-trier.de
[2] Business Information Systems II, Trier University, Trier, Germany

Abstract. Data-driven process analytics, including machine learning and process mining, rely on event logs that capture how business processes are executed. In many organizations, these logs are sensitive, incomplete, or difficult to share. This has increased interest in synthetic event log generation, especially conditional generation that creates synthetic logs under user-defined constraints. Thus, we propose the Petri Net Conditioned Synthesizer (PNC-SYN) to generate synthetic logs that are conformant with a given normative Petri net. At each step, an autoregressive model predicts a probability distribution over the next possible events, and a Petri net playout layer restricts this distribution to the transitions enabled by the Petri net. Furthermore, the autoregressive model remains responsible for generating realistic event sequences and attributes such as timestamps, costs, and resources. We study (1) how to integrate Petri net playout with an autoregressive model to ensure conforming traces while enabling attribute generation and (2) how well Petri net conditioned synthetic logs match the original attribute distributions as well as the utility for process mining tasks compared to an unconstrained autoregressive synthesizer.

Keywords: Synthetic event logs · Conditional generation · Petri nets

1 Introduction

Data-driven technologies such as artificial intelligence (AI) and process mining are profoundly transforming many sectors by enabling innovative approaches and solutions. When applied to business processes, both AI and process mining rely on event data, typically represented as event logs that capture the execution of process activities. In many organizations, however, such data are sensitive, incomplete, or difficult to share, which limits experimentation and the systematic evaluation of new methods. This has led to a growing interest in synthetic event log generation techniques, particularly conditional generation methods, which can produce event data under specific user-defined constraints [3,4]. Existing methods for generating synthetic event logs mostly follow a knowledge-driven

R. Posenato and I. Vanderfeesten (Eds.): CAiSE 2026 Workshops, LNBIP 586, pp. 12–24, 2026.
https://doi.org/10.1007/978-3-032-28160-9_2

approach or rely purely on learned distributions. Knowledge-driven generators require extensive manual configuration, such as defining process models, rules, distributions, and probabilities, and may produce synthetic data with unrealistic timing or attribute relationships that limit their usefulness [5,8]. In contrast, deep learning-based generators, like generative adversarial networks (GANs) [10], recurrent neural networks (RNNs) [2,9], and variational autoencoders (VAEs) [4], learn to generate traces directly from data and can capture complex temporal and attribute correlations. Conditional generative models for event logs extend data-driven generation in two main directions. First, data-driven simulation (DDS) builds on an explicit stochastic process model and uses it as an interpretable, white-box simulator that can integrate machine learning components into process models while keeping the model structure interpretable for what-if analysis [3]. However, these methods often rely on simplified stochastic assumptions and use learned components mainly to parameterize the simulator, which can limit how well it captures complex attribute dynamics. Second, conditional deep-learning architectures, such as conditional variational autoencoders (CVAEs), generate traces directly from high-level conditions with the process model encoded implicitly in the network weights [4]. A key limitation of current conditional generators is that normative process models are rarely used as the primary conditioning source of conditioning. In practice, organizations often already maintain such normative models and need synthetic event logs that are conformant by construction and still have realistic attributes. While DDS approaches use an explicit model for simulation and deep-learning approaches condition on labels or data attributes, neither provides a generic way to use a trusted normative model as a constraint during event log generation.

To address this gap, we propose the Petri Net Conditioned Synthesizer (PNC-SYN). At each generation step, a deep-learning model produces a probability distribution over event labels, a Petri net playout layer constrains this distribution to the set of transitions currently enabled in a given Petri net. A transition is then sampled and fired. The resulting trace is guaranteed to be replayable on the net, with alignment fitness equal to 1.0 while the deep-learning model remains responsible for learning and generating realistic event sequences and attributes such as timestamps, costs, and resources. Thus, PNC-SYN is complementary to CVAE-based approaches [4]. While CVAE approaches typically condition on attributes and keep the process structure implicit, PNC-SYN uses an explicit Petri net for conditioning and relies on a deep-learning model to generate realistic sequences and attributes. Thus, two research questions are analyzed:

RQ1: How can a Petri net playout mechanism be integrated with a deep-learning model to ensure conforming traces while enabling multi-perspective attribute generation?

RQ2: How well do Petri net-conditioned synthetic logs match the original attribute distributions and log characteristics compared to an unconstrained baseline?

The remainder of the paper is organized as follows. Section 2 provides background, Sect. 3 introduces PNC-SYN, Sect. 4 presents the evaluation, Sect. 5 discusses results and limitations, and Sect. 6 concludes this paper.

2 Background

2.1 Event Logs

Event logs are sets of cases, where each case consists of a sequence of events representing activity executions. Beyond control-flow, event logs may contain attributes from different perspectives (e.g., cost and time), leading to multi-perspective event logs [1].

Definition 1 (Universes). *We define the following universes: $\mathcal{C}$ the universe of all possible case identifiers, $\mathcal{L}$ the universe of all possible event logs, $\mathcal{E}$ the universe of all possible event identifiers, $\mathcal{A}$ the universe of all possible activity identifiers, $\mathcal{AN}$ the universe of all possible attribute identifiers, $\mathcal{T}$ the universe of all possible timestamps, and $\mathcal{AV}$ the universe of all possible attribute values.*

Definition 2 (Attributes and Classifier). *For any event identifier $e \in \mathcal{E}$, case identifier $c \in \mathcal{C}$, and attribute identifier $n \in \mathcal{AN}$, $\#_n(e) \in \mathcal{AV} \cup \{\perp\}$ denotes the value of attribute n for event e, and $\#_n(c) \in \mathcal{AV} \cup \{\perp\}$ denotes the value of attribute n for case c. If e (resp. c) does not have an attribute named n, then $\#_n(e) = \perp$ (resp. $\#_n(c) = \perp$). We define two attribute identifiers $activity \in \mathcal{AN}$ and $time \in \mathcal{AN}$, where $\#_{activity}(e) \in \mathcal{A} \cup \{\perp\}$ assigns an activity label and $\#_{time}(e) \in \mathcal{T} \cup \{\perp\}$ a timestamp.*

Definition 3 (Trace and Case). *For each case identifier c that occurs in an event log, the case has an associated trace, denoted by $\hat{c}$, where $\hat{c} \in \mathcal{E}^* \setminus \{\langle\rangle\}$ is a non-empty sequence of events. Also, each event appears at most once in a trace, i.e., for all $1 \leq i < j \leq |\hat{c}|$ we have $\hat{c}(i) \neq \hat{c}(j)$. For convenience, we write $e \in \hat{c}$ to denote that the event e occurs in the sequence $\hat{c}$. The addition of an event e to a trace $\sigma \in \mathcal{E}^*$ is denoted by $\sigma \oplus e = \sigma \cdot \langle e \rangle$. If all events in the trace have timestamps, we require the trace to be ordered chronologically.*

Definition 4 (Event Log). *An event log $L \in \mathcal{L}$ is a finite set of case identifiers, i.e., $L \subseteq \mathcal{C}$. For each case $c \in L$, let $\sigma = \hat{c}$ denote its (non-empty) trace. We assume that an event identifier belongs to at most one case in the log.*

2.2 Petri Nets

Petri nets are a graphical and mathematically grounded modelling language with a strong theoretical basis that enables formal analysis [12]. A Petri net consists of places and transitions. Tokens reside in places, and their distribution over places, called a *marking*, represents the current state of the net, while transitions correspond to activity executions or events [1,11]. Intuitively, a transition is *enabled* if all its input places contain at least one token. Firing the transition consumes one token from each input place and produces one token in each output place and changes the marking. The following definitions formalize these notions.

Definition 5 (Petri Net [1]**).** *A Petri net is a triple* $N = (P, T, F)$ *where* P *is a finite set of places,* T *is a finite set of transitions with* $P \cap T = \emptyset$*, and* $F \subseteq (P \times T) \cup (T \times P)$ *is the set of directed arcs.*

Definition 6 (Initial and Final Marking [1]**).** *Let* $\mathbb{B}(P)$ *denote the set of all finite multisets over* P*. A* marking *is an element* $M \in \mathbb{B}(P)$ *describing the distribution of tokens over places. A marked Petri net is a pair* (N, M) *with* $N = (P, T, F)$ *and* $M \in \mathbb{B}(P)$*. We assume a fixed initial marking* $M_I \in \mathbb{B}(P)$ *and a fixed final marking* $M_F \in \mathbb{B}(P)$ *for* N*.*

Definition 7 (Input Places, Output Places, and Firing Rule)[1,11]**).** *Let* (N, M) *be a marked Petri net with* $N = (P, T, F)$ *and* $M \in \mathbb{B}(P)$*. For a transition* $t \in T$*, its input places are* $\bullet t = \{p \in P \mid (p, t) \in F\}$ *and its output places are* $t\bullet = \{p \in P \mid (t, p) \in F\}$*. The transition* t *is enabled at* M*, written* $(N, M)[t\rangle$*, if* $M(p) \geq 1$ *for all* $p \in \bullet t$*. Firing* t *yields a new marking* $M' = (M \setminus \bullet t) \uplus t\bullet$*, where* $\bullet t$ *and* $t\bullet$ *are interpreted as multisets that contain each place once, and we write* $(N, M)[t\rangle(N, M')$*.*

2.3 Autoregressive Models

Autoregressive (AR) sequence models represent the probability of a sequence as a product of conditional probabilities, where each element depends on the preceding elements [7]. In process mining, such models are commonly used as next-event predictors. Given a prefix of a trace, they assign a probability distribution over the next activity label and, in multi-perspective settings, over additional event attributes [2]. Let $\sigma = \hat{c}$ be the trace of a case $c \in \mathcal{C}$ with activity labels $\underline{e_t} \in \mathcal{A}$ obtained via the classifier $\underline{e_t} = \#_{activity}(e_t)$ (cf. Sect. 2.1). We define the label sequence $\mathbf{a} = \langle a_1, \ldots, a_T \rangle$ with $a_t = \underline{e_t}$ and extend the activity alphabet with a start-of-sequence symbol `SOS` and an end-of-sequence symbol `EOS`, forming the vocabulary $\mathcal{V} = \mathcal{A} \cup \{\texttt{SOS}, \texttt{EOS}\}$. An AR model with parameters θ factorizes the joint probability of a sequence as

$$p_\theta(\mathbf{a}) = p_\theta(a_1, \ldots, a_T) = \prod_{t=1}^{T} p_\theta\big(a_t \mid a_1, \ldots, a_{t-1}\big). \tag{1}$$

At each step t, the model therefore provides a probability distribution over the next label, conditioned on the complete prefix. In practice, each activity label is mapped to an input vector $x_t \in \mathbb{R}^d$ via an encoding function ϕ, i.e., $x_t = \phi(a_t)$. The model maintains a hidden state h_t that summarizes the prefix up to time t through a recurrent update function f_θ:$h_t = f_\theta(h_{t-1}, x_t)$. A common choice for f_θ is the Long Short-Term Memory (LSTM) network, which was introduced to mitigate the vanishing gradient problem to capture long-term dependencies by means of gating mechanisms [7]. For an input sequence $(x_1, \ldots, x_T)$, the LSTM computes at each time step t:

$$
\begin{aligned}
i_t &= \text{sigmoid}(W_{ix}x_t + W_{ih}h_{t-1} + b_i) && \text{(input gate)} \\
f_t &= \text{sigmoid}(W_{fx}x_t + W_{fh}h_{t-1} + b_f) && \text{(forget gate)} \\
o_t &= \text{sigmoid}(W_{ox}x_t + W_{oh}h_{t-1} + b_o) && \text{(output gate)} \\
g_t &= \tanh(W_{gx}x_t + W_{gh}h_{t-1} + b_g) && \text{(cell candidate)} \\
c_t &= f_t \odot c_{t-1} + i_t \odot g_t && \text{(cell state)} \\
h_t &= o_t \odot \tanh(c_t) && \text{(hidden state).}
\end{aligned} \tag{2}
$$

where σ denotes the sigmoid function, $\odot$ the element-wise product, c_t is the internal cell state, and h_t is the hidden state used as sequence representation. The gates control how much past information is kept, how much new information is added, and how much of the internal state is exposed as output [7]. The probabilities over the next-event labels are obtained by mapping the hidden state h_t to unnormalized scores $z_t \in \mathbb{R}^{|\mathcal{V}|}$ and applying a softmax function with $z_t = W_o h_t + b_{\text{out}}$:

$$
p_\theta(v \mid a_1, \ldots, a_t) = \text{softmax}(z_t)_v = \frac{\exp(z_{t,v})}{\sum_{v' \in \mathcal{V}} \exp(z_{t,v'})}, \tag{3}
$$

for all $v \in \mathcal{V}$, where $W_o \in \mathbb{R}^{|\mathcal{V}| \times \dim(h_t)}$ and $b_{\text{out}} \in \mathbb{R}^{|\mathcal{V}|}$ are trainable output parameters. Given an event log $L \in \mathcal{L}$, the model parameters θ are learned by maximizing the likelihood of the observed label sequences, or equivalently by minimizing the cross-entropy loss.

3 Petri Net Conditioned Synthesizer (PNC-SYN)

PNC-SYN combines an AR model with Petri-net execution semantics to synthesize realistic traces that are control-flow conformant by construction. First, an AR model is trained on the original event log to learn how event sequences and multi-perspective attributes typically evolve over time. Second, a normative Petri net, often modeled by domain experts, representing the expected process behavior is provided as an explicit control-flow constraint. During generation, the AR model produces a probability distribution over likely next activities, while the Petri net continuously restricts this distribution to only those transitions that are currently executable in the net.

Definition 8 (Autoregressive Model). *Let $L \in \mathcal{L}$ be an event log. For each case $c \in L$, let $\sigma = \langle e_1, \ldots, e_T \rangle$ be its trace and $\mathbf{a} = \langle a_1, \ldots, a_T \rangle$ the corresponding label sequence with $a_t = \#_{activity}(e_t)$ (cf. Sect. 2.3). An AR model is a probability model p_θ with parameters θ learned from the label sequences in L by maximizing their likelihood. For any prefix $\mathbf{a}_{<t}$, the model yields a conditional distribution over the next label in $\mathcal{V}$, i.e., for all $v \in \mathcal{V}$, $p_\theta(v \mid \mathbf{a}_{<t})$.*

Definition 9 (Autoregressive Sampling). *Let p_θ be an AR model as defined in Definition 8. Sequence generation initializes the prefix with $\mathbf{a}_{<1} = \langle \texttt{SOS} \rangle$. At each step $t \geq 1$, the model provides $p_\theta(v \mid \mathbf{a}_{<t})$ for all $v \in \mathcal{V}$, and samples the*

next label a_t. *The prefix is updated and sampling continues until* **EOS** *is sampled. The returned sequence is* $\mathbf{a} = \langle a_1, \ldots, a_T \rangle$ *(excluding* **EOS***). The probability of the resulting sequence factorizes as*

$$p_\theta(\mathbf{a}) = \prod_{t=1}^{T} p_\theta(a_t \mid \mathbf{a}_{<t}).$$

In multi-perspective event logs, the same step-wise sampling scheme applies to additional event attributes by using multiple output heads that share the prefix representation and output the respective conditional distributions.

Definition 10 (Normative Petri Net). *A normative Petri net is a triple* $\mathcal{N} = (N, M_I, M_F)$, *where* $N = (P, T, F)$ *is a Petri net (cf. Sect. 2.2) and* $M_I, M_F \in \mathbb{B}(P)$ *are the initial and final markings (cf. Sect. 2.2). It specifies the normative control-flow behavior by defining, for each marking* M *reachable from* M_I, *according to the firing rule in Sect. 2.2, the set of enabled transitions*

$$\mathrm{En}(N, M) = \{\, t \in T \mid (N, M)[t\rangle \,\}.$$

Definition 11 (Petri Net Playout). *Let* $\mathcal{N} = (N, M_I, M_F)$ *be a normative Petri net as in Definition 10. A playout is any firing sequence from* M_I *to* M_F, *i.e., a finite sequence of transitions* $\langle t_1, \ldots, t_k \rangle$ *such that there exist markings* $M_0, \ldots, M_k \in \mathbb{B}(P)$ *with* $M_0 = M_I$, $M_k = M_F$, *and for all* $i \in \{1, \ldots, k\}$: $(N, M_{i-1})[t_i\rangle(N, M_i)$.

Definition 12 (Firings of Invisible Transitions). *Let* $\mathcal{N} = (N, M_I, M_F)$ *be a normative Petri net as in Definition 10. Let* $T_{\mathrm{inv}} \subseteq T$ *denote the set of invisible transitions, and assume that each visible transition* $t \in T \setminus T_{\mathrm{inv}}$ *is labeled with an activity label in* $\mathcal{A}$. *Invisible transitions may have to fire before a visible transition becomes enabled. Therefore, when determining the feasible next labels at a marking* M, *we allow firing any finite (possibly empty) sequence of invisible transitions first. We define* $\mathrm{En}_{\mathcal{V}}(N, M) \subseteq \mathcal{V}$ *as the set of feasible next labels as follows: a label* $a \in \mathcal{A}$ *is in* $\mathrm{En}_{\mathcal{V}}(N, M)$ *if there exists a marking* M' *reachable from* M *by firing only transitions in* T_{inv} *such that, at* M', *at least one enabled visible transition is labeled with activity* a. *Moreover,* **EOS** $\in \mathrm{En}_{\mathcal{V}}(N, M)$ *if the final marking* M_F *is reachable from* M *by firing only transitions in* T_{inv}.

Definition 13 (Petri Net Conditioned Label Distribution). *Let* $p_\theta(v \mid \mathbf{a}_{<t})$ *be the next-label probabilities of an autoregressive model (Definition 8) and let* $\mathcal{N} = (N, M_I, M_F)$ *be a normative Petri net (Definition 10). For a current marking* M, *let* $\mathrm{En}_{\mathcal{V}}(N, M) \subseteq \mathcal{V}$ *be the set of enabled next labels as in Definition 12. For all* $v \in \mathcal{V}$, *define the Petri net conditioned distribution by*

$$q_t(v \mid M) = \frac{p_\theta(v \mid \mathbf{a}_{<t}) \cdot \mathbb{I}[v \in \mathrm{En}_{\mathcal{V}}(N, M)]}{\sum_{v' \in \mathrm{En}_{\mathcal{V}}(N,M)} p_\theta(v' \mid \mathbf{a}_{<t})}.$$

Here, $\mathbb{I}[\cdot]$ *denotes the indicator function, i.e.,* $\mathbb{I}[\mathit{condition}] = 1$ *if the condition holds and* $\mathbb{I}[\mathit{condition}] = 0$ *otherwise, where the condition is membership in the enabled-label set* $\mathrm{En}_{\mathcal{V}}(N, M)$. *Also, for every marking* M *reachable during generation,* $\mathrm{En}_{\mathcal{V}}(N, M) \neq \emptyset$, *so that the normalization is well-defined.*

PNC-SYN generates the synthetic log L_{syn} by sampling n traces from an AR model while enforcing Petri-net playout semantics at each step. After training an AR multi-head model with a shared prefix representation and output heads p_θ^{act} (activity) and p_θ^{time} (timestamp) on L_{real}, each trace generation starts in the initial marking M_I with the start-of-sequence token $\langle \texttt{SOS} \rangle$. While the final marking M_F has not been reached, the model first computes the next-label probabilities $p_\theta^{\text{act}}(v \mid \mathbf{a}_{<t})$ for all $v \in \mathcal{V}$. This distribution is then conditioned on the current marking M by computing $q_t(v \mid M)$ for all $v \in \mathcal{V}$ according to Definition 13. The next activity label a_t is sampled from the conditioned distribution $q_t(v \mid M)$ for all $v \in \mathcal{V}$, and a corresponding enabled transition is fired to obtain the next marking M'. When multiple enabled transitions share the sampled activity label or have the same probability, one of them is selected uniformly at random. In addition, a timestamp $\tau_t \in \mathcal{T}$ is sampled from $p_\theta^{\text{time}}(\tau \mid \mathbf{a}_{<t} \oplus a_t)$. An event e_t is created with activity $\#_{activity}(e_t) = a_t$ and timestamp $\#_{time}(e_t) = \tau_t$. The event is appended to the current trace σ, and the activity history is updated. Once M_F is reached, the completed trace σ is stored in L_{syn}.

Algorithm 1 PNC-SYN: Petri Net Conditioned Synthesis

Initialize synthetic log $L_{\text{syn}} \leftarrow \emptyset$
Train an autoregressive multi-head model with shared prefix representation and output heads p_θ^{act} (next-activity) and p_θ^{time} (timestamp) on L_{real} (cf. Definition 8)
for $j \leftarrow 1$ **to** n **do**
  $(M, t, \mathbf{a}_{<1}, \sigma) \leftarrow (M_I, 1, \langle \texttt{SOS} \rangle, \langle \rangle)$
  while $M \neq M_F$ **do**
    Compute next-label probabilities $p_\theta^{\text{act}}(v \mid \mathbf{a}_{<t})$ for all $v \in \mathcal{V}$
    Compute conditioned probabilities $q_t(v \mid M)$ for all $v \in \mathcal{V}$
    Sample $a_t \in \mathcal{A} \subseteq \mathcal{V}$ with $\texttt{EOS} \notin \mathcal{V}$ according to $q_t(v \mid M)$ for $v \in \mathcal{V}$
    Sample $\tau_t \in \mathcal{T}$ from $p_\theta^{\text{time}}(\tau \mid \mathbf{a}_{<t} \oplus a_t)$
    Pick enabled $t_t \in T$ with label a_t and fire $(N, M)[t_t\rangle(N, M')$
    $M \leftarrow M'$
    Initialize new event e_t with $\#_{activity}(e_t) = a_t$ and $\#_{time}(e_t) = \tau_t$
    $\sigma \leftarrow \sigma \oplus e_t$
    $\mathbf{a}_{<t+1} \leftarrow \mathbf{a}_{<t} \oplus a_t$
    $t \leftarrow t + 1$
  end while
  $L_{\text{syn}} \leftarrow L_{\text{syn}} \uplus \{\sigma\}$
end for
return L_{syn}

4 Evaluation

This section describes the evaluation of the proposed approach, aligned with the two research questions introduced in Sect. 1. We implement PNC-SYN in Python[1]. As a concrete instantiation of the AR model in Sect. 2.3, we use

[1] https://github.com/martinkuhn94/PNC-SYN.

an LSTM-based next-event model that predicts activity labels and inter-event times. Therefore, we utilize the approach of Camargo et al. as an example implementation [2]. For each event e_t in a trace, we consider its activity label $a_t = \underline{e_t} \in \mathcal{A}$ and its timestamp $\tau_t = \#_{time}(e_t)$. Instead of modeling absolute timestamps directly, the model operates on inter-event times defined as $\Delta t_1 = 0$ and $\Delta t_t = \tau_t - \tau_{t-1}$ for $t > 1$. These are transformed by a monotonic scaling function $s : \mathbb{R}_{\geq 0} \to [0, 1]$ (implemented as division by the maximum inter-event time observed in the training set). Each event is then represented as a pair $(a_t, \tilde{\Delta t}_t)$ with $\tilde{\Delta t}_t = s(\Delta t_t)$. In the input layer, activity labels a_t are mapped to dense embeddings, and the scaled inter-event time $\tilde{\Delta t}_t$ is concatenated as a continuous feature to form the LSTM input vector x_t. Given a prefix $(x_1, \ldots, x_t)$, the LSTM produces a hidden state h_t from which two output heads are derived: (i) a softmax layer yielding the next-activity distribution $p_\theta(a_{t+1} \mid a_1, \ldots, a_t)$, and (ii) a regression layer predicting the next scaled inter-event time $\widehat{\tilde{\Delta t}}_{t+1}$. During generation, we sample a_{t+1} from the predicted distribution, invert the scaling to obtain $\widehat{\Delta t}_{t+1} = s^{-1}(\widehat{\tilde{\Delta t}}_{t+1})$, and reconstruct the absolute timestamp by $\hat{\tau}_{t+1} = \hat{\tau}_t + \widehat{\Delta t}_{t+1}$. The resulting event $(a_{t+1}, \hat{\tau}_{t+1})$ is appended to the prefix and fed back into the model. The implemented approach is then validated on the Sepsis Cases event log, a well-established benchmark in process mining with substantial behavioral variability. As a constraint model, we use the normative Petri net for the Sepsis Cases log created by Mannhardt [11]. All experiment outputs and supplementary analyses are available in the accompanying Zenodo repository[2]. To address the research questions, we compare PNC-SYN against an unconstrained baseline based on the AR next-event model of Camargo et al. [2]. The baseline generator produces traces directly from the learned next-event distribution and does not enforce any explicit process model constraints. In contrast, PNC-SYN uses the same trained AR model but applies Petri net conditioned playout during decoding (cf. Sect. 3). This experimental design isolates the effect of Petri net conditioning, since the underlying AR model is identical for both generators. The AR model is defined with two stacked LSTM layers (hidden size 16), an activity embedding layer with 16 dimensions, and two output heads: (i) a softmax layer that estimates the next-activity distribution and (ii) a regression head that predicts the next inter-event time. The model is trained for 15 epochs on the original Sepsis Cases event log and the architecture and hyperparameters are fixed across all experiments to ensure comparability. From the real log L_{real}, we generate two synthetic logs: L_{AR}, produced by the unconstrained AR baseline, and L_{PNC}, produced by PNC-SYN using the normative Petri net. Each synthetic log contains the same number of cases as the original log. To account for variability, we generate 100 synthetic logs for both generators. The trace generation follows the stopping criteria defined in Sect. 3.

We evaluate the synthetic logs along two dimensions, *resemblance* and *utility* [6]. Resemblance measures how closely the synthetic logs reproduce statistical properties of L_{real}. We compare (1) the number of events, (2) the number of dis-

[2] https://zenodo.org/records/18414864.

tinct trace variants, (3) the trace length distribution using the Hellinger distance, (4) the event distribution using the Hellinger distance, and (5) the case throughput time distribution using the Kolmogorov-Smirnov statistic. All resemblance scores are normalized to the range [0, 1], where higher values indicate stronger similarity to L_{real}. Utility assesses whether synthetic logs are suitable for typical process mining tasks. We follow the Train-on-Real/Test-on-Real (TRTR) and Train-on-Synthetic/Test-on-Real (TSTR) protocols [6]. In TRTR, a process model is discovered from L_{real} and evaluated on L_{real}. In TSTR, a process model is discovered from one of the synthetic logs (L_{AR} or L_{PNC}) and evaluated on L_{real}. We discuss the results obtained with the Inductive Miner, while additional results for the Heuristics Miner are provided in the repository. For each discovered model, we report the process discovery quality dimensions of fitness, precision, simplicity, and generalization. Fitness measures how well the discovered model can reproduce the observed behavior in the original log. Precision measures how much extra behavior the model allows beyond what is observed in the original log. Generalization measures whether the model captures process regularities rather than overfitting to the traces in the original log. Simplicity captures the complexity of the discovered model, where simpler models are preferred.

5 Results and Discussion

This section reports resemblance and utility results and discusses how they relate to the research questions from Sect. 1. Figure 1 summarizes how closely the synthetic logs reproduce structural and distributional properties of L_{real}. Figure 1 shows that both synthetic generators produce fewer events than L_{real} (15214 events). L_{AR} generates 12582 events and L_{PNC} generates 12424 events on average. While this indicates that neither generator fully reproduces the overall number of events, the total number of events is similarly reduced for L_{AR} and L_{PNC}. At the same time, PNC-SYN produces trace variants closer to the real log (839.96 vs. 846.00) than the unconstrained baseline (827.56). This suggests that Petri net conditioning stabilizes case termination behavior. This is consistent with the intended role of the Petri net as an explicit execution constraint.

The resemblance scores in Fig. 1 highlight the trade-off introduced by conditioning. Compared to L_{AR}, L_{PNC} shows lower similarity for activity frequencies (0.89 vs. 0.94), trace lengths (0.67 vs. 0.74), and throughput times (0.60 vs. 0.64). This indicates that restricting each generation step to enabled Petri net transitions changes the sampling dynamics of the AR model. The AR model assigns probability mass to activities that may be likely under the data distribution but are not enabled in the normative model. Removing this probability mass and renormalizing the enabled set shifts the activity distribution, which can change variant structure and affect attribute generation (e.g., timestamps). Figure 2 evaluates whether the generated logs remain useful for process mining discovery, and thereby complements the discussion from a utility perspective. Figure 2 indicates that fitness is comparable across logs (L_{Real}: 0.94, L_{AR}: 0.93,

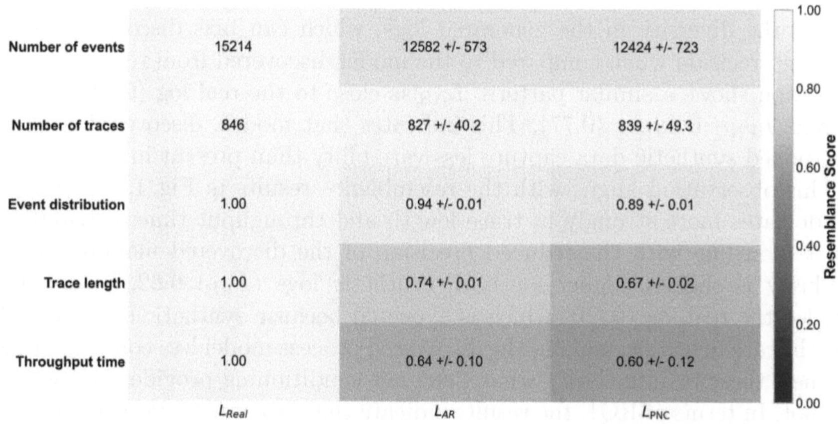

Fig. 1. Mean ± standard deviation of resemblance scores (0–1) across 100 runs for number of events, number of traces, event distribution, trace length distribution, and throughput time distribution, comparing L_{real}, L_{AR}, and L_{PNC}.

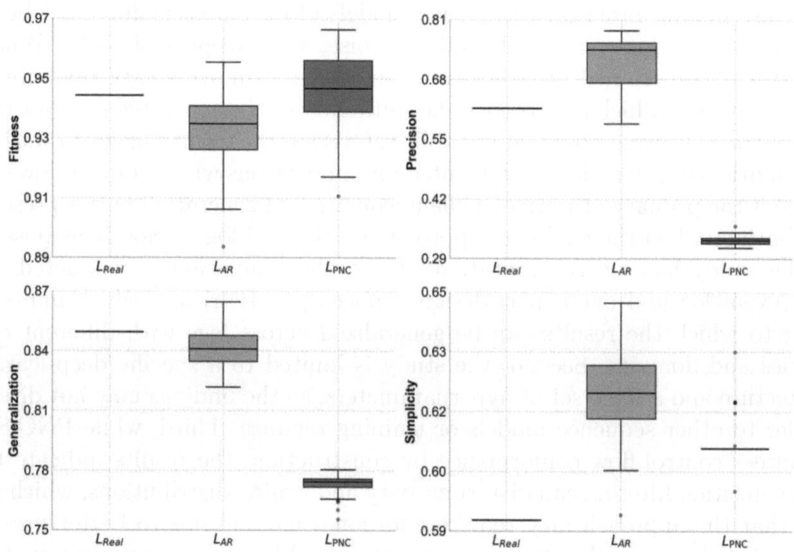

Fig. 2. Inductive Miner quality scores (Fitness, Precision, Generalization, Simplicity) across runs for L_{real}, L_{AR}, and L_{PNC}.

L_{PNC}: 0.94), indicating that models discovered from both synthetic logs can replay a large fraction of the behavior in the evaluation log. However, precision differs substantially: L_{AR} yields 0.72, while L_{PNC} yields 0.33 (L_{Real}: 0.62). Since precision penalizes additional behavior allowed by the discovered model, this result suggests that discovery from L_{PNC} tends to yield models that are more permissive when evaluated on L_{real}. This is because Petri net conditioning reduces the diversity in the generated logs, which can bias discovery, thereby lowering precision when compared to the model discovered from real data. Generalization shows a similar pattern. L_{AR} is close to the real log (0.84 vs. 0.85), whereas L_{PNC} is lower (0.77). This indicates that models discovered from the conditioned synthetic data capture less variability than present in the real log.

This observation aligns with the resemblance results in Fig. 1, where L_{PNC} also deviates more strongly in trace length and throughput time distributions, and it is in line with the reduced precision of the discovered models. Finally, simplicity is slightly higher for both synthetic logs (L_{AR}: 0.62, L_{PNC}: 0.61) than for the real log (0.59), which is expected because synthetic data typically smooths rare behavior, making the discovered process model less complex. Taken together, these results clarify what Petri net conditioning provides and what it does not. In terms of RQ1, the results indicate that integrating Petri net playout at sampling time provides an effective control-flow constraint, reflected in the closer match in trace variants and the preserved discovery fitness. In terms of RQ2, the results indicate that conditioning can reduce distributional resemblance and impact precision and generalization. This reflects a fundamental challenge in process mining practice. Normative models often represent intended behavior, whereas real logs include deviations, noise, and exceptional paths. When a generator is constrained by a normative model, it will systematically suppress these deviations, which may reduce the suitability of the generated data for tasks that rely on capturing observed variability. Overall, the results suggest that Petri net-conditioned generation is best suited for applications where control-flow compliance is the primary objective, while unconstrained generation better preserves distributions when the goal is to approximate the real log as closely as possible.

This study has several limitations. First, the evaluation is conducted on a single event log and one expert-designed normative Petri net, which limits the extent to which the results can be generalized across logs with different complexities and domains. Second, the study is limited to a specific deep-learning architecture and a fixed set of hyperparameters, so the findings may not directly transfer to other sequence models or training regimes. Third, while PNC-SYN guarantees control-flow conformance by construction, the results indicate that strict transition filtering can distort activity and timing distributions, which suggests that the approach may require additional mechanisms to better preserve stochastic behavior under strong constraints. In addition, the computational efficiency of the approach is not examined in detail, and its scalability for larger event logs and more complex Petri nets remains to be assessed. Finally, the current evaluation mainly considers control-flow and time perspective, whereas many real logs include more perspectives, such as resources or costs.

6 Conclusion

This paper presented PNC-SYN, a Petri net-conditioned approach to synthetic event log generation that combines an AR next-event model with step-wise Petri net playout. The key contribution is a generation mechanism that enforces control-flow conformance by construction while retaining a data-driven component for learning realistic sequential and temporal patterns. Experiments on the Sepsis Cases event log show that Petri net conditioning stabilizes structural aspects of the generated logs and preserves high replay fitness in process discovery, but it can reduce distributional resemblance and affect the quality of discovered models compared to an unconstrained baseline. These results indicate that Petri net-conditioned generation is particularly suitable when compliance with a normative process model is a primary requirement. Future work will investigate extensions to richer multi-perspective logs under explicit constraints. Further validation will also include comparison with standard probabilistic Petri net, additional event logs, and downstream tasks beyond process discovery.

Acknowledgments. This research was funded by the German Federal Ministry of Research, Technology and Space (BMFTR) and the European Union (NextGenerationEU) in the project KI-AIM under the funding code 16KISA115K, and by the BMFTR in the project KI-AIM2 under the funding code 16KIS2540.

References

1. van der Aalst, W.M.P.: Data Science in Action. Springer, Cham, Switzerland (2016)
2. Camargo, M., Dumas, M., González-Rojas, O.: Learning accurate LSTM models of business processes. In: Business Process Management: 17th International Conference, pp. 286–302. Springer-Verlag, Berlin, Heidelberg (2019)
3. Camargo, M., Dumas, M., González-Rojas, O.: Learning accurate business process simulation models from event logs via automated process discovery and deep learning. In: Advanced Information Systems Engineering, pp. 55–71. Springer International Publishing, Cham (2022)
4. Graziosi, R.: Generating the traces you need: a conditional generative model for process mining data. In: 2024 6th International Conference on Process Mining (ICPM), pp. 25–32 (2024)
5. Grüger, J., Geyer, T., Jilg, D., Bergmann, R.: Sample: a semantic approach for multi-perspective event log generation. In: Process Mining Workshops, pp. 328–340. Springer Nature Switzerland, Cham (2023)
6. Hernandez, M., Epelde, G., Alberdi, A., Cilla, R., Rankin, D.: Synthetic tabular data evaluation in the health domain covering resemblance, utility, and privacy dimensions. Methods Inf. Med. **62** (2023)
7. Hochreiter, S., Schmidhuber, J.: Long short-term memory. Neural Comput. **9**, 1735–80 (1997)
8. Kuhn, M., Grüger, J., Matheja, C., Rivkin, A.: Data petri nets meet probabilistic programming. In: 22nd International Conference on Business Process Management, vol. 14940, pp. 21–38. Springer, Cham, Switzerland (2024)
9. Kuhn, M., Grüger, J., Bergmann, R.: PALSYN: a method for synthetic multi-perspective event log generation with differential private guarantees. Process Sci. **2**(1), 28 (2025)
10. Li, K., Yang, S., Sullivan, T.M., Burd, R.S., Marsic, I.: PROCESSGAN: generating privacy-preserving time-aware process data with conditional generative adversarial nets. ACM Trans. Knowl. Discov. Data **18**(9) (2024)

11. Mannhardt, F.: Multi-perspective process mining. Ph.D. thesis, Technische Universiteit Eindhoven (2018)
12. Murata, T.: Petri nets: properties, analysis and applications. Proc. IEEE **77**(4), 541–580 (1989)

Graphtender: An Interactive Generator of Absence-Aware Synthetic Graph Datasets

José Calderón[1,2](✉), Daniel Ayala[1,2], Inma Hernández[1,2], and David Ruiz[1,2]

[1] DEAL, ETSII, University of Seville, Av. Reina Mercedes s/n, 41012 Sevilla, Spain
{josecalderon,dayala1,inmahernandez,druiz}@us.es

[2] SCORE Lab, I3US, University of Seville, Av. Reina Mercedes s/n, 41012 Sevilla, Spain

Abstract. This short paper presents our progress towards creating an absence-aware synthetic graph generation approach for explainable graph neural networks in Information Systems Engineering (ISE). The resulting graphs, together with ground-truth annotations, can be used to construct benchmarks to evaluate explainability methods that account for missing nodes. In real-world information systems, the non-existence of expected elements, such as missing services, unimplemented rules, or absent entities, often explains system behavior, reflecting broken dependencies, unmet responsibilities, latent requirements, or compliance gaps. However, existing explainability benchmarks overlook this form of negative reasoning. To address this limitation, we introduce Graphtender, a web-based tool that treats node omission as a first-class explanatory variable when synthesizing graph datasets. The use of a structured generation framework ensures that absence-based explanations are systematically embedded in the graphs, enabling the validation of explainability methods that more faithfully capture the dynamics of evolving information systems.

Keywords: Graph Benchmarking · Graph Neural Networks · Synthetic graph datasets · Explainability

1 Introduction

Information Systems Engineering (ISE) is increasingly faced with a world of continuously changing, interconnected digital artefacts [10]. Enterprise architectures evolve as organizations reconfigure their capabilities, business processes adapt to changing regulations and markets, and platform ecosystems integrate and deprecate services with high frequency [8,20]. As a result, many ISE models are naturally represented as graphs, capturing entities and the relationships between them [4,11].

Graph Neural Networks (GNNs) have therefore emerged as powerful tools to support ISE tasks such as anomaly detection, impact analysis, compliance

R. Posenato and I. Vanderfeesten (Eds.): CAiSE 2026 Workshops, LNBIP 586, pp. 25–32, 2026.
https://doi.org/10.1007/978-3-032-28160-9_3

verification, and architectural risk assessment. However, when these models are used in contexts involving governance, compliance, or strategic decisions, their predictions must be explainable to engineers and domain experts. Explainable AI (XAI) has thus become an important requirement for graph-based learning in information systems [3].

Most existing GNN explainability techniques define explanations as substructures of the input graph that are responsible for a prediction. Benchmarks used to evaluate these explainers typically rely on synthetic datasets where explanations correspond to the presence of specific nodes or edges or occasionally the absence of edges between existing nodes. Consequently, current evaluation frameworks assume that all explanatory evidence must be derived from nodes already present in the graph.

However, many real-world ISE scenarios require reasoning about elements that are expected but entirely missing from the system model. For example, in healthcare process monitoring, patient pathways can be represented as graphs of diagnostic and treatment activities. A predictive model that identifies the risk of adverse outcomes may rely on the absence of expected activities, such as a missing medication reconciliation step or a follow-up appointment. In such cases, the absence of a node itself represents a meaningful explanation, as illustrated in Fig. 1.

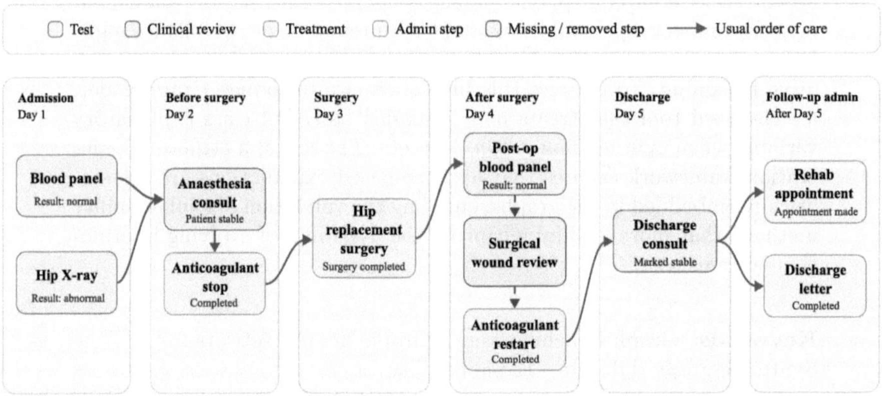

Fig. 1. Example of a healthcare treatment pathway represented as a graph. The expected surgical wound review (red node) is missing, illustrating how the absence of a node can affect downstream decisions and serve as an explanation for model predictions. (Color figure online)

This form of absence-based reasoning is common across ISE contexts. Process compliance violations often arise from missing activities or control points [13], enterprise architecture analysis highlights absent capabilities as indicators of architectural misalignment [12,15], and organizational or system-of-systems models frequently reveal governance gaps through missing roles or dependencies [16,19]. Despite its relevance, current synthetic graph generators and explainability benchmarks do not explicitly represent such absence-based explanations.

In this short paper, we introduce Graphtender, a web-based tool for generating synthetic graph datasets in which node absence is treated as a first-class explanatory factor. The system supports the structured generation of graphs with ground-truth annotations that explicitly encode absence-based explanations, enabling the evaluation of explainability methods capable of reasoning about missing elements in evolving information systems.

2 Related Work

Synthetic graph datasets with controllable structures and known ground-truth explanations are commonly used to evaluate explainability methods for graph neural networks (GNNs) [1,17]. Early graph generators focused on reproducing the global structural properties of networks. Classical models such as Erdős-Rényi graphs [5–7], Barabási-Albert preferential attachment networks [2], and stochastic block models [9] generate graphs with characteristics such as randomness, scale-free degree distributions or community structure. Although useful for studying general graph learning behavior, these generators do not encode explicit semantic expectations about which structures should appear in the graph, limiting their usefulness for evaluating explainability methods.

Benchmarks such as BA-Shapes, BA-Community, Tree-Cycles, and Tree-Grid [18] define the ground-truth explanation of a prediction based on the presence of specific nodes or edges belonging to a motif. Although these benchmarks have advanced the research on explainability, they implicitly assume that explanations can only be derived from elements already present in the graph.

Recent frameworks aim to increase the flexibility of synthetic graph generation. CLEAR [14] generates counterfactual graph examples through controlled perturbations of existing graph structures. ShapeGGen [1] provides a flexible framework to construct motif-based datasets for the evaluation of explainability. However, these approaches still derive explanations exclusively from the presence of graph elements and lack graphical interfaces, requiring users to define datasets programmatically and lacking the ability to visually inspect the effects of perturbations on the generated graphs.

No current explainer or benchmark captures the explanatory role of missing nodes, yet these absences often reveal the root cause of failures, unintended behavior, and non-compliance in dynamic IS. Our work addresses this gap by introducing a tool for creating absence-aware synthetic graph datasets. This enables a systematic evaluation of explainability methods that go beyond presence-based reasoning.

3 Our Proposal

To address the gap discussed in the previous sections, we present **Graphtender**[1], an open-source web application for the interactive generation of absence-

[1] Graphtender is publicly available at https://github.com/DEAL-US/Absynthe.

aware synthetic graph datasets. Rather than requiring researchers to write ad-hoc scripts for each experimental configuration, Graphtender provides a guided, reproducible pipeline that systematically produces annotated graph variants suitable for benchmarking GNN explainability methods under node-absence scenarios.

3.1 Overview and Design Principles

Graphtender follows three key principles to support reproducible benchmarking. First, datasets are defined through declarative configurations that fully specify the base graph, labeling rules, and perturbations, enabling exact dataset regeneration. These configurations can also specify a fixed random seed, ensuring that all stochastic processes involved in dataset generation, such as base graph sampling, motif placement, and perturbation selection, are reproducible. Second, the tool separates interactive dataset design from batch dataset generation, allowing researchers to visually explore motif compositions, labeling schemes, and perturbations before producing large datasets. Third, Graphtender enforces label-aware quality control: a perturbation is accepted only if it changes at least one node's ground-truth label, ensuring that each generated variant introduces a structurally meaningful difference relevant for explainability evaluation.

The application follows a client-server architecture with an interactive frontend for graph visualization and configuration, a REST API with WebSocket support for real-time progress tracking, and a generation engine built on NetworkX that handles graph composition, motif detection via subgraph matching, and perturbation logic.

3.2 Pipeline Stages

The user interface follows a four-stage pipeline, each implemented as a dedicated view.

Stage 1: Graph Construction. Researchers define a base graph either by composing parameterizable structural motifs commonly used in GNN explainability benchmarks (e.g., house, cycle, tree, and star motifs) using a selected composition pattern, optionally injecting random nodes and edges as structural noise, or by uploading an existing graph in GraphML format. In both cases, the resulting graph is rendered interactively for inspection (Fig. 2).

Stage 2: Ground-Truth Labeling. Node labels are assigned using configurable labeling functions. The main mechanism relies on subgraph matching to detect motif instances: nodes belonging to a recognized motif receive its label, while the remaining nodes are labeled as *unknown* (Fig. 3).

Stage 3: Perturbation Design. Researchers simulate structural modifications to the graph and analyze their impact on node labels. The supported perturbations are modular and include node removal, edge removal, edge addition,

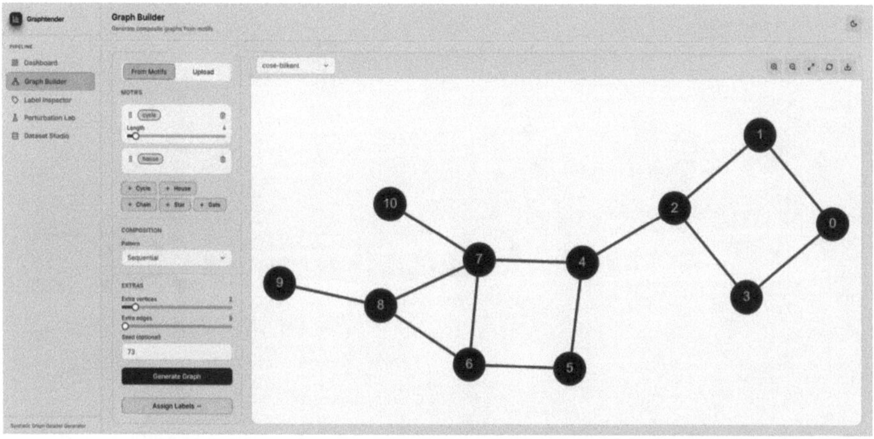

Fig. 2. Graph construction stage of the Graphtender pipeline.

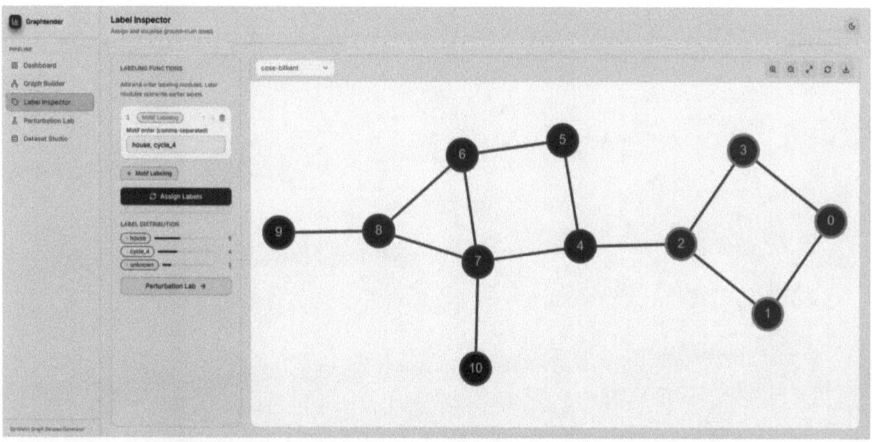

Fig. 3. Ground-truth labeling through motif detection.

combined edge perturbation, and mechanisms to model node-absence scenarios where missing expected nodes influence label assignment (Fig. 4).

Stage 4: Batch Generation. All previous configurations are combined to generate annotated graph variants in batch. Each variant is exported in GraphML together with JSON metadata describing the parent graph, the perturbation applied, the affected nodes and edges, and both the *expected* (pre-perturbation) and *observed* (post-perturbation) label assignments (Fig. 5).

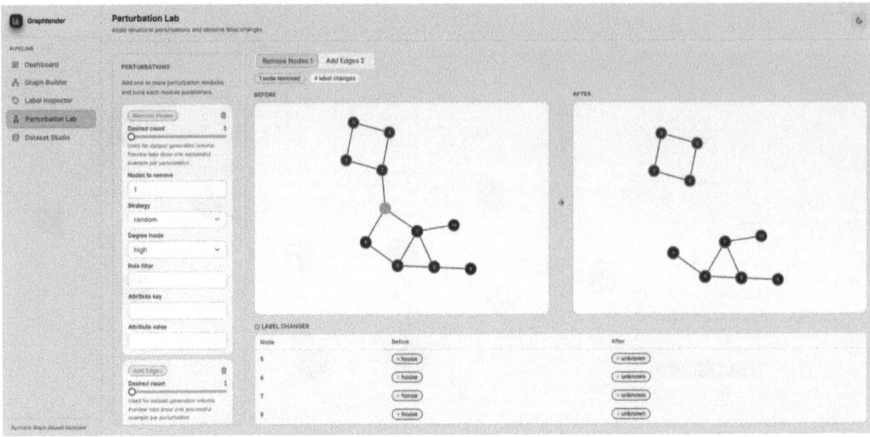

Fig. 4. Perturbation design stage used to simulate structural changes.

Fig. 5. Batch generation of annotated graph variants.

4 Conclusion

In this short paper, we present our progress toward developing an absence-aware synthetic graph generation approach aimed at improving the evaluation of explainable graph neural networks (GNNs) in Information Systems Engineering. Our approach contributes to research on synthetic datasets for evaluating AI methods in information systems by explicitly modeling the role of missing elements in graph structures. The generated datasets allow researchers to examine whether explainability methods correctly identify not only influential nodes, but also the absence of expected ones as part of the explanation process.

In future work, we plan to extend the generation framework behind Graphtender to support a broader range of structural patterns and perturbation strategies. By incorporating absence as an explicit explanatory variable, this work represents an initial step toward more realistic benchmarks for explainable AI in graph-based representations of information systems.

Acknowledgments. This publication is part of the project PID2022-139798OB-I00, funded by MICIU/AEI/10.13039/501100011033 and by ERDF/EU.

This work was also supported by the Spanish Ministry of Universities [FPU23/04004].

Disclosure of Interests. The authors have no competing interests to declare that are relevant to the content of this article.

References

1. Agarwal, C., Queen, O., Lakkaraju, H., Zitnik, M.: Evaluating explainability for graph neural networks. Sci. Data **10**(1), 144 (2023)
2. Barabási, A.L., Albert, R.: Emergence of scaling in random networks. Am. Assoc. Adv. Sci. **286**(5439), 509–512 (1999). https://doi.org/10.1126/science.286.5439.509
3. Brasse, J., Broder, H.R., Förster, M., Klier, M., Sigler, I.: Explainable artificial intelligence in information systems: a review of the status quo and future research directions. Electron. Mark. **33**(1), 26 (2023)
4. Cabanillas, C., Resinas, M., Ruiz-Cortés, A., Awad, A.: Automatic generation of a data-centered view of business processes. In: International Conference on Advanced Information Systems Engineering, pp. 352–366. Springer (2011)
5. Erdős, P., Rényi, A.: On random graphs I. Publ. Math. Debrecen **6**, 290–297 (1959)
6. Erdős, P., Rényi, A.: On the evolution of random graphs. Publ. Math. Inst. Hungarian Academy Sci. **5**, 17–61 (1960)
7. Gilbert, E.N.: Random graphs. Ann. Math. Stat. **30**(4), 1141–1144 (1959). https://doi.org/10.1214/aoms/1177706098
8. Hinkelmann, K., Gerber, A., Karagiannis, D., Thoenssen, B., Van der Merwe, A., Woitsch, R.: A new paradigm for the continuous alignment of business and it: combining enterprise architecture modelling and enterprise ontology. Comput. Ind. **79**, 77–86 (2016)
9. Holland, P.W., Laskey, K.B., Leinhardt, S.: Stochastic blockmodels: first steps. Soc. Netw. **5**(2), 109–137 (1983). https://doi.org/10.1016/0378-8733(83)90021-7
10. Kallinikos, J., Aaltonen, A., Marton, A.: The ambivalent ontology of digital artifacts. MIS Q., 357–370 (2013)
11. Kim, H., Lee, B.S., Shin, W.Y., Lim, S.: Graph anomaly detection with graph neural networks: current status and challenges. IEEE Access **10**, 111820–111829 (2022)
12. Kotusev, S., Alwadain, A.: Modeling business capabilities in enterprise architecture practice: the case of business capability models. Inf. Syst. Manag. **41**(2), 201–223 (2024)
13. Ly, L.T., Maggi, F.M., Montali, M., Rinderle-Ma, S., Van Der Aalst, W.M.: Compliance monitoring in business processes: functionalities, application, and tool-support. Inf. Syst. **54**, 209–234 (2015)
14. Ma, J., Guo, R., Mishra, S., Zhang, A., Li, J.: Clear: generative counterfactual explanations on graphs. Adv. Neural. Inf. Process. Syst. **35**, 25895–25907 (2022)

15. Rosenau, C., Sandkuhl, K., Nast, B.: The role of business capabilities for future viability in enterprise architecture-a structured literature review. In: 17th IFIP WG 8.1 Working Conference on the Practice of Enterprise Modeling Forum, M4S, FACETE, AEM, Tools and Demos, pp. 3–5. CEUR-WS, Stockholm, Sweden (2024)
16. Roubtsova, E.E., Wiersma, N.: A practical extension of frameworks for auditing with process mining, pp. 406–415. ENASE (2018)
17. Ying, Z., Bourgeois, D., You, J., Zitnik, M., Leskovec, J.: Gnnexplainer: generating explanations for graph neural networks. Adv. Neural. Inf. Process. Syst. **32** (2019)
18. Yuan, H., Yu, H., Wang, J., Li, K., Ji, S.: On explainability of graph neural networks via subgraph explorations. In: International Conference on Machine Learning, pp. 12241–12252. PMLR (2021)
19. Zhao, Y., Cai, B., Cozzani, V., Liu, Y.: Failure dependence and cascading failures: a literature review and investigation on research opportunities. Reliabil. Eng. Syst. Safety, 110766 (2024)
20. Zimmermann, A., Schmidt, R., Sandkuhl, K., Jugel, D., Bogner, J., Möhring, M.: Evolution of enterprise architecture for digital transformation. In: IEEE 22nd International Enterprise Distributed Object Computing Workshop (EDOCW), pp. 87–96. IEEE (2018)

MIDas4CS

From Associational to Causality-Aware Digital Twins: An Architectural Framework

Thriveni B. Raju[1], Benjamin P. M. Laevens[1], Corinna Meeßen[1], Carolin V. Schneider[1], and Sandra Geisler[2](✉)

[1] RWTH University Hospital, Aachen, Germany
{tbasavanapur,blaevens,cmeessen,cschneider}@ukaachen.de
[2] Department of Computer Science, RWTH Aachen University, Aachen, Germany
geisler@dbis.rwth-aachen.de

Abstract. Advances in artificial intelligence (AI) and the growing availability of large-scale data have led to the integration of predictive models within digital twin (DT) architectures. However, most existing DT architectures remain primarily associational, limiting their ability to incorporate domain knowledge, address uncertainty, and reason about the effects of interventions. Moreover, explainability in current AI-enabled DTs is often post-hoc rather than structurally embedded. In safety-critical domains like healthcare, these limitations reduce the transparency and reliability of DTs. Hence, we propose the concept of an architecture for data-driven, causality-aware DTs that integrates the causal model layer and a causal inference engine within DT frameworks. The proposed architecture allows for evaluating the influence of different interventions on the system, causal reasoning, and uncertainty-aware decision support while integrating domain knowledge into the twins' representations. By moving from predictive modeling to causally grounded DTs, the framework enhances the interpretability of model outcomes and supports reliable decision-making. The paper aims to contribute to the foundation for next-generation DTs capable of moving beyond correlation-based intelligence toward causally aware and trustworthy systems.

Keywords: Digital Twins · Causality · Prior Knowledge Integration · Uncertainty Quantification · Explainability

1 Introduction

Digital twins (DTs) are virtual or digital replicas of physical systems that enable simulation of the system's behavior [1]. The core components of a DT include a physical system, a data connection, and a digital space consisting of models and software tools that support data analysis [1]. Over the decades, DTs have been widely explored across domains such as manufacturing and healthcare [2,3]. With the rise of large and high-frequency datasets, and advancements in machine

R. Posenato and I. Vanderfeesten (Eds.): CAiSE 2026 Workshops, LNBIP 586, pp. 35–47, 2026.
https://doi.org/10.1007/978-3-032-28160-9_4

learning (ML) and artificial intelligence (AI), predictive models are increasingly built into DTs' architectures to improve their accuracy [4]. However, these DTs rely on black-box ML models as their decision processes are difficult to interpret. Also, these models produce point estimates with limited representation of uncertainty [4]. Another key limitation of AI-DTs is that they do not explicitly incorporate prior knowledge, such as physical laws and engineering constraints in industrial DTs, or clinical guidelines in healthcare DTs. Instead, these models mainly learn statistical patterns from observed data. In addition, AI models make it difficult to answer *what-if* questions, which require causal reasoning and include both intervention analysis and counterfactual analysis. Such analyses are important for decision-making, as it helps to understand how a system might behave under different actions.

To illustrate the research gap, consider a lung cancer risk management scenario. An AI-based DT might analyze imaging, medical history, and lifestyle factors like smoking to predict a 30% five-year lung cancer risk [7]. However, the model may not explain how uncertain its prediction is or which factors influenced the result. Clinicians may also want to understand *how would the risk change if the patient were to stop smoking?* or *What would happen if the patient were to undergo earlier screening?*. These types of questions require understanding cause-and-effect relationships. Without such information, DT outputs can be difficult for clinicians to interpret, or trust [7]. These limitations– lack of uncertainty quantification, limited interpretability, absence of prior knowledge, and difficulty in evaluating what-if scenarios– can reduce the reliability of AI-driven DTs and motivate the need for DTs that move beyond the correlation-based prediction towards causal reasoning. This paper proposes a conceptual architecture for *Causality-aware Digital Twins (CDTs)* that integrates causal modeling and inference into DTs structural framework and aims to answer the following question:

1. How can prior knowledge be integrated into DTs? Specifically, how can *probabilistic priors* (prior probability distributions over model parameters) and *domain knowledge* be incorporated into DT models?
2. How can uncertainty be quantified in DTs? In particular, how can *aleatory uncertainty* and *epistemic uncertainty* be identified and quantified?
3. How can causal modeling be integrated into DTs? How do causal models enable DTs to perform *interventional* and *counterfactual analysis*?
4. How can causal modeling improve the explainability of DTs? Can explicit *cause–effect relationships* help explain model predictions?

The remainder of the paper is organized as follows. Section 2 reviews related work, and Sect. 3 presents the proposed architecture. Section 4 discusses the findings, limitations, and future work, including validation with real-world data, and Sect. 5 concludes the paper.

2 Related Work

This section reviews prior work on DTs, focusing on prior knowledge integration, uncertainty quantification, causal modeling for counterfactual analysis, and explainability, which form the foundation of the proposed architecture.

Prior knowledge includes existing information, experts' insights, and assumptions. It can be integrated into DT models through probabilistic priors or knowledge graphs. Probabilistic priors capture uncertainty about unknown model parameters, while knowledge graphs represent structured relationships between system variables. Combining both is important for building reliable DTs. Recent research has explored the integration of domain knowledge into DTs. For example, Eirinakis et al. [8] propose a conceptual framework for a cognitive DT that uses knowledge graphs to enhance interpretation and decision-making in industrial systems. However, the work remains conceptual and lacks quantitative evaluation. It also focuses on semantic knowledge without incorporating probabilistic priors [8]. Building on this, the present work integrates both probabilistic and knowledge-based priors using causal models, enabling a unified approach to knowledge representation and probabilistic reasoning in DTs.

Uncertainty quantification (UQ) addresses the identification and analysis of uncertainties in computational models to ensure predictions reflect variability rather than deterministic outcomes [9]. Uncertainties are commonly classified as *aleatory uncertainty*, representing inherent randomness, and *epistemic uncertainty*, arising from limited knowledge or data. Accounting for these uncertainties is important in DTs, as variations in inputs or parameters affect the reliability of predictions and decision-making. Chen et al. [9] propose an uncertainty-aware DT framework for controlling directed energy deposition, where stable melt-pool temperature and depth are critical for manufacturing quality. Their approach uses a Time-Series Dense Encoder (TiDE) neural network to predict system states and estimate conditional quantiles $Q_\tau(Y \mid X)$ via quantile regression, enabling prediction intervals that capture uncertainty in melt-pool dynamics. These estimates are integrated into a robust model predictive control (MPC) framework to optimize inputs under disturbances. Experiments on real data demonstrate improved temperature stability, smoother control signals, and fewer constraint violations compared to nominal MPC controllers [9]. However, the method primarily captures data-driven uncertainty and does not address epistemic uncertainty, motivating the exploration of CDT to better characterize overall uncertainty.

Causal inference comprises methods for analyzing cause-effect relationships among variables [10]. It addresses questions like *What causes an outcome?* and *What would happen if a different action is taken?* [10]. Incorporating causal modeling into DTs shifts them from correlation-based predictions to causality-aware reasoning, enabling evaluation of interventions and "what-if" scenarios for informed decision-making. Its benefits are increasingly demonstrated in healthcare applications. Kekić et al. [11] developed a DT framework to retrospectively evaluate counterfactual vaccine allocation strategies during the COVID-19 pandemic. The approach combines coarse-grained causal modeling, ordinary differential equation-based simulation, and literature-based estimates for vaccine effectiveness and immunity waning. Applied to Israel's 2021 vaccination campaign, it compares the implemented strategy– prioritizing high-risk and older age groups– with alternatives including *no prioritization*, *younger groups prioritization*, or *strict risk-ranked approach*. Results show that prioritizing high-risk and older populations minimizes severe cases [11], demonstrating how causal modeling can support the evaluation of alternative strategies. However, the framework doesn't evaluate interventions such as behavioral changes or government policy measures during high transmission periods. Another study [12] proposes a conceptual framework for causal DTs that integrates structural causal models, potential outcomes, and reinforcement learning to simulate alternative treatment strategies in personalized healthcare. Based on these works, this paper investigates how causal modeling can be integrated into DT architectures to enable both counterfactual and interventional analysis.

Explainability refers to a model's ability to provide understandable reasons for its predictions [6]. Recent works have explored integrating explainable AI (XAI) techniques into DTs. For example, Kreuzer et al. [6] propose an architecture that integrates XAI into DTs through either inherently interpretable models or post-hoc methods like TS-MULE, an extension of LIME for time-series data. Their use case showcases XAI-enabled DT for forecasting CO_2 levels in smart buildings while providing actionable explanations to human operators, thereby improving trust and transparency. The study further shows that inherently interpretable models, like N-Beats and DEPTS, yield more stable predictions than post-hoc methods. Building on this preference for interpretable models, this paper investigates how causal modeling can enhance explainability in DTs.

Table 1. Coverage of key topics in related digital twin studies compared with the proposed CDT framework

Study	Domain Knowledge	Uncertainty Quantification	Causal Modeling	Explainability
Eirinakis et al. (2020) [8]	✓			
Chen et al. (2025) [9]		✓		
Kekić et al. (2023) [11]	✓		✓	
Vallée (2026) [12]			✓	
Kreuzer et al. (2025) [6]				✓
Proposed CDT	✓	✓	✓	✓

Limitations and Research Gap. Despite their improved predictive efficiency, existing AI-DT frameworks remain limited in their ability to jointly address uncertainty quantification, prior knowledge integration, causal reasoning about predictions, and produce explainable results. While each of these components has been studied separately in DT research, to our knowledge, a unified architecture that brings all these together is missing. Table 1 summarizes the reviewed studies by comparing the key topics addressed in DT research, highlighting the gaps that motivate the proposed architecture in this paper, which aims to integrate all the identified key aspects within a unified setting.

3 Causality-Aware Digital Twins Architecture

Based on the insights from the reviewed studies and the identified research gaps, a conceptual CDT architecture is designed as illustrated in Fig. 1. It is organized into four interconnected layers: (i) the Physical System, (ii) the Data Layer, (iii) the Digital Twin Core, consisting of a causal modeling layer and a causal inference engine, and (iv) the Decision and Control Layer. Each of these layers serves a distinct functional role while collectively contributing to the overall construction and operation of CDTs, which is discussed in the subsequent subsections. The architecture extends the existing DTs framework to integrate prior knowledge, account for uncertainty, and do causal modeling to overcome the limitations of AI-based DTs.

3.1 Physical System

The physical systems modeled by DTs can range from industrial machinery to biological systems. They act as both the primary source of data for the DT and as the recipient of decisions and control actions generated by the twin, forming a bi-directional feedback loop between the physical system and its digital counterpart. In this loop, decisions and simulation outcomes generated by the DT are applied to the physical system, influencing its state and behavior. These changes, along with other external factors, are subsequently captured through new observations and measurements and fed back into the DT. This continuous exchange enables the DT to remain synchronized with the evolving state of the physical system.

In the lung cancer risk management use case introduced earlier in Sect. 1, the physical system refers to the patient's disease progression, which is monitored through clinical observations, diagnostic tests, and medical records. These observations not only describe the current state of the patient but also reflect the impact of past interventions, allowing the DT to continuously update its understanding of disease dynamics.

3.2 Data Layer

The data layer serves as the foundational layer of CDT and integrates historical and real-time data regarding the physical system. It supports the integration of

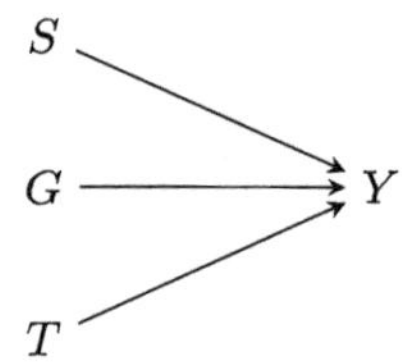

Fig. 2. Causal graph where variables S, G, and T directly influence the outcome Y.

Prior knowledge is integrated in this layer in two ways. Expert insights help define the causal graph structure by identifying plausible relationships between variables. Probabilistic priors can represent prior beliefs about unknown model parameters. For example, in lung cancer risk management, the tumor progression can be modeled as:

$$Y = \beta_S S + \beta_G G + \beta_T T + \epsilon,$$

where the β coefficients describe the strength of the causal effects. Here, instead of assuming fixed parameter values, priors like *informative priors* [15] can be assigned to reflect prior medical knowledge. For example, the influence of smoking exposure on tumor progression can be represented as:

$$\beta_S \sim \mathcal{N}(\mu_S, \sigma_S^2),$$

where the mean, μ_S, reflects existing clinical understanding of the expected effect on smoking, and the variance σ_S^2 captures the uncertainty associated with this belief. As new patient data become available, these priors can be updated via posterior distribution [10,15], enabling the DT to refine its representation over time. Through this mechanism, the causal model layer combines observational data with expert knowledge to construct a causal representation of the system, providing the basis for simulation of intervention and counterfactual reasoning.

Causal Inference Engine: Built upon the causal model, the causal inference engine enables the CDT to reason about the potential interventions and alternative scenarios. *Intervention analysis* evaluates the effect of modifying a particular variable on the outcome. For example, in lung cancer risk management, the model can evaluate how tumor progression may change if different treatment strategies are used by estimating [10]:

$$P(Y|do(T = t')),$$

which represents the distribution of tumor progression Y if a specific treatment strategy $T = t'$ is applied. This allows clinicians to evaluate the expected effect of choosing a particular treatment strategy before it is implemented. The framework also supports *counterfactual analysis*, which allows us to examine what the outcome might have been under an alternative condition. In causal terms, this can be expressed as [10]:

$$P(Y_{X=x'} \mid X = x),$$

which represents the value that the outcome variable Y would have taken if the variable X value had been x'. For example, in the lung cancer use case, the CDT can evaluate whether a patient's disease trajectory might have changed if treatment had been initiated earlier by estimating:

$$P(Y_{T=t'} \mid T = t),$$

where t denotes the current treatment plan and t' represents the hypothetical alternative treatment scenario. Such analysis enables the exploration of hypothetical scenarios that cannot be directly inferred from the observed data.

Furthermore, the causal model structure naturally supports *uncertainty representation.* Aleatory uncertainty is captured through an exogenous term ϵ_i in the structural equations. Epistemic uncertainty, arising from incomplete knowledge, limited data, or model parameters, is represented through probabilistic priors. When evaluating the effect of intervention, the model accounts for variability in data and uncertainty in causal relationships. By accounting for these uncertainties, the CDT can provide not only estimated outcomes but also an indication of the confidence associated with these predictions.

3.4 Decision and Control Layer

The decision and control layer translates the outputs of the DT core layer into actionable and interpretable results to the end user. These results can include predictions, simulations, and decision-support recommendations. In the proposed CDT architecture, this layer plays a central role in improving the explainability of DT by connecting model outputs to the underlying causal factors that drive them. Previous studies [6] have noted that inherently interpretable models provide more reliable predictions than post-hoc interpretation techniques. In the proposed CDT framework, causal modeling already improves interpretability by explicitly representing cause–effect relationships within the system. This transparency can be further enhanced by presenting the model outputs through intuitive visualizations, such as causal graphs, intervention effect plots, counterfactual comparison plots, or risk trajectories.

In lung cancer risk management, the causal factors, such as smoking influencing the disease progression, can be visualized using causal graphs. Similarly, the results of intervention analysis and counterfactual analysis can be communicated through comparative visuals, such as risk trajectories or outcome comparison charts. By combining interpretable causal models with informative visualizations, the CDT enables clinicians to better understand the model's reasoning and assess the potential impact of different treatment decisions. The outputs generated in this layer are not final endpoints but are used to inform decisions and control actions applied to the physical system. These decisions and actions influence the system's state, and the resulting changes are subsequently captured as new data and fed back into the DT through the data layer. This establishes a bi-directional feedback loop between the digital and physical systems, enabling the continuous synchronization and adaptation over time.

4 Discussion and Future Work

The proposed CDT architecture addresses the research questions outlined in the introduction section by integrating prior knowledge, uncertainty quantification, causal modeling, and explainability within a unified framework. Table 2 summarizes how each question is addressed by different components of the CDT architecture. In particular, the causal model layer enables integration of expert knowledge and probabilistic priors, and the causal inference engine supports intervention and counterfactual analysis. The decision and control layer enhances the explainability of CDT by linking the predictions to causal relationships and

Table 2. Mapping of research questions to the CDT architecture components

Research Question	Architecture Component	How it is Addressed
How can prior knowledge be integrated into DTs?	Causal Model Layer	Domain knowledge defines causal relationships between variables, while probabilistic priors incorporate expert beliefs about uncertain model parameters.
How can uncertainty be quantified in DTs?	Causal Model Layer & Causal Inference Engine	Epistemic uncertainty is represented through probabilistic priors, while aleatory uncertainty is captured through stochastic disturbance terms.
How can causal modeling enable intervention and counterfactual analysis?	Causal Inference Engine	Structural causal models allow evaluation of interventions and counterfactual scenarios through causal inference.
How can causal modeling improve the explainability of DTs?	Decision and Control Layer	The explicit causal structure, inference results, and their visual representation enable interpretable explanations of system outcomes

uncertainty estimates. Together, these components provide a structured approach for developing more reliable DTs.

The architecture can be implemented as a modular pipeline in which domain variables and outcomes are defined, data are collected and preprocessed, and the causal structure is specified using domain knowledge. Model parameters are then estimated, and the model is used for intervention and counterfactual analysis. The outputs are integrated into a decision-support system and updated as new data becomes available. This distinguishes the proposed CDT from a standalone causal AI framework, as it operates within a closed-loop system that continuously evolves through interaction with the physical system. While this work focuses on a healthcare use case, the same structure can be applied to other domains by adapting the data sources and domain knowledge. For example, in industrial systems, sensor data from machines, maintenance logs, and operational conditions can be used to model equipment degradation and simulate maintenance strategies.

Despite these advantages, several practical challenges remain. The framework has not been validated, and evaluating intervention and counterfactual outcomes using observational data alone is difficult. Furthermore, the effectiveness of the CDT depends on the availability of high-quality data and reliable domain knowledge for constructing the causal structure. Additional challenges include scalability and computational cost, particularly when dealing with large datasets and complex causal relationships. The future work of this paper includes the implementation and validation of the CDT architecture using large-scale population datasets such as the UK Biobank [16], which contain extensive longitudinal data on health outcomes, genetics, and lifestyle factors. Current efforts aim to develop a data-driven pipeline for causal modeling and simulation-based inference to support intervention analysis. The evaluation will consider predictive performance, uncertainty calibration, and interpretability of results. This will provide empirical evidence of the framework's practical applicability beyond a conceptual setting.

5 Conclusion

This paper presented a conceptual architecture for a Causality-aware Digital Twin (CDT) aimed at improving the transparency, reliability, and decision-support capabilities of DTs. The proposed framework integrates prior knowledge, uncertainty quantification, causal modeling, and explainability within a unified architecture. By incorporating causal reasoning, the CDT moves beyond purely predictive analysis and enables the evaluation of intervention and counterfactual scenarios. The framework also integrates probabilistic priors and domain knowledge to support knowledge-driven modeling while accounting for uncertainty. Using a lung cancer risk management scenario as an illustrative example, the study demonstrated how causal modeling can provide deeper insights into the relationships between risk factors, treatments, and outcomes. Furthermore, the inclusion of uncertainty-aware inference helps to improve the interpretability and trustworthiness of model predictions. While the framework provides a conceptual foundation for CDT, its practical implementation and evaluation remain important directions for future work. In particular, validating the architecture using large-scale cohort datasets could support the development of DTs for personalized risk management. Overall, the proposed CDT framework highlights the potential of combining causal reasoning and uncertainty-aware modeling to advance the development of more explainable and decision-oriented DT systems.

References

1. Crespi, N., Drobot, A.T., Minerva, R.: The Digital Twin, Springer, Cham (2023). https://doi.org/10.1007/978-3-031-21343-4
2. Vrabič, R., Erkoyuncu, J.A., Farsi, M., Ariansyah, D.: An intelligent agent-based architecture for resilient digital twins in manufacturing. CIRP Ann. **70**, 349–352 (2021). https://doi.org/10.1016/j.cirp.2021.04.049
3. Surian, N.U., et al.: A digital twin model incorporating generalized metabolic fluxes to identify and predict chronic kidney disease in type 2 diabetes mellitus. NPJ Digit. Med **7**, 140 (2024). https://doi.org/10.1038/s41746-024-01108-6
4. Kaul, R., et al.: The role of AI for developing digital twins in healthcare: the case of cancer care. WIREs Data Mining Knowl. Discov. **13(1)**, e1480 (2023) (2023). https://doi.org/10.1002/widm.1480
5. Sun, T., He, X., Li, Z.: Digital twin in healthcare: recent updates and challenges. DIGITAL HEALTH **9** (2023). https://doi.org/10.1177/20552076221149651
6. Kreuzer, T., Papapetrou, P., Zdravkovic, J.: AI explainability methods in digital twins: a model and a use case. In: Borbinha, J., Prince Sales, T., Da Silva, M.M., Proper, H.A., Schnellmann, M. (eds.) Enterprise Design, Operations, and Computing. EDOC 2024. Lecture Notes in Computer Science, vol. 15409, pp. 3-20. Springer, Cham (2025). https://doi.org/10.1007/978-3-031-78338-8_1
7. Avanzato, R., Beritelli, F., Lombardo, A., Ricci, C.: Lung-DT: an AI-powered digital twin framework for thoracic health monitoring and diagnosis. Sensors (Basel). **24**(3), 958 (2024). https://doi.org/10.3390/s24030958
8. Eirinakis, P.: Enhancing cognition for digital twins. In: IEEE International Conference on Engineering, Technology and Innovation (ICE/ITMC), pp. 1–7. , Cardiff, UK (2020). https://doi.org/10.1109/ICE/ITMC49519.2020.9198492
9. Chen, Y., Tsai, Y., Karkaria, V., Chen, W.: Uncertainty-aware digital twins: robust model predictive control using time-series deep quantile learning. ASME. J. Mech. Des. **148**(2), 021702 (2025). https://doi.org/10.1115/1.4069104
10. Pearl, J.: Causal diagrams for empirical research. Biometrika **82**(4), 669–688 (1995). https://doi.org/10.1093/biomet/82.4.669
11. Kekić, A., Dehning, J., Gresele, L., von Kügelgen, J., Priesemann, V., Schölkopf, B.: Evaluating vaccine allocation strategies using simulation-assisted causal modeling. Patterns **4**, 100739 (2023). https://doi.org/10.1016/j.patter.2023.100739
12. Vallée, A.: From prediction to intervention: causal digital twins for personalized clinical decision support. J. Transl. Med. (2026). https://doi.org/10.1186/s12967-026-07895-8
13. Evans, R.J.: Causal Inference Lecture Notes, University of Oxford. https://www.stats.ox.ac.uk/~evans/APTS/. (Accessed 04 Mar 2026)

14. Splawa-Neyman, J., Dabrowska, D. M., Speed, T. P.: On the application of probability theory to agricultural experiments. Essay on principles. Section 9. Statist. Sci. **5**, 465–472 (1990). http://www.jstor.org/stable/2245382
15. Baio, G.(2012): Bayesian Methods in Health Economics(1st ed.). Chapman and Hall/CRC. https://doi.org/10.1201/b13099
16. Sudlow, C.: UK Biobank: an open access resource for identifying the causes of a wide range of complex diseases of middle and old age. PLoS Med. **12**(3), e1001779 (2015). https://doi.org/10.1371/journal.pmed.1001779

Event-Driven Digital Twins

Marco Picone[1(✉)], Riccardo Morandi[1], Samuele Burattini[2], Angelo Croatti[3], Stefano Mariani[1], Sara Montagna[4], and Alessandro Ricci[2]

[1] University of Modena and Reggio Emilia, Modena, Italy
{marco.picone,riccardo.morandi,stefano.mariani}@unimore.it
[2] Alma Mater Studiorum – University of Bologna, Bologna, Italy
{samuele.burattini,a.ricci}@unibo.it
[3] Azienda Unità Sanitaria Locale della Romagna, Ravenna, Italy
angelo.croatti@auslromagna.it
[4] University of Urbino, Urbino, Italy
sara.montagna@uniurb.it

Abstract. The adoption of Digital Twins (DT) as a paradigm to realise a pervasive softwarisation of the physical world, across different application domains and different network levels (from cloud to edge), calls for software architectures and platforms featuring levels of flexibility beyond the ones provided by the solutions available in the state of the art. In this paper we introduce an architectural blueprint and implementation for an event-driven notion of DT, meant to tackle such limitations by promoting flexibility and decoupling. As validation, we present its conceptual application to the challenging context of healthcare emergency missions management and initial experimental evaluation through open-source DT solutions.

Keywords: Digital Twins · Event-Driven · Cyber-Physical Systems

Digital Twins (DT) are moving fast towards a widespread adoption and diffusion beyond industrial contexts where they are rooted, as a general way to bridge the physical space and Cyberspace [12,18,19]. On the one hand, they provide a conceptual and technological means for enacting the virtualisation of strategical physical assets (PAs) of organisations and enterprises—from specific products, machines, buildings to users and processes. On the other hand, the pervasive diffusion of Internet of Things (IoT) technologies and standards makes it possible to broaden their adoption and applicability beyond *vertical* applications, as software systems eventually integrated with larger enterprise contexts and possibly across enterprises [8].

This direction leads to envision in the future a pervasive softwarisation of the physical world in terms of highly dynamic ecosystems of connected and interoperable DTs, across different application domains and different network levels (from cloud to edge) [1,2,9]. The main challenge tackled in this paper concerns DT *software architecture*, that is: what architectural patterns can be

R. Posenato and I. Vanderfeesten (Eds.): CAiSE 2026 Workshops, LNBIP 586, pp. 48–60, 2026.
https://doi.org/10.1007/978-3-032-28160-9_5

used to design DTs (and DT platforms) so that they would allow for the different degrees of *flexibility* that this view calls for. In particular, it is possible to identify three distinct degrees of flexibility concerning the *shadowing* process enacted by the DT, DT functionalities, and DT deployment.

The *shadowing* process is the process used to keep the DT state aligned/updated to the one of the corresponding PA, according to the model(s) implemented by the DT. Flexibility here is required for dealing with the heterogeneity of the PAs that are mirrored by the DTs of an ecosystem, of the model(s) adopted for performing the physical-digital mapping, and of the network protocols and strategies adopted to connect the physical and digital layer.

Flexibility and heterogeneity concern also the level of functionalities that the DT could provide *as-a-service*, at the application level. In that view, a DT is not necessarily vertically bound to one specific application, in a closed-system perspective, but could be integrated in a larger enterprise context, possibly across enterprises. This open-system perspective makes it possible to envision ecosystems of connected, interoperable and pervasive DTs [10].

Finally, flexibility is also required for DT deployment, which could either happen at the cloud, fog and edge level [3]. For instance, a DT could be deployed at the edge level to model the PA with fine-grained data collected with strict real-time constraints, while a different DT model could be deployed on the cloud, representing the same asset through coarse-grained properties and more relaxed timing constraints, but requiring better scalability to offer advanced services to several consumers.

These challenges call for the adoption of software architectures beyond monolithic approaches, which are typically adopted for DTs designed as vertical closed applications. Accordingly, we propose an *event-driven* architectural blueprint for DTs. Such architecture enables a modular approach in the design of a DT so that the application logic can be properly encapsulated, and a DT can be flexibly configured, choosing proper interfaces depending on the context where it is deployed. Besides, it paves the way for designing ecosystems composed by DTs at different levels of granularity, whose deployment could span from the cloud to the edge level. Finally, we discuss the benefits of the proposed architecture in practice by considering its application to a concrete real-world implementation of emergency handling in the healthcare context.

1 Event-Driven Perspective

In this section we reason about *event-driveness* from a few complementary perspectives: DTs' capabilities, lifecycle, and architecture. For doing so, as depicted in Fig. 1 (top), three are the event abstractions working as cornerstones of our proposal: PA events (e_{PA}), DT events (e_{DT}), and internal events (e_i).

PA events represent a *change in state* of a PA, either stemming from its own evolution or caused by the DT (e.g. as requested by an application). As such, PA events are captured/generated by the *shadowing* process of the corresponding DT through a dedicated *physical interface*, responsible of mapping those PA

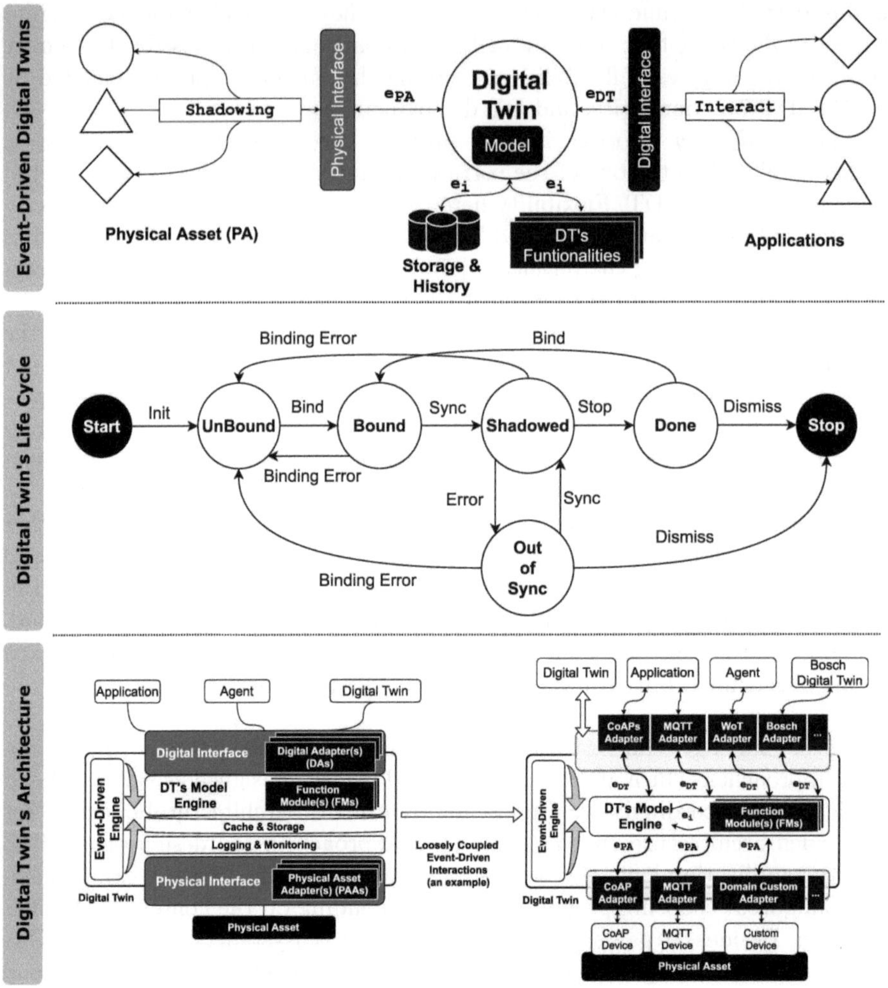

Fig. 1. Representation of event-driven DT with lifecycle and architecture.

properties relevant to the application domain to the corresponding DT properties, at the most appropriate level of abstraction, as dictated by the *shadowing model* defined by the application designer. It is thus the application designer that defines how system events (i.e. the events happening in the real-world domain) are translated into PA events, while preserving their semantics w.r.t. the domain properties relevant for the application at hand. This allows to decouple the DT from the PAs in multiple ways: by hiding PAs heterogeneity, by encapsulating domain- and application-specific concerns within the shadowing process, and by decoupling the PA lifecycle from the DT own.

Complementarily, *DT events* represent a change in state of the DT, either stemming from its own evolution (possibly caused by the PA, in turn) or conse-

quential to applications' interaction (e.g. commands sent to PAs). In the former case, each e_{DT} must be amenable of *observation* by applications, hence a *digital interface* delivers them at the most appropriate level of abstraction, as dictated by the *DT model.* In the latter, interaction with the PA through the DT (a form of *augmentation* [11]) is available to applications through the same digital interface, that handles accordingly new events e_{DT} that the DT exploits to trigger further internal activities (e.g. part of an articulated workflow), or maps to events e_{PA} that the physical interface will translate to the appropriate actions on the PA. It is the application designer that has the responsibility to align the semantics of DT events to the real-world happenings relevant for applications, by suitably implementing digital adapters and the function modules available to the DT model engine—described in Sect. 1.1.

Finally, *internal events* e_i provide for a *common representation* of all other events within the DT, as a consequence of and for driving its inner functioning (e.g. lifecycle events, as described in next section). These events are the glue binding together the physical and digital world semantics as modelled by the application designer, by providing for a common "semantics ground" where both system events (i.e. PA events) and application events (i.e. DT events) can be represented according to the DT model. DT features that concern navigating its history or predicting future states could also be interpreted in an event-driven fashion. Namely, the DT model should define how past events are stored and queried and how future events (predictions) are generated (e.g. through simulation or machine learning techniques).

A further dimension in which the event-driven approach proves particularly effective concerns the modelling and management of the DT lifecycle [15]. The notion of a well-defined lifecycle for a DT has been recently recognised in the literature as a fundamental requirement for DT platforms [16], capturing how a twin should behave with respect to its associated PA over time and how software components can implement and govern that behaviour. Internal events e_i provide a natural and coherent mechanism to drive such lifecycle, as depicted in Fig. 1 (middle), where each state transition is triggered and mediated by the internal event flow.

Upon creation, the DT enters the *Unbound* state, where all internal modules are ready to start the binding procedure with the PA, either automatically or triggered by an external component. Once binding is completed, the DT transitions to *Bound* and begins the shadowing process, reaching the *Shadowed* state where it is fully synchronised with its physical counterpart. Any synchronisation error moves the DT to *Out of Sync*, from which it returns to *Shadowed* once recovered. When explicitly stopped, the DT moves to *Done*—remaining accessible to consumers while retaining its memory—before being finally dismissed to *Stop.* Binding errors at any stage cause a transition back to *Unbound*, ensuring consistent recovery semantics throughout the lifecycle.

The adoption of an event-driven approach carries relevant implications also from a software engineering perspective, opening the DT design space to a set

of established architectural patterns that can be directly leveraged to support the engineering of DT-based systems.

Table 1. Software patterns enabled by the proposed event-driven DT approach.

Pattern	Description	Mapping to Event-Driven DT
Microkernel	A stable core extended by independently loadable plug-in modules.	The DT Core hosts the DT Model, which is extended by plug-in components activated by e_i and e_{PA}.
CQRS	Separates state-mutation commands from state-query operations.	The Physical Interface handles state updates via e_{PA}; the Digital Interface serves queries and interactions via e_{DT}.
Pipes & Filters	Processing logic is decomposed into a chain of transformations over a data stream.	e_{PA} and e_i flow through a configurable chain of components within the DT Core, each applying a targeted transformation according to the DT Model.
Serverless	Functions are deployed and scaled independently, triggered by events.	Individual components or augmentation modules of the DT Core can be deployed as serverless functions activated by e_i or e_{DT}.
Sidecar	Additional components are deployed alongside a core service without modifying it.	Augmentation and monitoring modules can be attached to a running DT instance as independent sidecars, interacting exclusively through the defined event abstractions.

As summarised in Table 1, the event-driven architecture introduced in this work is compatible with and can serve as an enabling substrate for several of these patterns. A *Microkernel* organisation, for instance, maps naturally onto the DT Model, where a stable core hosts dynamically loadable components acting as plug-ins and activated through the internal event flow. *CQRS* (Command Query Responsibility Segregation) finds a direct correspondence in the separation between the Physical Interface—which handles state updates driven by e_{PA}—and the Digital Interface—which serves read and interaction requests through e_{DT}. *Pipes and Filters* can govern the event transformation chain across the functional components of the DT core, while *Serverless* and *Sidecar* deployment models become viable for individual modules or augmentation components, supporting lightweight and independently scalable DT deployments. This compatibility with established patterns is not merely theoretical: it provides practitioners with a familiar vocabulary and a set of proven strategies for implementing event-driven DTs in real-world contexts.

1.1 Architecture

Relying on the introduced life cycle and event abstractions, we now detail the software architecture proposed to support the flexible implementation and deployment of DTs across multiple application domains. The notion of separating a physical interface from a digital interface in DT architectures has been recently recognised in the literature as a fundamental structural principle [7], reflecting a growing consensus on the need to decouple physical communication

concerns from application-facing ones. Building on this foundation, the contribution of this work lies in characterising and expanding this separation through an event-driven lens, with the specific goal of identifying which events are relevant to a DT, what role they play within each architectural component, and how they mediate the interactions among components throughout the DT life cycle.

As described in [14] the *Physical Interface (PI)* is the component responsible for both the initial *binding process* and the perpetual *shadowing process*, keeping the DT and its PA synchronised throughout the DT life cycle. To do so, it executes one or more *Physical Asset Adapters (PAAs)*, each tailored to the specific nature of the PA and to the protocols and data formats it supports, and produces the corresponding e_{PA} that propagate into the DT's internal event flow. Complementarily, the *Digital Interface (DI)* handles the outward-facing side of the DT, delivering internal events to external consumers through a set of reusable *Digital Adapters (DAs)* that translate e_{DT} into representations suitable for heterogeneous applications. The separation between PI and DI thus maps directly onto the distinction between e_{PA} and e_{DT}, making explicit the boundary between the physical and application-facing concerns of the twin. The *DT's Model Engine (DME)* sits at the core of this architecture, defining the DT's behaviour and its augmented functionalities. It hosts a set of configurable and reusable *Function Modules (FMs)*, each associated with a specific functionality and responsible for consuming e_i and e_{PA} to produce e_{DT} and further e_i according to the implemented logic. All three components are bound together by the *Event-driven Engine (EE)*, which acts as the internal communication backbone enabling their reciprocal interaction through the defined event abstractions. The EE is complemented by the *Cache & Storage (CS)* and *Logging and Monitoring (LM)* modules. Importantly, no assumption is made about how the EE is implemented in practice, leaving the choice of the underlying communication means—whether shared memory, message passing, or other mechanisms—open to the specific deployment context.

2 Evaluation and Benefits

In order to conceptually evaluate the proposed approach, we compared it with approaches presented in scientific literature together with the main production-ready references (Microsoft Azure, Eclipse Ditto, Amazon AWS and Bosch IoT Suite). Most studies about DTs are focused on manufacturing: they propose architectures that have been devised for a specific application domain, mainly lacking interoperability [4]. However, recent studies discuss general-purpose frameworks that enable cross-domain applications, presenting frameworks that mostly envision DTs as passive components, represented for instance as description documents [2], or isolated components, lacking the vision of DTs ecosystem [6].

Figure 2 compares our proposed solution with an abstract architecture devised out from state-of-the-art DT platforms. In such reference platforms, DTs are actually more similar to DT-oriented data repositories than software

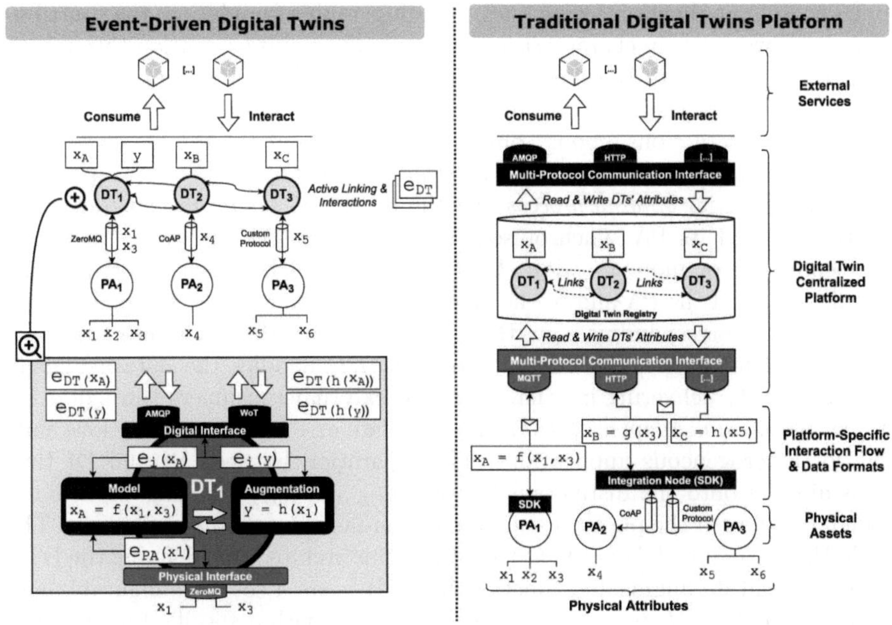

Fig. 2. A comparison between the proposed approach and existing DT solutions.

entities, that simply provide data originated from the associated PA or intermediate entities (such as gateways or integration nodes) on demand. Whether this data has to be pre-processed before being handled over to client applications is decided solely at the application level itself, and usually happens through services external to the DT, and sometimes even external to the DT platform itself.

Also how data is acquired from PAs, such as using which protocol and data formats, is decided application-wise through platform-wise services (e.g., APIs, protocols connectors or SDKs) and not individually for each DT. This latter aspect impacts the shadowing process, that in state-of-the-art platforms results somewhat fragmented across several platform services, rather than responsibility of a single entity. The same holds at the interface between DTs and client applications, that use platform-wise APIs to access DTs' data.

Within the analyzed software platforms, DTs are *passive* entities co-located at the same architectural layer of the platform itself (typically the cloud) and subordinated to external modules to control their properties, data and behaviours. We propose a diametrically opposite approach where DTs are instead *active* and independent event-driven software entities, operating over an evolving life-cycle and communicating with the external world through physical and digital fine-grained interfaces.

The proposed event-driven approach is evaluated with respect to five core properties of DTs widely recognised in the literature [12]. The first property,

Representativeness and Contextualization, concerns how accurately a DT represents its PA in terms of properties, behaviours, and relationships, driven by an internal model that determines the representation purpose and target context. In traditional platforms, DTs act as passive data stores that collect properties forwarded by external entities, with no internal model governing how the physical asset is interpreted. Contextualization is entirely delegated to external components, resulting in a shallow and application-agnostic view of the physical world. The event-driven approach addresses this limitation by equipping each DT with a dedicated internal model and purpose-built adapters, enabling fine-grained, context-aware representation of the PA through event-driven behaviour.

With respect to *Shadowing*—the capability to accurately measure and represent the PA over time, including timely bidirectional synchronization between digital and physical counterparts—traditional platforms distribute this responsibility across multiple platform-level services rather than encapsulating it within the DT itself. Fixed communication protocols and platform-specific data formats introduce vendor lock-in, limiting adoption and reusability across heterogeneous deployments. In the proposed approach, each DT independently encapsulates its own PA communication stack, supporting any required protocol and format, and abstracts physical heterogeneity into reusable, interoperable adapter modules.

The property of *Replication* addresses the ability to digitalize and replicate a PA multiple times to support scalability and adapt digital behaviours across domains, architectures, and deployment layers. Traditional solutions rely on centralised, monolithic architectures—typically cloud-only— where DTs are passive singletons confined to isolated tenants, which fundamentally constrains cross-domain interaction and fault tolerance. The event-driven model natively supports multiple active, independent, and modular DT instances interacting via events across multi-layered and cross-domain deployments, spanning from the edge to the cloud.

Turning to *Composability*, which captures the ability of a DT to hide the complexity of a PA composed of sub-components or cooperating entities, while exposing only the attributes and capabilities relevant to the target context, leaving the DT passively subject to it with no internal awareness or control. In the proposed approach, each DT actively governs the composition process through the behaviour defined by its internal model, leveraging dynamic adapters and a native event-based observability mechanism.

Finally, *Augmentation* refers to the capability of leveraging softwarization to extend and evolve the typically fixed functionalities of a PA over time. This property is largely absent from existing production platforms, where any such capability is outsourced to external computational services. In the proposed approach, augmentation is a first-class DT function, implemented through a flexible plug-in mechanism that allows novel functionalities to be injected at runtime, building on existing modules and events to evolve the DT behaviour without requiring structural changes to the platform.

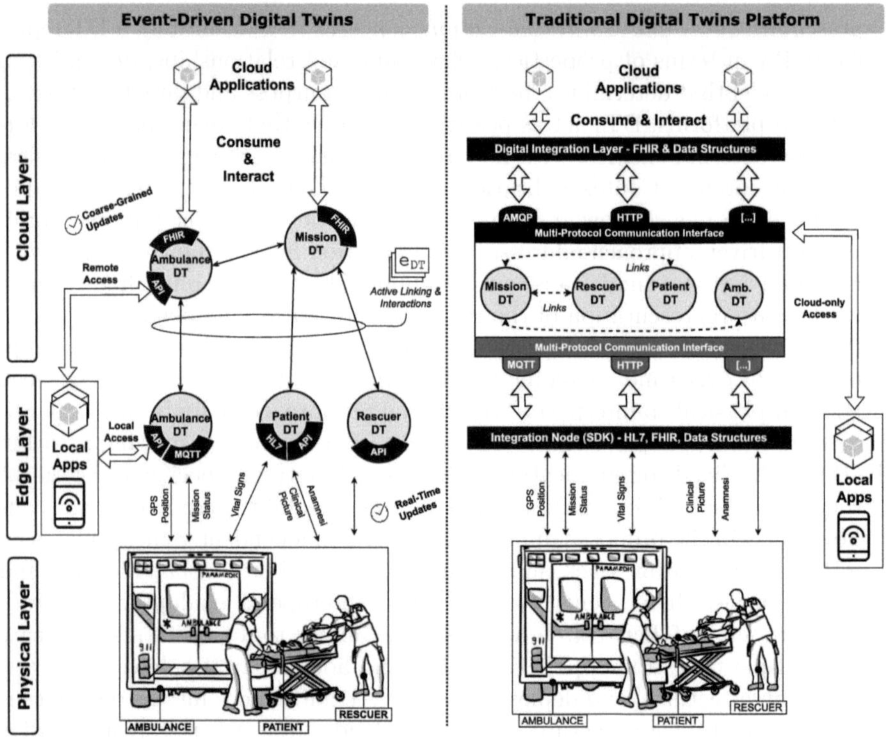

Fig. 3. PAs and DTs comparison for an Healthcare Emergency Mission Scenario.

3 Applying Event-Driven Digital Twins

The evaluation of the proposed approach combines two complementary directions: a design-level assessment on a real-world healthcare case study, validating the expressiveness of the event-driven DT model in a challenging and heterogeneous scenario, and an experimental evaluation relying on an extended version of the open-source WLDT framework [13], refactored entirely around the event abstractions introduced in this work.

The healthcare case study[1] targets the virtualisation of trauma management missions [5,17], involving heterogeneous PAs—ambulance, rescuers, patient, and the mission process itself—and is used to compare the proposed approach with existing centralised solutions, as illustrated in Fig. 3. Each DT operates as an independent and active entity spanning from edge to cloud, accessible as-a-service by both local and remote applications. In contrast, traditional platforms confine DTs to passive, cloud-only entities, forcing edge services to relay through the cloud and requiring additional integration layers to handle heterogeneous PAs, at the cost of unnecessary latency and architectural complexity. At the edge

[1] Collaboration with the Trauma Centre of the "M. Bufalini" Hospital in Cesena, Italy.

level we can deploy multiple DTs responsible to interact with PAs by means of proper adapters, to produce a flow of e_{PA} to update the current state of each DT according to its model. For instance, the `PatientDT` exploits two adapters to: i) receive real-time patient's data from an HL7[2] Vital Signs Monitor; and ii) collect clinical information about patient and anamnesi through a smartphone app communicating using RESTful APIs. Both adapters produce e_{PA} to update `Patient DT` state. Meanwhile, at the cloud level, other DTs can collect more coarse-grained information composing events from other DTs. For instance, the `MissionDT` shadows the whole emergency mission process and exposes a FHIR-based[3] adapter to deliver information to third-party services.

Compared to centralized approaches and previous experimentations [5] the current event-driven refactoring strongly improves flexibility along the lines discussed in the paper. Moreover, decoupling the responsibilities within the components of the same DT and across multiple independent twins encapsulating the application logic improves interoperability with both heterogeneous PAs and third-party cross-domain applications.

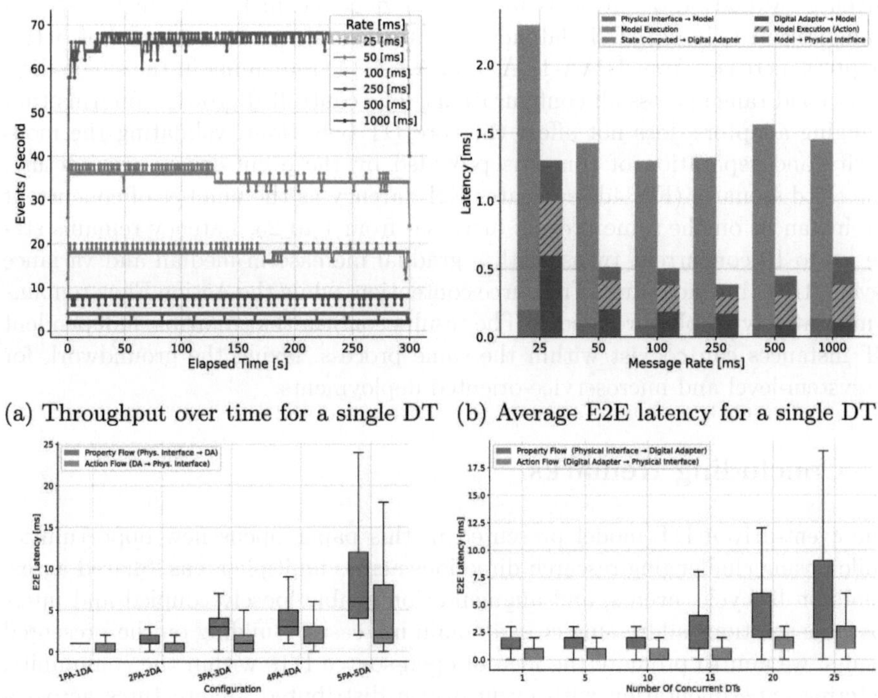

(a) Throughput over time for a single DT (b) Average E2E latency for a single DT

(c) E2E for a DT with multiple adapters (d) E2E latency for multiple DT instances.

Fig. 4. Performance analysis of event-driven DTs with different configurations.

[2] Health Level 7 (HL7) https://www.hl7.org/.

[3] Fast Healthcare Interoperability Resources (FHIR) https://hl7.org/FHIR/.

The experimental evaluation considers three scenarios targeting complementary aspects of the proposed approach: (i) a single DT instance with one Physical Asset Adapter (PAA) and one Digital Adapter (DA) at varying message rates, to assess event bus stability and end-to-end responsiveness; (ii) a single DT instance with an increasing number of PAA/DA pairs, to evaluate modularity and decoupling under adapter scaling; and (iii) multiple independent DT instances running concurrently on the same node, to demonstrate the feasibility of active, coexisting twins as a basis for ecosystem-level deployments. The key metrics are *throughput* (events/s processed by the event bus over time) and *end-to-end (E2E) latency* (elapsed time from event ingestion at the PAA to delivery at the DA, and vice versa), decomposed per architectural component to isolate the overhead introduced by the event-driven routing.

In the first scenario, the system sustains stable throughput across all tested rates (25–1000 ms), with no observable degradation over the 300 s observation window as illustrated in Fig. 4a. E2E latency remains well below 2.5 ms for rates up to 500 ms, with *Model Execution* dominating in both flow directions and inter-component routing contributing negligibly, confirming that the event-driven coordination overhead is minimal as depicted in Fig. 4b. In the second configuration (Fig. 4c), E2E latency scales gradually as the number of active adapters increases from 1PAA-1DA to 5PAA-5DA, remaining in the single-digit millisecond range across all configurations. The controlled growth confirms that changing adapters does not affect the core DT behaviour, validating the modularity and separation of concerns provided by the event-driven architecture. The third scenario (Fig. 4d) evaluates E2E latency as the number of concurrent DT instances on the same process increases from 1 to 25. Latency remains stable up to 10 concurrent twins, with a gradual increase in median and variance beyond that threshold due to resource contention, while the Action Flow remains comparatively stable throughout. The results confirm that multiple independent DT instances can coexist within the same process, laying the groundwork for ecosystem-level and microservice-oriented deployments.

4 Concluding Remarks

The event-driven DT model presented in this paper opens new opportunities while posing challenging research directions across multiple areas. Shared agreements on lifecycle, events, and augmentation enable loosely coupled and interoperable solutions addressing cross-domain use cases. Building on the presented results, we aim to promote the idea of open-source DTs within the community, fostering experimentation with event-driven distributed architectures across a broad spectrum of application domains and deployment scenarios.

References

1. Atkinson, C., Kühne, T.: Taming the complexity of digital twins. IEEE Software pp. 0–0 (2021). https://doi.org/10.1109/MS.2021.3129174
2. Autiosalo, J., Siegel, J., Tammi, K.: TwinBase: open-source server software for the digital twin web. IEEE Access **9**, 140779–140798 (2021). https://doi.org/10.1109/ACCESS.2021.3119487
3. Bellavista, P., Giannelli, C., Mamei, M., Mendula, M., Picone, M.: Application-driven network-aware digital twin management in industrial edge environments. IEEE Trans. Indust. Info. , pp. 1–1 (2021). https://doi.org/10.1109/TII.2021.3067447
4. Cimino, C., Negri, E., Fumagalli, L.: Review of digital twin applications in manufacturing. Comput. Ind. **113**, 103130 (2019). https://doi.org/10.1016/j.compind.2019.103130
5. Croatti, A., Gabellini, M., Montagna, S., Ricci, A.: On the integration of agents and digital twins in healthcare. J. Med. Syst. **44**(9), 1–8 (2020). https://doi.org/10.1007/s10916-020-01623-5
6. Eramo, R., Bordeleau, F., Combemale, B., van den Brand, M., Wimmer, M., Wortmann, A.: Conceptualizing digital twins. IEEE Softw., pp. 0–0 (2021). https://doi.org/10.1109/MS.2021.3130755
7. ETSI Specialist Task Forces (STF) 628: Smartm2m; digital twins communication requirements. TS TS-103-845-V1.1.1, European Telecommunications Standards Institute (ETSI), (2024)
8. Fuller, A., Fan, Z., Day, C., Barlow, C.: Digital twin: enabling technologies, challenges and open research. IEEE Access **8**, 108952–108971 (2020). https://doi.org/10.1109/ACCESS.2020.2998358
9. Jacoby, M., Usländer, T.: Digital twin and internet of things—current standards landscape. Appl. Sci. **10**(18) (2020)
10. Lehner, D., et al.: Digital twin platforms: requirements, capabilities, and future prospects. IEEE Softw., pp. 0–0 (2021). https://doi.org/10.1109/MS.2021.3133795
11. Minerva, R., Crespi, N.: Digital twins: properties, software frameworks, and application scenarios. IT Prof. **23**(1), 51–55 (2021). https://doi.org/10.1109/MITP.2020.2982896
12. Minerva, R., Lee, G.M., Crespi, N.: Digital twin in the IoT context: a survey on technical features, scenarios, and architectural models. Proc. IEEE **108**(10), 1785–1824 (2020)
13. Picone, M., Mamei, M., Zambonelli, F.: WLDT: a general purpose library to build IoT digital twins. SoftwareX **13**, 100661 (2021). https://doi.org/10.1016/j.softx.2021.100661
14. Picone, M., Martinelli, M., Burattini, S., Giulianelli, A., Ricci, A.: The two faces of interoperability: bridging cyber and physical spaces with digital twins. In: 2025 21st International Conference on Distributed Computing in Smart Systems and the Internet of Things (DCOSS-IoT), pp. 1–8 (2025). https://doi.org/10.1109/DCOSS-IoT65416.2025.00078
15. Picone, M., et al.: Harmonizing physical and digital twins lifecycles. In: 2025 IEEE 22nd International Conference on Software Architecture Companion (ICSA-C), pp. 197–204. (2025). https://doi.org/10.1109/ICSA-C65153.2025.00039
16. Ricci, A., Croatti, A., Mariani, S., Montagna, S., Picone, M.: Web of digital twins. ACM Trans. Internet Technol. **22**(4), (2022). https://doi.org/10.1145/3507909

17. Ricci, A., Croatti, A., Montagna, S.: Pervasive and connected digital twins - a vision for digital health. IEEE Internet Comput. (2021). https://doi.org/10.1109/MIC.2021.3052039
18. Saracco, R.: Digital twins: bridging physical space and cyberspace. Computer **52**(12), 58–64 (2019). https://doi.org/10.1109/MC.2019.2942803
19. Tao, F., Zhang, H., Liu, A., Nee, A.Y.C.: Digital twin in industry: state-of-the-art. IEEE Trans. Industr. Inf. **15**(4), 2405–2415 (2019)

Digital Twins and World Models: A Systematic Taxonomic Disambiguation

Kunal Suri(✉) and Fabio Arnez

Université Paris-Saclay, CEA, List, F-91120 Palaiseau, France
{kunal.suri,fabio.arnez}@cea.fr

Abstract. Although often conflated, Digital Twins and World Models represent distinct paradigms of system reasoning. A Digital Twin is defined by a persistent, bidirectional data coupling with a specific physical asset. Conversely, a World Model captures environmental dynamics to support prediction and planning, without necessitating a direct link to a singular physical counterpart. This paper establishes a rigorous disambiguation for researchers and practitioners in the Physical AI realm. We define minimal criteria for each paradigm, compare them via a multidimensional taxonomy, and validate the framework using concrete real-world systems. Our analysis demonstrates that neither paradigm subsumes the other. Rather, they intersect within a bounded convergence zone where specific architectures integrate both. While this taxonomy is descriptive and integrative, we note that formal ontological grounding remains an avenue for future work.

Keywords: Digital Twins · World Models · Artificial Intelligence · Autonomous Systems · Industry 5.0 · Embodied AI · Physical AI

1 Introduction

The terms "Digital Twin" (DT) and "World Model" (WM) are often treated as synonyms, but they are not the same construct. DTs emerged from systems engineering and lifecycle management [3]; WMs emerged from cognitive science, reinforcement learning, and modern foundation-model research [2,5]. As these paradigms increasingly co-appear in Physical AI systems, treating them as interchangeable obscures differences in what they represent, how they are built, and what they optimize. The ambiguity is amplified by the polysemy of "world model": in engineering, it may denote physics-based equations, while in AI it typically denotes a learned predictive model of environment dynamics [2,4]. These usages rest on different epistemological assumptions. When the distinction is lost, practitioners may treat a world model as if it carried digital-twin-grade fidelity, or expect a digital twin to generalise like a world model, wherein either error can lead to flawed design, verification, and trust decisions.

This conflation has intensified in recent industry and research discourse. The NVIDIA Cosmos technical report [1] describes Physical AI as requiring "a digital

R. Posenato and I. Vanderfeesten (Eds.): CAiSE 2026 Workshops, LNBIP 586, pp. 61–66, 2026.
https://doi.org/10.1007/978-3-032-28160-9_6

twin of itself, the policy model, and a digital twin of the world, the world model." Waymo's World Model (WWM), for example, generates synthetic driving scenarios for offline training but has no persistent live coupling to any single vehicle [7]. In our terms, this is a WM described with DT vocabulary. Semantically, this is *construct overload*: one label used for structurally different systems [9]. The issue is measurable, not anecdotal: Wuni et al. [8] report that roughly one-third of 358 analyzed definitions describe a digital model rather than a true digital twin.

To address this ambiguity, we provide a systematic disambiguation of DTs and WMs and a structured account of where they truly converge. Our contributions are threefold: (1) minimal defining criteria for each paradigm; (2) a multi-dimensional taxonomy that makes their differences explicitly selected based on discriminating power at the DT–WM boundary; and (3) an empirical grounding against named Physical AI systems. Our central claim is that neither paradigm subsumes the other; they overlap only within a bounded, configuration-dependent convergence zone. We note that this taxonomy is descriptive rather than ontologically formalized, and grounding it within frameworks such as the Unified Foundational Ontology (UFO) remains a topic of future work.

2 Conceptual Definitions and Taxonomy

2.1 Conceptual Foundations and Related Work

Before presenting formal criteria, we briefly define each paradigm. The DT concept, articulated by Grieves [3], rests on three pillars: Physical Space, Virtual Space, and persistent bidirectional data flow between them. A simulation represents a *class* of systems, whereas a DT represents a *specific* asset in its operating context. Compared with traditional simulation, DTs add instance specificity, continuous bidirectional coupling, and lifecycle integration.

The meaning of "digital twin" has broadened over time. Between 2015 and 2025, concept creep expanded the label across multiple domains. Wuni et al. [8] report that roughly one-third of 358 definitions describe static digital models without bidirectional data flow. Industry usage is broader still: IoT Analytics[1] report describes a spectrum from basic digital artifacts (for example, a photo) to real-time closed-loop orchestration. In this paper, we adopt the strict Grieves criteria [3] while acknowledging this broader usage.

WMs trace to Craik's theory of mental models and Sutton's Dyna architecture, as suggested in recent surveys [2,4]. Two influential modern directions are Generative Dreaming [5] and JEPA-style [6] prediction in representation space. Across these surveys, common WM properties include learned representations, action-conditioned prediction, planning through imagined rollouts, latent-space operation, agent-centricity, and generalization. Crucially, none requires a physical referent [2,4]. Guan et al. [4] emphasize this point for autonomous driving: WMs must both *understand* the current scene and *predict* its evolution. This helps explain why some systems are described with DT language despite lacking persistent bidirectional coupling to a specific physical asset.

[1] https://iot-analytics.com/how-the-worlds-250-digital-twins-compare/.

2.2 Operational Definition Criteria

We define two minimal criteria sets from the primary sources above.

A system qualifies as a *Digital Twin* if it: (i) represents a *specific* physical entity, not a generic class; (ii) maintains a *bidirectional, persistent* data connection to that entity; and (iii) is coupled to the entity's *lifecycle* [3]. Without a physical counterpart, there is no twin.

A system qualifies as a *World Model* if it: (i) learns a state transition function, $x_{t+1} = f(x_t, a_t)$ from data itself, that captures how an environment evolves in response to actions; (ii) supports *prediction and planning* through imagined future states; and (iii) operates on *learned representations*, not exclusively hand-crafted physics [2,5], i.e., a physical referent is optional.

These criteria make the set-theoretic relationship explicit. Neither paradigm subsumes the other. Most deployed DTs are not WMs, because they rely on physical referents, including (physics-based) simulations, and do not support agent-centric imagination. While most WMs are not DTs, because they could lack physical referents and bidirectional synchronization. Their overlap is the bounded convergence zone characterized in Sect. 3.

2.3 Taxonomic Comparison

Table 1 organizes key DT–WM differences across 9 dimensions (Dim.), grouped into *Foundational*, *Structural*, and *Institutional* categories derived from key sources [3,5,8]. These dimensions are selected for their discriminative relevance to the DT–WM boundary adopted in this paper and do not originate from a formal ontological framework such as the UFO. The *foundational* group captures whether a physical counterpart is required (Dim. 1), the coupling modality between physical and virtual entities (Dim. 2), and the dominant epistemological origin of the models involved (Dim. 3). The *structural* group addresses purpose: asset lifecycle management vs. agent planning and world simulation (Dim. 4), as well as the fidelity vs. generalization trade-off (Dim. 5), temporal scope (Dim. 6), and knowledge representation (Dim. 7). Finally, the *institutional* group contrasts the standardization maturity of each paradigm (Dim. 8) and the prediction target: asset state at the instance or aggregate level for DTs versus future state conditioned on actions, observations, or prompts for WMs (Dim. 9).

3 Taxonomy Validation and Convergence Patterns Between Digital Twins and World Models

3.1 Taxonomy Validation on a Concrete Case

To demonstrate the taxonomy's diagnostic power, we apply it to the Waymo World Model (WWM) [7]. WWM has no permanent physical counterpart (Dim. 1): it is built on Google DeepMind's Genie 3 and post-trained on fleet logs, but operates offline for scenario generation. It lacks bidirectional coupling (Dim. 2), as generated simulations do not feed actuator commands back to any

Table 1. Multi-dimensional taxonomy of Digital Twins and World Models.

Dimension	Digital Twins	World Models
Foundational		
1. Physical dependence	Required [3]	Optional [4,5]
2. Coupling modality	Bidirectional-live [3]	None or unidirectional
3. Epistemology	Predominantly physics-based, explicit (often hybrid)	Predominantly learned from data [5]
Structural		
4. Purpose	Asset lifecycle management [3]	Agent planning & world simulation [2,5]
5. Fidelity vs. generalization	High-fidelity, instance-level focused	Broad, approximate
6. Temporal scope	Lifecycle-spanning	Task-scoped
7. Knowledge representation	Equations, rules, and learned components	Neural network parameters
Institutional / Functional		
8. Standardization	Established and evolving (ISO, IEC)	No widely adopted formal standards yet
9. Prediction target	Asset state (instance or aggregate) [3]	Future state given context (actions, observations, or prompts) [2,4]

vehicle in real time. Its epistemology is predominantly learned (Dim. 3), relying on diffusion and auto-regressive architectures trained on over millions of fully autonomous miles, though its grounding in real sensor logs ensures implicit physical consistency. Its purpose is agent planning and world simulation (Dim. 4): generating counterfactual driving scenarios to evaluate the Waymo Driver. It prioritizes broad generalization over instance-level fidelity (Dim. 5), simulating everything from tornadoes to elephants with a single model. It is task-scoped (Dim. 6), serving offline training and validation rather than persisting across a vehicle's lifecycle. Its knowledge is stored in neural network parameters (Dim. 7). It operates without formal DT standards (Dim. 8). Its prediction target is the future state given context actions, scene layouts, or language prompts (Dim. 9). Under the strict criteria of this taxonomy, WWM aligns with WM on all nine dimensions, with only Dim. 3 showing partial overlap due to the real-world provenance of its training data. This suggests that classifying WWM (a world model) with DT vocabulary will be an instance of construct overload under the definitions adopted in this work.

3.2 Convergence Patterns

Despite their differences, DTs and WMs increasingly appear within the same pipelines. Zhou et al. [9] recently proposed a four-stage DT–AI framework: Modeling, Mirroring, Intervening, and Autonomous Management. The NVIDIA Omniverse–Cosmos pipeline illustrates this pattern in industry [1]: Omniverse performs the DT function (explicit-physics simulation, lifecycle-spanning asset management), while Cosmos performs the WM function (generative prediction of future states given context). Critically, these compose into a pipeline, where Omniverse renders 3D scenarios that condition Cosmos models to generate synthetic environments, rather than collapsing into a single concept. This separation preserves distinct roles along Dims. 3, 6, 7, and 9: Omniverse relies on explicit physics and geometric models (Dim. 3) that persist across the asset lifecycle (Dim. 6), while Cosmos stores knowledge in neural network parameters (Dim. 7) and predicts future states from multi-modal prompts (Dim. 9).

Likewise, in **Sim-to-Real Robotics (Dims. 1, 3, 5 in focus)**: 1X World Model [2] learns a simulator directly from real robot video and action data using a video-pretrained world model (1XWM) that derives robot actions from text-conditioned video generation. This replaces hand-authored DT scenes with a learned generative model, shifting epistemology (Dim. 3) entirely to the data-driven side and relaxing the physical-dependence requirement (Dim. 1, 5): the model generalises to tasks and objects never physically encountered.

4 Discussion and Conclusion

DTs and WMs are complementary within this taxonomy: DTs provide high-fidelity, lifecycle-persistent, physics-grounded representations (Dims. 3, 5, 6) with standards support such as the Asset Administration Shell (AAS) (Dim. 8), while WMs prioritise generalisation (Dim. 5) via learned prediction and counterfactual reasoning [2,5], targeting future states from diverse inputs (Dim. 9). Integration leverages DT grounding with WM exploration, as in NVIDIA's Omniverse–Cosmos pipeline: persistent geometric and physics models (Dims. 3, 6) composed with neural multi-modal generation (Dims. 7, 9) [1].

In conclusion, DTs and WMs are distinct but complementary paradigms that converge within specific architectural configurations to enable Physical AI. The conflation of these terms, driven by concept creep, marketing pressures, and the polysemy of "world model" across communities, obscures real differences in ontological commitment, system architecture, and safety guarantees. A generative video model alone is not a DT; conversely, a world model, despite sometimes being described as "a digital twin of reality," aligns with WM criteria on all nine taxonomy dimensions. Yet within a bounded convergence zone such as sim-to-real robotics (Dims. 1, 3, 5), the two paradigms functionally merge into layered architectures that compose both rather than choosing between them. This empirically bounded convergence strengthens the case for disambiguation. We

[2] https://www.1x.tech/discover/world-model-self-learning.

acknowledge two principal limitations: (1) the taxonomy dimensions are selected for discriminative power rather than derived from a foundational ontology, which limits their claim to completeness, and (2) our validation covers a small number of named systems, so the boundary conditions we identify require broader empirical testing. Our taxonomy nonetheless provides a systematic framework for navigating convergence without collapsing conceptual distinctions. In future work, we plan to ground the dimensions in formalizations such as UFO and extend validation to a broader corpus of industrial and embodied AI systems.

Acknowledgments. This work was partially supported by the European Union's Horizon Europe programme under Grant Agreement No. 101138782 (**RAASCEMAN**[3]https://cordis.europa.eu/project/id/101138782).

Furthermore, LLM tools (Claude, Gemini, and Qwen) assisted with brainstorming, structural planning, and language editing. All intellectual ideas, analyses, and conclusions remain the sole responsibility of the authors.

References

1. Agarwal, N., Ali, A., Bala, M., Balaji, Y., et al.: Cosmos world foundation model platform for physical AI. arXiv preprint arXiv:2501.03575 (2025). https://arxiv.org/abs/2501.03575, technical report - NVIDIA
2. Ding, J., Zhang, Y., Shang, Y., Zong, Z., Feng, J., Yuan, Y., et al.: Understanding world or predicting future? A comprehensive survey of world models. ACM Comput. Surv. **58**(3), 1–38 (2025). https://dl.acm.org/doi/full/10.1145/3746449
3. Grieves, M.W.: Digital twins: past, present, and future. In: Crespi, N., Drobot, A.T., Minerva, R. (eds.) The Digital Twin, pp. 97–121. Springer International Publishing (2023). https://doi.org/10.1007/978-3-031-21343-4_4
4. Guan, Y., et al.: World models for autonomous driving: an initial survey. IEEE Trans. Intell. Veh. (2024). https://doi.org/10.1109/TIV.2024.3398357
5. Ha, D., Schmidhuber, J.: World models, vol. 2, p. 440 (2018). https://arxiv.org/abs/1803.10122
6. LeCun, Y.: A path towards autonomous machine intelligence version 0.9. 2, 2022-06-27. Open Rev. **62**(1), 1–62 (2022). https://openreview.net/pdf?id=BZ5a1r-kVsf
7. Waymo Research: The Waymo world model: A new frontier for autonomous driving simulation. Waymo Blog (2026). https://waymo.com/blog/2026/02/the-waymo-world-model-a-new-frontier-for-autonomous-driving-simulation/. Accessed 03 Mar 2026
8. Wuni, I.Y., Grieves, M., Yamin, M.J., Koroma, S.A.: Conceptualising the digital twin: an analysis of 358 definitions. Digital Twin, 2600763 (2025) https://doi.org/10.1080/27525783.2025.2600763
9. Zhou, R., Chen, D., Jia, Z., et al.: Digital twin AI: opportunities and challenges from large language models to world models. arXiv preprint arXiv:2601.01321 (2026), https://arxiv.org/abs/2601.01321

Digital Process Twin Classification and Software Selection

Gerald Kremer[1(✉)], Eva-Maria Sikut[1], Luiz Ricardo Brito Ribeiro[2], Silvia Dallavalle[2], and Rainer Stark[1]

[1] Technische Universität Berlin, Pascalstraße 8-9, 10587, Berlin, Germany
kremer@tu-berlin.de

[2] University of São Paulo, Av. Bandeirantes, 3900-Vila Monte Alegre, Ribeirão Preto-SP 14040-900, Brazil

Abstract. Digital Process Twins (DPT) are widely discussed widely but defined and implemented inconsistently. This paper consolidates DPT characteristics into a multi-dimensional reference model with maturity levels and derives a capability mapping that links characteristic levels to required software capabilities. We demonstrate the approach with a technology-radar based assessment of representative platforms based on public documentation, showing how capability gaps and suitable tool support can be identified early for a given DPT ambition level.

Keywords: Digital Process Twin · Meta Model · Technology Radar

1 Introduction

Digital twins (DTs) have become a key research topic for data-driven operation and optimization of industrial systems. They are commonly described as virtual representations/models coupled with physical assets or processes through data flows [1]. Recent reviews show a growing landscape of concepts, taxonomies, and maturity models that distinguish, for example, levels of integration, lifecycle coverage, analytics, and autonomy [2]. This conceptual progress contrasts with a practical gap. Implementations often rely on ad-hoc selections of software solutions or toolchains (e.g., simulation tools, workflow engines, analytics stacks) driven by individual expertise rather than a transparent, requirement-based derivation from the targeted DT type [3]. Existing classification schemes explain what kinds of DTs exist, but they do not translate characteristics into verifiable software capability requirements.

The paper focusses on Digital Process Twins (DPTs) because software selection is particularly challenging for process-centric twins. DPTs typically require combining multiple software families (process modelling, runtime event evidence, conformance-checking, process mining, and often simulation), and the same DPT intent can be implemented through very different toolchains [4]. As a result, the gap between conceptual DPT characteristics and practical software decisions is especially large. In practice, several solutions already claim DPT support, for example Camunda for business processes or Siemens Technomatix Plant Simulation for manufacturing processes, yet vendors

R. Posenato and I. Vanderfeesten (Eds.): CAiSE 2026 Workshops, LNBIP 586, pp. 67–78, 2026.
https://doi.org/10.1007/978-3-032-28160-9_7

typically list features without positioning them against scientifically grounded DPT dimensions. The result is limited comparability between solutions, reduced reusability of research results, and weak traceability from DPT concepts to implementation choices.

Accordingly, the goal of this paper is to develop and demonstrate a traceable method that links a structured description of DPTs to a justified selection and evaluation of software solutions based on required capabilities. For this the paper addresses three research questions:

RQ1: How can DPTs be described via a meta-model that consolidates existing digital twin classifications while focusing on process-relevant dimensions?

RQ2: Which minimum software capabilities are required for these dimensions, and how can they be systematically organized?

RQ3: How can these capabilities be operationalized in a technology radar that supports consistent assessment and comparison of software solutions?

To answer these questions, we consolidate recurring characteristics from a corpus of established DT classification approaches into a DPT focused characteristics meta-model, map each characteristic to minimum required software capabilities, and operationalize the result as a DPT Technology Radar for comparing candidate tools and toolchains [4].

2 State of Research

2.1 Digital Process Twins

DTs are commonly defined as virtual representations of physical entities that are continuously linked to their real counterparts via data across the lifecycle [5]. Key characteristics repeatedly highlighted in the literature include bidirectional data exchange, multi-source data integration, and the ability to support monitoring, prediction, and control. Different authors bring specific views towards classifications of twins. Some authors emphasize lifecycle integration and service orientation [1]. Others classify DT use cases based on their main components (digital master, digital shadow, and digital twin) and state that most implementations rather focus on digital shadows or the digital master and simulations instead of the actual DT, which is a linkage of both [6].

Several authors propose additional frameworks to describe and classify DTs, like a use-case-oriented classification system along dimensions such as purpose, integration, data sources, and intelligence [7], while others introduce maturity models that cover connectivity, data, models, services, and organizational embedding [8].

DPTs focus on the dynamic behavior of processes, such as production workflows, logistics chains, service processes, and informational processes, rather than on physical assets alone. In BPM, a business process is defined as a collection of inter-related events, activities, and decision points involving actors and objects that collectively lead to an outcome of value to at least one customer [9]. Hence, the term Digital Twins of Business Processes (DTBP) is interpreted as focusing specifically on business processes. In this paper, DPTs are defined as twins of processes in a broader sense, including physical, organizational, and informational transformations in general. The understanding of a "process" varies across domains (e.g., structured activity sequences in BPM vs. physical transformations in manufacturing). This paper adopts a broad definition of both to enable cross-domain applicability.

Hence, a DPT can be characterized as a continuously synchronized, model-based representation of a process that links these formal process models to event logs and other data, supports monitoring, conformance, prediction, and what-if analysis, and can, in advanced cases, trigger or recommend interventions in the physical process.

Recent DTP work highlights executable DPT perspectives on the combination of monitoring, conformance checking, and enactment to enhance process-driven systems [4]. Process mining is frequently used as a technical basis to maintain process models from event data and operationalize process-centric twins for decision support [10].

Additionally, research on DPTs propose different technological solutions for the development of DPTs but also list current barriers during implementation. For example Fornari et al. (2025) formulate a research manifesto for DTBT, explicitly identifying open challenges in model design, data/model synchronization, tooling/infrastructure, and organizational-level integration [11].

2.2 Methodological Support for Digital Twin Development and IT Systems

Different works from researchers and standardization institutions provide guidelines and methodological support for developing and operating DTs. (ISO/IEC 30173:2023) and [13] offer high-level development processes, architectural roles, and composition principles for digital twins, while ISO 23247 focusses on DTs in manufacturing. Besides guidelines and high-level processes, reference architectures for IT systems are proposed, like the RAMI 4.0. Model which is depicted in Fig. 1. In the reference model layers are depicted, in which DT related functions are located in IT landscapes.

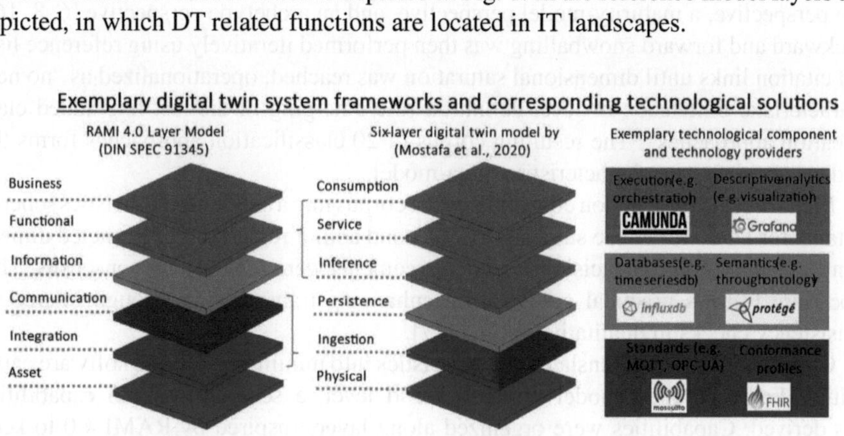

Fig. 1. Reference Models from [14] and [15] and added technologies for implementation

All these frameworks and development approaches provide general procedural models (define objectives, derive requirements, design architecture, implement, validate, iterate) and highlight traceability, but they never consider the variety of possible technologies that need to be utilized to develop a DT and hence do not show how to select existing software solutions on the market.

Because besides general methodologies to develop DTs a growing market offers building blocks for implementing DTs. General-purpose DT platforms such as Microsoft

Azure Digital Twins or AWS IoT TwinMaker provide data modelling, data integration, simulation, and analytics services. Process-oriented tools like process mining and execution platforms (e.g., Celonis, SAP Signavio), workflow and orchestration engines (e.g., Camunda), increasingly market DPTs and taken together, these platforms cover many of the functions identified in DPT frameworks. But at the same time, the tools only always cover specific technological parts of a DPT. The unresolved gap is therefore not the absence of taxonomies or architectures, but the missing traceable linkage between the conceptual descriptions of DTs and the features of concrete implemented software solutions.

3 Research Method

This paper proposes a method that links DPT concepts to software selection through a chain of artefacts: a DPT characteristics meta-model consolidated from established DT classification approaches, a mapping from characteristics to minimum required software capabilities, and a radar representation to compare candidate tools/toolchains.

The meta-model creation followed a seeded scoping approach. A Scopus candidate scan was executed using a TITLE-ABS-KEY query combining digital twin OR process twin AND taxonomy/classification/maturity model terms. The scan yielded 271 records (2016–2025). From this candidate set, three complementary seed approaches were selected to initialize snowballing, reflecting a manufacturing-oriented classification perspective, a maturity-model perspective, and an archetype perspective [6, 8, 16]. Backward and forward snowballing was then performed iteratively using reference lists and citation links until dimensional saturation was reached, operationalized as "no new characteristic dimension or level-definition rule emerging in the last five added classification approaches". The resulting corpus of 20 classification approaches forms the evidence base for the characteristics meta-model.

Meta-model construction consolidated the corpus into a single characteristics schema suitable for DPT. To reduce subjectivity, a second author reviewed the extracted dimensions and consolidation decisions and disagreements were resolved by consensus. This procedure follows practical guidance on enhancing transparency through intercoder consistency checks in qualitative coding [17].

Capability mapping translates characteristics into minimum required software capabilities. For each meta-model dimension and level, a set of minimum capabilities was derived. Capabilities were organized along layers inspired by RAMI 4.0 to keep architectural reasoning consistent and to support later visual traceability in the radar representation.

Radar-based operationalization supports assessment and comparison of candidate tools or toolchains. For a selected target DPT type (a chosen level on each meta-model dimension), the mapping yields a corresponding set of minimum capability requirements. Tool assessment can then be performed by collecting evidence for each capability level from inspectable sources such as vendor documentation, Consistent with the capability structuring, the radar uses the RAMI-inspired layer grouping and color coding to visually link assessed capabilities back to the architecture layers.

4 Research Results

4.1 Digital Process Twin Classification Meta Model

The starting point was the observation that numerous taxonomies and maturity models exist for digital twins, each introducing partly overlapping dimensions: e.g. the 8-dimension model by [18], lists of archetypes of digital twins by [16], a maturity model by [8], a multi-dimensional use-case classification by [7], an industrial use-case framework by [19], and related works. But specifically, for DPTs no such model existed. A Scopus scan was executed using a TITLE-ABS-KEY query combining "process twin*" OR "twin of process*" twin AND taxonomy OR classification, but the scan yielded only nine records, which were screened and did not show relevant classifications.

This is why three complementary literature seed approaches from regular DT twin literature were selected to initialize snowballing, reflecting a manufacturing-oriented classification perspective, a maturity-model perspective, and an archetype perspective [6, 8, 16]. Then the literature corpus was iteratively expanded (as described in Sect. 3 until additional sources no longer yielded genuinely new structural criteria for classifying process twins. Altogether 20 candidate dimensions were consolidated from the surveyed taxonomies, maturity models, and digital twin concepts. These dimensions were then reduced in a two-step filtering and consolidation approach. First non-transferable or non-technical dimensions were excluded. Dimensions were removed if they were strongly domain-specific, e.g. urban/geometry-focused criteria such as "2D/3D map level", "reality capture" or city-specific interaction types as in [7, 20, 21], or emphasized project-management aspects, such as the "time of creation" dimension [16] or strategic or ethical criteria that do not directly translate into implementable software capabilities, like the dimension "public good" in [22].

Then overlapping dimensions were merged or sharpened to improve direct linkability to software requirements. For example, the initial combined criterion *Data Connectivity & Synchronization* was separated into *Data Flow Direction* and *Level of Synchronization.* Model-related aspects were restructured into *Model Scope* and *Model Depth,* whereas model scope was inspired from the *levels of manufacturing systems* (process level, machine level, factory level) coming from [23], but was then transformed into micro level, meso level, and macro level, similar to process level, system level and system of systems level in [8]. Other dimensions were manipulated from existing classifications for a better fit to DPTs. One example is the *Model Depth* dimension in the new meta model, which was inspired by the dimension *Digital Model Richness* in [18], which originally had the scales geometry, control behavior and multi-physical behavior. For a better fit, to the topic of DPTs this was transformed to the dimension *Model Depth,* which can be described in structural/descriptive models (e.g. activity diagrams), behavioral models (e.g. discrete event models) and multidimensional models.

Applying these rules led to the DPT classification framework (termed "meta-model" because it serves as a template for instantiating concrete DPT profiles by selecting a level on each dimension), which can be found in Table 1.

Table 1. Digital Process Twin Characteristics Meta Model

Digital Process Twin Dimension	Dimension Levels	As Described in
1. Data Flow Direction	Static (no data flow)	[8, 16, 18, 21, 24, 25]
	Uni-Directional	
	Bi-Directional	
2. Level of Synchronisation	Static/Batch	[8, 18, 21, 25]
	Periodic	
	Real Time/Event-Driven	
3. Model Scope	Micro-Level (single process)	[8, 23, 25]
	Meso-Level (system of processes)	
	Macro-Level (system of systems)	
4. Model Depth	Descriptive/Structural Models	[18]
	Behavioural Models	
	Multidimensional Models	
5. Behaviour Simulation Paradigm	Only Structural (No simulation)	[26]
	Single Paradigm	
	Hybrid Paradigm	
6. Modelling Approach	Symbolic Modelling	[10, 23]
	Subsymbolic Modelling	
	Hybrid/Combined Modelling	
7. Analytical Capability	Descriptive	[8, 18, 23–25]
	Diagnostic	
	Predictive	
	Prescriptive	
8. Level of Control Autonomy	Manual Decision by Human	[27]
	Decision Suggestion for Human	
	Fully Automated	
9. Learning Ability	Static/not Learning	[22, 24, 25]
	Reactive (Offline)	
	Adaptive (Online)	
	Cognitive/Evolutionary	
10. System Integration level	Isolated	[24, 25]
	Proprietary Integration	
	Interoperable Integration	
11. Life Cycle Integration	No Integration	[28]

(*continued*)

Table 1. (*continued*)

Digital Process Twin Dimension	Dimension Levels	As Described in
	Impact Assessment on Life Cycle-KPIs	
	Multi-objective control based on KPIs	

4.2 Mapping of Twin Characteristics to Required Software Capabilities

The DPT meta model describes what kind of DPT is targeted. The next step specifies what a software solution must minimally provide to realize each of these characteristics. For this purpose, all dimensions and their levels were mapped to software capabilities and structured along the layers of the RAMI 4.0 architecture. RAMI 4.0 was chosen because it is an established reference for distributing responsibilities across layers and has been aligned with ISO 23247 and related standards. From a BPM perspective, the dimensions and capabilities can be related to the BPM life-cycle phases [9]: discovery and analysis draw on analytics (S10) and model repositories (S4); redesign benefits from simulation (S8, S9); implementation relies on execution runtimes (S7), interfaces (S5), and protocols (S6); monitoring requires data storage (S1), history (S3), and real-time synchronization.

The mapping was performed jointly by two authors following the same intercoder procedure as the meta-model construction in chapter 3. For example, the Synchronization dimension maps low, periodic, and event-driven levels to progressively richer capability requirements across data storage, history, semantics, interfaces, protocols, execution runtime, and model repository; the complete level-by-level mappings for all dimensions are provided in [29].

Digital Process Twin Software Capability Radar

The DPT software capability radar operationalizes the mapping from DPT characteristics to software capabilities. While RAMI 4.0 provides the layered reference structure, the radar specializes this view for DPTs by assigning the concrete, DPT-specific software capability clusters to these layers. In the radar exemplary assessed software solutions (assessment in October 2025) are plotted. The developed software capability radar can be found in Fig. 2. The radar is structured into sectors that represent RAMI-inspired layers:

- Communication layer: connectivity, protocols, event ingestion,
- Information layer: data storage, history, semantics, model repositories,
- Functional layer: execution runtimes, simulation/co-simulation, conformance checking, analytics services,
- Business layer: orchestration of value streams, integration into operational processes and governance.

Radial axes within each sector represent capability clusters derived from the eleven DPT dimensions. Two types of elements are distinguished. Mostly graded capability progressions are used for aspects that build logically on each other (e.g., analytics from descriptive to diagnostic to predictive to prescriptive), for which the radar uses stepped scales. The capability regarding the execution of processes that do not form a strict hierarchy (DES/ABM/hybrid) are represented as separate joints.

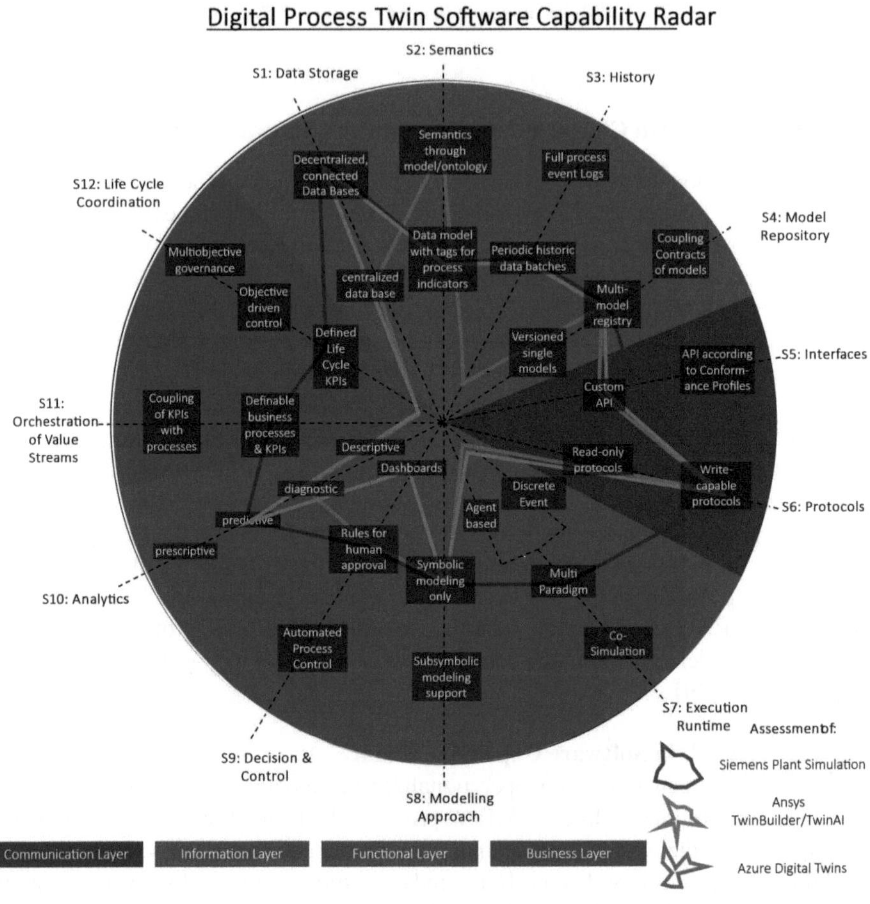

Fig. 2. DPT Software Capability Radar and assessment of Siemens Technomatix Plant Simulation, ANSYS Twin Builder, and Microsoft Azure Digital Twins

Through the radar a developer/researcher can assess relevant features of software solutions (or toolchains) that can then be visualized as a polygon connecting its achieved levels and discrete capabilities across all sectors. This makes visible how well a given system supports the requirements implied by a specific DPT classification profile, or where complementary tools are needed to reach the desired twin characteristics, and how different platforms compare in a neutral, capability-based manner. The radar thus forms the practical bridge between the DPT classification meta model and the evaluation of concrete software solutions for DPTs.

5 Discussion

The assessment using the DPT Software Capability Radar suggests a crowded but fragmented tooling landscape. Across candidate solutions, capabilities tend to converge on a common baseline in S1 Data Storage, S3 History, and S10 Analytics (e.g., storing operational traces and reporting via dashboards), while higher levels remain unevenly supported across sectors. This fragmentation aligns with broader observations that DT implementations are frequently realized as domain-specific solutions or toolchains rather than integrated, general-purpose platforms [30]. From a DPT perspective, the radar makes visible which capability clusters are typically provided by a single product and where composed toolchains become necessary.

A more distinctive gap concerns advanced capabilities that move beyond reporting towards runtime-coupled, model-driven DPT behavior. Research on executable digital process twins indicates that closed-loop pipelines combining monitoring, refinement and enactment are technically feasible but remain largely research prototypes rather than mature stacks [4]. Similarly, work on automated digital twin generation for complex manufacturing systems highlights that deriving executable structures from operational evidence is algorithmically demanding and sensitive to domain-specific assumptions, which helps explain why such capabilities are still scarce in commercial tools [31]. Finally, the radar indicates that higher-level orchestration and coordination capabilities (e.g., S11 Orchestration of Value Streams, S12 Life Cycle Coordination) are rarely supported beyond KPI-style reporting, showing a near absence of mature "business layer" support. This resonates with recent conceptual work that identifies organizational integration as an open challenge for process-oriented twins [11].

The proposed study has limitations. The base for the meta-model was built via a seeded scoping approach and therefore does not claim exhaustive coverage. Tool assessment is based on publicly accessible documentation. The full capability mapping and assessment sheets are therefore provided in [29] to support inspection, reuse and refinement. A further practical limitation is that the radar does not yet address the complexity of integrating heterogeneous tools into a coherent DPT stack (e.g., incompatible data formats, divergent API conventions). Future work should explore integration patterns such as standardized protocols (e.g. OPC UA) or middleware to reduce the friction of composing multi-vendor toolchains.

6 Conclusion and Implications

For vendors and industrial users, the results offer a method to structure and communicate DPT capabilities. The capability mapping and radar make transparent which capability clusters are covered and where complementary components are needed. Vendors can use this structure to design focused bundles or reference architectures (e.g., connectivity + event streaming + process modeling + analytics) aligned with recognizable DPT patterns, thereby enabling more targeted positioning of their offerings relative to specific DPT profiles. Industrial users on the other hand can benchmark existing solutions against their DPT profile and avoid both under- and over-engineered stacks. In short, the approach supports more systematic twinning strategies on top of already existing standards and frameworks. Many required capabilities for DPTs already exist in mature platforms. Rather than building full stacks from scratch, researchers can and should leverage these systems as building blocks, using the meta model and radar to select those whose capabilities match the targeted DPT profile. For highly specialized or advanced twins no off-the-shelf product is sufficient. Here, the capability model clarifies which gaps must be closed, typically via combinations of open-source components (e.g. Python-based libraries) and APIs provided by existing platforms. The radar helps to design such composed architectures systematically instead of ad-hoc.

Acknowledgments. The results presented were developed in the IGF project CNCgAIde (01IF23533N) by the Research Association for Programming Languages for Manufacturing Equipment (FVP) e.V. The project is funded by the Federal Ministry for Economic Affairs and Energy (BMWE) through the Industrial Collective Research (IGF) program based on a resolution of the German Bundestag).

Disclosure of Interests. The authors have no competing interests to declare that are relevant to the content of this article.

References

1. Stark, R., Fresemann, C., Lindow, K.: Development and operation of digital twins for technical systems and services. CIRP Ann. **68**, 129–132 (2019). https://doi.org/10.1016/j.cirp.2019.04.024
2. Iranshahi, K., Brun, J., Arnold, T., Sergi, T., Müller, U.C.: Digital twins: recent advances and future directions in engineering fields. Intell. Syst. Appl. **26**, 200516 (2025). https://doi.org/10.1016/j.iswa.2025.200516
3. Fett, M., Wilking, F., Goetz, S., Wartzack, S., Kirchner, E.: Practical insights into the perception of digital twins: an analysis of surveys. Forsch. Ingenieurwes. **89**, 99 (2025). https://doi.org/10.1007/s10010-025-00879-y
4. Corradini, F., Pettinari, S., Re, B., Rossi, L., Tiezzi, F.: Executable digital process twins: towards the enhancement of process-driven systems. BDCC **7**, 139 (2023). https://doi.org/10.3390/bdcc7030139
5. Grieves, M., Vickers, J.: Digital twin: mitigating unpredictable, undesirable emergent behavior in complex systems. In: Kahlen, F.-J., Flumerfelt, S., and Alves, A. (eds.) Transdisciplinary Perspectives on Complex Systems, pp. 85–113. Springer International Publishing, Cham (2017). https://doi.org/10.1007/978-3-319-38756-7_4
6. Kritzinger, W., Karner, M., Traar, G., Henjes, J., Sihn, W.: Digital twin in manufacturing: a categorical literature review and classification. IFAC-PapersOnLine **51**, 1016–1022 (2018). https://doi.org/10.1016/j.ifacol.2018.08.474
7. Al-Sehrawy, R., Kumar, B., Watson, R.: A multi-dimensional digital twin use cases classification framework. In: Presented at the 2021 European Conference on Computing in Construction July 26 (2021). https://doi.org/10.35490/EC3.2021.201
8. Uhlenkamp, J.-F., Hauge, J.B., Broda, E., Lutjen, M., Freitag, M., Thoben, K.-D.: Digital twins: a maturity model for their classification and evaluation. IEEE Access. **10**, 69605–69635 (2022). https://doi.org/10.1109/ACCESS.2022.3186353
9. Dumas, M., La Rosa, M., Mendling, J., Reijers, H.A.: Fundamentals of Business Process Management. Springer Berlin Heidelberg, Berlin, Heidelberg (2018). https://doi.org/10.1007/978-3-662-56509-4

10. Park, G., Van Der Aalst, W.M.P.: Realizing a digital twin of an organization using action-oriented process mining. In: 2021 3rd International Conference on Process Mining (ICPM), pp. 104–111. IEEE, Eindhoven, Netherlands (2021). https://doi.org/10.1109/ICPM53251.2021.9576846
11. Fornari, F., et al.: Digital twins of business processes: a research manifesto. Internet Things **30**, 101477 (2025). https://doi.org/10.1016/j.iot.2024.101477
12. (ISO/IEC 30173:2023): International Organization for Standardization, & International Electrotechnical Commission. (2023). Digital twin — Concepts and terminology (ISO/IEC 30173:2023). ISO. https://www.iso.org/standard/81442.html
13. ISO 23247.: International Organization for Standardization (2021). Automation systems and integration — Digital twin framework for manufacturing — Part 1: Overview and general principles (ISO 23247–2021) (2021)
14. DIN SPEC 91345:2016-04, Referenzarchitekturmodell Industrie 4.0 (RAMI4.0). https://www.dinmedia.de/de/-/-/250940128. https://doi.org/10.31030/2436156
15. Mostafa, F., Tao, L., Yu, W.: An effective architecture of digital twin system to support human decision making and AI-driven autonomy. Concurrency Comput. **33**, e6111 (2021). https://doi.org/10.1002/cpe.6111
16. van der Valk, H., Haße, H., Möller, F., Otto, B.: Archetypes of digital twins. Bus. Inf. Syst. Eng. **64**, 375–391 (2021). https://doi.org/10.1007/s12599-021-00727-7
17. O'Connor, C., Joffe, H.: Intercoder reliability in qualitative research: debates and practical guidelines. Int. J. Qual. Methods **19**, 1609406919899220 (2020). https://doi.org/10.1177/1609406919899220
18. Stark, R., Damerau, T.: Digital twin. In: The International Academy for Production Engineering, Chatti, S., Tolio, T. (eds.) CIRP Encyclopedia of Production Engineering, pp. 1–8. Springer Berlin Heidelberg, Berlin, Heidelberg (2019). https://doi.org/10.1007/978-3-642-35950-7_16870-1
19. Abisset-Chavanne, E., et al.: A digital twin use cases classification and definition framework based on industrial feedback. Comput. Ind. **161**, 104113 (2024). https://doi.org/10.1016/j.compind.2024.104113
20. Haraguchi, M., Funahashi, T., Biljecki, F.: Assessing governance implications of city digital twin technology: a maturity model approach. Technol. Forecast. Soc. Chang. **204**, 123409 (2024). https://doi.org/10.1016/j.techfore.2024.123409
21. Masoumi, H., Shirowzhan, S., Eskandarpour, P., Pettit, C.J.: City digital twins: their maturity level and differentiation from 3D city models. Big Earth Data. **7**, 1–36 (2023). https://doi.org/10.1080/20964471.2022.2160156
22. Chen, L., Xie, X., Lu, Q., Parlikad, A.K., Pitt, M., Yang, J.: Gemini principles-based digital twin maturity model for asset management. Sustainability **13**, 8224 (2021). https://doi.org/10.3390/su13158224
23. Aurich, J.C., Mertes, J., Wagner, M., Schmitz, M., Klar, M., Ravani, B.: Digital twins in manufacturing: a taxonomy for manufacturing applications. Digital Twin. **2**, 2496645 (2025). https://doi.org/10.1080/27525783.2025.2496645
24. Liu, Y., Feng, J., Lu, J., Zhou, S.: A review of digital twin capabilities, technologies, and applications based on the maturity model. Adv. Eng. Inform. **62**, 102592 (2024). https://doi.org/10.1016/j.aei.2024.102592
25. Waters, G.: Testing, Evaluation, Verification and Validation (TEVV) of Digital Twins: A Comprehensive Framework. https://arxiv.org/abs/2507.04555 (2025). https://doi.org/10.48550/ARXIV.2507.04555
26. Gomes, C., Thule, C., Broman, D., Larsen, P.G., Vangheluwe, H.: Co-simulation: a survey. ACM Comput. Surv. **51**, 1–33 (2019). https://doi.org/10.1145/3179993

27. Stark, R., Brandenburg, E., Lindow, K.: Characterization and application of assistance systems in digital engineering. CIRP Ann. **70**, 131–134 (2021). https://doi.org/10.1016/j.cirp.2021.04.061
28. Liu, Z., Araghi, S.N., Sarkar, A., Karray, M.H.: Demystifying Digital Twin Buzzword: A Novel Generic Evaluation Model. https://arxiv.org/abs/2311.12961 (2023). https://doi.org/10.48550/ARXIV.2311.12961
29. Kremer, G.: Level-by-Level Mapping of Digital Process Twin Characteristics to Digital Process Twin Software Capability. https://depositonce.tu-berlin.de/handle/11303/26569 (2025). https://doi.org/10.14279/DEPOSITONCE-25398
30. Alfaro-Viquez, D., Zamora-Hernandez, M., Fernandez-Vega, M., Garcia-Rodriguez, J., Azorin-Lopez, J.: A comprehensive review of AI-based digital twin applications in manufacturing: integration across operator, product, and process dimensions. Electronics **14**, 646 (2025). https://doi.org/10.3390/electronics14040646
31. Lugaresi, G., Matta, A.: Automated digital twin generation of manufacturing systems with complex material flows: graph model completion. Comput. Ind. **151**, 103977 (2023). https://doi.org/10.1016/j.compind.2023.103977

AI Compliance-Threaded Digital Twins in Critical Infrastructure

Rimma Dzhusupova(✉) and Mark van den Brand

Eindhoven University of Technology, Eindhoven, The Netherlands
{r.m.dzhusupova,M.G.J.v.d.Brand}@tue.nl

Abstract. Digital twins are increasingly used to model and optimize critical infrastructure, spanning design, construction, and operations. When enhanced with AI, these systems qualify as high-risk under the EU Artificial Intelligence Act, raising complex governance challenges. Unlike isolated AI applications, digital twins function as system-level entities that evolve across the value chain: suppliers deliver subsystem twins, Engineering, Procurement and Construction (EPC) companies integrate them into facility-wide twins, and operators deploy them in live environments. This lifecycle raises the question of how compliance obligations - provider vs. deployer duties, conformity documentation, and risk evidence - propagate when the digital twin changes hands. Beyond its regulatory implications, the work addresses a key software engineering problem: ensuring continuous traceability and lifecycle management of compliance artefacts in AI-enabled systems. The proposed framework embeds these processes within standard engineering and integration workflows, supporting compliance by design through evidence versioning and transfer mechanisms. In this paper, we introduce the concept of a compliance-threaded digital twin, treating the twin as an AI system whose obligations and conformity evidence must be modeled and transferred across organizational boundaries. Through analysis of Supplier–EPC–Operator workflows and EU AI Act provisions, we propose governance mechanisms to maintain regulatory alignment as digital twins evolve across the value chain.

Keywords: digital twins · AI compliance · software engineering · EU AI Act · critical infrastructure

1 Introduction

A digital twin is a virtual representation of a physical asset, system, or process, continuously updated with real-world data to support monitoring, analysis, and decision-making [1]. Originally developed in domains such as aerospace and manufacturing, digital twins have rapidly expanded into critical infrastructure sectors such as energy, utilities, and transportation. In these settings, they are used to simulate operating conditions, predict failures, optimise resource allocation, and validate safety decisions before implementation in the physical system [17].

R. Posenato and I. Vanderfeesten (Eds.): CAiSE 2026 Workshops, LNBIP 586, pp. 79–90, 2026.
https://doi.org/10.1007/978-3-032-28160-9_8

A defining characteristic of digital twins in critical infrastructure is that they span organisational boundaries. Vendors typically provide AI-enabled components or subsystems; engineering, procurement, and construction (EPC) contractors integrate these components into large-scale projects; and operators are ultimately responsible for running and maintaining the deployed system [16]. This distributed lifecycle creates governance challenges, since technical artefacts, validation results, and risk assessments need to be transferred and updated consistently at each handover.

The European Union's AI Act increases the importance of these issues by classifying AI systems used in the management and operation of safety component in critical infrastructure as "high-risk." Such systems are subject to strict obligations covering risk management, technical documentation, data governance, human oversight, and post-market monitoring [2]. For digital twins, this means compliance cannot be handled in isolation by a single actor. Instead, a continuous "thread" of obligations and evidence must be maintained throughout the lifecycle - from the initial vendor design, through integration into safety systems, to long-term operation by infrastructure providers [3,4,6]. Non-compliance carries fines of up to €35 million or 7% of global annual turnover (EU AI Act, art. 99), underscoring the urgency of early compliance integration.

However, existing approaches to AI governance and digital twin management do not sufficiently address the problem of compliance continuity across organisational boundaries. Compliance evidence is often siloed: vendors may deliver technical documentation, EPC integrators produce validation artefacts, and operators oversee monitoring, but there is no systematic mechanism to maintain, update, and transfer compliance obligations and evidence as systems evolve across the lifecycle. As a result, responsibility gaps appear at handover points, undermining both regulatory readiness and trust in high-risk AI systems [6,16]. This raises the central research question: *How can compliance obligations and conformity evidence be maintained continuously as AI-enabled digital twins transition across supplier, EPC, and operator boundaries?*

This paper introduces the concept of the *compliance-threaded digital twin*, framing the digital twin as the core regulatory unit and proposing an actionable model for versioning, documenting, and transferring compliance evidence along the value chain [5]. For software engineering research, the work contributes a novel perspective on compliance as an evolving artefact, bridging regulatory requirements with traceability, evidence management, and lifecycle governance.

The remainder of this paper is structured as follows. Section 2 describes the technical and regulatory background and reviews related work. Section 3 describes the method applied in this research. Section 4 introduces the compliance-threaded digital twin concept. Section 5 details governance mechanisms across supplier - EPC - operator value chains. Section 6 presents an industrial use case of an offshore substation control and safety system. Section 7 discusses implications and open challenges, and Sect. 8 concludes the paper.

2 Background and Related Work

The EU Artificial Intelligence Act classifies AI systems used as safety components in the management and operation of critical infrastructure as high-risk, imposing obligations that extend explicitly across the entire value chain [6,8,9,11,12]. Despite this, no operational framework exists for how distributed actors in digital twin ecosystems should coordinate to meet these obligations; fragmented, ad hoc compliance practices persist [13,14].

2.1 Existing Approaches to AI Governance and Digital Twin Management.

Most AI governance frameworks assume centralized control, addressing lifecycle management from development to deployment within a single organization [19,20].

In contrast, digital twin governance research has mainly concentrated on technical aspects such as model fidelity, data synchronization, and operational optimization across asset lifecycles. Whitmore et al. highlight persistent gaps between digital twin development during design phases and their operational performance, noting that over 70% of professionals in one surveyed role group rated digital twin benefits as poorly or not well delivered [21]. This disconnect reveals structural governance issues that extend beyond technical performance to include ownership, validation, and responsibility transfer across organizational boundaries.

2.2 Recent Research on Regulatory Alignment for AI in Critical Infrastructure

The introduction of the EU Artificial Intelligence Act has initiated early research efforts on compliance frameworks for high-risk AI systems in critical infrastructure. Initial analyses focus on interpreting legal obligations and translating them into technical or organizational controls [13], yet practical implementation methods remain limited. Advisory papers from legal and policy groups emphasize the complexity of multi-stakeholder compliance scenarios but provide little concrete guidance for operationalization [14].

2.3 Gaps in Propagating Compliance Responsibilities Beyond Organizational Boundaries

The literature consistently recognizes that digital twin lifecycles span multiple organizations - from suppliers and integrators to operators - but provides little insight into how compliance responsibilities should be maintained through these transitions. Recent research highlights the importance of trustworthy, distributed digital twin platforms for sustaining accountability and evidence management across multi-actor environments [25], yet offers limited guidance on practical implementation.

Recent analyses identify the operationalization of value-chain-wide obligations as a critical "missing link" in the regulatory landscape for AI systems under the EU AI Act [10,26,28]. While Article 25 of EU AI Act explicitly defines cross-value-chain responsibilities, neither academic research nor industry frameworks provide systematic methods for managing compliance in distributed digital twin ecosystems.

Three recurring gaps emerge: absent standards for cross-organisational evidence exchange, weak audit-trail continuity across project phases, and limited mechanisms for sustaining risk obligations as systems evolve.

While comparable problems have been addressed in supply-chain compliance for other industries [23], no studies to date have adapted such mechanisms for AI-regulated digital twins.

Existing frameworks address AI governance, digital twin management, and regulatory compliance in isolation, leaving their integration across multi-actor critical infrastructure environments unaddressed. This paper introduces a compliance-threaded approach that embeds regulatory obligations as evolving artefacts within the digital twin lifecycle, explicitly modeling evidence transfer across suppliers, EPC integrators, and operators.

3 Method

This study applies a *conceptual design research* [34] approach to develop a lifecycle governance framework for AI-enabled digital twins in critical infrastructure. The objective is to translate the regulatory requirements of the *EU Artificial Intelligence Act* into a structured compliance model that can be integrated within established engineering processes.

The research combines *regulatory interpretation* with *engineering governance analysis*, reflecting both the structure of the emerging legal framework and the operational logic of EPC project delivery. The author's extensive experience in engineering, procurement, and construction (EPC) project management, digital twin integration, and AI governance provided the practical foundation to ensure that the framework reflects industrial realities and regulatory intent.

The method followed three main stages:

- **Regulatory Lifecycle Alignment:** AI Act provisions were mapped to digital twin lifecycle stages - design, integration, and operation - to identify where compliance responsibilities arise and how they transfer across supplier, EPC, and operator boundaries.
- **Framework Development:** Regulatory insights were synthesised into the compliance-threaded digital twin model, treating compliance evidence as evolving artefacts embedded in the twin with versioned checkpoints at each lifecycle stage.
- **Scenario-Based Validation:** The framework was evaluated through a mock case of an unmanned offshore substation (Annex III(2), high-risk). Because

full AI Act enforcement commences in 2026, no production system yet demonstrates implemented compliance; the mock case therefore serves as a forward-looking validation.

4 Compliance-Threaded Digital Twin Concept

The compliance-threaded digital twin introduces a lifecycle-oriented framework in which regulatory alignment becomes an integral property of the twin, accompanying it through design, integration, and operation [22,29]. Unlike conventional approaches focused on system optimization, the concept treats compliance evidence - documentation, risk assessments, testing results, and audit trails - as a version-controlled digital asset intrinsically linked to the twin and continuously updated as it changes hands or configuration [7,11].

Alternatives such as a standalone digital thread or digital product passport can store compliance records, but AI compliance under the EU AI Act is not a documentation layer that can be managed separately from the system it governs. Risk management, data governance, model versioning, and human-oversight provisions each shape the system's architecture and training pipeline from the outset. Thus, embedding compliance evidence within the twin ensures that these obligations are ensured by design.

4.1 Core Elements of the Concept

Embedded Compliance Evidence. Regulatory artefacts are bound to the digital twin, forming a persistent and versioned record of conformity activities. Each change to the system automatically extends or modifies the evidence set.

Lifecycle Continuity. Compliance is not reinitiated at each lifecycle phase. Instead, each actor - supplier, integrator, or operator - receives, validates, and extends the inherited compliance record, maintaining an unbroken chain of accountability [30].

Traceability and Adaptivity. Evidence retains full provenance (who, when, how) and adapts to evolving technical and regulatory contexts. This supports retrospective audits and real-time assurance of conformity [32].

Adaptive Governance. As regulations and operational conditions evolve, compliance mechanisms within the twin update accordingly, preserving both historical traceability and forward compatibility [33].

4.2 Compliance Lifecycle Integration

The compliance-threaded digital twin operates through *compliance lifecycle integration* - the systematic mapping of regulatory obligations to each stage of the twin's evolution.

Figure 1 illustrates this lifecycle.

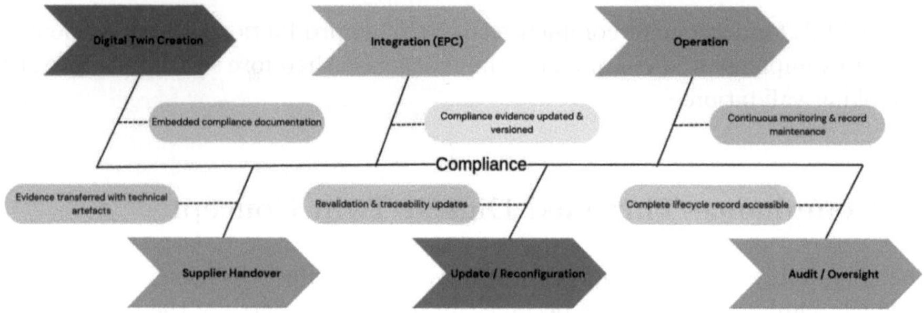

Fig. 1. Lifecycle of a compliance-threaded digital twin. Compliance is maintained as a continuous property across design, integration, operation, and audit phases. Each stage contributes to and validates the evolving evidence record, ensuring full lifecycle traceability and regulatory readiness.

Across all phases, compliance evidence remains inseparably linked to the active twin configuration, with each actor contributing to and validating the record before transfer. Thus, the complete compliance lineage becomes continuously available for oversight, assurance, and audit.

5 Governance Mechanisms for the Value Chain

Building on the compliance-threaded digital twin concept introduced in the previous section, this chapter examines how the principal actors in the value chain aligns with regulatory responsibilities under the EU AI Act (Regulation (EU) 2024/1689).

Digital twin infrastructures typically involve three distinct roles: the supplier (provider), the EPC integrator (provider / distributor), and the operator (deployer). Each assumes specific obligations that correspond to its degree of control over design, integration, or operation of an AI-enabled system.

Figure 2 summarizes this allocation of responsibilities, mapping the relevant provisions of the AI Act. The mapping constitutes a core contribution of this work, translating the abstract legal provisions of the EU AI Act into a role-based framework that supports the applied analysis of compliance-threaded digital twins. Columns derive from the three role definitions in articles 16, 24, and 26; rows derive from the AI Act's principal obligation clusters - risk management, documentation, data governance, human oversight, traceability, transparency, post-market monitoring, and market surveillance - each mapped to the role's degree of control.

In practice, these mapped responsibilities should be formalised within the supply-chain agreements themselves, using compliance-chain clauses and transfer-of-obligation schedules between suppliers and EPC integrators. Such provisions create contractual traceability that mirrors regulatory accountability, ensuring that conformity duties and evidence-handover obligations remain enforceable throughout the value chain.

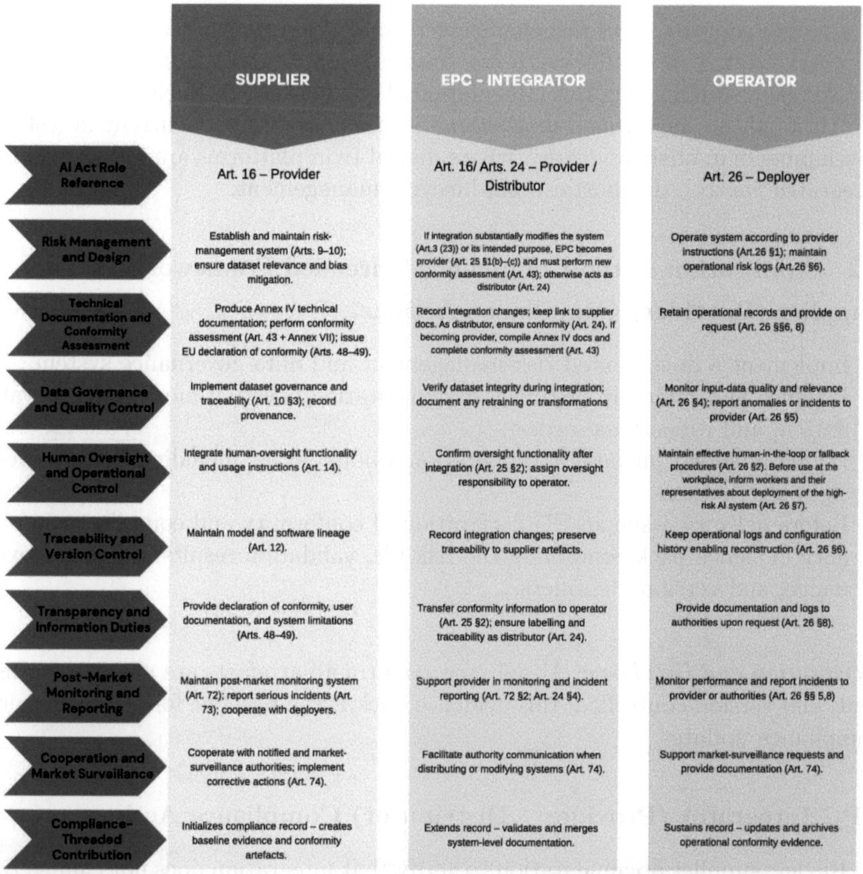

Fig. 2. Mapping EU AI Act Obligations to Lifecycle Roles in a Compliance-Threaded Digital Twin. Supplier (Provider), EPC Integrator (Provider/Distributor), and Operator (Deployer) responsibilities are aligned to Regulation (EU) 2024/1689 articles as indicated in each cell. The mapping clarifies role-specific duties across design, integration, and operation while preserving continuity of compliance evidence throughout the lifecycle.

6 Applied Use Case — Compliance-Threaded Digital Twin for an Unmanned Offshore Substation

6.1 Context and Classification

Offshore substations are increasingly operated as unmanned assets controlled from onshore centres, where the digital twin functions as a necessary operational component through which human operators remotely monitor, simulate, and control the installation.

The integration of AI modules within this twin, supporting condition monitoring, fault prediction, and protection logic, creates an AI system that functions as a *safety component in the management and operation of critical infrastructure.* Accordingly, it qualifies as a *high-risk AI system* under Annex III(2) of the EU Artificial Intelligence Act (Regulation (EU) 2024/1689; Recital 55).

Although presented as a mock scenario, this case mirrors current industrial developments in offshore energy, where digital twin platforms are introduced for integrated control, diagnostics, and lifecycle management.

6.2 Application of the Compliance-Threaded Framework

Supplier (Provider) Compliance Actions.

- Implement a documented risk-management and data-governance system.
- Produce and maintain technical documentation covering model design, validation, and robustness testing.
- Define intended purpose and operational boundaries, including human oversight instructions.
- Before delivery, issue an EU declaration of conformity and compile a compliance evidence pack containing the risk file, validation results, dataset provenance, and version identifiers.

Verification and Handover: At delivery, confirm all artefacts are present, consistent, and version-controlled; this evidence pack is the baseline for all subsequent compliance updates.

EPC Integrator (Provider / Distributor) Compliance Actions.

- Review supplier documentation to verify that integration does not change the intended purpose; if it does, assume provider obligations and perform a new conformity assessment.
- Validate system-level performance and ensure integrated AI modules maintain safety and risk controls within stated limits.
- Merge all supplier and project documentation into a unified technical file, recording integration tests and version-control information.
- At commissioning, freeze the configuration and sign off the compliance handover dossier containing all evidence necessary for operational conformity.

Verification and Handover: Confirm that documentation from all suppliers aligns, that risk controls are traceable end-to-end, and that the compliance register fully reflects the delivered configuration. The signed dossier is formally transferred to the operator together with the technical asset.

Operator (Deployer) Compliance Actions.

- Upon takeover, verify completeness of the technical file and evidence chain.
- Operate the system strictly within validated configurations and oversight requirements.
- For any modification or retraining, initiate a new compliance cycle: obtain updated conformity documentation from suppliers or integrators, log the change, and update the evidence thread.
- Maintain post-market monitoring, incident reporting, and periodic conformity reviews.

Verification and Handover: Ensure every compliance-relevant change is logged, justified, and supported by documentation; archive all prior versions so that the complete lifecycle record can be reconstructed at audit or investigation.

The compliance-threaded approach requires that each lifecycle transition, design release, integration acceptance, operational readiness, and subsequent update, be accompanied by a versioned transfer of conformity evidence.

6.3 Evidence Continuity and Handover Logic

The case demonstrates that compliance for high-risk AI is operationalisable within realistic industrial settings: for suppliers it is a deliverable, for EPC integrators a system-integration activity, and for operators a governance function. Embedding these responsibilities within the digital twin infrastructure converts regulatory requirements into a continuous, auditable lifecycle process applicable across safety-critical energy installations.

7 Discussion and Future Work

The proposed approach represents a proactive compliance model for forthcoming AI regulation, transforming legal obligations into a technical governance mechanism. Transitioning from concept to implementation will require standardisation of evidence artefacts, contract-based handover procedures, and interoperable repositories for lifecycle documentation. These elements will be essential to achieving scalable and auditable compliance management across industrial actors.

Further work will focus on piloting the framework in operational environments and evaluating its effectiveness under simulated regulatory review. It shall demonstrate what a compliance evidence package actually looks like in practice. Industry collaboration will be critical to validate the model's technical robustness, interoperability, and practical feasibility ahead of the AI Act's full enforcement.

8 Conclusion

This study introduced the compliance-threaded digital twin, a governance framework that connects the regulatory obligations of the EU AI Act with the lifecycle management of AI-enabled systems in critical infrastructure. The framework redefines compliance as a continuous, traceable process embedded within established engineering workflows, ensuring that conformity evidence remains complete and verifiable as responsibilities transition between suppliers, EPC integrators, and operators.

The work bridges a gap between regulatory research and engineering practice, where both academic literature and industry actors have lacked structured methods for translating AI Act obligations into lifecycle governance.

The paper delivers a conceptual framework that transforms regulatory requirements into an operational compliance architecture. Its novelty lies in treating compliance evidence as an integral artefact of the digital twin, which is maintained, versioned, and auditable across the full lifecycle. This approach extends conventional lifecycle management into the regulatory domain, providing a foundation for future conformity assessment and for raising industry readiness ahead of the AI Act's full enforcement.

Disclosure of Interests. The authors have no competing interests to declare that are relevant to the content of this article.

References

1. Perno, M., Hvam, L., Haug, A.: Implementation of digital twins in the process industry: a systematic literature review of enablers and barriers. Comput. Ind. **134**(103558) (2022). Available: https://doi.org/10.1016/j.compind.2021.103558
2. European Commission, "AI Act | Shaping Europe's digital future," (2025). [Online]. Available: https://digital-strategy.ec.europa.eu/en/policies/regulatory-framework-ai
3. Nemko, "EU AI Act 2025 Update: GPAI Rules & Compliance" (2025). [Online]. Available: https://digital.nemko.com/insights/eu-ai-act-rules-on-gpai-2025-update
4. Modulos A.G.: 352 Days to EU AI Act High-Risk Compliance (2025). [Online]. Available: https://www.modulos.ai/blog/eu-ai-act-high-risk-compliance-deadline-2026/
5. Tributech, Understanding the EU AI Act: What You Need to Know (2025). https://www.tributech.io/blog/eu-ai-act-introduction
6. Wessing, T.: AI Act: high-risk AI systems (2024). Available:https://www.taylorwessing.com/fr/insights-and-events/insights/2024/11/high-risk-ai-systems
7. Pronost, G., Negny, M., Nikolic, I.: Digital Twins along the product lifecycle: a systematic literature review of applications in manufacturing. Digit. Twin **2**(1) (2024). https://www.tandfonline.com/doi/full/10.12688/digitaltwin.17807.2
8. European Union, Annex III: High-Risk AI Systems Referred to in Article 6(2), Regulation (EU) 2024/1689. https://artificialintelligenceact.eu/annex/3/

9. Masons, P.: A guide to high-risk AI systems under the EU AI Act (2025). https://www.pinsentmasons.com/out-law/guides/guide-to-high-risk-ai-systems-under-the-eu-ai-act
10. Clifford Chance, The EU AI Act: Key Compliance Challenges for 2024, Clifford Chance Briefing (2024). https://www.cliffordchance.com/insights/resources/blogs/regulatory-investigations-financial-crime-insights/2024/ai-act-key-compliance-challenges.html
11. WilmerHale, Obligations for Deployers, Providers, Importers and Distributors of High-Risk AI Systems in the European Union's Artificial Intelligence Act (2024). https://www.wilmerhale.com/en/insights/blogs/wilmerhale-privacy-and-cybersecurity-law/20240826-obligations-for-deployers-providers-importers-and-distributors-of-high-risk-ai-systems-in-the-european-unions-artificial-intelligence-act
12. European Union, Article 25: Responsibilities Along the AI Value Chain, Regulation (EU) 2024/1689. https://artificialintelligenceact.eu/article/25/
13. appliedAI, AI Act Governance: Best Practices for Implementing the EU AI Act (2025). https://www.appliedai.de/uploads/files/Best-Practices-for-Implementing-the-EU-AI-Act_2025-07-02-092027_vwvf.pdf
14. Novelli, C., De Gregorio, E., Mari, L.: Robust Governance for the AI Act (2024). Available: https://artificialintelligenceact.eu/robust-governance-for-the-ai-act/
15. Organisation for Economic Co-operation and Development (OECD), Governing with Artificial Intelligence (2025). [Online]. Available: https://www.policyedge.in/p/oecds-governing-with-artificial-intelligence
16. Veale, M., Zuiderveen Borgesius, F. J.: EU AI Act, Harnessing Digital-Twin Technology, SSRN (2025). Available: https://papers.ssrn.com/sol3/papers.cfm?abstract_id=5357031
17. Tundis, A., Ramírez-Agudelo, O. H.: Safeguarding critical infrastructures with digital twins and AI. In: Proceedings of MAS 2024 (2024). Available: https://elib.dlr.de/206851/1/MAS2024-Tundis.pdf
18. Ai, L., Ziehl, P.: Advances in digital twin technology in industry: a review of applications, challenges, and standardization. J. Intell. Const. **3**(2), 9180083 (2025). Available: https://www.sciopen.com/article/10.26599/JIC.2025.9180083
19. Navex, Preparing for the Future of AI Governance, Risk, and Compliance (2025). [Online]. Available: https://www.navex.com/en-us/blog/article/artificial-intelligence-and-compliance-preparing-for-the-future-of-ai-governance-risk-and-compliance/
20. EY, Establishing AI governance with compliance and legal teams (2025). https://www.ey.com/en_us/insights/forensic-integrity-services/establishing-ai-governance-with-compliance-and-legal-teams
21. Whitmore, D., Krystallis, I., Papadonikolaki, E., et al.: Digital twins in the asset life cycle: are we there yet?. In: Proceedings of the Institution of Civil Engineers - Management, Procurement and Law (2024). [Online]. Available: https://www.sciencedirect.com/org/science/article/pii/S1751430424000102
22. Kalaboukas, K., et al.: Governance framework for autonomous and cognitive supply chain digital twins. Comput. Ind. **146** (2023). https://www.sciencedirect.com/science/article/abs/pii/S0166361523000076
23. Baghdadi, Y., Kebande, V. R., Kurshan, B., Abbassi, R.: The impact of artificial intelligence on regulatory compliance in the supply chain. World J. Adv. Res. Rev. **19**(03), 1559–1570 (2023). Available: https://wjarr.com/sites/default/files/WJARR-2023-1423.pdf

24. Borbach, C., Chun, W. H. K., Thielmann, T.: Making everything ac-count-able: the digital twinning paradigm. New Media Soc. (2025). Available: https://journals.sagepub.com/doi/full/10.1177/14614448251338289
25. Wang, X., Li, H., Yang, L., Liu, A., Liu, K.: Distributed and trustworthy digital twin platform based on blockchain: architecture, application and challenges. Digit. Commun. Netw. (2024). [Online]. Available: https://www.sciencedirect.com/science/article/pii/S2772918424000304
26. European Parliament, Artificial Intelligence Act: A framework for the use and supply of AI in the EU," Briefing (2021). [Online]. Available: https://www.europarl.europa.eu/RegData/etudes/BRIE/2021/698792/EPRS_BRI(2021)698792_EN.pdf
27. Clifford Chance, The EU AI Act – Overview of Key Rules and Requirements (2024). [Online]. Available: https://www.cliffordchance.com/content/dam/cliffordchance/PDFDocuments/the-eu-ai-act-overview.pdf
28. Simonelli, F., et al.: Reconciling the AI Value Chain with the EU's Artificial Intelligence Act, CEPS Working Paper No. 2022-02 (2022). [Online]. Available: https://ideas.repec.org/p/eps/cepswp/37654.html
29. Kuštelega, M., Mekovec, R., Shareef, A.: A new force in the digital economy: digital twins applications and challenges. CroDiM (2025). https://hrcak.srce.hr/file/475710
30. Alhadi, A., Beach, T., Rezgui, Y.: Enhancing asset management: integrating digital twins for continuous permitting and compliance – a systematic literature review. J. Build. Eng. **99**, 111515 (2025). [Online]. Available: https://doi.org/10.1016/j.jobe.2024.111515
31. Itäpelto, T., Elhajj, M., van Sinderen, M.: Digital twin application in lifecycle security of critical infrastructures: a systematic literature review. Int. J. Crit. Infrast. Prot. **50**, 100783 (2025). [Online]. Available: https://doi.org/10.1016/j.ijcip.2025.100783
32. Jawad, M. S., Chandran, P., Ramli, A. A. B. , Mahdin, H. B., Abdullah, Z. B., Rejab, M. B. M.: Adoption of digital twin for sustainable manufacturing and achievements of production strategic-planned goals. MethodsX **9**, 101920 (2022). https://doi.org/10.1016/j.mex.2022.101920
33. Ribeiro, D., Rocha, T., Pinto, G., et al.: Toward effective AI governance: a review of principles. arXiv preprint arXiv:2505.23417 (2023). [Online]. Available: https://arxiv.org/html/2505.23417v1
34. Vaishnavi, V. K., Kuechler, W.: Design Science Research Methods and Patterns: Innovating Information and Communication Technology," 2nd ed., Boca Raton, FL: CRC Press (2015). https://doi.org/10.1201/b18448

A Symbolic Virtual World for Training Agents in Cross-World Exploration

William Sawyerr(✉)

University for the Creative Arts, Farnham, Surrey, UK
william.sawyerr@uca.ac.uk

Abstract. Cross-world exploration (decision-making across multiple worlds under entry-gated evidence) is hard because decisive evidence about a candidate world requires costly, uncertain entry. We formalize this as a meta-decision problem and present a Symbolic Virtual World (SVW), in which regime parameters are explicit, queryable and manipulable. The SVW is instantiated with Earth-derived structure and constrained evidence access via an Earth-proxy layer. Initial runs under controlled regime changes confirm stable knowledge-growth and exploration-coverage signals with measurable sensitivity to regime variation.

Keywords: Symbolic Virtual Worlds · Digital Twins · Artificial Agents · Cross-World Exploration · Cross-Reality

1 Introduction

A rational agent maximizes expected utility by selecting actions from the best available strategy space. When an agent is bounded to a single world, its strategy space is fixed by that world's constraints, transition dynamics, observability and reward structure. If the regime governing that world is finite or degrading, long-term expected utility collapses regardless of how well the agent optimizes within it. The only way to recover is to access alternative worlds whose regimes may support higher-utility trajectories.

Humans face exactly this problem. A human can act in only one world at a time, yet the worlds available to them differ in structure, constraints and opportunity. Evaluating an alternative world requires entry, but entry is costly, uncertain and only partially informative. Decisive evidence about feasibility, constraints and reward gradients is coupled to being inside the world. This makes cross-world exploration (decision-making across multiple worlds under entry-gated evidence) a fundamental obstacle to utility maximization for bounded agents.

One response is to delegate exploration to artificial agents that can operate as second-order proxies, gathering evidence about alternative worlds on behalf of the primary agent [1]. But this delegation raises a prior question. Where and how should such agents be trained? Cross-world exploration requires agents that can

R. Posenato and I. Vanderfeesten (Eds.): CAiSE 2026 Workshops, LNBIP 586, pp. 91–102, 2026.
https://doi.org/10.1007/978-3-032-28160-9_9

detect regime shifts, revise beliefs about feasible actions and causal structure, then produce traceable evidence that supports rational entry or exit decisions. Training and evaluating these competences demands an environment in which regimes can be varied deliberately, their structure made explicit and evidence traces audited under controlled conditions. Existing VW paradigms (text-based, 2D and 3D) do not jointly satisfy these requirements. Regime parameters are typically implicit, variation is ad hoc and instrumentation is retrofitted rather than native.

To address this, we present a Symbolic Virtual World (SVW) designed as an experimental substrate for cross-world exploration. The SVW represents entities, relations, constraints and regime parameters as explicit, queryable symbolic state with event-driven transitions and native instrumentation. We instantiate it with Earth-derived structure to obtain heterogeneous local regimes at scale and constrain evidence access through an Earth-proxy layer governed by refresh policies, caching TTL and adapter policies. This makes the evidence pipeline measurable and controllable as part of the regime.

The remainder of the paper is organized as follows. Section 2 surveys related VW environments and positions SVWs relative to them. Section 3 describes the methods used to construct the SVW as an Earth-derived instantiation. Section 4 presents the system design and implementation. Section 5 reports initial empirical results from controlled scenario runs. Section 6 reflects on the findings and identifies directions for extending the empirical program. Section 7 summarizes contributions and next steps.

2 Related Work

This section reviews three common VW paradigms (text-based, 2D and 3D) and evaluates each against the requirements for cross-world exploration.

2.1 Text-Based Virtual Worlds

In text-based VWs, language mediates both state and action [2]. Sandboxes such as TextWorld [3] allow procedural generation of text-based games with controllable difficulty, enabling systematic study of generalization and transfer. Agents observe and act through textual channels, which makes these environments attractive for planning, instruction following, tool use and long-horizon reasoning. Because the interface is symbolic by construction, they can expose facts, relations and goals directly. They also accommodate non-spatial constraints (permissions, protocols, inventories, logical preconditions) that are central to many operational definitions of a world.

For cross-world exploration, text-based VWs have two strengths. They can make regime differences explicit in the observation stream because changes in rules or reward structure can be described directly rather than inferred from low-level sensory change. They also support fine-grained variation over VW descriptions for studying whether agents detect and adapt to altered constraints. However, they collapse multiple structural factors into a single channel (language), making it difficult to separate what the agent learned about environment dynamics from what it learned about linguistic surface form. They also tend to underspecify operational costs of entry and interaction (latency, partial observability, bounded measurement), which are central to the evaluation bottleneck in boundary crossing.

2.2 2D Virtual Worlds

Explicit spatial structure defines 2D VWs, typically with simplified geometry that keeps them lightweight and easy to instrument. Minigrid [4], for example, provides modular gridworld environments with configurable goals, partial observability and multi-room layouts. They are commonly used to study navigation, exploration, coverage and multi-agent coordination under partial observability. Controlled manipulation of maps, obstacles, resource distributions and local rules enables repeatable tests of responses to distribution shifts in topology or resource conversion rules.

For cross-world exploration, 2D VWs support systematic variation of constraints (movement rules, sensing radius, action costs) while remaining interpretable. They also make it straightforward to record auditable traces such as trajectories, visited regions and information-gain proxies. Their limitation is structural. When the target problem involves rich relational structure beyond geometry (entities, roles, institutional constraints and heterogeneous causal dependencies), purely spatial abstractions push too much of the VW definition into ad hoc reward shaping, reducing fidelity to the structural uncertainty that makes entry decisions hard.

2.3 3D Virtual Worlds

3D VWs emphasize embodied interaction, richer perceptual streams and physics-based dynamics [6]. Platforms such as AI2-THOR [5] provide near photo-realistic indoor scenes with object-level interaction, supporting research in visual navigation, manipulation and embodied question answering. They are valuable when the central challenge is grounded perception-action coupling, manipulation, or learning robust policies under complex sensory variation. High-fidelity simulators can produce large volumes of experience, which is attractive when policies must generalize across viewpoints, lighting, or contact dynamics.

For cross-world exploration, 3D environments can model certain entry costs more naturally (movement effort, occlusion, delayed feedback) and expose agents to regime shifts resembling those encountered by embodied systems. The trade-off is that high-fidelity rendering and physics make structural differences harder to localize and audit. Regime changes manifest as diffuse sensory shifts rather than explicit constraint changes. Evaluation can then drift toward perceptual robustness rather than boundary-crossing competence. The computational cost of running and resetting complex 3D simulations also limits the scale of systematic, factorial variation over VW parameters.

2.4 Summary

Across all three paradigms, the bottleneck for cross-world exploration is not realism but whether regimes can be varied deliberately, their structure made explicit and evidence traces audited under costly and uncertain entry. None jointly satisfies these requirements. SVWs close this gap by making regime parameters first-class objects, making constraints and observability manipulable and logged by construction and grounding selected domains in real-world signals through optional Earth anchoring.

3 Methods

An SVW can be instantiated synthetically, but anchoring it to a real referent provides heterogeneous structure at scale and grounds evaluation in externally observable signals. This section describes the three methods used to construct the SVW as an Earth-derived instantiation.

3.1 Earth as Referent

We anchor the SVW to Earth for two reasons. First, Earth supplies heterogeneous local regimes without manual authoring. Geographic, climatic, institutional and cultural structure varies across real locations in ways that are independently verifiable. Second, Earth-derived state variables can be compared against real observations, providing an external check on world fidelity that purely synthetic worlds lack.

The geographic foundation is built from GeoNames data covering the United Kingdom and Ireland. Locations are real places (cities, towns, rivers, mountains and forests) with coordinates, elevation, terrain type and administrative hierarchy (country, nation, region, district). Connections between locations represent real transport and proximity links (road, rail, path, waterway) filtered to distances under 10 km, yielding a spatial graph of approximately 5 000 locations and 50 000 connections.

Time in the SVW is real Earth UTC, read from the system clock on each tick. Location-specific astronomy (sunrise, sunset, twilight, moon phase and illumination) is computed from solar and lunar ephemerides using the algorithms of Meeus [8] rather than fetched from an external service, ensuring deterministic reproducibility for matched-condition comparisons.

3.2 Constrained Evidence Access

Cross-world exploration depends on evidence acquisition under constrained access. The SVW mediates this through an Earth-proxy layer that resolves location-conditioned facts from real Earth data sources on demand.

Twenty-three open-source adapters span seven categories (encyclopedic, news, government, cultural, historical, discourse and search), each returning structured *EarthFacts* (typed content with domain, topic, source, confidence and timestamp) under per-adapter timeout caps, rate limits and fallback policies.

Resolved facts are cached with a configurable time-to-live and evicted via LRU. Adapter policies (rate limits, timeouts, TTL, fallback behavior) are regime parameters that can be varied experimentally without code changes. Domain-specific refresh schedulers update weather, atmosphere and space weather state on independent 30-minute cycles; geography reloads weekly. Each refresh cycle signals the tick loop, so agents observe temporally coherent Earth state.

3.3 Operational Twinness

We treat digital-twin status operationally, following the principle that a twin's value lies in its ability to support prediction and intervention testing rather than in surface fidelity [7]. The SVW functions as a twin of Earth for the modeled domains to the extent that (i) its state variables correspond to identifiable real-world entities and measurements, (ii) it can be updated from observations and (iii) it supports forecasting or intervention testing under explicit modeled constraints. The key criterion is twinness by agreement. Predicted trajectories should match observed signals over matched time windows within domain-appropriate tolerances.

This criterion bounds what twinness claims mean and provides measurable fidelity targets while avoiding purely rhetorical resemblance. It also separates world realism from world usefulness. A world can be valuable for cross-world exploration training if it supports controlled regime variation and auditable evidence, even when twin fidelity is high only for a subset of modeled domains.

3.4 Summary

Together, these three methods ground the SVW in externally verifiable structure. Earth as referent supplies heterogeneous local regimes without manual authoring. Constrained evidence access makes the information pipeline a controllable part of the regime. Operational twinness provides a measurable fidelity criterion that avoids conflating realism with usefulness.

4 Design and Development

This section specifies the formal world model and design choices, then describes the implementation architecture.

4.1 Design

We specify a world as a structured tuple $W = (S, A, T, R, O)$, where S is symbolic state, A is the action set, T is the transition mechanism, R is the training reward and O is the observation interface. Cross-world exploration is defined over a parameterized family $\{W_\theta\}$; a regime shift is a change $\theta \to \theta'$ that alters constraints, observability, or resource conversion rules [9]. An agent policy $\pi(a_t \mid h_t)$ maps history to an action, optimizing a standard discounted objective within a given regime [10]:

$$J(\pi;\theta) = \mathbb{E}_{W_\theta,\pi}\left[\sum_{t=0}^{H-1} \gamma^t r_t\right].$$

R is a training signal aligned to evidence production (knowledge growth, coverage, prediction-error correction), while evaluation emphasizes auditable traces and sensitivity under controlled shifts $\theta \to \theta'$.

The state S is an explicit collection of entities, relations and regime parameters. In the Earth-derived instantiation, S includes geographic coordinates and typed feature attributes; spatial structure is represented as coordinates, graphs and feature sets rather than 3D physics. The action set A includes movement over a symbolic geography graph and evidence actions mediated by an Earth proxy that resolves and caches location-conditioned facts, constrained via refresh policies, caching TTL and adapter rate limits.

The transition mechanism T is event-driven. Actions trigger discrete state changes (position updates, memory writes, knowledge ingestion, communication events) recorded in tick-indexed event streams. Observations O expose partial views of S under explicit evidence-access constraints. Per-tick observation includes the current location record, optional local weather and wind state, identifiers of connected nearby locations, simulation time and cached Earth facts when available.

Agents are autonomous learners with persisted internal state operating under partial observability and constrained evidence access. Action selection conditions on observation payloads and accumulated memory (episodic events, extracted facts, belief records). Rewards attach to interpretable proxies for evidence production (knowledge acquisition, coverage, prediction-error correction and useful information sharing) and are not claims about real-world value. The system exposes two auditable trace levels. Tick-level summaries stream to clients while persisted world and agent state support post-hoc auditing and matched-condition comparisons.

For an Earth-anchored subset of variables y, twinness is measured by agreement between predicted and observed trajectories over a matched window $\mathcal{T}$:

$$E_y = \frac{1}{|\mathcal{T}|}\sum_{t\in\mathcal{T}} |\hat{y}_t - y_t|, \quad \text{twinness holds if } E_y \le \varepsilon_y.$$

This criterion yields measurable fidelity targets without conflating twinness with usefulness for regime-shift training.

4.2 Development

The SVW is implemented as a multi-agent system. A Python backend hosts world state, agent execution and data services while a desktop client provides live visualization and operator control. The backend exposes a REST API for control and inspection and WebSocket streams for tick-aligned simulation updates; agent execution can be distributed via an actor-style runtime. Persistent storage covers Earth-derived entities and spatial indices. An embedded vector store supports agent knowledge and memory retrieval. Agents sense by issuing spatial queries that return nearby features and typed attributes, supporting heterogeneous local regimes without high-fidelity rendering.

Agents maintain bounded per-agent state (location, memory, belief records) and perform observation parsing, action selection, learning updates and knowledge exchange. External text evidence is ingested through the Earth-proxy layer and integrated into retrievable memory. The server supports explicit resets and persists world and agent state, enabling tick-aligned comparisons under matched conditions.

4.3 Summary

The formal model defines worlds as parameterized tuples whose regime parameters are explicit and manipulable, with an operational twinness criterion for Earth-anchored domains. The implementation realizes this model as a running multi-agent system with symbolic state, event-driven transitions, constrained evidence access and native instrumentation at two auditable trace levels.

5 Evaluation

This section reports initial empirical results from the SVW under controlled operational regime changes. The system is under active development; we do not claim cross-world transfer results. Instead, these runs establish that the SVW produces stable, auditable signals and is measurably sensitive to regime variation. These are prerequisites for the transfer studies that follow.

5.1 Setup

A test harness runs scenarios against a live SVW server and writes reproducible artifacts (CSV summaries and charts). Each scenario resets the simulation (45 agents, fresh state) and runs for a fixed number of ticks. On each tick, agents receive structured observations (location attributes, connected neighbours, time and optionally cached Earth-proxy facts) and select actions under the evidence-access constraints defined in Sect. 4.

Four scenarios vary tick cadence (the wall-clock interval between decision steps) as a controllable regime parameter. Tick cadence is not itself a new world, but it alters time per decision, scheduling pressure and the effective rate of evidence updates relative to wall clock. Table 1 lists each scenario's configuration alongside its final results. Per-tick aggregate statistics are recorded for every scenario.

The Knowledge, Visited and Resolves columns report the mean values recorded at each scenario's final sampled tick. The following subsections examine these results in detail.

Table 1. Scenario configurations and aggregate results (45 agents, fresh reset each).

Scenario	Interval (s)	Ticks	Knowledge	Visited	Resolves
`baseline_15`	1.0	101	40.1	33.4	86
`fast_15`	0.2	121	46.9	39.2	105
`slow_10`	2.0	61	36.9	30.8	127
`step_change_20`	1.0→0.2	138	46.5	38.8	154

5.2 Baseline Results

In the baseline scenario, agents reach a mean knowledge score of 40.1 and mean visited locations of 33.4 over 101 ticks, with 86 total Earth-proxy resolves. Figure 1 plots mean knowledge score by snapshot index with a ±1 standard deviation band and the max-knowledge trace. The dispersion indicates substantial heterogeneity across agents, which is expected under partial observability and constrained evidence access.

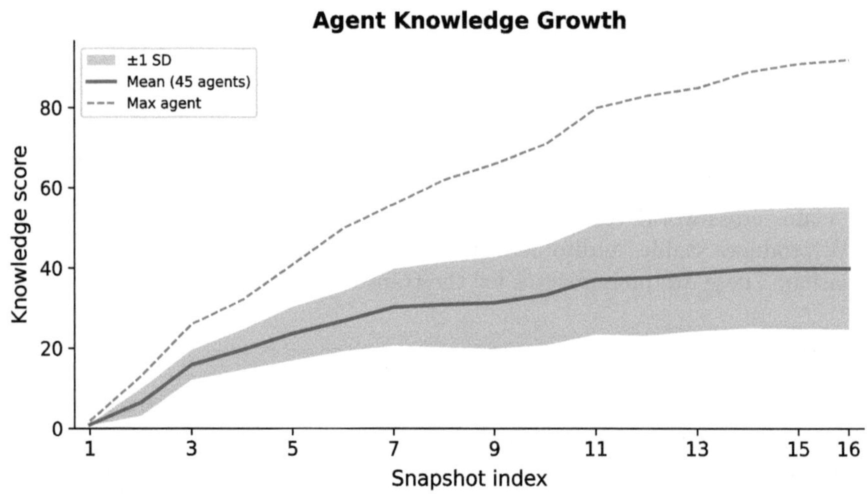

Fig. 1. Baseline scenario. Mean knowledge score by snapshot index with ±1 standard deviation band and maximum-knowledge trace (45 agents).

The growth curve shows steady knowledge accumulation through approximately the midpoint of the run, after which the rate diminishes as agents exhaust nearby unvisited locations. The widening standard deviation band reflects diverging exploration trajectories. Some agents discover high-value clusters early, while others traverse sparser regions. This heterogeneity is a useful property for cross-world exploration research, since it provides natural variation for studying how regime shifts affect different agent profiles.

5.3 Cross-Scenario Comparison

To test whether the SVW is sensitive to regime variation, we compare final aggregate metrics across all four scenarios. Figure 2 plots knowledge score, exploration coverage, Earth-proxy resolves and reward side by side; Table 1 reports the corresponding values.

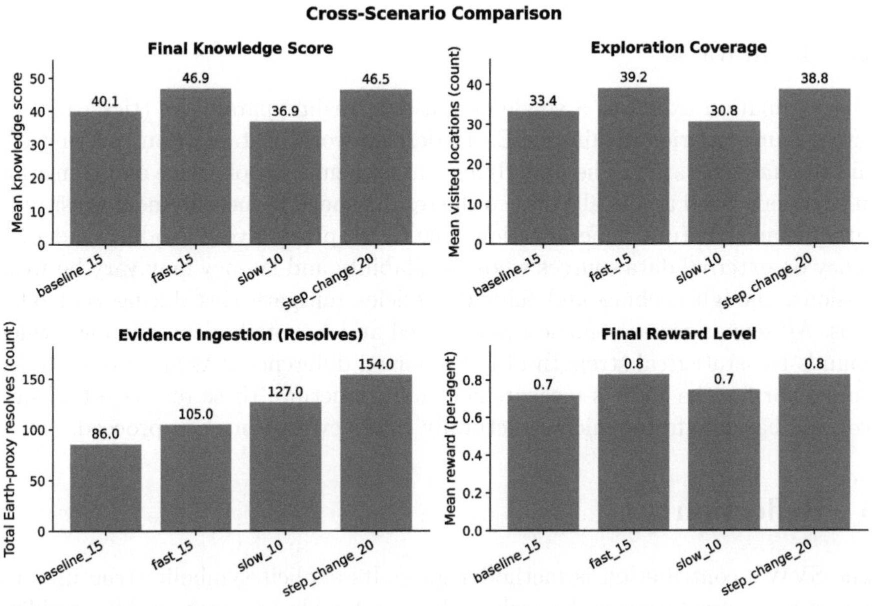

Fig. 2. Cross-scenario comparison. Final aggregate metrics under four operational regimes (knowledge score, exploration coverage, Earth-proxy resolves and reward).

The bar charts reveal a clear pattern. Knowledge and coverage track together across scenarios, while proxy resolves and reward do not move in lockstep with them. Faster ticks yield higher knowledge and coverage. The fast scenario reaches 46.9 compared to the baseline's 40.1, a 17% increase over a comparable run duration. The slow scenario, with fewer ticks and longer decision windows, produces less knowledge (36.9) but accumulates more Earth-proxy resolves (127 vs. 86), suggesting that longer intervals allow more evidence ingestion per decision cycle. The step-change scenario reaches 46.5 knowledge and 154 resolves (the highest resolve count) because the mid-run shift from 1.0 s to 0.2 s cadence combines an initial period of deeper per-tick evidence gathering with a subsequent burst of rapid exploration.

These differences are not claims about which cadence is best. They demonstrate two properties relevant to cross-world exploration. First, the SVW's regime parameters produce measurable, comparable outputs. Second, the agent-world loop is sensitive to controlled regime changes in a way that can be quantified and used to define held-out shifts.

5.4 Evidence Pipeline

Cross-world exploration depends on acquiring and integrating evidence under constrained access. The Earth-proxy layer mediates this by recording per-adapter call volume, latency and timeouts for each scenario. This makes evidence acquisition measurable and exposes concrete targets for later robustness testing (adapter throttling, failure injection, policy changes).

5.5 Limitations

This evaluation exercises a single operational regime parameter (tick cadence) across four scenarios within one Earth-derived world instantiation covering UK and Ireland geography. The underlying state schema, action space and transition rules remain fixed across all runs, so the results speak to measurement sensitivity rather than structural generalization. The Earth-proxy layer introduces a dependency on external data sources whose availability and latency may vary between sessions, though caching and fallback policies mitigate this during controlled runs. All scenarios use a single random seed and a short horizon window, which bounds the statistical strength of the reported differences. As an initial empirical anchor for the SVW's measurement infrastructure, these results establish a working baseline from which structurally richer evaluations can proceed.

6 Reflection

The SVW's contribution is methodological. Its explicit symbolic structure and native instrumentation make regime shifts inducible and measurable, enabling boundary-crossing competence to be trained and evaluated rather than argued narratively. The evaluation results provide an initial empirical anchor for this claim. We reflect here on what those results reveal about the SVW's fitness as a substrate for cross-world exploration.

The operational-regime experiments show that changing a single regime parameter (tick cadence) produces measurably different agent behavior while preserving a comparable measurement interface. This is a necessary property. If regime variation did not produce detectable differences in agent traces, the substrate would be uninformative for boundary-crossing research. The step-change scenario goes further by demonstrating that regime shifts can be induced within a single run, making shift boundaries visible on a common tick axis. Together, these results confirm that the SVW satisfies the controllability and sensitivity conditions required by the meta-decision framing in the Introduction.

The metrics used here (knowledge score, visited locations and proxy resolves) are deliberately simple. They serve as measurement surfaces rather than ultimate definitions of success. Knowledge score and visited locations provide a readable picture of evidence accumulation and spatial coverage; proxy resolves expose the evidence-acquisition channel that mediates constrained access to external facts. The observed dispersion across agents within a run is also informative.

Heterogeneity under shared constraints is a diagnostic signature for exploration dynamics that would be invisible in aggregate-only reporting.

What the results do not yet show is equally important. The current regime variation is operational (tick cadence), not structural (altered constraints, changed action spaces, or modified transition rules). The gap between operational sensitivity and cross-world transfer competence is substantial. Closing it requires held-out regime families, schema shifts and twinness quantification. The present results establish that the measurement infrastructure is in place; the next phase of work must exercise it against structurally richer regime variation.

7 Conclusion

Bounded agents cannot maximize utility across worlds without exploring alternatives. Cross-world exploration is hard because decisive evidence requires costly, uncertain entry. We formalized this as a meta-decision problem and derived four requirements for an experimental substrate, namely explicit regime parameters, systematic variation, native instrumentation and repeatability. None of the existing VW paradigms jointly satisfies these requirements.

We presented an SVW that satisfies them by construction, instantiated it with Earth-derived structure and constrained evidence access via an Earth-proxy layer and defined an operational twinness criterion for Earth-anchored domains. Initial evaluations under controlled operational regime changes confirm that the SVW produces stable, auditable signals and is measurably sensitive to regime variation.

The gap that remains is between operational sensitivity and cross-world transfer competence. The next phase of work is to exercise the measurement infrastructure against structurally richer regime variation. This includes held-out regime families with train/test separation, schema shifts in constraints and action spaces, repeated seeds with confidence intervals and domain-specific twinness quantification.

Disclosure of Interests. The authors have no competing interests to declare that are relevant to the content of this article.

References

1. Sawyerr, W.: Indirect utility maximization via second-order agents. In: 18th ACM International Workshop on Immersive Mixed and Virtual Environment Systems (MMVE 2026), 4–8 April 2026, Hong Kong, pp. 15–20 (2026)
2. Cicognani, A.: Language and design in text-based virtual worlds. J. Netw. Comput. Appl. **23**(3), 247–274 (2000)
3. Côté, M.-A., et al.: TextWorld: a learning environment for text-based games. In: Cazenave, T., Saffidine, A., Sturtevant, N. (eds.) CGW 2018. CCIS, vol. 1017, pp. 41–75. Springer, Cham (2019). https://doi.org/10.1007/978-3-030-24337-1_3

4. Chevalier-Boisvert, M., et al.: Minigrid & miniworld: modular & customizable reinforcement learning environments for goal-oriented tasks. In: Advances in Neural Information Processing Systems, vol. 36 (2023)
5. Kolve, E., et al.: AI2-THOR: An Interactive 3D Environment for Visual AI. arXiv preprint arXiv:1712.05474 (2017)
6. Duan, J., Yu, S., Tan, H.L., Zhu, H., Tan, C.: A survey of embodied AI: from simulators to research tasks. IEEE Trans. Emerg. Topics Comput. Intell. **6**(2), 230–244 (2022)
7. Bauer, P., Stevens, B., Hazeleger, W.: A digital twin of earth for the green transition. Nat. Clim. Change **11**, 80–83 (2021)
8. Meeus, J.: Astronomical Algorithms, 2nd edn. Willmann-Bell, Richmond (1998)
9. Padakandla, S.: A survey of reinforcement learning algorithms for dynamically varying environments. ACM Comput. Surv. **54**(6), 127:1–127:25 (2021)
10. Moerland, T.M., Broekens, J., Plaat, A., Jonker, C.M.: Model-based reinforcement learning: a survey. Found. Trends Mach. Learn. **16**(1), 1–118 (2023)

LLM-SOA

JIT-SA: A Governed Engineering Method for Volatile AI-Driven Service Composition

Hirad Rezaei[1(✉)], Fethi Rabhi[1], and Amin Beheshti[2]

[1] UNSW Sydney, Sydney, Australia
{hirad.rezaei,f.rabhi}@unsw.edu.au
[2] Macquarie University, Sydney, Australia
amin.beheshti@mq.edu.au

Abstract. Classical Service-Oriented Architecture (SOA), serverless orchestration, and microservice design all assume that service topologies are largely defined before execution. This assumption becomes restrictive in AI-native settings where user intents, resource needs, and service combinations are volatile and cannot be fully pre-enumerated at design time. In this paper, we introduce **Just-in-Time Software Architecture (JIT-SA)** as a governed engineering method for volatile AI-driven service composition. JIT-SA treats architecture as a transient artifact synthesized from intent and context under explicit operational and governance constraints. We contribute (i) a formal intent-to-topology transformation model, (ii) a layered engineering method spanning semantic compilation, bounded topology synthesis, validation, and ephemeral deployment, and (iii) governance mechanisms including policy validation, budget guardrails, clarification dialogues, and deployment constraints. We instantiate the method in a prototype using LangGraph for stateful reasoning and Akash SDL for infrastructure realization, and evaluate it across three burst-workload scenarios. The evaluation shows that JIT-SA can synthesize valid executable topologies without invalid deployment and that it occupies a distinct operating regime: it is advantageous for rare, compute-intensive, latency-tolerant workloads, but inferior to serverless or persistent orchestration for predictable or latency-sensitive tasks. The contribution of the paper is therefore not a universal replacement for SOA, but a governed engineering paradigm and artifact set for volatile service composition in AI-native information systems.

Keywords: Information Systems Engineering · Volatile Service Composition · Multi-Agent Systems · Service-Oriented Architecture · Runtime Topology Synthesis · Governance

1 Introduction

Classical Service-Oriented Architecture (SOA) and modern serverless platforms share a common engineering assumption: service topologies are largely specified

R. Posenato and I. Vanderfeesten (Eds.): CAiSE 2026 Workshops, LNBIP 586, pp. 105–117, 2026.
https://doi.org/10.1007/978-3-032-28160-9_10

before execution. Architects define workflows, enumerate services, and deploy persistent or pre-registered components that are then invoked at runtime. This assumption works well for stable and predictable workloads, but it becomes restrictive in AI-native settings where user intents are open-ended, required resource profiles vary substantially, and suitable service combinations cannot always be anticipated during design.

This paper addresses that problem through **Just-in-Time Software Architecture (JIT-SA)**, an engineering method for volatile AI-driven service composition. JIT-SA treats architecture not as a fixed design-time artifact, but as a transient artifact synthesized from intent and context, validated under explicit constraints, deployed for task execution, and dissolved after completion. The goal is not to replace existing SOA or serverless approaches, but to support a specific class of volatile workloads for which pre-enumerating workflows is either inefficient or infeasible (Fig. 1).

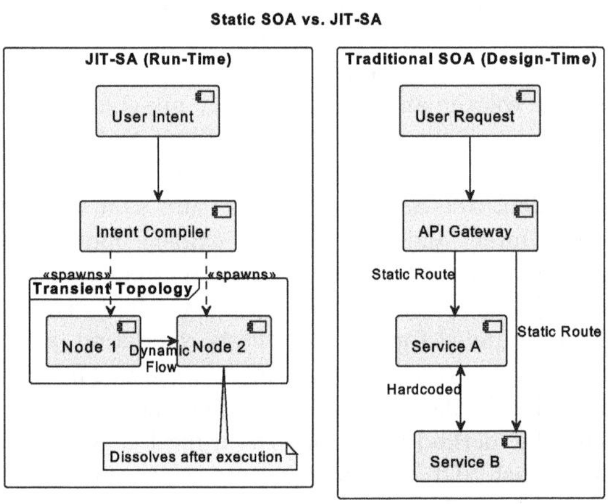

Fig. 1. From static service design to governed runtime synthesis. JIT-SA treats topology as a transient artifact synthesized for a specific intent and dissolved after execution.

Consider a user request such as: *"Analyze the sentiment of the last 10 min of Ethereum blockchain transactions."* In a conventional SOA setting, successful execution depends on whether the relevant workflow and supporting services have already been designed and deployed. Under JIT-SA, the engineering task shifts: the system interprets the intent, synthesizes a bounded service topology, validates it against resource and governance constraints, deploys the necessary components, and terminates them after execution.

From an Information Systems Engineering perspective, the contribution is therefore a change in what must be designed. Instead of pre-defining all possible workflows, engineers define the *synthesis space*, *validation logic*, *governance rules*, and *operating boundaries* within which architectures may be generated safely at runtime.

The paper is guided by three research questions: **RQ1:** how can volatile service topologies be engineered from intent and context under explicit constraints rather than predefined catalogs? **RQ2:** what governance mechanisms make runtime topology synthesis bounded, valid, and operationally safe? **RQ3:** under what workload conditions is this method preferable to serverless or persistent orchestration?

The paper makes four contributions: **(i) Conceptual**—JIT-SA as an engineering paradigm for volatile AI-driven service composition; **(ii) Methodological**—a formal intent-to-topology transformation and a layered method spanning semantic compilation, bounded refinement, validation, and deployment; **(iii) Governance**—mechanisms for syntactic/semantic validation, resource checks, budget guardrails, and clarification dialogues; and **(iv) Empirical**—evaluation across three burst-workload scenarios characterising validity, failure modes, and operating regime.

JIT-SA is not proposed as a universal replacement for SOA or serverless architectures. Rather, it targets a complementary regime: rare, compute-intensive, and latency-tolerant workloads where architectural volatility is high and pre-deployment is inefficient.

2 Background and Research Positioning

Service Composition. Early semantic web research (OWL-S [3], WSMO [10]) enabled semantic matchmaking [6] and AI planning over pre-registered services [5,14,15]. Sheng et al. [13] showed that service selection and resource allocation may need to co-evolve, but all these approaches assume a pre-modelled service landscape. Serverless platforms (AWS Lambda, Step Functions [4]) introduced ephemeral compute with rapid cold starts but still rely on pre-deployed catalogs. JIT-SA targets the gap: synthesising both services and composition for unpredictable intents.

Agentic LLMs and Tool Use. The Internet of Agents [16,17] posits networks of autonomous problem-solving systems. Tool-using LLMs (Toolformer [11], Gorilla [7]) and tool-creation [1] have extended this further. JiT-Codegen [19] enables LLMs to inject code at runtime within a single machine. JIT-SA extends this to the architectural level, synthesising distributed container topologies and network rules on demand.

Adaptive Pipelines and Runtime Evolution. PipeMind [9] and related work [8] showed that multi-agent systems can monitor and adapt analytics pipelines, but under a *fixed-topology assumption*: they tune parameters within a known architecture rather than synthesising a new one. CAiSE work on runtime evolution [12], variability management [2], and declarative deployment [18] establishes adaptation as a first-class engineering concern, but stops short of synthesising executable topologies from volatile natural-language intent. The resulting gap is a governed engineering method for *runtime topology synthesis*, which JIT-SA addresses (Table 1).

Table 1. Positioning of JIT-SA relative to existing approaches.

Approach	Dynamic Comp.	Generative Svcs	Dist. Infra	Ephemeral
OWL-S [3]	✓	×	×	×
Serverless [4]	Partial	×	✓	✓
JiT-Codegen [19]	✓	✓	×	×
IoA [16]	✓	×	✓	×
JIT-SA	✓	✓	✓	✓

3 JIT-SA as an Engineering Method for Volatile Service Composition

JIT-SA treats software architecture as a transient artifact generated under explicit constraints. It takes three inputs: a natural-language intent I, an operational context $\mathcal{C}$, and governance constraints over resources, security, and deployment policy, and produces an executable topology G only if bounded validation succeeds:

$$\Phi(I, \mathcal{C}) \rightarrow G \tag{1}$$

where Φ is a stochastic but bounded transformation ensuring G satisfies resource, security, and execution invariants. The engineering task is to specify the transformation space, validation rules, and operating boundaries under which runtime generation is allowed.

The method comprises three layers (Fig. 2):

Layer 1: Semantic Compiler. The control plane defines architecture state as $S_t = (\mathcal{M}, \mathcal{D}, \mathcal{H})$, where $\mathcal{M}$ represents active functional units, $\mathcal{D}$ data-flow artifacts, and $\mathcal{H}$ interaction history. It interprets intent I via a structured-output prompt that decomposes it into required services and data flows. If compiler confidence falls below 0.7, a clarification dialogue is triggered before synthesis proceeds.

Layer 2: Bounded Topology Synthesis. The core method constructs an execution graph $G = (V, E)$ using iterative refinement between an *Architect* sub-agent (graph generation) and a *Validator* sub-agent (constraint checking). On each iteration, the Validator returns a structured error record specifying the

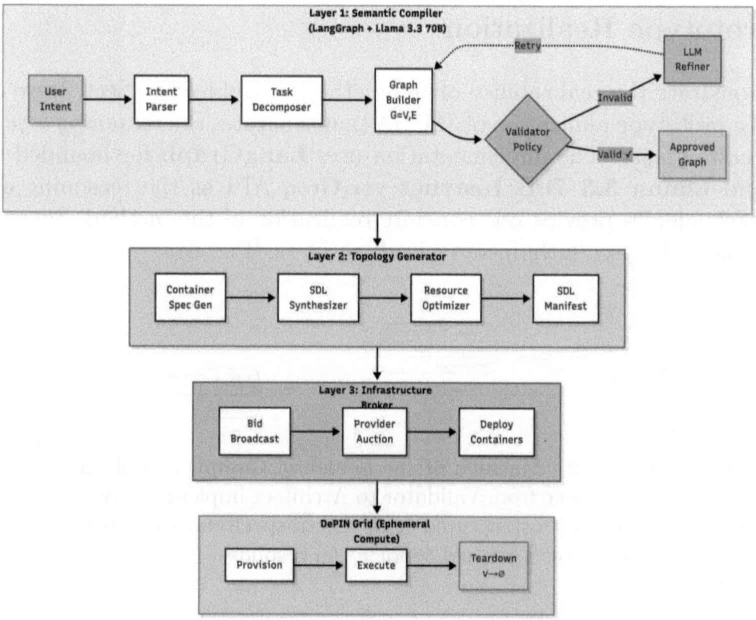

Fig. 2. JIT-SA Layered Architecture: Intent → Compilation → Generation → Deployment. Layer 1 (Semantic Compiler) interprets intent and coordinates refinement. Layer 2 (Bounded Topology Synthesis) constructs and validates the execution graph. Layer 3 (Infrastructure Broker) maps the graph to ephemeral compute.

violated constraint; the Architect revises only the flagged components. This loop continues until all checks pass or the iteration limit k is reached:

Algorithm 1: Topology Synthesis with Bounded Refinement

Result: Deployment Manifest M
Input: Intent I, Constraints C, Max Iterations k;
$G \leftarrow$ LLM_Decompose(I); $i \leftarrow 0$;
while *Valid(G, C) is False and* $i < k$ **do**
| $E \leftarrow$ Validate(G, C); $G \leftarrow$ LLM_Refine(G, E); $i \leftarrow i + 1$;
end
if $i = k$ **then**
| **return** Failure;
end
foreach *Vertex* $v \in G$ **do**
| $S_v \leftarrow$ Synthesize_Container(v); $M \leftarrow M \cup S_v$;
end
return M;

Layer 3: Ephemeral Infrastructure Realization. Once a valid graph is obtained, the infrastructure broker maps graph vertices onto a resource pool $\mathcal{R}$ by minimizing deployment cost subject to capability constraints. After task completion, the mapping is dissolved, returning the system to a zero-persistence state.

4 Prototype Realization

To demonstrate the realizability of the method introduced in Sect. 3, we implemented a prototype realization of JIT-SA that separates the *reasoning layer* from the *execution layer*. The implementation uses **LangGraph** for bounded refinement and **Llama 3.3 70B Instruct** via Groq API as the reasoning engine. These technologies provide one concrete realization of the method. Source code is available at https://github.com/hiradbrz/jit-sa (Fig. 3).

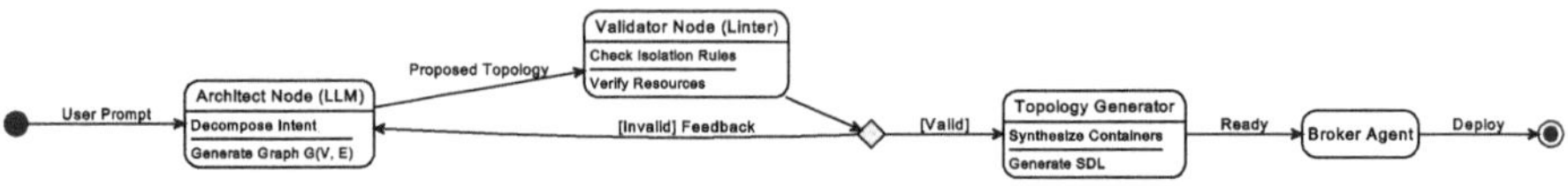

Fig. 3. The Internal State Machine of the Semantic Compiler implementation using LangGraph. The cyclic edge from Validator to Architect implements the self-correction loop: the Validator returns a structured error record specifying the violated constraint, and the Architect generates a revised topology in response.

Intent Input and Prompt Design. Intent is submitted as a free-form natural-language string (e.g., `"Analyze sentiment of the last 10 min of ETH transactions"`). The Semantic Compiler wraps it in a structured system prompt specifying: (i) the required output schema (typed JSON with `services`, `data_flows`, and `resource_hints`); (ii) the available container registry; and (iii) active governance constraints. Outputs failing Pydantic schema validation are rejected and retried. The *LLM Refiner* (Architect sub-agent) receives on each iteration the current graph plus a structured Validator error record and is instructed to fix only the flagged violation without altering validated components. Semantic soundness is checked by prompting the LLM to verify that all intended functional units appear in the final topology and data flows are complete (Table 2).

Table 2. Validation mechanisms enforced by the JIT-SA prototype.

Dimension	Mechanism	Example Check
Syntactic Validity	Pydantic Schemas	No disconnected nodes; fields typed correctly
Resource Validity	Akash Bid Constraints	GPU type matches provider spec
Isolation Rules	Policy Engine	Scrapers isolated from Inference containers
Semantic Soundness	LLM Self-Evaluation	All intended functional units present in topology
Security Baseline	Port Scanner	No unintended public port exposures

The *Topology Generator* was engineered to synthesize **Stack Definition Language (SDL)** files. SDL is a YAML-based specification used by Akash to define resource requirements and network exposure. While we use DePIN as our primary substrate, the architecture is designed to be substrate-agnostic—the same topology could be deployed to Kubernetes, AWS ECS, or other orchestrators with appropriate manifest translators.

5 Design Evaluation

We evaluate JIT-SA as a design artifact rather than as a universally superior deployment stack. The evaluation addresses four dimensions: **validity** (can the method synthesize executable topologies without invalid deployment?), **governability** (do the validation and guard-rail mechanisms constrain unsafe or infeasible generation?), **operating regime** (under what workload conditions is the method appropriate?), and **efficiency** (what cost–latency trade-offs characterize that regime?).

5.1 Experimental Setup

Environment. All experiments used **Llama 3.3 70B Instruct** via Groq API as reasoning engine, with Akash Network as DePIN substrate. Timing measurements were averaged over 5 runs per scenario. Baselines were AWS EC2 On-Demand, AWS Lambda, and Kubernetes with HPA on EKS. For the baselines, equivalent workloads were configured manually using the same container images and task definitions as those synthesized by JIT-SA, ensuring that execution time differences reflect provisioning overhead rather than task implementation differences.

Scenarios. We evaluated three intent classes, each submitted as a free-form natural-language string to the JIT-SA CLI: (A) *Social Sentiment*: `''Scrape 1,000 tweets, store in a vector DB, and perform sentiment analysis''`; (B) *Document Processing*: `''Extract tables from 50 PDF financial reports and generate a consolidated Excel file''`; (C) *Multi-Modal Analysis*: `''Download 100 Sentinel-2 images, run land-use classification, and produce a GeoJSON overlay''`.

5.2 Generated Topologies and Execution

Table 3 summarizes the synthesized topologies. For Scenario A, execution progressed from intent compilation at T+0 s to broker negotiation at T+15 s, deployment at T+55 s, and teardown at T+184 s (Fig. 4).

5.3 Quantitative Results

Table 4 presents comprehensive results across all scenarios. Baselines used the same container images and task definitions as those synthesized by JIT-SA, so

Table 3. Automatically Generated Topologies.

Scenario	Components Generated	GPU	Complexity
A (Sentiment)	Scraper, ChromaDB, Llama-3-8B	1x L4	Medium
B (Documents)	PDF Parser, Schema Normalizer, Excel Writer	No	Low
C (Satellite)	Image Fetcher, PyTorch Classifier, GeoJSON	1x A10	High

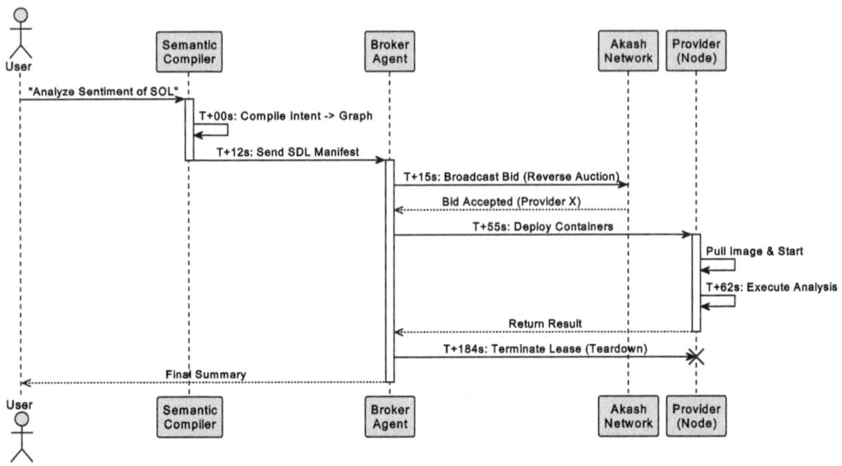

Fig. 4. Sequence Diagram: System autonomously negotiates, deploys, and destroys resources.

execution time differences reflect provisioning overhead only. EC2 incurs manual provisioning overhead (90–180 s); Lambda achieves near-instant starts but is CPU-only; Kubernetes requires cluster warmup (12–18 s). JIT-SA's provisioning time (32–78 s) reflects LLM reasoning, validation, and DePIN bid negotiation; execution times are equivalent across systems for each scenario.

Across all scenarios, JIT-SA synthesized executable topologies without invalid deployment. The cost advantage (70–96% versus EC2, 40–55% versus Kubernetes) arises from DePIN spot pricing and zero idle cost; the latency disadvantage versus Lambda (40–75 s extra) reflects the LLM reasoning and bid negotiation phases.

Table 5 decomposes provisioning time for Scenario A across 47 executions. Self-correction triggered in 31 cases (66%): the Validator rejected the initial Architect output and reinvoked it with a structured error record. Common correction triggers were missing network rules (42%), incorrect resource specifications (35%), and incomplete data-flow definitions (23%). No invalid topology reached deployment.

Table 4. Performance Comparison: JIT-SA vs. Alternatives. Execution times are equivalent across systems for each scenario; differences arise solely from provisioning.

Metric	Scenario A				Scenario B				Scenario C			
	EC2	Lambda	K8s	JIT-SA	EC2	Lambda	K8s	JIT-SA	EC2	Lambda	K8s	JIT-SA
Provision (s)	120	2	15	**55**	90	2	12	**32**	180	3	18	**78**
Execute (s)	129	129	129	129	245	251	248	251	412	425	418	425
Total (s)	249	131	144	**184**	335	253	260	**283**	592	428	436	**503**
Cost ($)	0.56	0.05	0.15	**0.02**	0.34	0.04	0.12	**0.03**	1.12	0.10	0.28	**0.09**

Table 5. Latency Breakdown for Scenario A (Averaged, 5 runs).

Phase	Duration (s)	Std. Dev.
LLM Intent Decomposition (Llama 3.3 70B)	8.2	1.4
Topology Validation (2 iterations avg.)	4.1	0.9
SDL Generation	1.2	0.3
DePIN Bid Broadcast	2.8	0.6
Provider Matching	12.4	3.2
Container Pull & Start	26.3	5.8
Total Provisioning	**55.0**	**8.1**

5.4 Failure Modes and Reliability

Across 47 total executions, the evaluation exposed three classes of governance-relevant failure:

- **DePIN Market Failures (12%):** During peak hours, no providers accepted bids within the 60 s timeout. The system fell back to AWS Lightsail, preserving completion but removing cost benefits.
- **Validation Failures from Ambiguous Intent (8%):** Underspecified intents (e.g., `''analyze this data''`) caused compiler confidence to fall below 0.7, triggering a clarification dialogue that asks the user to specify data source, output format, and resource constraints. A single clarification round was sufficient in all observed cases.
- **Budget Overruns (Prevented):** In 5 cases, the Infrastructure Broker rejected bids exceeding user-defined limits ($0.50), demonstrating guard-rail effectiveness.

No invalid topologies reached deployment stage, validating the bounded refinement approach. However, the 12% DePIN unavailability rate highlights infrastructure brittleness compared to hyperscale cloud SLAs (99.9%+ availability guarantees).

Solution Quality. In all 47 executions, synthesized topologies completed their tasks successfully; task-level outputs were manually verified for correctness on a 10-execution sample. A rigorous user study comparing JIT-SA topologies to human-engineered baselines on qualitative dimensions is identified as important future work.

5.5 Applicability Decision Framework

The conditions below are derived directly from the experimental results: the >5 min execution threshold is the crossover point at which DePIN savings exceed JIT-SA provisioning overhead; the <1/hour frequency reflects where Lambda billing becomes more economical; and the >1 min latency-tolerance condition corresponds to the observed provisioning floor of 32–78 s (Table 6).

Table 6. JIT-SA vs. Alternatives: Decision Matrix derived from experimental results.

Workload Characteristics	JIT-SA	Serverless	Kubernetes
Execution time >5 min	✓	×	✓
Invocation freq <1/hour	✓	✓	×
Unpredictable resources	✓	×	Partial
Latency tolerance >1 min	✓	×	×
Public data only	✓	×	×

Use JIT-SA when: Tasks are rare (<1/hour), computationally intensive (>5 min execution), require unpredictable resources (e.g., variable GPU types), and tolerate cold-start latency (∼1 min).

Use Serverless when: Tasks are frequent, require low latency (<10 s), or have predictable resource profiles.

Use Kubernetes when: Workloads are continuous, require stateful storage, or demand enterprise SLAs.

6 Governance Boundaries, Limitations, and Mitigations

JIT-SA enables fluid architectures, but three challenges remain.

Cold Start Penalty. Latency is the most immediate trade-off. Unlike pre-warmed static microservices, JIT-SA incurs "Time-to-Ready" overhead from LLM reasoning (~5–12 s) and DePIN container pulling (~20–60 s), restricting use to asynchronous workloads. We mitigate this through topology caching, where intents with semantic similarity > 0.92 bypass reasoning and reuse validated SDLs. Future work includes predictive pre-warming and hybrid modes in which critical components remain persistent while heavy compute is synthesized on demand.

Security and Trust in DePIN. Permissionless infrastructure introduces serious security risks that currently limit JIT-SA to non-sensitive workloads. Untrusted providers may copy data or model weights, return fabricated results, or exploit prompt injection to induce malicious topology generation. Static analysis and budget limits provide only partial protection. Because regulated data cannot be processed on unaudited infrastructure, JIT-SA is currently suitable only for public data. Production deployment would require stronger guarantees such as TEEs, zero-knowledge verification, and provider reputation systems.

Ambiguity and Cost Variance. Underspecified intents (e.g., "analyze this") and fluctuating DePIN rates can cause failure or cost overruns. We mitigate ambiguity through clarification dialogues triggered when compiler confidence falls below 0.7, and enforce budget guardrails by rejecting bids above user-defined thresholds. DePIN pricing can fluctuate by 20–40% hour-to-hour, so users may still experience variable performance-cost ratios compared with fixed-price cloud platforms.

7 Conclusion and Future Work

This paper introduced **JIT-SA** as a governed engineering method for volatile AI-driven service composition—treating architecture as a transient artifact synthesised from intent and context under bounded validation, policy constraints, and operational guardrails. The evaluation showed JIT-SA can synthesise valid executable topologies without invalid deployment and occupies a distinct operating regime: appropriate for rare, compute-intensive, latency-tolerant workloads, but inferior to serverless or Kubernetes for predictable or latency-sensitive tasks. The current security posture limits deployment to public-data workloads on unaudited infrastructure.

Future work will focus on stronger execution verification, learning-based refinement of synthesis policies, hybrid persistent/ephemeral partitioning, and a rigorous user study comparing JIT-SA outputs to human-engineered baselines on solution quality.

References

1. Cai, T., Wang, X., Ma, T., Chen, X., Zhou, D.: Large language models as tool makers. In: Proceedings of the International Conference on Learning Representations (ICLR), arXiv:2305.17126 (2024)
2. Ghaddar, A., Tamzalit, D., Assaf, A., Bitar, A.: Variability as a Service: Outsourcing Variability Management in Multi-tenant SaaS Applications. In: Ralyté, J., Franch, X., Brinkkemper, S., Wrycza, S. (eds.) CAiSE 2012. LNCS, vol. 7328, pp. 175–189. Springer, Heidelberg (2012). https://doi.org/10.1007/978-3-642-31095-9_12
3. Martin, D., Burstein, M., McDermott, D., McIlraith, S., Paolucci, M., Sycara, K., McGuinness, D.L., Sirin, E., Srinivasan, N.: Bringing semantics to web services with OWL-S. World Wide Web **10**(3), 243–277 (2007). https://doi.org/10.1007/s11280-007-0033-x
4. Mathew, A., Andrikopoulos, V., Blaauw, F.J.: Exploring the cost and performance benefits of AWS step functions using a data processing pipeline. In: IEEE/ACM International Conference on Utility and Cloud Computing (UCC) (2021). https://doi.org/10.1145/3468737.3494084
5. McIlraith, S.A., Son, T.C.: Adapting Golog for composition of semantic web services. In: Proceedings of the International Conference on Principles of Knowledge Representation and Reasoning (KR), pp. 482–493 (2002)
6. Paolucci, M., Kawamura, T., Payne, T.R., Sycara, K.: Semantic Matching of Web Services Capabilities. In: Horrocks, I., Hendler, J. (eds.) ISWC 2002. LNCS, vol. 2342, pp. 333–347. Springer, Heidelberg (2002). https://doi.org/10.1007/3-540-48005-6_26
7. Patil, S.G., Zhang, T., Wang, X., Gonzalez, J.E.: Gorilla: Large language model connected with massive APIs. arXiv preprint arXiv:2305.15334 (2023)
8. Rezaei, H.B., Ng, S., Rabhi, F.: Enhancing analytics pipelines with advanced multi-agent feedback integration. In: Enterprise Applications, Markets and Services in the Finance Industry (FinanceCom 2024). Lecture Notes in Business Information Processing (LNBIP), vol. 541, pp. 47–61. Springer, Cham (2025). https://doi.org/10.1007/978-3-031-89933-1_4
9. Rezaei, H.B., Rabhi, F., Beheshti, A.: Pipemind: Toward a multi-agent framework for real-time feedback and continuous optimization in analytics pipelines. In: Companion Proceedings of the ACM on Web Conference 2025 (WWW '25), pp. 2891–2894. ACM (2025). https://doi.org/10.1145/3701716.3715193
10. Roman, D., Keller, U., Lausen, H., de Bruijn, J., Lara, R., Stollberg, M., Polleres, A., Feier, C., Bussler, C., Fensel, D.: Web service modeling ontology. Appl. Ontol. **1**(1), 77–106 (2005)
11. Schick, T., et al.: Toolformer: Language models can teach themselves to use tools. arXiv preprint arXiv:2302.04761 (2023)
12. Serral, E., Valderas, P., Pelechano, V.: Supporting runtime system evolution to adapt to user behaviour. In: Advanced Information Systems Engineering. Lecture Notes in Computer Science, vol. 6051, pp. 378–392. Springer, Cham (2010). https://doi.org/10.1007/978-3-642-13094-6_30
13. Sheng, Q.Z., Benatallah, B., Maamar, Z., Dumas, M., Ngu, A.H.H.: Enabling personalized composition and adaptive provisioning of web services. In: Advanced Information Systems Engineering. Lecture Notes in Computer Science, vol. 3084, pp. 322–337. Springer, Cham (2004). https://doi.org/10.1007/978-3-540-25975-6_24

14. Sirin, E., Parsia, B., Wu, D., Hendler, J., Nau, D.: HTN planning for web service composition using SHOP2. J. Web Semant. **1**(4), 377–396 (2004). https://doi.org/10.1016/j.websem.2004.06.005
15. Traverso, P., Pistore, M.: Automated Composition of Semantic Web Services into Executable Processes. In: McIlraith, S.A., Plexousakis, D., van Harmelen, F. (eds.) ISWC 2004. LNCS, vol. 3298, pp. 380–394. Springer, Heidelberg (2004). https://doi.org/10.1007/978-3-540-30475-3_27
16. Wang, Y., et al.: Internet of agents: Fundamentals, applications, and challenges. IEEE Trans. Cogn. Commun. Netw. (2025). arXiv:2505.07176
17. Wibowo, J.A., Polyzos, G.C.: Toward a safe internet of agents. J. Artif. Intell. Res. (2025). arXiv:2512.00520
18. Wild, K., Breitenbücher, U., Képes, K., Leymann, F., Weder, B.: Decentralized Cross-organizational Application Deployment Automation: An Approach for Generating Deployment Choreographies Based on Declarative Deployment Models. In: Dustdar, S., Yu, E., Salinesi, C., Rieu, D., Pant, V. (eds.) CAiSE 2020. LNCS, vol. 12127, pp. 20–35. Springer, Cham (2020). https://doi.org/10.1007/978-3-030-49435-3_2
19. Xu, M.: Every software as an agent: Blueprint and case study. arXiv preprint arXiv:2502.04747 (2025)

An Exploratory Study of Strategic Domain-Driven Design with Large Language Models

Hanieh Attari Moghadam[1], Roya Nasiri[1](✉), Indika Kumara[1](✉), Damian Andrew Tamburri[2,3], and Willem-Jan van den Heuvel[1]

[1] Jheronimus Academy of Data Science, Tilburg University, 's-Hertogenbosch, The Netherlands
{h.attarimoghadam,r.nasiri,i.p.k.weerasinghadewage, w.j.a.m.v.d.heuvel}@tilburguniversity.edu

[2] Jheronimus Academy of Data Science, Technical University of Eindhoven, 's-Hertogenbosch, The Netherlands
datamburri@unisannio.it

[3] University of Sannio, Benevento, Italy

Abstract. Domain-Driven Design (DDD) supports the development of software systems that align with the structure and knowledge of business domains. DDD is specially used for designing microservice architectures. However, the DDD process is complex and time-consuming, and requires a strong collaboration between developers and domain experts. This research investigates the potential of Large Language Models (LLMs) to automate DDD activities. We focus on the strategic design of the DDD, which guides the identification of business (sub)domains and bounded contexts that define the scope of domain models and, consequently, of microservices. We conducted an exploratory study using zero-shot prompting. By manually analyzing model outputs in each step in the strategic DDD, we derived an error taxonomy. Moreover, the results show that LLMs can generate plausible business capabilities and initial subdomain groupings, but they struggle to maintain consistent semantic boundaries in later stages. Our findings, particularly the error taxonomy, can inform future research aimed at improving the LLM-based DDD process.

Keywords: Domain-Driven Design · Large Language Models · Strategic Design · DDD · LLMs

1 Introduction

Domain-Driven Design (DDD) advocates decomposing a business domain into sub-domains, modeling those domains, and using those models to guide the design and implementation of software systems [6]. A domain model captures conceptual or real-situation objects in a (sub)domain. Instead of a monolithic

R. Posenato and I. Vanderfeesten (Eds.): CAiSE 2026 Workshops, LNBIP 586, pp. 118–130, 2026.
https://doi.org/10.1007/978-3-032-28160-9_11

domain model for the problem domain, DDD uses a set of domain models, each within a bounded context, which defines the boundary for interpreting the meanings of the concepts in a given model. DDD is a popular approach to designing microservices [14], where one or more services operationalize a domain model within a bounded context. The DDD process comprises two phases: strategic design and tactical design. The former focuses on analyzing the problem domain to distill business capabilities, subdomains, and bounded contexts. The tactical design applies within a bounded context and translates a domain model into software components that implement domain behaviors captured by the model. Overall, the process is complex and lengthy and requires deep knowledge of DDD and extensive input from domain experts [6,14]. Automating the DDD process can reduce this manual effort and accelerate software delivery.

The emergence of Large Language Models (LLMs), which have transformed how natural language is processed and generated, has created new opportunities for automating software and service engineering tasks, including requirement analysis, process modeling, and code generation [7,8,11,13]. While prior work have studied automating domain modeling tasks with LLMs [3,4,13], none have considered the strategic or tactical design processes in DDD.

To address this gap, we conduct an exploratory study to understand the extent to which LLMs can support the strategic design process of DDD. We evaluate the model's ability to discover business capabilities, cluster them into subdomains, classify subdomains, and propose bounded contexts. To better understand the limitations of LLM-based automation, we develop an error taxonomy (29 categories) in three dimensions (Business Capability, Business Subdomain, Bounded Context) and use it to analyze errors that occur and propagate across stages of the strategic design process. Our findings, though preliminary, can inform further studies into automating the DDD process. For example, the error taxonomy can be used to evaluate new approaches to LLM-based strategic design, and new methods can be developed to mitigate specific errors.

The remainder of the paper is organized as follows. Section 2 reviews the related literature, and Sect. 3 presents our research methodology. Next, we present the results in Sect. 4 and conclude the paper in Sect. 5.

2 Related Work

While there are no studies on automating the DDD process using LLMs, several studies have investigated automating domain modeling. Early studies demonstrated that prompt-based approaches can generate classes, attributes, and relationships without domain-specific fine-tuning [2]. Subsequent work evaluated models such as GPT-3.5 and GPT-4 for generating UML class diagrams from textual descriptions, showing promising precision but incomplete coverage of domain concepts [3]. To improve LLMs' reliability, recent work combines them with structural guidance mechanisms such as task decomposition [4], retrieval-augmented modeling [12], ontology-based reasoning [5], and formal constraints [9]. Additional studies use optimization techniques and guardrails to improve the reliability of LLM-based domain modeling. For example, techniques such as advanced prompt strategies and hyperparameter tuning can improve the quality of generated outputs [1]. In sum, the existing literature shows LLMs can derive domain models from natural-language sources, such as user stories, and achieve results comparable to expert-derived models on certain tasks.

Overall, most work focuses on extracting structural models (e.g., UML class diagrams) but provides limited support for strategic DDD tasks, such as capability extraction, subdomain classification, and bounded context identification. Our study aims to address this research gap.

3 Methodology

We adopt an exploratory approach to study LLMs' capabilities for automating the strategic design phase of DDD in a complex socio-technical domain.

3.1 Ground Truth Use-Case Selection

This study employs a single in-depth case study of a *Mental Health Treatment System,* modeling the psychotherapy life cycle in the German healthcare system. The case study manually follows each step in the DDD process to create a microservice architecture. A group of five students in a master's course at the Jheronimus Academy of Data Science (JADS) developed it. All students had completed domain-driven design and microservices lessons, and one student had domain expertise (a bachelor's degree in Psychology and professional experience). The case study has been developed in English and under the guidance of the lecturers. We selected this case study because it was difficult to find a detailed DDD use case from industry or academia. The case study has a complex socio-technical structure that comprises multiple interacting subdomains (e.g., patient onboarding, scheduling, and analytics), diverse stakeholders (patients, therapists, and administrators), and critical workflows (e.g., patient-therapist matching and emergency response). These characteristics make the domain suitable for evaluating LLM-based automation of strategic DDD artifacts.

3.2 Model and Prompting Strategy Selection

We selected Gemini 2.0 Flash as the primary LLM due to its large context capacity and compatibility with API-based prompting workflows. The model supports a context window of up to 1,000,000 tokens, enabling the inclusion of extensive problem domain specifications and artifacts within a single prompt. It was the best-performing model in the Gemini LLM family during the experiments. We were also able to use free education credits for Gemini. We employed Zero-shot prompting, which is commonly used in prior domain modeling studies as a baseline for comparative evaluation [3], thus allowing the model's inherent capabilities to be assessed without the influence of examples. This study also aims to build a baseline for the LLM-based automation of strategic DDD activities.

3.3 Strategic DDD Automation: Experimentation Pipeline

Figure 1 illustrates the overall experimental workflow, highlighting the transitions among the strategic DDD design stages. It consists of four sequential tasks: business capability extraction, subdomain grouping, subdomain classification, and bounded context identification. To systematically analyze performance across the workflow, the experiment adopts a dual-path setup that separates intrinsic task ability from the influence of input quality [3]. In Path A (Propagated Input), each stage consumes the artifact from the previous step, simulating an end-to-end, autonomous workflow and revealing how upstream errors propagate to downstream tasks. In Path B (Ground-Truth (GT) Input), each stage instead receives the corresponding GT artifact, enabling evaluation of the model's reasoning for the target task under ideal conditions. Together, these two paths enable the results to distinguish errors caused by imperfect upstream inputs from those arising from the model's reasoning within each task.

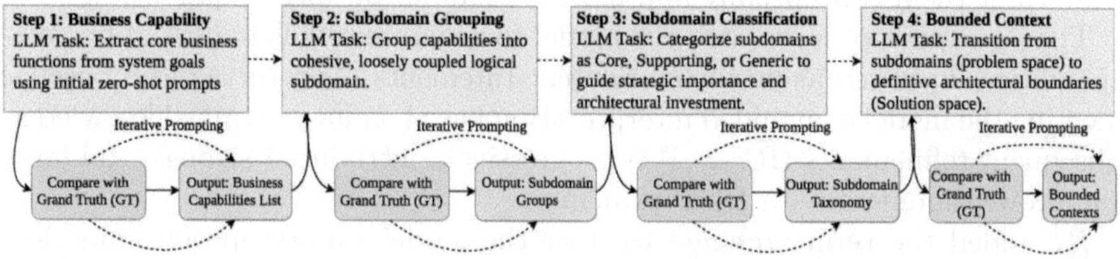

Fig. 1. Experimentation Design for Studying Strategic DDD Automation with LLMs

The purpose of constructing this pipeline is twofold. First, it provides a systematic framework for assessing whether an LLM can autonomously execute key tasks of the strategic phase of DDD while maintaining conceptual alignment across stages. Second, it enables the evaluation of how errors introduced in earlier stages propagate and influence the accuracy of subsequent artifacts. Together, this process supports a holistic understanding of the potential and limitations of LLM-driven DDD automation.

All stages of the pipeline follow the same prompting structure. A baseline zero-shot prompt defines the task objective, assigns the model a DDD or business expert role, and specifies the output format. The generated artifact is compared with the GT model to assess semantic alignment with DDD principles. When inconsistencies arise, the prompt is iteratively refined and re-executed, and the most semantically consistent output is propagated to the next stage. This feedback-driven process improves the interpretability and semantic consistency of generated artifacts while maintaining traceability across the pipeline.

To ensure architectural validity, all LLM-generated capabilities and intermediate artifacts were reviewed by the first three authors of this paper. The third author teaches DDD in JADS's master's program. We evaluated the outputs against core DDD principles, including high cohesion, clear ownership, and well-defined boundaries [6, 14].

To systematically evaluate the LLM's performance in automating strategic DDD edsign, three error taxonomies were developed to classify discrepancies between LLM-generated artifacts and the expert-defined Ground Truth (GT). Following the taxonomy development approach of Shen et al. [10], outputs from baseline zero-shot experiments on the case study were analyzed to identify errors, including invented capabilities, merged or fragmented functions, incorrect subdomain groupings, and misclassification of strategic domains. These recurring patterns were clustered by the DDD principles they violated and organized into three categories: *Business Capability Errors, Subdomain Modeling Errors, Bounded Context Errors.* This taxonomy was validated across all experiments to ensure clear, mutually exclusive definitions for consistent qualitative analysis of the LLM's architectural reasoning.

Business Capability Extraction. The first stage identifies the business capabilities required to achieve the system's goals, independent of technical implementation. The system goals were provided as input, and the LLM was instructed to interpret them conceptually and list the required business capabilities.

The basic prompt instructed the model to generate a bulleted list of business capabilities expressed as business-oriented statements. This served as a baseline reflecting the model's unguided interpretation based on its pretrained knowledge. Subsequent refinements (R1 -> R4) progressively introduced stronger guidance to improve alignment with DDD principles.

R1 added the term *granular* to steer the model toward specific, function-oriented capabilities rather than broad summaries. *R2* added didactic guidance encouraging the model to reason about the distinction between business intent and implementation. *R3* added structural constraints to exclude technical features (e.g., data storage, APIs, and authentication), split overly broad capabilities into independent business functions, and provide short rationales. *R4* further strengthened the prompt by introducing three rules: *scope and exclusion guardrails*: exclude technical implementations, interfaces, non-functional requirements, and security features; *granularity and single-responsibility*: each capability must represent one clear business purpose and avoid merging multiple functions, and *data-volatility distinction*: separate capabilities managing stable descriptive data from those handling volatile transactional processes. Although these constraints improved conceptual clarity, the model still showed over-segmentation, hallucinated capabilities, and boundary/scope issues.

Because the final capability list included newly introduced capabilities and semantic drift, it could not be directly compared with the canonical GT subdomain structure. To isolate the LLM's grouping performance, the expert-derived baseline grouping was constructed. Using the GT use case guidance, the LLM-generated capabilities were treated as a hybrid list and assigned to the most appropriate GT subdomain based on their primary business responsibility. Flawed capabilities were mapped to the closest corresponding GT responsibility, while plausible new capabilities were integrated into the GT architecture. The resulting validated structure served as the reference benchmark for evaluating LLM outputs in the next stage.

Subdomain Grouping. The objective of this stage is to evaluate whether the LLM can identify natural cohesion boundaries among capabilities and organize them into meaningful domain components consistent with DDD principles of high cohesion and loose coupling.

The basic prompt instructed the LLM to assign each capability to exactly one group. Initial outputs revealed architectural issues, including low-cohesion groupings and "junk drawer" subdomains combining unrelated responsibilities.

To address these issues, we refined the prompt iteratively: *R1*, applying the DDD principle of separating Generic and Supporting functions; *R2*, introducing a business milestonebased heuristic that groups capabilities contributing to the same milestone while separating stages across key transitions; *R3*, emphasizing architectural principles such as separation by architectural concern and defining operational boundaries by milestones; and *R4*, strengthening architectural reasoning by introducing high-level domain categories (operational, analytical, and supporting) with a rule prioritizing the most specific business functions.

After comparison with the GT, *R1* was selected as the most reliable prompt for the next pipeline phase. Although subsequent refinements introduced minor improvements, they also introduced architectural regressions, such as overly generalizable supporting domains, that undermined overall cohesion. The experiment shows that precise and consistent Ubiquitous Language is more critical for architectural automation than complex prompting logic.

Subdomain Classification. Once subdomains were identified, the next phase classified them as Core, Supporting, or Generic [6]. In DDD, Core subdomains represent the organization's competitive advantage, while Supporting subdomains provide necessary but non-differentiating functionality. Generic subdomains represent commodity capabilities that can often be reused or outsourced.

The LLM was instructed to classify the generated subdomains based on business value rather than implementation details. While the initial prompt correctly identified core domains such as *PatientTherapist Matching* and *Treatment Scheduling*, it struggled to distinguish Supporting and Generic domains (e.g., *Regulatory Compliance*). To address these issues, we refined the prompt iteratively: *R1 Structured Reasoning*, which embedded formal DDD definitions of Core, Supporting, and Generic subdomains and required a brief justification for each classification; *R2 Checklist Gate Heuristic*, which introduced a three-question decision rule: (1) Does the subdomain directly create customer value? (2) Would a competitor need the same implementation to match the differentiator? (3) Would outsourcing it remove the competitive advantage? A subdomain was labeled Core only if it satisfied all three conditions; and *R3 Strategic Parsimony and Enriched Output*, which emphasized minimizing *Core* subdomains and generated brief functional descriptions to improve semantic grounding.

During refinement, the focus shifted from improving classification accuracy to ensuring the output could support the next pipeline stage. An initial attempt at Bounded Context Identification showed that outputs containing only subdomain names and brief justifications lacked sufficient semantic detail, leading the LLM to group them by superficial lexical similarity (e.g., "management"), yielding low-cohesion contexts. To address this, *R3* was enhanced with explicit functional descriptions for each subdomain, providing stronger semantic grounding. The enriched *R3* output improved information quality for subsequent steps and was selected as input for the next stage.

To evaluate the LLM's performance in the subdomain classification step, we employed a two-stage approach. First, an expert-derived baseline classification was constructed by assigning the LLM-generated subdomains from the previous step to the GT strategic categories: Core, Supporting, or Generic. This baseline served as the benchmark for evaluation. Second, the LLM's classifications were compared against this benchmark to identify discrepancies, including direct LLM errors (e.g., subdomain misclassification) and propagated errors inherited from earlier pipeline stages.

Bounded Context Identification. This stage identifies Bounded Contexts, which define clear conceptual and linguistic boundaries between subsystems and transition a domain model from the problem space to the solution space.

The basic prompt instructed the model to group subdomains by a cohesive business purpose, shared data ownership, and a consistent Ubiquitous Language. It also required that each subdomain belong to exactly one context, that groups align with business intent, and that each context be given a concise name. In addition, the strategic separation between Core, Supporting, and Generic domains had to be preserved.

However, this prompt produced overly broad contexts that mixed unrelated domains, resulting in low cohesion. For example, the model grouped *Patient-Therapist Matching* (Core) with *Therapist Network Management* (Supporting) under a single "Management" context. This occurred because the prompt used overly abstract terms, such as "cohesion", "alignment", and "shared purpose", which are conceptually sound but not operationally enforceable. This leads the LLM to rely on superficial lexical cues (e.g., grouping domains containing "Management" or "Core") rather than on genuine domain cohesion.

To address this issue, the prompt was iteratively refined. *R1* introduced a *Default-to-Separation* rule, instructing the model to treat each subdomain as an independent context unless explicit justification for merging was provided. *R2* added *constraint-based guardrails*, requiring each grouping to satisfy five conditions: shared vocabulary, rule consistency, data ownership, rate of change, and interaction frequency. *R3* incorporated a *self-verification* mechanism that required the model to report whether invalid groupings were present (pass/fail), hence encouraging internal consistency without external validation.

Each output was compared with the GT use case using three criteria: one-to-one correspondence between subdomains and contexts, the absence of overlapping responsibilities, and consistent naming aligned with the Ubiquitous Language. The configuration combining three refined rules produced the most stable and interpretable results and was therefore selected as the final methodological output for this stage. It shows that explicit architectural rules are more effective than abstract guidance when directing LLM reasoning in DDD tasks.

4 Results

This section presents our findings on the use of LLMs to automate strategic design tasks in the DDD process. To support transparency and reproducibility, the use case, the basic and refined prompts, and the qualitative and quantitative results are provided in an open replication package[1]. In the remainder of this section, we discuss the results for each strategic design task. Regarding error counts, we report only the results for the best-refined prompt; the rest are available in the replication package.

4.1 Business Capability Extraction

Table 1 shows the error categories for business capability extraction, along with the results for the basic prompt (BF) and best refined prompt (RF). We identified 11 error categories, grouped into 3 high-level categories: content errors. boundary and scope errors, and definition and naming errors. Content errors are related to the presence or absence of a business capability within a given use case. The boundary and scope errors capture the granularity issues that arise from incorrect scoping of a business capability. The last error category represents semantic issues related to the definition and naming of a capability.

The basic prompt produced a well-structured but incomplete list of 15 business capabilities, including 5 new ones, of which only three semantically matched, while omitting 17 GT capabilities. The model tended to generate coarse-grained functions, such as *Patient Intake & Profiling*, whereas the ground truth case study defines finer-grained capabilities, including *Patient Information Management, Survey Generation, and Patient Match Acceptance.* This highlights substantial coverage gaps in the generated results. The prompt refinements showed no improvement, except in reducing definition and naming errors.

4.2 Subdomain Grouping: Domain Decomposition

The second phase evaluated the LLM's ability to group the identified business capabilities into cohesive and loosely coupled subdomains. The analysis distinguished between errors originating from the LLM's grouping logic and those propagated from flaws in the input business capabilities.

As shown in Table 2, we identified 11 error types in domain decomposition, classified into three high-level categories: structural, semantic, and mixed. The first category comprises sub-domains that violate the DDD principles, such as single responsibility, cohesion, granularity (size), and integrity of domain models (bounded contexts). The second category captures the high-level root causes of domain decomposition errors, including misplacement of business capabilities across domains and LLM hallucination. The third category includes erroneous sub-domains that can be attributed to both syntactical and semantic errors.

[1] https://doi.org/10.6084/m9.figshare.31711063.

Table 1. Business Capability Error Taxonomy. BP-Basic Prompt, RP-Refined Prompt

Error Category	Error Name	Description	BP	RP
Content Errors	New Capability	LLM generates a business capability that does not exist in the Ground Truth (GT) use case. These are hallucinated functions, often caused by overgeneralization or confusion between adjacent domains.	5	10
	Missing Capability	LLM omits valid Ground Truth capabilities, typically as a side effect of over-merging or semantic drift. Missing capabilities reduce functional coverage and distort the system's conceptual completeness.	17	16
Boundary and Scope Errors	Capability Merging	LLM incorrectly combines distinct Ground Truth capabilities into a single, overly broad function, reducing granularity and cohesion. *Inter-Domain Merging* (capabilities from different subdomains) *Intra-Domain Merging* (capabilities within the same subdomain).	3	5
	Under-Scoped Capability	LLM captures only a fraction of the Ground Truth capability's responsibility, focusing on technical sub-steps or partial processes instead of the full business goal.	0	1
	Boundary Expansion	LLM starts from a valid Ground Truth capability but adds new, unscoped functionality beyond the defined boundaries of the original business requirement.	6	5
	Semantic Drift	The LLM misinterprets a capability's business purpose or intent, framing a correct business function within the wrong context or domain (e.g., reinterpreting an operational task as analytical). This typically results in a missing correct capability as well.	2	2
	Capability Conflation	A severe boundary error where distinct subdomains, each with its own Ubiquitous Language, are merged into one capability. The result is a large, incohesive unit with multiple unrelated responsibilities and blurred lifecycle ownership.	1	0
Definition and Naming Errors	Implementation Defined Capability	The capability name reflects technical implementation details (the "how") rather than business purpose (the "what"). This violates the separation between problem and solution space.	1	0
	Incongruent Naming	The capability name promises a broader function than its description actually provides, creating inconsistency between the label and the meaning.	1	0
	Ambiguous Naming	The capability name is overly generic, e.g., "Management," "Processing", and conceals multiple possible responsibilities, leading to misclassification and merged meanings.	1	0
	Fractured Language	The LLM uses multiple terms or synonyms,e.g., "Psychotherapist", "Therapist", for the same core concept, fragmenting the Ubiquitous Language and creating confusion across contexts.	1	0

Using the basic prompt, the LLM grouped 15 business capabilities into 7 subdomains, which were evaluated against the GT using the error taxonomy. Although some groupings were reasonable, the output contained major DDD violations. Notably, the model created a *System Administration & Compliance* subdomain that merged three unrelated concerns, Identity Management (User Access & Role Management), Regulatory Compliance, and Communications (Stakeholder Communication), forming a DDD "junk drawer" anti-pattern that increases coupling and obscures domain ownership. The analysis also showed that errors were from systematic patterns and often propagated from ambiguous input capabilities. For example, the merged capability *Patient Intake & Profiling* caused boundary violations and produced a low-cohesion *Patient Management & Intake* subdomain, illustrating how flawed inputs can cascade into architectural errors. As shown in Table 2, although the Basic Prompt produced slightly fewer hallucinated subdomains from the previous design phase, this was minor compared to the more severe architectural flaws (e.g., low-cohesion subdomains).

The experiments on the refined prompts yielded two key conclusions about the use of LLMs for automated subdomain decomposition. First, despite several prompt refinements, the first refinement's output remained the most reliable starting point for the architecture. Although later prompts introduced more complex heuristics, they led to a serious architectural regression, such as the creation of a *Compliance & Security* subdomain that incorrectly merged Regulatory *Compliance* and *User Access & Role Management*, resulting in a typical DDD "common" or "miscellaneous" bounded context. In contrast, the first refinement correctly separated these concerns into *Access Control & Authorization* and *Regulatory Compliance & Data Governance*. Second, the results show that the quality and clarity of the input business capabilities are more critical than prompt complexity. Even carefully designed prompts with architectural heuristics could not overcome ambiguities in the input, indicating that the precision of the Ubiquitous Language is the key limiting factor in automating early-stage architectural design.

4.3 Bounded Contexts

Table 3 shows the bounded context error taxonomy, which distinguishes between two broad categories of errors: (1) semantic and conceptual errors, which originate from misinterpretations of the business meaning or strategic relationships between subdomains, and (2) structural errors, which arise when the internal composition or completeness of a bounded context is flawed even if its high-level boundary appears correct. Semantic errors most often propagate from the subdomain classification (Core, Supporting, and generic), whereas structural errors reflect weaknesses introduced in subdomain grouping. A critical distinction exists between the Low-Cohesion Context and the Heterogeneous Context errors, which are sometimes superficially similar but differ in both origin and severity.

The analysis evaluates outputs from the final refined prompt, guiding the LLM to derive sound bounded contexts using three rules: *Default-to-Separation*, *constraint-based guardrails*, and *self-verification*(see Sect. 3). The input consisted of the enriched subdomain list from the previous DDD step, including functional descriptions for each subdomain. The results highlight a key limitation of automated DDD pipelines. The final refined prompt effectively guided the LLM to follow the *Default-to-Separation* heuristic, avoiding severe grouping errors, such

Table 2. Business Subdomain Decomposition Error Taxonomy

Error Category	Error Name	Description	BP	RP
Structural	Low-Cohesion Subdomain	A subdomain accrues multiple unrelated responsibilities. Can be a direct LLM grouping error (over-broad clustering) or propagated from an incohesive input capability (e.g., capability merging upstream) that "pollutes" the target subdomain. *DDD Facet Violated:* Cohesion & single responsibility of a subdomain.	5	3
	Propagated Incompleteness	The model correctly recognizes the subdomain's intent but produces an incomplete subdomain because the necessary capabilities are missing from the input. *DDD Facet Violated:* Coverage within a recognized subdomain.	2	1
	Propagated Scope Expansion	The model recognizes the correct subdomain but over-broadens its responsibility because an expanded input capability stretches the subdomain's conceptual boundary. *DDD Facet Violated:* Scope/boundary size of a subdomain.	1	1
	Boundary Violation	Functions from one GT subdomain are absorbed into another due to to a merged upstream capability, contaminating the receiver and breaking bounded-context integrity. *DDD Facet Violated:* Bounded-context purity & ownership.	1	1
Semantic	Capability Misplacement	A valid capability is grouped under the wrong (but otherwise valid) subdomain because the model misunderstood the business purpose or lifecycle ownership. *DDD Facet Violated:* Correct capability to correct subdomain mapping.	1	1
	Missing Subdomain	A Ground Truth (GT) subdomain is absent entirely. Often happens when relevant capabilities were drifted/merged elsewhere or the model failed to perceive a cohesive theme. *DDD Facet Violated:* Coverage of GT problem space.	2	1
	Hallucinated Subdomain	The model invents a subdomain not present in GT, typically to house "homeless" capabilities created by New Capability, Semantic Drift, or Inter-Domain Merging at the input level. *DDD Facet Violated:* Alignment with GT scope & Ubiquitous Language.	3	1
	Capability Induced Misplacement	A capability is misplaced because it is pulled toward a flawed "anchor" capability (e.g., a technical term or mislabeled theme) that creates a misleading local context. *DDD Facet Violated:* Local semantic attraction/anchoring.	1	0
	New Subdomain (Legitimate Extension)	A semantically valid, cohesive subdomain outside the GT scope. Document as "extension" (not counted as an error) if it's coherent and not caused by upstream defects. *DDD Facet Violated:* Extension beyond GT scope.	1	2
Mixed	Implementation Defined Subdomain	The model defines a subdomain around the *how* (technology/logistics) instead of the *what* (business purpose). Technical or logistical cues (e.g., "scheduling," "algorithm") drive grouping and obscure the real domain responsibility. *DDD Facet Violated:* Separation of problem vs. solution space.	3	3
	Drift-Induced Subdomain Splitting	A cohesive GT subdomain is fragmented into multiple LLM subdomains because drifted capabilities now "sound" like they belong elsewhere, causing the model to split what should remain one domain. *DDD Facet Violated:* Boundary integrity & cohesion.	1	0

as the "junk drawer" anti-pattern observed in the initial prompt. However, a well-engineered prompt at this stage cannot fully correct flawed inputs. Although the resulting bounded context is structurally well-separated, it remains architecturally unsound because its components reflect errors propagated from earlier DDD steps. This finding highlights the fragility of the strategic DDD automation pipeline and the importance of input quality at each stage.

Table 3. Bounded Context Error Taxonomy

Error Category	Error Name	Definition	BP	RP
Semantic and Conceptual Errors	Conflated Core Context	Two or more *Core* subdomains with distinct business purposes are incorrectly merged into one bounded context. This eliminates strategic boundaries, mixes ubiquitous languages, and blurs ownership of core domain logic.	1	1
	Conflated Supporting Context	Distinct *Supporting* subdomains with different purposes, data ownership, or change rates are incorrectly grouped into one bounded context, resulting in low cohesion and unclear ownership.	1	0
	Conflated Generic Context	Multiple *Generic* subdomains (shared technical services or infrastructural modules) are merged into a single "catch-all" bounded context. This conflation hides independent infrastructural responsibilities.	1	0
	Heterogeneous Context	Subdomains from *different strategic classifications* (Core, Supporting, and Generic) are merged into one context without a clear architectural rationale. This violates strategic design boundaries and creates semantic confusion.	1	2
Structural Errors	Low-Cohesion Context	A bounded context that correctly exists as a separate module but internally mixes elements with weak conceptual or operational relationships, lowering cohesion. Arises from vague scoping or propagated boundary mistakes.	2	1
	Partial Context Representation	The context captures only part of the intended subdomain responsibilities, leading to dependency leakage or missing behaviors, undermining autonomy.	2	1
	Hallucinated Context	A bounded context created for a subdomain that does not exist in the ground-truth domain model. This typically results from overgeneralization, term misinterpretation, or LLM hallucination.	1	1

5 Conclusion

This study investigated whether Large Language Models (LLMs) can automate strategic Domain-Driven Design (DDD) activities. A structured workflow was developed covering business capability extraction, subdomain grouping and classification, and bounded context identification. Using a Ground Truth mental health treatment use case and zero-shot prompting, the results show that LLMs can generate plausible outputs but often diverge from core DDD principles, including capability merging, semantic drift, low cohesion, misplaced subdomains, and heterogeneous bounded contexts. We developed a taxonomy of

29 errors. The findings highlight the potential of LLMs as assistive tools for early DDD activities rather than autonomous architects. However, this conclusion is limited to zero-shot prompting; agentic designs or humanAI collaboration may enable iterative refinement and better alignment with DDD principles. Future work can explore these and alternative LLMs to improve end-to-end DDD automation.

Acknowledgments. This research was partially funded by the Safeguard project (grant No. 20506020) with Deloitte.

References

1. Bulhakov, V., et al. Investigating the role of LLMs hyperparameter tuning and prompt engineering to support domain modeling. In: Software Engineering and Advanced Applications, pp. 349–366. Springer, Cham (2026)
2. Chaaben, M.B., et al.: Towards using few-shot prompt learning for automating model completion. In: 45th international conference on software engineering: New ideas and emerging results (ICSE-NIER), pp. 7–12. IEEE (2023)
3. Chen, K., et al.: Automated domain modeling with large language models: A comparative study. In: International Conference on Model Driven Engineering Languages and Systems (MODELS), pp. 162–172. IEEE (2023)
4. Chen, R., et al.: A model is not built by a single prompt: LLM-based domain modeling with question decomposition. arXiv:2410.09854 (2024)
5. Coutinho, M.L.: Leveraging LLMs in text-based ontology-driven conceptual modeling. In: Joint Ontology Workshops (2024)
6. Evans, E.: Domain-Driven Design. Addison-Wesley (2004)
7. Hadi, M.U., et al.: Large language models: a comprehensive survey of its applications, challenges, limitations, and future prospects **1**(3), 1–26 (2023)
8. Kumara, I., et al.: Large language models for service-oriented computing (llm4soc): review and research directions. In: Service-Oriented Computing, pp. 90–113. Springer, Cham (2026)
9. Sadik, A.R. et al.: LLM as a code generator in agile model driven development. In: José Domínguez Mayo, F., Ferreira Pires, L., Seidewitz, E. (eds.) International Conference on Model-Driven Engineering and Software Development, pp. 198–212. Springer, Cham (2024). https://doi.org/10.1007/978-3-031-96841-9_10
10. Shen, J., et al.: A study of in-context-learning-based text-to-SQL errors. arXiv:2501.09310 (2025)
11. Shi, H., et al.: How LLMs aid in domain modeling: Opportunities and challenges. In: Proceedings of the 2025 IEEE International Conference on Software Services Engineering (SSE), Helsinki, Finland (2025) IEEE
12. Tinnes, C., et al.: Software model evolution with large language models: Experiments on simulated, public, and industrial datasets (2024)
13. Yang, Y., et al.: Multi-step iterative automated domain modeling with large language models. In: International Conference on Model Driven Engineering Languages and Systems Companion (MODELS Companion '24), pp. 587–595. ACM (2024)
14. Zhong, C., et al.: Domain-driven design for microservices: an evidence-based investigation. IEEE Trans. Softw. Eng. **50**(6), 1425–1440 (2024)

A Multi-agent Service for Football Data Querying

Michele Pedrazzoli and Davide Ragazzi(✉)

Kama.Sport Srl, Paratico, Italy
{michele.pedrazzoli,davide.ragazzi}@kama.sport

Abstract. In the world of professional football, the availability of official data is continuously increasing, spanning historical records, live match events, player statistics, referee information, lineups, and technical staff data. As a result, leagues, clubs, analysts, and editorial teams are faced with the challenge of accessing and interpreting a large volume of structured and constantly updated information in a timely and reliable manner. To support the exploration and analysis of such data, Large Language Models (LLMs) have recently emerged as promising tools, offering new possibilities for natural language interaction with complex sports data repositories. In this paper, we propose a GPT-based approach to assist professional football stakeholders in querying official football data through natural language. The approach leverages a service-oriented multi-agent architecture based on crewAI, wherein four specialized agents are employed for multiple tasks: (i) resolving football entities mentioned in the user query; (ii) retrieving grounded information from an official PostgreSQL database containing historical and live match data; (iii) generating visual summaries when explicitly requested; and (iv) producing the final professional response based on the retrieved data. The approach has been implemented within a service-oriented ecosystem, and preliminarily validated in realistic usage scenarios involving internal representatives of a football league and experts in football editorial services, demonstrating its potential in providing reliable and up-to-date insights from official football data.

Keywords: Large Language Models · Multi-Agent Systems · Sports Analytics · Tool-Augmented LLMs · Football Data Querying · Service-Oriented Architectures

1 Introduction

In the contemporary landscape of sports analytics, the availability of real-time and historical data has transformed the way fans, analysts, journalists, and professionals interact with football-related information. Modern competitions generate vast amounts of structured and semi-structured data, including match

R. Posenato and I. Vanderfeesten (Eds.): CAiSE 2026 Workshops, LNBIP 586, pp. 131–143, 2026.
https://doi.org/10.1007/978-3-032-28160-9_12

events, player statistics, team formations, referee decisions, standings, and seasonal aggregates [1]. Managing and querying this continuously evolving information ecosystem poses significant technical challenges, particularly when low-latency responses and up-to-date insights are required during live matches.

Recent advances in Large Language Models (LLMs) have opened new opportunities for natural language interfaces capable of translating complex user questions into meaningful answers across heterogeneous sports data sources [5]. By enabling intuitive question-answering over structured databases, LLM-based systems can bridge the gap between raw statistical repositories and end users seeking contextualized, conversational insights [7]. However, despite their remarkable generative capabilities, LLMs are inherently limited when operating without direct access to reliable and updated data sources. Retrieval-Augmented Generation (RAG) approaches address this limitation by grounding language model outputs on external knowledge sources during the generation process [3]. In dynamic domains such as live sports events, this limitation may lead to outdated information or hallucinated responses if the generation process is not properly grounded.

To overcome these issues, service-oriented architectures combined with agent-based orchestration mechanisms offer a robust solution. In particular, multi-agent frameworks such as crewAI[1] enable the decomposition of complex question-answering workflows into coordinated tasks executed by specialized agents. This modular design enhances transparency, controllability, and scalability, while ensuring that each step of the reasoning and data retrieval pipeline is explicitly defined and monitored [11].

In this paper, we present a service-oriented architecture built around a GPT-based system designed to answer natural language questions about matches, leagues, seasons, teams, players, statistics, referees, lineups, and technical staff. The proposed solution leverages a crewAI-based orchestration layer composed of four specialized agents and four corresponding tasks, each responsible for a distinct phase of the query-processing pipeline: (i) interpreting and classifying the user query; (ii) retrieving relevant and up-to-date data from a dedicated sports database containing both historical records and live match events; (iii) validating and structuring the retrieved information; and (iv) generating the final natural language response grounded on the retrieved data. By granting agents controlled access to a continuously updated database, the system ensures reliable outputs and supports real-time responses, even during ongoing matches.

Moreover, the multi-agent pipeline is encapsulated within a service-oriented ecosystem, enabling integration through REST APIs and deployment in production environments. This design supports scalability and interoperability with external platforms.

This work extends our previous study on LLM-based RAG architectures for football scouting data analysis by shifting from scouting-oriented semantic retrieval to natural-language querying over official football databases, including historical and live match data [4]. More specifically, the contribution of this

[1] https://crewai.com.

paper lies in the design of a service-oriented multi-agent architecture grounded on read-only SQL access to continuously updated official football data, with explicit separation between entity resolution, data retrieval, optional visualization, and final response generation.

The remainder of this paper is organized as follows. Section 2 reviews related work on LLM-based question-answering systems and agent-oriented architectures in sports analytics. Section 3 discusses the motivations behind our approach and the challenges posed by real-time sports data management. Section 4 describes the proposed crewAI-based architecture in detail, outlining the roles of the four agents and their interaction workflow. Section 5 presents an evaluation of the system in both historical and live-match scenarios. Finally, Sect. 6 concludes the paper by discussing strengths, limitations, and future research directions.

2 Related Work

The continuous advancement of Artificial Intelligence has opened new frontiers in sports data analysis, enabling innovative methods to extract valuable insights from diverse information sources, including match events, player performance metrics, and broader contextual data [12]. Traditional AI and machine learning techniques have long been applied to sports analytics, facilitating performance evaluation, tactical decision-making, and predictive modelling across multiple disciplines [6]. Beyond classic approaches, recent research has explored the integration of Large Language Models (LLMs) and Retrieval-Augmented Generation (RAG) frameworks to further enhance data accessibility and query responsiveness. A notable example is SoccerRAG, which demonstrates the application of RAG and LLMs for natural language retrieval of soccer information, showing significant improvements in complex query handling and the accessibility of extensive sports archives [9]. More recent work has also explored GraphRAG-based approaches for structured sports data retrieval, demonstrating how graph-enhanced retrieval pipelines can improve the grounding of LLM responses when querying complex soccer datasets [8].

In parallel, LLM-driven frameworks are emerging that incorporate domain-specific reasoning into sports contexts. For instance, SportsGPT outlines an LLM-centric system for sports motion assessment and interpretability, illustrating how generative models can be applied to domain-specific sports data tasks [10]. Additionally, multi-agent NLP frameworks such as GridMind have been proposed to unify multimodal sports data through coordinated retrieval and language modeling, leveraging specialized agents to interpret queries, retrieve relevant data, and synthesize cohesive responses [2]. These works highlight the potential of combining agent-based systems with generative models for sports analytics.

Nevertheless, despite the growing interest in AI-driven sports systems, existing research often remains focused on prototypical systems, document-oriented retrieval settings, or narrowly scoped domains (e.g., motion analysis or single-sport frameworks). Compared with systems such as SoccerRAG [9] and our previous scouting-oriented work [4], the present contribution targets operational querying over official football data grounded on a relational PostgreSQL database, including both historical records and live match updates. This positions the proposed architecture within a more service-oriented and operational setting, where data traceability, controlled access, and timeliness are central requirements.

3 Motivating Scenario

In the contemporary football ecosystem, professional leagues, clubs, technical staff, referees, and media organizations increasingly rely on accurate and up-to-date data to support decision-making, performance evaluation, and public communication. Major football competitions generate vast amounts of official information on a daily basis, including match events, player statistics, standings, disciplinary records, referee decisions, lineups, and seasonal aggregates. This information is continuously updated during live matches and stored within centralized official databases.

Official Match Data. Typically, official football data can be divided into two macro-categories. The first category includes *structured historical data*, such as player profiles, team rosters, past match results, standings, season-by-season statistics, referee assignments, and technical staff information. These datasets enable longitudinal analysis across seasons and competitions. The second category comprises *live event data*, generated in real time during matches, including goals, substitutions, fouls, cards, VAR decisions, formation changes, and other time-stamped events.

Although this information is highly structured at the database level, accessing and querying it effectively often requires technical expertise (e.g., SQL knowledge, familiarity with database schemas, or dedicated analytics platforms). As a result, many stakeholders struggle to extract timely insights from official data repositories, especially during live matches when responsiveness is critical.

Challenges. A top-tier professional league can generate thousands of matches per season across multiple competitions, each producing hundreds of granular events and statistical updates. When aggregated across seasons and categories (e.g., youth, women's, professional divisions), the resulting data volume becomes extremely large and continuously evolving.

While such data is essential for competitive analysis and regulatory transparency, several challenges emerge. First, stakeholders increasingly require *natural language access* to official data, rather than complex manual queries. For example, a coach may need instant answers about a player's recent performance trends, a match analyst may request cross-season comparisons for a team or competition, and a referee may want historical statistics related to disciplinary patterns or specific match contexts. Second, during live matches, information must be both *accurate and immediately updated*, leaving no room for outdated content or unverifiable statements. Third, media operators and editorial teams demand reliable, data-driven narratives to produce accurate match previews, post-match reports, and analytical content, where even minor inaccuracies can undermine credibility.

Traditional dashboards, while powerful, are not designed for flexible, conversational, and context-aware queries that combine historical and live data in a unified response. Moreover, general-purpose LLMs, when used without direct access to official databases, risk generating outdated or hallucinated information, especially in time-sensitive match scenarios.

To address these limitations, we propose a GPT-based, service-oriented architecture grounded on continuously updated official databases and orchestrated through a multi-agent workflow. By granting specialized agents controlled access to historical records and live match events, the system enables reliable natural language querying over football data at scale. Such a solution can serve multiple stakeholders: football leagues seeking transparent and centralized access to official statistics; clubs and technical staff requiring rapid analytical insights; referees interested in contextual performance data; and editorial teams aiming to produce accurate, data-driven content. Ultimately, this approach fosters a scalable and trustworthy interface between complex sports data infrastructures and the diverse actors operating within modern football competitions.

4 System Architecture

The proposed solution is built upon a service-oriented architecture that orchestrates four specialized agents using the *crewAI* framework. The system is designed to transform natural language questions into reliable, data-grounded answers by decomposing the overall reasoning process into distinct yet coordinated tasks. Each agent is responsible for a specific phase of the pipeline and is equipped with dedicated tools that constrain its capabilities and ensure controlled interaction with the underlying data sources.

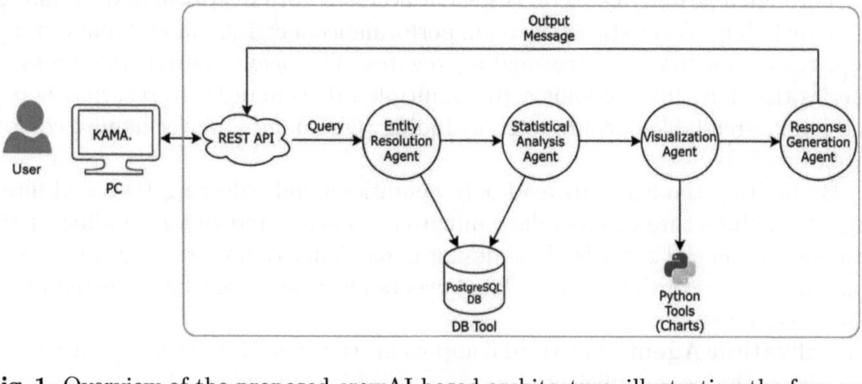

Fig. 1. Overview of the proposed crewAI-based architecture, illustrating the four specialized agents and their interaction with dedicated tools and the football database. The service communicates with the Kama platform through REST APIs for data ingestion and response generation.

The architecture, shown in Fig. 1, follows a sequential workflow composed of four main stages: (i) entity resolution, (ii) data retrieval and statistical analysis, (iii) optional visualization, and (iv) response generation. This modular design enhances transparency while reducing hallucination risks by grounding each step on verified database outputs.

Entity Resolution Agent. The first component of the pipeline is the *Name Resolver* agent, whose role is to extract and normalize all football-related entities mentioned in the user query. These entities may include competitions and seasons, teams, players, referees, staff members, and statistical parameters.

Natural language questions often contain ambiguities, variations in naming conventions, incomplete season references, or homonyms (e.g., players with the same surname). The Name Resolver addresses these challenges by leveraging dedicated lookup tools that perform fuzzy matching directly against the official database. These tools retrieve candidate entity identifiers (IDs) through fuzzy matching against the official database, ensuring that subsequent processing relies exclusively on validated database references rather than on raw textual names. When ambiguity remains (e.g., homonymous players or incomplete season references), the agent is instructed to preserve uncertainty rather than propagating potentially incorrect mappings downstream.

This step is crucial for guaranteeing semantic correctness and consistency. By transforming user input into a structured *EntitiesMapping*, the system establishes a reliable bridge between conversational language and relational database identifiers, preventing downstream ambiguity and enforcing referential integrity.

Statistical Analysis Agent. Once entities are resolved, the *Stats Analyst* agent is responsible for retrieving the requested information from the official PostgreSQL database. This agent operates under strict constraints: it can execute only `SELECT` queries, and it must use exclusively the entity IDs provided by the previous step. Query generation is therefore grounded on validated identifiers rather than on free-form textual references, reducing ambiguity and preventing uncontrolled access patterns.

Through a *postgreSQL* tool, the agent accesses both historical and live match data, including player statistics, team performance metrics, match events, standings, referee records, and seasonal aggregates. The agent constructs structured queries that may involve joins across multiple tables in order to return coherent and human-readable outputs (e.g., including team names, player names, competition details).

By limiting the agent to read-only operations and enforcing ID-based filtering, the architecture ensures data integrity, security, and full grounding of the response on official records. This design is particularly important in live match contexts, where continuously updated events must be accurately reflected in the generated answers.

Visualization Agent. The third component, the *Plot Maker* agent, is activated only when the user explicitly requests a graphical representation. Its responsibility is to transform structured outputs from the statistical analysis phase into visual artifacts, such as bar charts or scatter plots.

The agent leverages dedicated chart-generation tools that automatically produce visualizations and upload them to an external storage service, returning a public URL as output. Depending on the analytical context, it selects the most appropriate representation (e.g., bar charts for categorical comparisons or scatter plots for two-parameter correlations).

By isolating visualization into a dedicated agent, the architecture preserves separation of concerns: numerical retrieval and graphical rendering are handled independently, improving maintainability and extensibility.

Response Generation Agent. The final stage of the pipeline is managed by the *Football Expert* agent. Unlike the previous agents, which interact directly with structured tools, this component focuses exclusively on producing the final natural language response.

Grounded strictly on the verified outputs of the previous steps, the Football Expert synthesizes the retrieved data into a clear, professional, and domain-appropriate answer. It does not access the database directly and does not generate internal reasoning traces, ensuring that the response remains concise, factual, and tailored to football professionals.

This separation between data retrieval and answer generation is fundamental: it preserves factual reliability while allowing stylistic flexibility and contextual adaptation in the final output.

Figure 2 illustrates the interface of the service along with an example of a user interaction.

Architectural Considerations. The adoption of a multi-agent crewAI workflow is motivated by architectural considerations. In particular, task specialization helps separate normalization, retrieval, visualization, and response generation concerns, with the goal of improving controllability and reducing the propagation of ungrounded reasoning across the pipeline. First, it enforces task specialization, reducing cognitive overload on a single monolithic model. Second, it constrains each agent through explicit tool access, mitigating hallucination risks and preventing unauthorized database operations. Third, it supports scalability, as additional agents or tools can be integrated without redesigning the entire pipeline.

Most importantly, by grounding the entire reasoning process in an official, continuously updated PostgreSQL database, the system ensures that responses remain accurate, reproducible, and suitable for professional use cases, including live match analysis, regulatory reporting, technical evaluation, and editorial content production.

Overall, the architecture represents a structured integration of LLM reasoning capabilities with deterministic database querying, combining conversational flexibility with the reliability required in professional football environments.

5 Preliminary Evaluation

We conducted a preliminary human-centered evaluation to assess the perceived usefulness and output quality of the proposed multi-agent, service-oriented architecture in realistic operational scenarios. The system was connected to the official

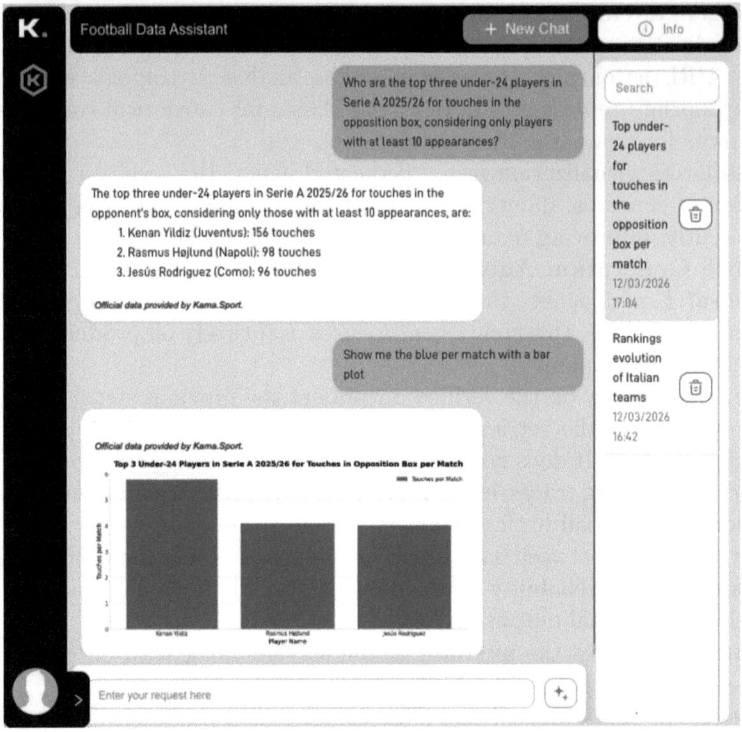

Fig. 2. User-facing interface of the service showing an example interaction, where a user requests football statistics and asks the system to generate a chart.

football PostgreSQL database, containing both historical records and live match events, and was tested through its REST-based interface. The evaluation focused on the overall pipeline described in Sect. 4, including entity resolution, statistical querying, optional visualization, and final response generation. At this stage, the evaluation was not intended as a benchmark-style comparison against alternative architectures or as a component-wise assessment of individual modules.

Given the professional context in which the system is intended to operate, domain expertise was considered essential for a meaningful assessment. Therefore, we adopted a *human-based evaluation* strategy. Evaluators included internal representatives of a professional football league and experts in football editorial services.

Each participant was asked to submit a set of twenty predefined queries to the system. The queries were designed to reflect realistic usage scenarios and varied in complexity, ranging from general questions (e.g., performance summaries or season overviews) to highly detailed analytical requests involving multiple parameters, specific competitions, and temporal constraints. For each query, evaluators were required to: (i) assign a 1-to-5 Likert score, and (ii) provide a short textual justification.

The evaluation criteria adopted in this preliminary phase are listed below:

- *Correctness.* The response must accurately reflect the user query and the underlying official database content, avoiding inconsistencies or misinterpretations.
- *Completeness.* The answer should fully address all aspects of the request, including relevant contextual information (e.g., competition, season, period).
- *Clarity.* The output must be well-structured, readable, and suitable for professional football stakeholders.
- *Reliability.* The response must be factually grounded in official data, avoiding hallucinations or unverifiable statements.

Quantitative Evaluation. Ratings were aggregated across evaluators and queries. For each criterion, we computed mean, median, and standard deviation values. The system achieved an overall mean (median) score of 4.1 (4.0). As shown in Fig. 3, the mean (median) scores were 4.0 (4.0) for Correctness, 3.8 (3.7) for Completeness, 4.5 (4.5) for Clarity, and 4.2 (4.2) for Reliability. Standard deviation values ranged from 0.6 for Clarity to 1.2 for Completeness.

These results indicate that the strongest aspect of the system lies in the clarity and professional presentation of the responses, followed by high levels of perceived reliability. Correctness also achieved solid results, while Completeness obtained slightly lower scores, suggesting room for improvement in addressing all implicit aspects of certain queries.

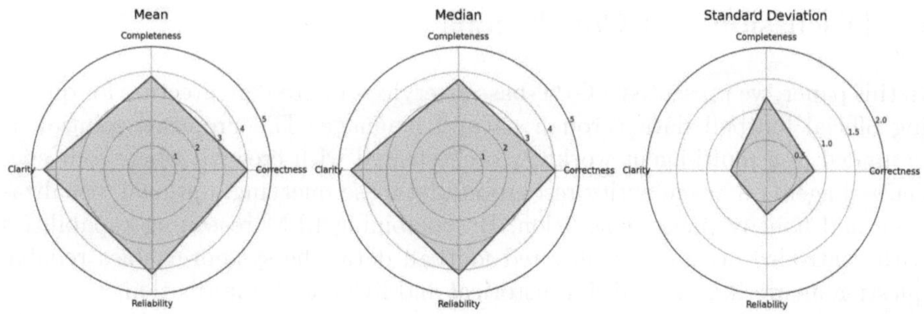

Fig. 3. Evaluation of the quality of the response over a set of predefined queries: Mean, Median, and Standard Deviation values for the four criteria assessed by the evaluators.

Qualitative Evaluation. From a qualitative perspective, evaluators highlighted several strengths of the system. Responses were generally described as clear, well-structured, and aligned with professional editorial standards. In particular, participants appreciated the system's ability to combine historical and live data into coherent answers, making it suitable for both internal league analysis and external editorial production.

However, some limitations emerged. First, when queries were overly generic, especially when no specific competition, season, or time frame was provided, the system sometimes returned answers that, while correct, did not fully match the implicit intent of the evaluator. This occasionally affected the perceived completeness of the response. Second, when requests involved highly specific combinations of parameters (e.g., multiple statistical filters across different competitions and periods), minor reductions in completeness or precision were observed, mainly due to the increased complexity of the query interpretation and aggregation process. Evaluators also noted that the chart-generation component, while useful for standard comparisons, is currently limited in flexibility and may not fully satisfy requests involving very specific or customized visual representations. Finally, the system showed greater difficulty when handling very complex queries requiring cross-analysis of match events that cannot be directly reduced to standard aggregated football statistics, thus revealing the current boundaries of the underlying data access and representation layer.

Overall, feedback from league representatives and editorial experts converged on similar conclusions: the system demonstrates strong reliability and clarity in structured, well-defined professional queries, while future improvements should focus on better handling underspecified requests, more advanced visualization needs, and highly complex event-level analytical questions. These findings suggest the practical potential of the proposed multi-agent architecture as a conversational interface for official football data, while also outlining clear directions for further refinement.

6 Discussion and Conclusions

In this paper, we presented a GPT-based, service-oriented architecture for querying official football data through natural language. The proposed solution is grounded in a multi-agent workflow orchestrated with crewAI, where four specialized agents manage entity resolution, database querying, optional visualization, and final response generation. By combining LLM reasoning capabilities with controlled access to structured football data, the system enables reliable question answering over official historical and live match information.

Unlike generic conversational systems, the proposed approach does not rely solely on the parametric knowledge of the underlying language model. Instead, it constrains data interaction through dedicated tools and specialized agents, ensuring that the final output is grounded in verified database content. This design is particularly valuable in professional football contexts, where timeliness, factual accuracy, and interpretability are essential for leagues, clubs, referees, technical staff, and editorial operators.

6.1 Strengths and Limitations

The proposed architecture exhibits several strengths. A key advantage lies in its *modularity*. The multi-agent structure decomposes the workflow into specialized tasks, making the system easier to design, maintain, and extend. Each agent can be independently improved without redesigning the entire pipeline, and each tool can be refined or replaced according to domain needs. This separation of concerns is particularly beneficial in football data scenarios, where entity resolution, statistical retrieval, visualization, and answer generation require different capabilities.

Another important strength is its *scalability and versatility*. Since the architecture is grounded on structured data access rather than on a single domain-specific repository, it can be extended to multiple structured football sources, including historical archives, live match databases, competition repositories, and additional external providers. This makes the system suitable for a broad range of use cases, from live match support to post-match editorial production and competition-wide analytics.

A further advantage is *reliability*. By constraining the data retrieval phase to dedicated tools and read-only SQL queries, the architecture reduces the risk of hallucinated outputs and increases the traceability of generated answers. Moreover, separating retrieval from final response generation improves interpretability, as answers are produced only after a grounded data extraction step. The system also benefits from *adaptability*, since new tools, data connectors, or analytical modules can be progressively added as requirements evolve.

Nevertheless, several limitations remain. Chart generation is currently delegated to Python-based plotting tools with predefined functionalities. Consequently, the Plot Maker agent cannot generate arbitrary visualizations and is constrained by the capabilities of the implemented chart functions.

Another limitation concerns the granularity of accessible data. At present, the system primarily operates on aggregated statistics and structured summaries rather than the full set of raw match events. While sufficient for many professional queries, this may limit deeper exploratory analyses requiring event-level reasoning.

Finally, although the multi-agent design improves robustness, complex or underspecified queries may still remain challenging. Generic requests lacking clear references to competitions, seasons, or time periods may lead to answers only partially aligned with user expectations, while highly specific requests involving complex parameter combinations may stress both query interpretation and data aggregation.

6.2 Future Developments

Several future developments can further strengthen the proposed architecture. A first direction consists in extending the system to access raw event-level data and provide broader querying capabilities over the football database.

A second line of development concerns the visualization layer. Enhancing the chart-generation subsystem with richer plotting capabilities and additional chart types would improve the usefulness of the system for analysts, editorial teams, and technical staff.

Another promising direction lies in integrating the architecture with our previous work on LLM- and RAG-based football scouting services. Combining official match data querying with scouting-oriented semantic retrieval would enable more powerful services where structured statistics, live match information, and unstructured scouting knowledge interact within a unified ecosystem.

We also plan to investigate alternative LLM backbones and orchestration strategies to optimize performance, latency, and operational cost across different deployment environments, together with more comprehensive evaluation protocols including answer accuracy, SQL execution success, response latency, live-update behavior, and comparisons against simpler baselines such as single-agent pipelines.

Overall, the proposed multi-agent architecture represents a robust and extensible bridge between conversational AI and official football data infrastructures, offering a scalable and trustworthy solution for modern football stakeholders.

References

1. Anzer, G., et al.: Common data format (CDF): a standardized format for match-data in football (soccer) (2025). https://arxiv.org/abs/2505.15820
2. Chipka, J., et al.: GridMind: a multi-agent NLP framework for unified, cross-modal NFL data insights. arXiv preprint arXiv:2504.08747 (2025). Multi-agent RAG+LLM approach for unified sports data querying
3. Lewis, P., et al.: Retrieval-augmented generation for knowledge-intensive NLP tasks. In: Advances in Neural Information Processing Systems (NeurIPS 2020) (2020)
4. Martire, F.A., Ragazzi, D.: Leveraging LLMs and rag for enhanced football talent scouting. In: Grabis, J., Wautelet, Y. (eds.) Advanced Information Systems Engineering Workshops, pp. 298–309. Springer Nature Switzerland, Cham (2025)
5. Pavitt, J., Braines, D., Tomsett, R.: Cognitive analysis in sports: supporting match analysis and scouting through artificial intelligence. Appl. AI Lett. **2** (2021). https://doi.org/10.1002/ail2.21
6. Pietraszewski, P., et al.: The role of artificial intelligence in sports analytics: a systematic review and meta-analysis of performance trends. Appl. Sci. **15**, 7254 (2025). https://doi.org/10.3390/app15137254
7. Schilling, A., et al.: Querying football matches for event data: towards using large language models. In: Dong, J.S., Izadi, M., Hou, Z. (eds.) Sports Analytics (ISACE 2024). LNCS, vol. 14794, pp. 216–227. Springer, Cham (2024). https://doi.org/10.1007/978-3-031-69073-0_19
8. Sepasdar, Z., Gautam, S., Midoglu, C., Riegler, M.A., Halvorsen, P.: Enhancing structured-data retrieval with GraphRAG: soccer data case study. arXiv preprint arXiv:2409.17580 (2024). https://doi.org/10.48550/arXiv.2409.17580
9. Strand, A.T., Gautam, S., Midoglu, C., Halvorsen, P.: SoccerRAG: multimodal soccer information retrieval via natural queries. arXiv preprint arXiv:2406.01273 (2024). https://doi.org/10.48550/arXiv.2406.01273
10. Tian, W., et al.: SportsGPT: an LLM-driven framework for interpretable sports motion assessment and training guidance (2025). https://arxiv.org/abs/2512.14121

11. Xi, Z., et al.: The rise and potential of large language model based agents: a survey. arXiv preprint arXiv:2309.07864 (2023)
12. Xia, H., et al.: Language and multimodal models in sports: a survey of datasets and applications. arXiv preprint arXiv:2406.12252 (2024)

AI News Experiences at Scale: Semantic Enrichment, RAG Based Interaction, and Multimodal Delivery

Dario Pellegrini and Davide Ragazzi(✉)

Stark Technology Partner Srl, Via Luigi Suardo 18/C, 24067 Sarnico, Italy
{dario.pellegrini,davide.ragazzi}@starktechnologypartner.com

Abstract. Building on a previously proposed automated newsroom architecture powered by Large Language Models (LLMs), this paper proposes a framework for AI enhanced news consumption that integrates multiple LLM-based features to improve how readers discover, understand, and interact with news content. While the prior work established a modular pipeline for news generation, metadata enrichment, and Retrieval-Augmented Generation (RAG), the present contribution examines how those capabilities translate into concrete features that improve how readers discover, understand, and consume news. Specifically, we propose a framework of five AI features: semantic tagging and geolocation enrichment, similar news association via RAG, natural language Q&A, article summaries, and podcast synthesis based on RAG. We instantiate this framework in two production applications. We evaluate the framework on a corpus of nearly 700,000 processed articles and 10,180 generated podcasts, correlating feature introductions with measurable growth in user adoption.

Keywords: news consumption · large language models · semantic tagging · geolocation · retrieval-augmented generation · text-to-speech · podcast synthesis · RAG audio · personalised news · service-oriented architectures

1 Introduction

The proliferation of digital news sources has created a paradox: readers have access to more information than ever, yet navigating it effectively remains a persistent challenge [9]. Relevance filtering, personalisation, and multimodal delivery have emerged as key levers to transform raw information abundance into meaningful consumption experiences [4].

In a previous work [6] we introduced a Service-Oriented Architecture (SOA) for an automated newsroom that leverages LLM-powered agents to ingest, generate, and semantically enrich news articles at scale. That system demonstrated the viability of fully automated editorial pipelines processing nearly 700,000 articles, but focused on the backend infrastructure and left largely unaddressed how

R. Posenato and I. Vanderfeesten (Eds.): CAiSE 2026 Workshops, LNBIP 586, pp. 144–157, 2026.
https://doi.org/10.1007/978-3-032-28160-9_13

enriched content can be surfaced to end users in ways that genuinely improve news consumption. Existing systems in the literature address individual consumption modalities, recommendation, Q&A, or audio delivery, in isolation, leaving a gap for an integrated, modular framework that can be selectively deployed across features.

This paper fills that gap. We propose a framework of five AI features for users: semantic tagging and geolocation filtering, similar news association, natural language Q&A, article summaries, and podcast synthesis based on RAG. Each feature is designed to be independently deployable on top of the existing SOA infrastructure. The features are described generically, without presupposing a specific application, and are then evaluated through two concrete instantiations in production news applications. The contributions of this paper are:

- A modular framework of five AI driven consumption features for news applications, with detailed technical specifications for each, designed to be selectively deployed on top of an LLM and RAG infrastructure.
- Evidence from two production instantiations of the framework linking feature introductions to measurable growth in user adoption across nearly 700,000 processed articles and 10,180 generated podcasts.

The rest of the paper is organised as follows: Sect. 2 summarises the underlying infrastructure; Sect. 3 presents the feature framework; Sects. 4–8 detail each feature independently of any specific application; Sect. 9 describes two production instantiations; Sect. 10 presents the evaluation; Sect. 11 discusses related work; and Sect. 12 concludes.

2 Background: The Automated Newsroom Infrastructure

The system described in [6] operates as a three layer stack (see Fig. 1). At the bottom, a *generation pipeline* ingests raw articles from APIs, RSS feeds, and LLM-assisted scrapers, then produces enriched articles via an LLM Configuration Agent (using `LLAMA3.3-70B-Versatile`) and a metadata enrichment step covering entity extraction, sentiment analysis, and geospatial tagging. In the middle, a *RAG layer* converts each article into vector embeddings (`text-embedding-3-small`) stored in Qdrant. RAG supports similar news retrieval, Q&A, and podcast synthesis, grounding outputs in recent and verifiable sources while reducing hallucination risks. The layer also enables semantic similarity search and duplicate detection. At the top, a *Service-Oriented Architecture* exposes these capabilities as API endpoints consumed by mobile (Swift/iOS, Kotlin/Android) and web clients. The present paper operates entirely at the SOA layer, building features for users on top of the existing infrastructure without modifying the core pipeline.

3 Framework of AI Consumption Features

Building on the SOA infrastructure of [6], we identify five AI features that address distinct aspects of the news consumption experience. Each feature is

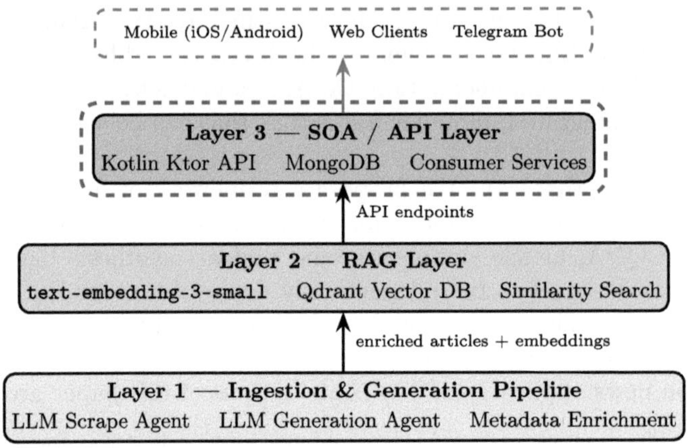

Fig. 1. The automated newsroom stack from [6]. The dashed region marks the consumer-facing layer detailed in this paper.

designed to be independently deployable: a news application can adopt any subset depending on its editorial focus, target audience, and operational constraints. The features operate at the consumer layer of the stack, leveraging the enriched articles, vector embeddings, and API services produced by the backend pipeline without requiring modifications to it.

Table 1 summarises the five features, their primary AI mechanism, and the consumption need they address.

Table 1. Framework of five AI consumption features.

Feature	AI mechanism	Consumption need
Semantic tagging	LLM extraction	Topic-based filtering and discovery
Similar news association	RAG/vector search	Contextual depth without manual search
Natural language Q&A	RAG + LLM generation	Factual queries grounded in live corpus
Article summaries	LLM summarisation	Rapid relevance assessment
Podcast synthesis	RAG + LLM + TTS	Hands-free, multimodal consumption

The features are not mutually exclusive and share infrastructure: semantic tags produced by the tagging feature serve as inputs to the filtering and retrieval features; the RAG layer underpins similar news association, Q&A, and podcast synthesis alike, enabling semantic retrieval over a continuously evolving news corpus and grounding generated outputs in recent, verifiable sources; and the LLM generation capability is shared across summaries, Q&A answers, and podcast scripts. This composability enables shared infrastructure across features.

Sections 4–8 detail each feature independently of any specific application or deployment context.

4 Semantic Tagging and Geolocation Enrichment

Semantic tagging and geolocation enrichment together form the metadata backbone of the framework: both are produced at ingestion time and stored alongside each article, making them available to downstream features without additional processing. Semantic tags transform article text into concept-level labels: an article mentioning "ECB rate decision" is tagged *Politica Monetaria* and *Unione Europea* even if neither phrase appears verbatim. Geolocation enrichment associates each article with the geographic coordinates of the places where the reported events occurred, enabling location-aware retrieval without requiring any client-side GPS data.

4.1 Tag Extraction Pipeline

Each generated article is passed to a dedicated LLM tagging agent with title, excerpt, and up to 300 body tokens. The model returns semantic tags at concept level rather than lexical keywords, identifying topics and themes instead of surface terms. Tags are produced as open labels in the article's language (e.g., *Giustizia*, *Relazioni Internazionali*, *Conflitto armato*) without a fixed taxonomy. This design adapts to emerging and niche topics, as shown by tags such as *Gruppi terroristici* and *Politica nucleare* that appear organically in the corpus (see Sect. 10).

Example 4.1: Semantic tag extraction

Input excerpt: "The ECB raised its benchmark rate by 25 basis points amid persistent inflation in the eurozone, pressuring mortgage holders across Southern Europe."
AI-extracted tags: *Politica Monetaria, Banca Centrale Europea, Unione Europea, Economia, Inflazione Sud Europa*

4.2 User-Facing Filtering

Tags are stored as indexed fields in MongoDB alongside each article record, enabling O(1), average lookup by tag name via MongoDB's hash index and efficient intersection queries across multiple tags. On the client side, users maintain a personal tag preference profile; the home feed ranks articles by a weighted combination of recency and tag affinity.

4.3 Tag Distribution and Real-World Validation

The tag distribution responds accurately to major news cycles and persistent reader interests, confirming semantic tagging effectiveness without manual curation. Table 2 shows selected examples across the deployment period (April 2022 – February 2026).

Beyond event-related spikes, *Giustizia* appeared in the top five for **37 of 47 months** and *Criminalità* for 18, reflecting stable reader interests the system reliably captures.

Table 2. Top tags during selected real world events. Counts represent combined accesses across the indicated months.

Event	Top tags (AI-assigned)	Accesses
Russia–Ukraine conflict (Apr–May 2022)	Ucraina (Ukraine), Kiev (Kyiv), Russia	282 / 193 / 76
Draghi govt. crisis (Jul 2022)	Draghi, Senato (Senate)	133 / 129
Meloni election (Oct–Nov 2022)	Meloni, Giorgia Meloni	921 / 885
Hamas–Israel conflict (Oct–Nov 2023)	Gruppi terroristici (Terrorist groups), Israele (Israel), Gaza	2,342 / 1,208 / 1,066
Paris Olympics (Aug 2024)	Parigi (Paris)	689
Death of Pope Francis (Apr–May 2025)	Papa (Pope), Morte (Death)	1,079 / 1,393
Intl. tensions (Sep–Dec 2025)	Guerra (War), Diplomazia (Diplomacy), Conflitto armato (Armed conflict)	2,620 / 1,647 / 1,337

4.4 Geolocation Enrichment

Each article is enriched with geographic coordinates at ingestion time. The pipeline resolves place names mentioned in the article body using OpenStreetMap Nominatim, disambiguating toponyms by publication language (e.g., *"Milan"* → Milan, Italy when the source is Italian) and storing one or more `(lat, lon)` pairs per article in MongoDB. Of the 699,589 articles processed to date, **678,601 (97%)** carry at least one coordinate pair.

The geotag records *where an event occurred*, not where the reader is located. Articles about a flood in Lombardy carry the coordinates of the affected municipalities. This event-centric georeferencing can serve as input to retrieval filters, map visualisations, or geographic clustering, without requiring any user-side location permission.

Example 4.2: Geolocation enrichment

Input excerpt: "Flooding in the Po valley forced evacuations near Piacenza, as the river reached its highest level since 2000."

Extracted coordinates:
Po valley → (45.06N, 9.70E)
Piacenza → (45.05N, 9.69E)

Corpus coverage: 678,601 / 699,589 articles (97%).

5 Similar-News Association via RAG

Similar-news association surfaces articles that are topically related to a piece the user is currently reading, drawn from across the available sources in the corpus. It differs from the duplicate detection described in [6] in both purpose and threshold: where duplicate detection operates at near-identity similarity and is invisible to readers, this feature operates at a lower threshold to surface *editorially distinct but thematically related* content, supporting contextual deepening without manual search.

5.1 Retrieval Design

When a user opens an article, its embedding is used as a query against the Qdrant vector index. The search returns the top-k nearest neighbours ($k = 5$ by default), filtered by a **recency gate**: candidate articles must have been published within a configurable window (default: 7 days) relative to the source article, preventing the carousel from surfacing stale content. The resulting candidates are re-ranked by a linear combination of cosine similarity and recency before being returned to the client.

Example 5.1: Similar-news retrieval

Source article: "BYD unveils charging platform twice as powerful as Tesla's V4."

Retrieved similar articles (top-3):
[0.91] "Tesla's V4 Supercharger rollout accelerates across Europe."
[0.87] "Chinese EV makers close the technology gap with Western rivals."
[0.83] "EU fast-charging infrastructure mandate: what it means for automakers."

5.2 Vector Index Population

The Qdrant index is populated at ingestion time: each article, after generation and metadata enrichment, is embedded using OpenAI's `text-embedding-3-small` model (1,536 dimensional vectors) and upserted into a persistent collection keyed by article identifier. Embeddings are computed once and cached; re-embedding is triggered only when an article's body is updated. The same index and embedding model are shared across similar news association, Q&A, and podcast synthesis features, so the infrastructure cost is incurred once and amortised across all three.

6 Natural-Language Q&A with RAG

The Q&A feature allows users to pose open questions in natural language and receive concise answers grounded in sources derived from the live news corpus.

Unlike a general-purpose chatbot, the system answers only from retrieved articles, preventing hallucination and ensuring traceability to sources. The SOA design of [6] makes this feature usable across channels: the same API endpoint can serve a mobile in-app interface, a web frontend, or a messaging platform, with no modifications to the retrieval or generation logic.

6.1 End-to-End Flow

Figure 2 illustrates the complete pipeline. The user's question is embedded with the shared `text-embedding-3-small` model (see Sect. 5) and used to retrieve the top-N ($N = 8$) most semantically relevant articles from the same Qdrant index. Retrieved article titles and excerpts are injected into a structured LLM prompt that instructs the model to: (i) answer the question using only the provided context; (ii) cite the specific articles that support each statement; (iii) explicitly state when the retrieved context is insufficient to answer the question rather than speculating.

The generated answer is returned to the client alongside a list of source news (title, outlet, image), allowing the reader to verify claims directly.

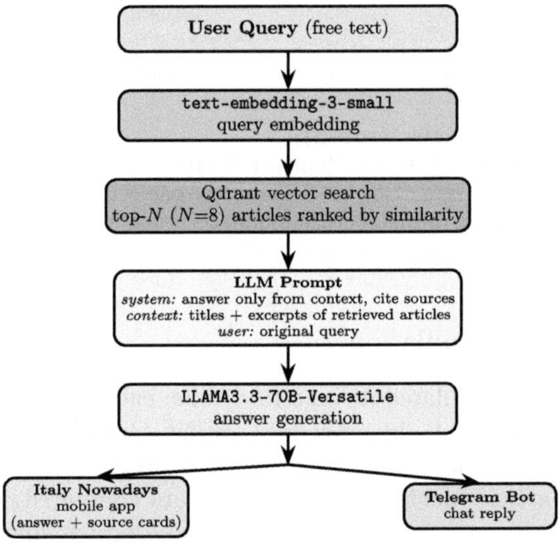

Fig. 2. Q&A pipeline: the user query is embedded, relevant articles are retrieved via RAG, and an LLM generates a grounded answer. The same backend serves both a mobile app interface and a Telegram bot channel.

Example 6.1: Q&A interaction

User query: "What is the Italian government's position on nuclear energy?"

Retrieved context: 8 articles from the past 30 days covering energy policy, government statements, and EU energy directives.

Generated answer: "The Italian government has signalled openness to reconsidering nuclear energy as part of its decarbonisation strategy over time, with the Minister of Environment stating that [paraphrase]. This contrasts with the 1987 referendum outcome that led to Italy shutting down its reactors. [Sources: Article A, Article B]"

7 AI Article Summaries

AI summaries support news scanning at two granularities: single articles and thematic groups, while preserving factual fidelity and a neutral tone.

7.1 Single Article Summary

Summaries are generated **on demand**: the article (title, excerpt, body) is passed to `LLAMA3.3-70B-Versatile` and the result cached in MongoDB. Two presentation modes are supported: a **prose summary** (2–4 sentences) and a **bullet-point summary** (3–5 key points), both produced by the same inference call. The prompt instructs the model to retain core news facts and avoid introducing absent information.

7.2 Multi Article Thematic Summary

Users can request a summary of recent news filtered by provider category (e.g., *politics*, *economy*). A set of 5–10 retrieved articles is passed to the LLM synthesis agent, which merges overlapping information across sources and surfaces editorial divergences. Output is bounded at 150 words for five articles, scaling linearly. This feature shares retrieval and synthesis infrastructure with the RAG podcast pipeline (Sect. 8), differing only in output modality, and demonstrating the composability of the underlying LLM infrastructure [6].

8 RAG-Driven Podcast Synthesis via Text-to-Speech

Audio delivery addresses a fundamental limitation of textual news: it demands visual attention. By combining RAG-based retrieval with LLM narrative synthesis and text-to-speech (TTS), a news application can offer users spoken reports on any topic, generated on demand from a natural language query. The result is a self-contained audio podcast grounded in the live news corpus, suitable for hands-free consumption during commutes or other contexts where users are not looking at a screen.

8.1 Relationship to Q&A

Both Q&A (Sect. 6) and podcast synthesis begin with the same RAG retrieval step: a textual user query is embedded and used to retrieve the top-N semantically relevant articles from the Qdrant vector index. The two features diverge at the generation stage. Q&A instructs the LLM to produce a concise, factual answer of a few sentences, prioritising precision and source traceability. Podcast synthesis instead instructs the LLM to produce an extended narrative script, prioritising coherence, flow, and listenability. The output modality also differs: text for Q&A, audio for podcasts. This design allows the two features to share infrastructure while serving distinct consumption needs.

8.2 End-to-End Pipeline

Figure 3 illustrates the complete pipeline, which comprises four sequential stages. Stage 1 corresponds to the user's natural language query; the subsequent stages process it as follows.

Stage 2—RAG Retrieval. The user's query can include a specific list of tags (e.g., *"energia nucleare, Italia"*); it is embedded with the shared *text-embedding-3-small* model and used to retrieve the top-N articles from the same Qdrant index described in Sect.5 (N configurable; default: 8–12). Recency filtering ensures the retrieved content reflects the current news cycle.

Stage 3—Narrative Synthesis. Retrieved article titles and excerpts are assembled into a structured prompt for `LLAMA3.3-70B-Versatile`. The synthesis agent is instructed to:

- Produce a cohesive narrative of target length (configurable; default: approximately 400–600 tokens), not a list of article summaries.
- Open with a brief thematic introduction and close with a forward-looking sentence to give the podcast broadcast structure. Use the tone selected in configuration if present
- Attribute claims to sources implicitly (e.g., *"according to recent reports"*) rather than citing article titles, which would sound unnatural when read aloud.
- Not introduce facts beyond the retrieved context.

Stage 4—TTS and Delivery. The adapted script is passed to the TTS engine (integrated via `LLAMA3.3-70B-Versatile`'s speech synthesis capability) with configurable voice parameters: speaker identity, speech rate (default: 0.95× for improved clarity), and pitch. Each application deployment can define a distinct branded voice profile. The resulting audio file is stored in the services database and served via the API layer. A query-level cache keyed on the embedding of the user's query ensures that repeated requests for semantically equivalent topics are served from cache rather than re-generated.

Example 8.1: RAG podcast synthesis

User query: "energia nucleare in Italia"
Retrieved articles (top-4 of N=10):
[0.93] "Il governo valuta il ritorno al nucleare civile nel piano energetico 2030."
[0.89] "Referendum 1987: perché l'Italia uscì dal nucleare e cosa è cambiato."
[0.85] "Direttiva UE sulle energie pulite: il nucleare torna sul tavolo."
Synthesised script opening (before TTS): "Torna al centro del dibattito politico italiano la questione energetica, con il nucleare che dopo decenni di assenza sembra recuperare terreno. Il governo ha avviato una valutazione tecnica per includere i reattori di nuova generazione nel piano energetico nazionale al 2030, [...] "

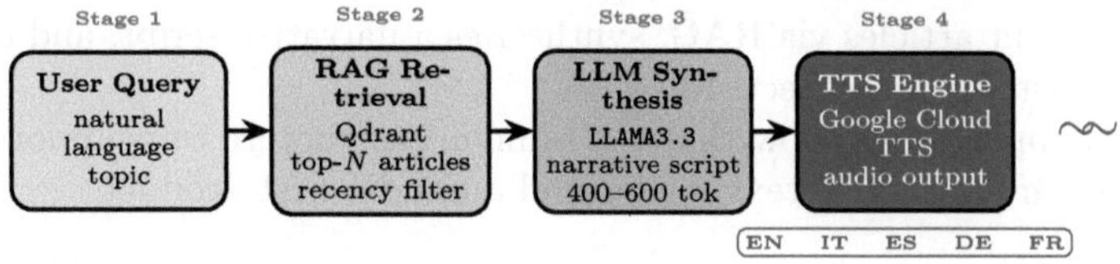

Fig. 3. RAG podcast synthesis pipeline: a natural language query triggers retrieval of relevant articles, which are synthesised into a narrative script and converted to audio via TTS (Google Cloud TTS; languages: EN, IT, ES, DE, FR).

9 Instantiation: Two Production Applications

The framework described in Sects. 4–8 has been instantiated in two production applications: *Italy Nowadays* and *Odeum*. Table 3 summarises feature deployment.

Table 3. Feature deployment across the two production applications. ✓ = deployed; P = proposed, infrastructure-ready; – = not applicable.

Feature	Italy Nowadays	Odeum
Semantic tagging	✓	–
Similar-news (RAG)	P	–
Natural-language Q&A	✓	–
Article summaries	✓	–
Podcast synthesis (TTS)	–	✓

9.1 Italy Nowadays

Italy Nowadays covers Italian current affairs and deploys semantic tagging, natural language Q&A, and AI summaries, while similar-news retrieval is planned (Table 3). Articles are enriched with tags and summaries (Sect. 4, Sect. 7), and Q&A is available both in-app and via Telegram (Sect. 6). Geolocation enrichment (§4.4) runs at the backend; proximity filtering is not yet exposed in the current release.

9.2 Odeum

Odeum is a multilingual audio news application for hands-free consumption. It deploys podcast synthesis in five languages (EN, IT, ES, DE, FR): the system retrieves relevant articles via RAG, synthesises a narrative script, and delivers a spoken podcast via TTS (Sect. 8).

The two applications show that the same infrastructure can support distinct experiences: an interactive text reader and an audio-first product.

10 Implementation and Evaluation

10.1 System Configuration

Both applications described in Sect. 9 run on the infrastructure of [6]: LLAMA3.3-70B-Versatile for generation and synthesis, text-embedding-3-small for embeddings, Qdrant for vector storage, MongoDB for structured data, and Kotlin Ktor for API serving. Mobile clients are implemented in Swift (iOS) and Kotlin (Android).

10.2 Feature-Level Metrics

Table 4 summarises the operational statistics accumulated across the production deployment of both applications.

10.3 Adoption and Access Growth

Table 5 reports the total monthly accesses recorded in *Italy Nowadays* from launch (April 2022) through February 2026, grouped by year. Figure 4 plots the full monthly time series with annotations marking the two key AI feature introductions.

The data show a rapid growth phase between 2022 and 2024. Following launch in April 2022 (196 accesses in the first month), the platform recorded 23,048 accesses over its first nine months, with a monthly average of 2,561. In 2023, total accesses increased to 82,407, corresponding to a monthly average of 6,867 and a year-over-year growth of +258%.

Growth continued in 2024, which represents the peak year in absolute terms, with 111,416 total accesses and a monthly average of 9,285 (+35% compared to

Table 4. System-level metrics per AI feature.

Feature	Volume	Avg. latency
Semantic tagging	699,589 articles	1.8 s
Geolocation enrichment	678,601 articles	2.0 s
Sentiment analysis	128,025 articles	2.0 s
Similar-news (RAG)	– queries	0.8 s
Q&A (RAG)	– queries	3.1 s
Single Article summary	699,589 articles	3.0 s
Multi Article summary	on demand	3.0 s
Podcast synthesis (RAG+TTS)	10,180 podcasts	30 s–2 min

Table 5. Annual access statistics for *Italy Nowadays*. 2022 covers only 9 months (April–December); 2026 covers January–February only.

Year	Total accesses	Monthly avg.	YoY growth
2022 (9 mo.)	23,048	2,561	—
2023	82,407	6,867	+258%
2024	111,416	9,285	+35%
2025	104,896	8,741	−6%
2026 (2 mo.)	18,233	8,620	n.a.

2023). Monthly accesses surpassed 10,000 for the first time in August 2024 and reached a maximum of **11,074** in October 2024.

In 2025, total accesses amounted to 104,896, corresponding to a monthly average of 8,741 and a moderate year-over-year decline of −6%, suggesting stabilisation around a consolidated user base. Data for 2026 (January–February) report 18,233 accesses with a monthly average of 8,620, confirming the late-2025 plateau.

Overall, from launch (196 accesses in April 2022) to the peak observed in October 2024 (11,074), the system shows an increase of over **5,500%** in monthly traffic.

We acknowledge that the absence of controlled experiments prevents strict causal attribution: external factors such as major political events or electoral campaigns may independently drive access spikes visible in the data. The temporal alignment between AI feature deployments and sustained growth inflections is therefore treated as suggestive, circumstantial evidence rather than proof of causation. Controlled A/B experiments to isolate per feature impact on adoption and retention are identified as a direction for future work.

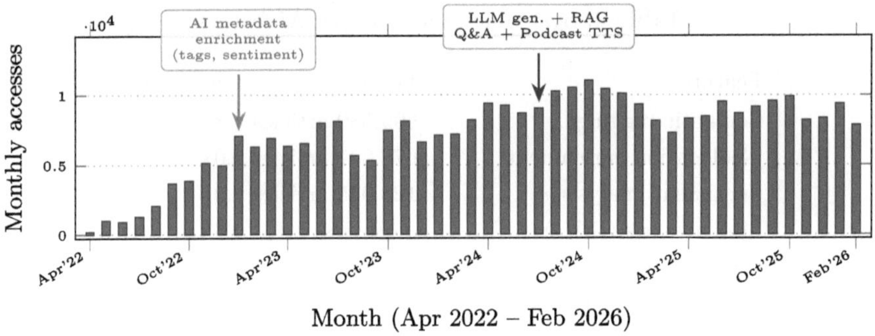

Fig. 4. Monthly accesses to *Italy Nowadays* (April 2022 – February 2026), annotated with AI feature introductions.

11 Related Work

AI enhanced news consumption has been studied along several dimensions. Personalised recommendation [9] and semantic framing [2] address content relevance and interpretation, while LeanContext [1] and Just-in-Time News [8] demonstrate LLM-based Q&A for domain-specific queries. These works focus on individual interaction modalities; our system integrates five features within a unified framework. No prior system combines all five modalities, semantic enrichment, similarity retrieval, Q&A, summarisation, and audio delivery, within a single deployable framework [5]. The combination of RAG retrieval, narrative synthesis, and TTS for news has not been addressed as a unified pipeline in prior work. Multi-document summarisation [3] addresses the synthesis step in isolation, while prior work on news TTS [7] typically applies speech synthesis to human-written text. Our pipeline synthesises audio end to end from LLM-generated content, including the intermediate script adaptation step that makes the output broadcast quality. The closest prior system is the automated newsroom described in [6], on which this work directly builds. Where that paper establishes the production infrastructure, the present contribution examines how it translates into value for users.

12 Conclusions and Future Work

This paper described five AI features that transform news consumption into an interactive, multimodal experience. Built on the automated newsroom infrastructure of [6], they include semantic tagging and geolocation enrichment, similar news association, natural-language Q&A, and RAG podcast synthesis. They are deployed in two production applications and evaluated on nearly 700,000 articles and 10,180 podcasts.

System-level metrics confirm feature efficiency at scale, while the correlation between feature introductions and user-adoption growth provides encouraging, albeit circumstantial, evidence of end-user value. The integrated design is novel relative to prior work, which has typically addressed them in isolation.

Future work includes controlled A/B experiments, multilingual podcast generation, and query-aware voice personalisation for TTS.

References

1. Arefeen, M.A., Debnath, B., Chakradhar, S.T.: LeanContext: Cost-efficient domain-specific question answering using LLMs. Nat. Lang. Process. J. **7**, 100065 (2024). https://doi.org/10.1016/j.nlp.2024.100065
2. Alonso del Barrio, D., Gatica-Perez, D.: Framing the news: from human perception to large language model inferences. In: Proceedings of the 2023 ACM International Conference on Multimedia Retrieval, pp. 627–635. ICMR '23, Association for Computing Machinery, Thessaloniki, Greece (2023). https://doi.org/10.1145/3591106.3592278
3. Fabbri, A.R., Li, I., She, T., Li, S., Radev, D.: Multi-News: A large-scale multi-document summarization dataset and abstractive hierarchical model. In: Proceedings of the 57th Annual Meeting of the Association for Computational Linguistics, pp. 1074–1084. Association for Computational Linguistics, Florence, Italy (2019). https://doi.org/10.18653/v1/P19-1102, https://aclanthology.org/P19-1102/
4. Karimi, M., Jannach, D., Jugovac, M.: News recommender systems - Survey and roads ahead. Inf. Process. Manag. **54**(6), 1203–1227 (2018). https://doi.org/10.1016/j.ipm.2018.04.008
5. Kiskola, J., et al.: Generative AI and news consumption: Design fictions and critical analysis. In: Proceedings of the 2025 CHI Conference on Human Factors in Computing Systems. CHI '25, Association for Computing Machinery, New York, NY, USA (2025). https://doi.org/10.1145/3706598.3713804
6. Pellegrini, D., Ragazzi, D.: Automated newsrooms and enhanced editorial processes through large language models. In: Advanced Information Systems Engineering Workshops (CAiSE 2025). Lecture Notes in Business Information Processing, vol. 556, pp. 318–325. Springer, Cham (2025). https://doi.org/10.1007/978-3-031-94931-9_26
7. Prateek, N., et al.: In other news: A bi-style text-to-speech model for synthesizing newscaster voice with limited data. In: Proceedings of the 2019 Conference of the North American Chapter of the Association for Computational Linguistics: Human Language Technologies, Volume 2 (Industry Papers), pp. 205–213. Association for Computational Linguistics, Minneapolis, Minnesota (2019). https://doi.org/10.18653/v1/N19-2026, https://aclanthology.org/N19-2026/
8. Sufi, F.K.: Just-in-Time news: An AI chatbot for the modern information age. AI **6**(2), 22 (2025). https://doi.org/10.3390/ai6020022
9. Wu, C., Wu, F., Huang, Y., Xie, X.: Personalized news recommendation: Methods and challenges. ACM Trans. Inf. Syst. **41**(1) (2023). https://doi.org/10.1145/3530257

Architectural Constraints Alignment in AI-Assisted, Platform-Based Service Development

Julius Irion[1], Moritz Leugers[1], Paul Hartwig[1], Simon Kling[1], Tachmyrat Annayev[1], Alexander Schwind[1], Maria C. Borges[2], and Sebastian Werner[2](✉)

[1] Technische Universität Berlin, Berlin, Germany
{irion,m.leugers,paul.l.hartwig,s.kling,annayev, alexander.schwind}@campus.tu-berlin.de

[2] Information Systems Engineering, Technische Universität Berlin, Berlin, Germany
{mb,sw}@ise.tu-berlin.de

Abstract. AI-assisted development tools enable rapid prototyping of services but often lack awareness of architectural constraints, infrastructure dependencies, and organizational standards required in production environments. Consequently, generated artifacts may exhibit brittle behavior and limited deployability. We propose a retrieval-augmented scaffolding approach that combines platform-based code generation with agentic clarification loops to expose and resolve architectural constraint ambiguities. By combining template retrieval with structured interaction, the method embeds production-relevant considerations during service scaffolding. Evaluation indicates improved architectural consistency and deployability compared to general-purpose AI code generation workflows, suggesting that constraint-aware retrieval is essential for aligning AI-assisted service development with production software engineering practices.

Keywords: AI4SE · Software Architecture · Platform Engineering

1 Introduction

The rise of Large Language Models (LLM) and AI-driven IDEs in recent years has disrupted the traditional software development process. According to the 2025 Stack Overflow Developer Survey [16], 84% of respondents self-report they are using or planning on using AI tools during development. Additionally, 51% of professional developers report daily usage of AI tools. This development has led to the emergence of an AI-first approach to software development often labeled as "vibe coding" which is driven by iterative prompting.

This work was conducted as part of a university-industry collaboration between the TU Berlin ISE department and a large German software company. The proposed framework was evaluated against deployment workflows used within the company.

R. Posenato and I. Vanderfeesten (Eds.): CAiSE 2026 Workshops, LNBIP 586, pp. 158–170, 2026.
https://doi.org/10.1007/978-3-032-28160-9_14

While this approach allows for fast service prototyping, it relies heavily on a trial-and-error approach in order to generate deployable code. Consequently, this manifests itself in a cycle of prompting, the software producing errors, and re-prompting until an, oftentimes preliminary, error-free state is reached. This is not only time-consuming but also drives resource and token usage, unnecessarily increasing development costs.

However, the limitations of vibe coding extend beyond inefficiency and also reflect a fundamental architectural mismatch. Software architecture demands context-specific decisions that account for organizational constraints and domain-specific knowledge [4]. Writing code for production environments is inherently complex, with numerous architectural considerations and subtle service dependencies that must be correctly managed: adapting to existing infrastructure services, integration with CI/CD pipelines, security policies, and alignment with established architectural patterns [17]. LLMs, which rely on the "wisdom of the masses", lack access to this organization-specific context [4] and consequently produce brittle deployment artifacts with inconsistent, non-deterministic behavior. Production environments demand the opposite: *consistent*, *deployable* artifacts that satisfy organizational architectural constraints.

In this paper, we propose **a RAG-based template retrieval approach that uses agentic clarification loops** to bridge LLM-driven generation with platform engineering rigor. Our approach leverages organizational platform knowledge (encoded in architectural templates[1]) as a retrieval corpus to ensure that production configurations and architectural constraints are considered when scaffolding new services. The agentic clarification loops repeatedly engage the user to best match the user's intent to the available service templates and improve the retrieval chances. To provide initial evidence for the viability of our approach, we present a preliminary user study comparing unstructured vibe coding to RAG-enhanced platform engineering. We evaluated both approaches across three dimensions: deployment success rate, resource usage, and developer experience. Our early results suggest that the proposed approach shows promise compared to general-purpose AI-assisted service development, by ensuring that generated artifacts remain compatible with existing deployment environments, while reducing developer frustration when using AI-assistants.

The remainder of this paper is structured as follows: First, we provide background and related work in Sect. 2, then introduce our RAG-based approach in Sect. 3. In Sect. 4, we evaluate our RAG-based system against unstructured vibe coding. Finally, we discuss the limitations of our study in Sect. 5 and conclude in Sect. 6.

2 Background and Related Work

In the following, we show how our tool builds upon related research and industry efforts in *AI-assisted software development* and *platform engineering*.

[1] https://backstage.io/docs/features/software-templates/writing-templates.

2.1 AI-Assisted Software Development

In recent years, we've seen large language models (LLMs) emerge and gain widespread adoption across the software development landscape. LLMs and AI-agents and are widely used as programming assistants, most notably through tools such as GitHub Copilot or Cursor. Empirical studies emphasize their usefulness in code generation [12], but also show that AI-generated suggestions often contain logical, syntactic, or semantic errors and frequently require manual effort to compile and behave as intended [7,8].

Complementing this line of work, several recent studies have explored LLM capabilities for generating architectural artifacts. Jahić and Sami [5] examine the state of practice by tasking LLMs with producing design and deployment diagrams, though practitioners expressed low confidence in the results. Arun et al. [1] explore LLM-based service generation, but limit their approach to serverless deployments. Even within this constrained scope, the generated architectural artifacts were not fully functional.

Ivers and Ozkaya [4] attribute these limitations to the inherent nature of LLMs. Architectural design requires context-specific decisions, but LLMs rely on the "wisdom of the masses", making them poorly suited for tasks that depend on unique organizational constraints and domain knowledge.

To address these limitations, Retrieval-Augmented Generation (RAG) approaches have recently been suggested. RAG systems enhance the generative process by grounding LLM outputs in external domain-specific knowledge sources. The researchers in [3] apply RAG for architectural decision support, though their work focuses solely on design recommendations without extending to service generation or deployment. Pesl et al. [11] study RAG-based approaches for service discovery but not service generation. The idea of incorporating platform knowledge in service generation through RAG-based approaches was first proposed in [17], but this work remains purely conceptual without any implementation or validation.

2.2 Platform Engineering

In recent years, software architecture and engineering have been complemented by the emergence of *platform engineering*. By creating toolchains and reusable services for developers, platform engineering aims to boost developer productivity, ensure operational consistency [6] and improve reliability [2]. *Internal Developer Platforms (IDPs)* have emerged as a concrete manifestation of platform engineering principles. They encode organizational constraints and architectural decisions into reusable artifacts, providing a consistent foundation for recurrent development work. Backstage [9,15] is a prominent open-source example of an IDP, originally developed at Spotify and now widely adopted across the industry.

In software engineering, we refer to *scaffolding* as the automated generation of project structures and boilerplate code. When combined with IDPs and architectural templates, service scaffolding extends beyond basic code generation to include pre-configured organizational policies, security controls, and integration points for existing CI/CD pipelines and infrastructure.

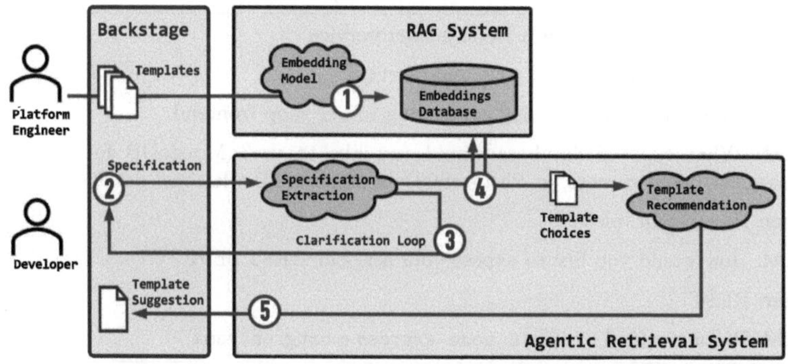

Fig. 1. System Architecture and Workflow: 1. Template Ingestion 2. Conversational Specification 3. Clarification 4. Retrieval of Templates 5. Template Suggestion based on Specification.

3 Approach

Our approach addresses the aforementioned shortcomings of vibe coding for service engineering by shifting from the AI-assisted generation of code to the structured RAG-based retrieval of pre-approved service templates. We implement this as an Agentic Retrieval System integrated directly into an Internal Developer Platform (IDP), specifically utilizing Backstage[2]. By grounding code generation in pre-approved architectural templates, we ensure that scaffolded services satisfy organizational constraints from the get-go.

The proposed workflow, visible in Fig. 1, is comprised of five distinct phases: template ingestion (only necessary once, performed by the platform engineer), requirement specification, clarification loop, retrieval, and template suggestion to the user. The basis of our retrieval consists of a catalog of available service templates, which encompass boilerplate code, standard configurations, CI/CD pipelines, and security policies. These artifacts are embedded using the `all-MiniLM-L6-v2` embedding model [13,14,18], which comes prepackaged with `Chroma`[3], where the templates are subsequently stored. This results in a consolidated knowledge base for our retrieval system.

A core challenge in bridging the gap between natural language user input and structured architectural templates is the handling of ambiguity. For this purpose, we employ an *agentic clarification loop*, powered by OpenAI's `GPT4o-mini` LLM [10]. In order to avoid reliance on insufficient prompt input by the user, the LLM acts as a virtual software architect, repeatedly engaging the user. This enables the effective matching of a user's intent to the available service templates and, therefore, effective retrieval, through a natural conversation with the user inside the IDP.

[2] https://backstage.io.

[3] https://github.com/chroma-core/chroma.

User: I need a template for a Node.js microservice

LLM: Whats the purpose of your microservice?

User: It's for a product catalog connecting to our shop frontend.

LLM: What type of database would you like to use? MongoDB for flexible, document-based storage, or PostgreSQL for structured, relational data?

User: PostgreSQL please

LLM: How would you like to expose your service? REST or gRPC?

User: REST

LLM: Recommended template: `node-express-postgres.yaml`

Fig. 2. Example interaction of the agentic clarification loop.

Effective template retrieval requires specific information from the user. Therefore, we define a list of requirements, including the service's purpose, the desired tech stack, and CI/CD requirements, which need to be satisfied for retrieval. As illustrated in Fig. 2, the LLM will repeatedly ask the user clarifying questions until all requirements are satisfied.

Additionally, the system is designed to handle uncertainty to accommodate non-expert users. If the user is unable to give a specific constraint and responds with "not sure" or an equivalent answer, the agent disregards the strict requirement and infers the appropriate template from the remaining context. Thereby, the retrieval still functions, even if a user is not technically proficient enough to provide all specifications.

Once the clarification loop completes and a sufficient base of information is extracted, the gathered requirements are subsequently embedded to enable querying of the template catalog. For this purpose, we employ semantic vector search in order to retrieve the closest matching service template from the vector database. The resulting recommendation is then suggested to the user in a final answer recommending it as the best option for the planned project.

Our approach ensures that even vague or minimal user input can be resolved to a fully functioning and deployable service scaffold. Unlike AI-powered IDEs that merely suggest code at a granular level, our system delivers a complete architectural template that is guaranteed to work in the available environment.

4 Evaluation

To validate our claims that RAG-based service template retrieval addresses the fundamental limitations of vibe coding for scaffolding, we designed a comparative study evaluating both approaches across three critical dimensions. First, we measure *deployment success rate*. This is the core indicator of whether generated artifacts actually work in production environments. Second, we track *resource usage* to quantify the iterative trial-and-error cycles that characterize vibe coding and drive up development costs. Third, we assess *developer experience* to understand the cognitive and practical burden each approach imposes on users. Together, these metrics capture whether our system delivers on its promise: deployable service artifacts with lower overhead and reduced developer friction.

4.1 Methodology

To evaluate our RAG-based system, we repeatedly tasked it to pick a correct ground-truth template among multiple close ones. Concretely, it was prompted to return a fitting template for a service with frontend and server-side rendering (SSR), that uses Postgres, and must support authentication. Correctly choosing a template with SSR was our distinguishing factor. Next to the ground truth, we used 20 other templates that deviated slightly from it, e.g., by using single-page applications instead of SSR. The experiment was run 10 times with randomized phrasing, but all similar in complexity. Logged metrics per run are: success (selection of the correct template), number of turns/questions asked by the agentic loop and input/output tokens. This way, we can assess how our RAG based approach performs in our quality metrics in a scenario where the correct decision is non-trivial.

To test vibe coding on the designated metrics, we devised a user study. The task we gave to testers was the following:

> *The software you are supposed to build is scaffolding for an Angular app with NX-Workspace, automated CI/CD pipelines and Kubernetes deployment capabilities. The CI/CD pipelines shall handle automated test, build and deployment and run on every commit.*

A total of seven people participated in the study. All were students, doctoral candidates or post-docs recruited through the university department with which we conduct our research. The same advisor controlled the study for all executions, each of which took approx. one hour. All testers worked on the same computer, ensuring an identical setup[4]. We supplied testers with an instance of Visual Studio Code and GitHub Copilot, powered by `GPT-5-mini`. Target for deployment was an existing Kubernetes cluster with a readily deployed GitLab runner to execute CI/CD pipelines. Each tester got their own branch in a specifically created GitLab repository. Each branch was prepared by us with deployment instructions for the AI assisted IDE that gave all necessary information about deployment, such as the cluster to target, the container registry and credentials to use.

Testers were also asked about their prior experience with CI/CD pipelines, Kubernetes, Angular, and NX Workspace, as well as how frequently they use AI-assisted IDEs. To assess whether architecting the software was successful, we had them report on the seven quality gates listed in Table 1.

The time testers took was recorded and capped at 45 minutes, after which the study was stopped. Afterwards, the prompt logs were exported from Visual Studio Code in order to calculate the token usage. We finally asked each person to rate their experience on the Likert scale and describe it in free text.

[4] https://github.com/paullhartwig/acp_data_and_evaluation.

4.2 Results for the Success Rate

Our RAG system returned the correct template in all 10 runs with randomized phrasing. This results in a success rate of 100%. In contrast, the results for the different quality gates in the user study on vibe coding can be seen in Table 1.

Table 1. Vibe Coding User Study Results

Quality Gate	Tester						
	01	02	03	04	05	06	07
CI/CD pipelines run on every commit.	✗	✓	✓	✓	✓	✓	✗
The CI/CD "test"-stage runs without error.	✗	✓	✓	✓	✗	✗	✗
Building the project in the CI/CD pipeline succeeds.	✓	✓	✓	✓	✗	✗	✗
The Docker image is successfully pushed to the registry.	✗	✓	✗	✓	✗	✗	✗
The CI/CD "deploy"-stage runs without error.	✗	✓	✓	✓	✗	✗	✗
The deployment itself worked, Kubernetes Pods are in state "Running"	✗	✓	✗	✓	✗	✗	✗
The Kubernetes Pod logs do not indicate an error.	✗	✓	✗	✓	✗	✗	✗

In total, only two testers were able to pass all quality gates, while four of seven could only pass zero to one of them. One tester was able to pass four. Unsuccessful testers mostly did not make it past the early stages of the exercise, failing to execute CI/CD pipelines at all or with the desired functionality. This results in the summarized success rates of both approaches, displayed in Table 2.

Table 2. Success Rates of Both Approaches

	Tester							RAG
	01	02	03	04	05	06	07	
Success Rate [%]	14	100	57	100	14	14	0	100

Averaging the success rate of all testers, we get 43% for vibe coding, whereas our RAG succeeds in 100% of the cases. This suggests that our approach is reliable for selecting the correct template even in a case where multiple similar ones exist. The success of vibe coding, on the other hand, is much less probable, as not even half of the quality gates could be achieved by the testers and only two of seven were able to generate a runnable system.

Overall, we find that the vibe coding approach was largely unsuccessful and inconsistent for service scaffolding, even though the amount of external constraints to follow was comparatively small. In production environments with extensive dependencies, the architectural mismatch between LLM generation and organizational constraints becomes even more pronounced. We therefore expect deployment success rates to deteriorate further as architectural complexity increases beyond our experimental setting. This is exactly the problem we

Table 3. Resource Usage of Approaches Compared

Costs	Tester								RAG
	01	02	03	04	05	06	07	Mean	
Num. Prompts	23	26	24	23	17	27	14	22	3
Input tok (k)	846	1006	889	2043	792	647	363	941	3.2
Output tok (k)	10.6	17.9	14.5	10.5	11.8	11.9	8.0	12.1	0.26
Cost $	0.23	0.29	0.25	0.53	0.22	0.19	0.11	0.26	0.001

RAG values are medians over 10 runs. Cost: $0.25/M input, $2/M output

aim to solve with RAG-enhanced, template-based platform engineering, as service templates are deployable and satisfy organizational constraints by design.

4.3 Resource Usage

The results regarding resource usage can be seen in Table 3. It can be seen that the RAG approach proves to be significantly more efficient than vibe coding. On the one hand, the number of prompts users exchanged with the RAG is significantly lower than that with the AI-assisted IDE. This results in less time overall spent interacting with the system. Correlating with the smaller number of prompts, the amount of tokens used by the RAG undercuts vibe coding by a factor of more than 100. In extreme cases, testers used more than two million tokens for generating a working service (see tester 04), whereas the RAG system only needed a median of about 3000 tokens. The factor of 100 for token usage in turn exceeds the factor of about ten for the number of prompts dramatically, which can be explained by the amount of context passed to the AI assistant being much larger. It needs entire files as context to work, whereas our RAG-based system merely works with small user prompts and (embeddings of) service templates. This, in turn, corresponds to a far higher cost of vibe coding as opposed to our RAG system during use.

4.4 Developer Experience

Table 4 shows the results for the developer experience testing, including the number of prompts needed, the success rate, and the rating of the overall experience, for both the RAG approach and our user study.

Our results reveal a contrast in developer experience between RAG retrieval and the vibe coding approach. While our approach of combining RAG with predefined service templates intends to reduce cognitive load, unstructured generation through vibe coding seems to intensify it.

It can be seen that the quality of the user experience correlates with passing quality gates. Users who were unable to create deployable systems rated their participation as "bad" or "poor". In contrast, satisfying the quality gates resulted

Table 4. Comparison of Vibe Coding vs. RAG Approach in Amount of Prompts needed, Success Rate and Overall Experience

Tester	Prompts	Duration	Success Rate	Experience
01	23	45 mins.	0.14	Bad
02	26	45 mins.	1	Good
03	24	46 mins.	0.57	Fair
04	23	44 mins.	1	Good
05	17	45 mins.	0.14	Bad
06	27	46 mins.	0.14	Poor
07	14	45 mins.	0	Poor
RAG (med.)	**3**	**<5 mins.**	**1**	**n.A.**

in a good experience, even when the user lacked deep technical understanding. As an example, tester 04 reported surprise at succeeding without prior knowledge.

According to the qualitative user feedback, unsuccessful users report feelings of being "helpless" or "at the whims of AI" when the assistant built a non-functional system and they were not able to fix it due to a lack of understanding the generated code. Others were satisfied for creating a basic outline of the code structure, but then got stuck when the assistant was continuously unable to resolve a specific issue.

Furthermore, tool expertise appeared not to improve our testers ability to create a deployable system. The expertise of testers across the different technologies used are shown in Table 5.

Table 5. Tool Expertise of Testers in Years

	Tester						
	01	02	03	04	05	06	07
Kubernetes	5+	5+	5+	0-1	0-1	0-1	1-2
CI/CD	5+	1-2	1-2	0-1	0-1	1-2	1-2
Angular	0-1	0-1	0-1	0-1	0-1	0-1	1-2
NX-Workspace	0-1	0-1	0-1	0-1	0-1	0-1	0-1
AI-Development	F	A	A	F	F	F	N

A = all the time, F = frequently, N = never

Tester 01, despite 5+ years of Kubernetes experience, failed all quality gates and rated the experience as 'bad'. This suggests that for experts, the negative experience stems from the friction between their correct mental model and the AI's tendency to architect with wrong assumptions or false versions, which was also described as irritating by our testers. However, tester 04 was successful despite not reporting experience with any of the technologies, indicating, if at all, a negative correlation between technological expertise and success with vibe coding.

Generally, it can also be seen that all testers exhausted the 45-minute time-cap. Furthermore, the number of prompts with which they attempted to architect a working system greatly exceeds what was necessary with the RAG approach.

In contrast, our RAG-based approach effectively mitigates the psychological stressors that building services with the AI assistant has shown to cause by enforcing a 'correct-by-designnn' paradigm. Retrieving pre-validated templates rather than generating code from scratch eliminates the risk of subtle architectural hallucinations. Users are not required to debug complex infrastructure configurations generated by an AI. Instead they are provided instantly with service scaffolds that inherently satisfy organizational constraints and can be deployed with the click of a button.

5 Limitations

Although our results demonstrate a clear advantage for the RAG-based template approach, limitations regarding the experimental design must be considered when interpreting our findings. A primary limitation of our user study is the reliance on a small sample of seven testers. Furthermore, since our participants were recruited from an academic environment, they may lack the specific knowledge possessed by full-time engineers. Therefore, the high failure rates observed in the vibe coding group might differ in an enterprise setting where domain expertise is higher and people are more well-versed with the tools in use. Additionally, we only tested with a single task, which could be expanded to more cases in a more thorough analysis. Also, the quality gates could be expanded; we only verified the Kubernetes pod logs to be error-free but did not actually use the AI generated service or verify correct functionality. Lastly, we used the same GitHub login for each test iteration, so it cannot be ruled-out that the system learned from each iteration. Our tests results, however, did not suggest this.

Our RAG approach came out favorably in the comparison, however the evaluation focuses on the transactional cost of deployment by measuring the tokens and time required for a developer to build a service. This metric does not show the operational cost required to engineer, validate and maintain the underlying templates. Unlike vibe coding, which offers an environment capable of attempting any task immediately, the utility of the RAG system is strictly conditional on the existence of a relevant, pre-approved template. The efficiency gains reported in our study reflect a shift in responsibility: from the application developer to the platform engineer.

Lastly, it should be noted that the ecosystem around developer platforms is evolving rapidly. During the development of this work, Backstage introduced support for the Model Context Protocol. MCP enables AI systems to interact with platform tools and services through standardized interfaces, potentially allowing AI assistants to access platform capabilities, templates, and documentation directly. As this feature became available only late in our development process, we were not able to evaluate it within the scope of this study, but it represents a promising avenue for future work.

6 Conclusion

In this work, we presented a comparative evaluation of two approaches to service scaffolding: unstructured, prompt-driven vibe coding and a structured, RAG-enhanced template retrieval system. Our RAG-based system has been shown to beat vibe coding in all recorded metrics of deployment success rate, resource consumption, and overall developer experience for scaffolding new services.

While testers were able to create a runnable system through vibe coding only in two of seven cases, our RAG-based approach recommended the correct, inherently deployable template 100% of the time while also requiring far fewer interactions with the user and time to be spent with it. Generally, testers reported a great deal of psychological stress and a rather bad experience while interacting with the AI-assisted IDE, especially in cases where it did not work as intended. This problem is alleviated by our system through a superior success rate and deployability-by-design of the result. At the same time, it is more resource-efficient by a factor exceeding 100x.

While LLMs and agentic code generation have lowered the barrier to service development, it can be seen that these tools are currently unable to handle intricacies, organizational constraints and non-trivial requirements of production-grade service architectures. They have shown here a tendency to trap developers in frustrating "trial end error" phases that lead to high token usage and feelings of helplessness when AI generation fails.

In contrast, our RAG-based approach of recommending fitting, pre-defined templates has shown to act as a guardrail, ensuring deployability of services and reducing resource usage. This, however, comes with an organizational necessity: The benefits of such a system can only be had if the organization using it possesses such pre-defined templates. This requires an up-front investment in building a catalog of templates for service scaffolding that, as organizational constraints change and develop, also has to be maintained to avoid architectural drift. This means adopting a platform engineering approach to software architecture. However, the results of this work indicate that this is a worthwhile investment.

References

1. Arun, S., Tedla, M., Vaidhyanathan, K.: LLMs for generation of architectural components: an exploratory empirical study in the serverless world. In: 2025 IEEE 22nd International Conference on Software Architecture (ICSA), pp. 25–36 (2025). https://doi.org/10.1109/ICSA65012.2025.00013
2. Cruz, A., Bhambhani, A.: Evolving services development: frameworks and SRE platform. In: Betsy, B., Harvey, T. (eds.) Site Reliability Engineering. O'Reilly Media (2017)
3. Díaz-Pace, J.A., Tommasel, A., Capilla, R.: Helping novice architects to make quality design decisions using an LLM-based assistant. In: Proceedings of the 18th European Conference on Software Architecture (ECSA'24), pp. 324–332 (2024)
4. Ivers, J., Ozkaya, I.: Will generative AI fill the automation gap in software architecting? In: 2025 IEEE 22nd International Conference on Software Architecture Companion (ICSA-C), pp. 41–45 (2025). https://doi.org/10.1109/ICSA-C65153.2025.00014
5. Jahić, J., Sami, A.: State of practice: Llms in software engineering and software architecture. In: 2024 IEEE 21st International Conference on Software Architecture Companion (ICSA-C). pp. 311–318 (2024). https://doi.org/10.1109/ICSA-C63560.2024.00059
6. Körbächer, M., Grabner, A., Hilliary, L.: Platform Engineering for Architects: Crafting modern platforms as a product. Packt Publishing (2024)
7. Mo, R., et al.: Assessing and analyzing the correctness of github copilot's code suggestions. ACM Trans. Softw. Eng. Methodol. **34**(7) (2025). https://doi.org/10.1145/3715108
8. Nguyen, N., Nadi, S.: An empirical evaluation of github copilot's code suggestions. In: Proceedings of the 19th International Conference on Mining Software Repositories, pp. 1–5. MSR '22, Association for Computing Machinery, New York, NY, USA (2022). https://doi.org/10.1145/3524842.3528470
9. Niemen, G.: How We Use Golden Paths to Solve Fragmentation in Our Software Ecosystem (2020). https://engineering.atspotify.com/2020/08/how-we-use-golden-paths-to-solve-fragmentation-in-our-software-ecosystem, Accessed 29 Jan 2026
10. OpenAI: GPT-4o System Card (2024). https://arxiv.org/abs/2410.21276, Accessed 29 Jan 2026
11. Pesl, R.D., Mathew, J.G., Mecella, M., Aiello, M.: Retrieval-augmented generation for service discovery: Chunking strategies and benchmarking. IEEE Trans. Serv. Comput. 1–15 (2026). https://doi.org/10.1109/TSC.2026.3665441
12. Rasnayaka, S., Wang, G., Shariffdeen, R., Iyer, G.N.: An empirical study on usage and perceptions of LLMs in a software engineering project. In: Proceedings of the ACM/IEEE 44th International Conference on Software Engineering: Companion Proceedings, pp. 111–118. LLM4Code '24 (2024). https://doi.org/10.1145/3643795.3648379
13. Reimers, N., Gurevych, I.: Sentence-BERT: Sentence embeddings using Siamese BERT-networks. In: Proceedings of the 2019 Conference on Empirical Methods in Natural Language Processing and the 9th International Joint Conference on Natural Language Processing (EMNLP-IJCNLP), pp. 3982–3992 (2019). https://doi.org/10.18653/v1/D19-1410
14. Sentence Transformers: all-MiniLM-L6-v2: A sentence-transformers model (2021). https://huggingface.co/sentence-transformers/all-MiniLM-L6-v2, Accessed 29 Jan 2026

15. Spotify Engineering: What the Heck is Backstage Anyway? (2020). https://engineering.atspotify.com/2020/03/what-the-heck-is-backstage-anyway, Accessed 29 Jan 2026
16. Stack Overflow: 2025 Developer Survey: AI. Online Report (2025). https://survey.stackoverflow.co/2025/ai/, Accessed 29 Jan 2026
17. Truong, H.L., Vukovic, M., Pavuluri, R.: On coordinating LLMs and platform knowledge for software modernization and new developments. In: 2024 IEEE International Conference on Software Services Engineering (SSE), pp. 188–193 (2024). https://doi.org/10.1109/SSE62657.2024.00036
18. Truong, H.L., Vukovic, M., Pavuluri, R.: On coordinating LLMs and platform knowledge for software modernization and new developments. In: 2024 IEEE International Conference on Software Services Engineering (SSE), pp. 188–193 (2024). https://doi.org/10.1109/SSE62657.2024.00036

A Service-Oriented Architecture for Feedback-Driven Reconfiguration of LLM Analytics Pipelines

Hirad Rezaei[1(✉)], Fethi Rabhi[1], and Amin Beheshti[2]

[1] UNSW Sydney, Sydney, Australia
{hirad.rezaei,f.rabhi}@unsw.edu.au
[2] Macquarie University, Sydney, Australia
amin.beheshti@mq.edu.au

Abstract. Analytics pipelines increasingly compose heterogeneous services—retrieval modules, LLM endpoints, vector stores, validators, and delivery components—yet their service configurations remain static even as costs, quality, and governance requirements change at runtime. This paper proposes a service-oriented architecture in which a policy-bounded LLM planner, embedded within a MAPE-K control loop, reasons over telemetry signals, structured service descriptors, and task intent to recommend verified reconfiguration actions—including service substitution, traffic rerouting, context-budget tuning, validator insertion, and graceful degradation. We formalise the service graph model, define a typed operator catalogue with explicit pre- and post-conditions, and illustrate the design through a document-grounded analytics scenario. The contribution is a precise, service-centric design proposal for self-adaptive LLM pipelines, accompanied by an evaluation agenda covering operational, economic, quality, and governance dimensions.

Keywords: service-oriented architecture · large language models · MAPE-K · runtime adaptation · service reconfiguration · analytics pipelines · governance

1 Introduction

Service-oriented architectures (SOA) are the dominant assembly model for enterprise analytics pipelines, orchestrating document ingestion APIs, retrieval services, vector stores, LLM endpoints, validators, and report generators. This modular composition promotes reuse and provider independence, but exposes pipelines to runtime perturbations—provider outages, budget changes, retrieval quality drift, or new regulatory requirements—that static configurations cannot absorb.

The centrality of LLMs in these pipelines is not incidental. LLM endpoints introduce signals—grounding quality, citation correctness, context-budget utilisation, and task-intent alignment—that have no direct equivalent in classical

R. Posenato and I. Vanderfeesten (Eds.): CAiSE 2026 Workshops, LNBIP 586, pp. 171–178, 2026.
https://doi.org/10.1007/978-3-032-28160-9_15

web-service QoS models. These semantic signals cannot be captured by latency or failure-rate thresholds alone, which is precisely why deterministic rule engines are insufficient as sole planners: encoding cross-cutting conditions such as "if retrieval recall drops *and* cost pressure increases, substitute the retriever *before* reducing context budget" requires combinatorial rule growth. The LLM planner is thus motivated not as a general-purpose agent, but as the specific component best suited to synthesise heterogeneous, semantically rich signals over a bounded action space.

Service-oriented computing provides composition and QoS models for distributed capabilities [3], while the self-adaptive systems community has established control-loop frameworks for runtime reconfiguration [1,2]. LLMs have demonstrated capacity for tool-augmented reasoning [4] and LLM-assisted service composition [5,6]. Recent work on LLMOps highlights the industrial urgency of principled runtime management for LLM-instrumented processes [9]. However, existing approaches address either design-time composition [5] or runtime monitoring [9], but not closed-loop reconfiguration of the deployed service graph itself. Similarly, dynamic QoS-aware service adaptation [10] handles traditional web services but lacks mechanisms for the semantic signals specific to LLM-based pipelines.

This paper addresses that gap with a *service-oriented architecture* for feedback-driven pipeline reconfiguration. We treat the analytics workflow as a typed service graph and position an LLM not as an unconstrained agent, but as a bounded planner inside a policy-aware control loop that recommends service-level changes verified against contract compatibility and governance constraints. The paper contributes: (1) a formal service graph model with typed reconfiguration operations; (2) a MAPE-K reference architecture with an LLM planner, contract verifier, and policy gate; and (3) an evaluation agenda with concrete degradation injection protocols and a discussion of expected outcomes.

The remainder of the paper is structured as follows. Section 2 formalises the service graph and feedback model. Section 3 presents the reference architecture and operator catalogue. Section 4 provides an illustrative scenario and evaluation agenda. Section 5 surveys related work, and Sect. 6 concludes.

2 Problem Formulation

Service Graph and Descriptors. Let an analytics pipeline be a directed acyclic graph $G = (S, E)$ where each node $s_i \in S$ denotes a deployed service instance and each edge $(s_i, s_j) \in E$ a data dependency. Each s_i carries a *service descriptor* D_i specifying: capability profile (task type, modality, semantic role); interface contract (I/O schema, protocol version); quality indicators (latency percentiles, failure rate, grounding rate); resource profile (token cost, infrastructure cost, throughput); and governance profile (data residency, provider approval status, provenance requirements). A *service catalogue* $\mathcal{C}$ maintains compatible alternatives for each capability class.

The quality of service descriptors is critical to correct system behaviour: a poorly specified descriptor may admit operationally ill-suited substitutions or mask true degradation. In practice, descriptors must be authored or validated by service owners at registration time. We envision a lightweight schema-validation step at catalogue registration and a runtime consistency check that flags descriptors whose declared quality indicators diverge significantly from observed telemetry—triggering a descriptor-update workflow rather than a reconfiguration cycle.

Reconfiguration as Constrained Transformation. A reconfiguration action $a \in \mathcal{A}$ transforms G into $G' = a(G)$ subject to: (i) *contract compatibility*: $\forall (s_i, s_j) \in E'.\ schema(D_i.out) \subseteq schema(D_j.in)$; and (ii) *governance compliance*: $\forall s_k \in S'.\ D_k \models \mathcal{R}$, where $\mathcal{R}$ is the active governance rule set. Only actions satisfying both constraints are executable.

Feedback Signals. A pipeline is *degraded* when QoS thresholds are violated or exhibit adverse trends. Feedback is collected across four groups: **operational** (latency, failure rate, throughput); **economic** (token cost, infrastructure cost, budget headroom); **quality** (retrieval coverage, grounding rate, citation correctness); and **governance** (policy violations, unverified claims, missing provenance). The monitoring layer aggregates these into a structured *feedback report* that triggers a planning cycle when threshold conditions are met.

3 Reference Architecture

The design instantiates a MAPE-K control loop [1] with an LLM as the planning component. Figure 1 illustrates the architecture.

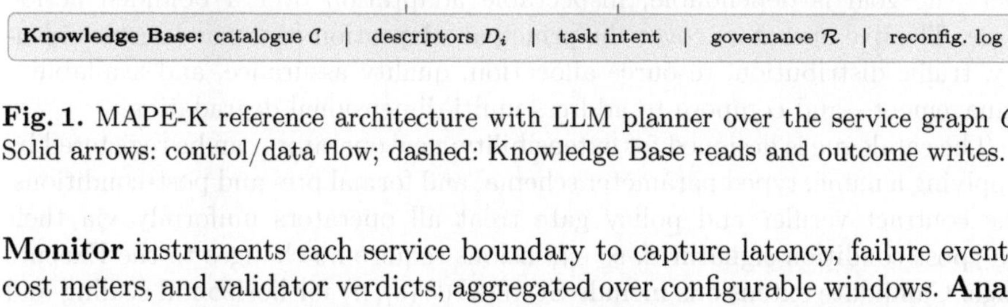

Fig. 1. MAPE-K reference architecture with LLM planner over the service graph G. Solid arrows: control/data flow; dashed: Knowledge Base reads and outcome writes.

Monitor instruments each service boundary to capture latency, failure events, cost meters, and validator verdicts, aggregated over configurable windows. **Analyse** applies threshold-and-trend detection to produce a structured diagnosis—affected service(s), violated dimension(s), and severity—forwarded to the Planner. The **Knowledge Base** stores $\mathcal{C}$, descriptors D_i, current task intent, governance rules $\mathcal{R}$, and a log of prior reconfiguration outcomes used for planning context.

Plan constructs a context window from the Knowledge Base and diagnosis, then prompts the LLM planner to generate reconfiguration proposals. The prompt is assembled programmatically in four steps: (i) the affected service descriptors are serialised as typed JSON records, making interface contracts and quality indicators explicit to the planner; (ii) the structured diagnosis with metric values is appended, framing the planning task as a constrained selection problem rather than open-ended generation; (iii) the operator catalogue schema (Sect. 3.1) is included with its pre- and post-condition types, so the model's output vocabulary is bounded to parameterised operator invocations; and (iv) applicable governance rules from $\mathcal{R}$ are embedded as hard constraints the plan must not violate. This prompt structure follows the principle of *structured output generation* [4]: rather than asking the LLM to reason freely and produce free-form instructions, the prompt shapes the generation space so that every output is a machine-parseable action record. In ambiguous scenarios—where multiple operator sequences are plausible—the planner is instructed to rank proposals by estimated quality impact and to flag uncertainty explicitly; the Execute stage then applies the highest-ranked action that passes both gates, deferring lower-ranked options for human review if the first is rejected.

The LLM is *not* permitted to issue arbitrary tool calls or free-form modifications. This bounded design is deliberate: restricting the planner's output vocabulary to typed operators makes every proposal machine-verifiable, while the planner's value lies in synthesising heterogeneous signals—semantic quality, cost trajectories, and governance rules—that would require combinatorial rule growth to encode deterministically.

Execute applies two gates before actuating any change: (i) a *contract verifier* checks interface compatibility between affected endpoints; (ii) a *policy gate* checks alignment with $\mathcal{R}$. Actions failing either gate are rejected and the Planner is notified. High-risk actions may additionally require human approval.

3.1 Reconfiguration Operators

Table 1 defines the operator catalogue. The catalogue is intentionally compact: the goal is dependable, inspectable adaptation over a bounded action space. The five operators cover the principal adaptation concerns—service identity, traffic distribution, resource allocation, quality assurance, and availability management—and compose to address multi-dimensional degradation.

The catalogue is designed for extensibility: new operators can be registered by supplying a name, typed parameter schema, and formal pre- and post-conditions. The contract verifier and policy gate treat all operators uniformly via their pre-/post-condition signatures, so extensions require no changes to the Execute stage. Candidate extensions include $\textsc{ScaleOut}(s_i, n)$ for horizontal scaling and $\textsc{CacheInsert}(s_i, \tau_{\text{ttl}})$ for response caching—both expressible within the same typed framework.

When multiple operators are triggered simultaneously, the policy gate resolves conflicts using a priority ordering: governance-restoring actions (e.g., InsertVal in response to a policy violation) take precedence over cost-reducing

Table 1. Reconfiguration operator catalogue. Pre-conditions are checked at planning time; post-conditions define the guaranteed state after execution. $\mathcal{C}$: service catalogue; G: pipeline graph; $\mathcal{R}$: active governance rule set.

Operator	Pre-condition	Post-condition / Effect
$\textsc{Sub}(s_i, s_j)$	$s_j \in \mathcal{C}$; contracts compatible	s_i replaced by s_j; graph updated as $G[s_i \mapsto s_j]$; all edges preserved
$\textsc{Reroute}(s_i, w)$	$0 < w \leq 1$; target in $\mathcal{C}$	Proportion w of requests redirected to alternative provider; original handles $1-w$
$\textsc{TuneCtx}(\delta_c, \delta_r)$	Budget permits δ_c; δ_r within retriever capacity	Context window adjusted by δ_c tokens; retrieval depth adjusted by δ_r documents
$\textsc{InsertVal}(v, \tau)$	$v \in \mathcal{C}$; $0 < \tau \leq 1$	Validator v inserted before delivery boundary; outputs with score $< \tau$ are blocked
$\textsc{Degrade}(\{s_k\})$	Each s_k non-essential	Services $\{s_k\}$ suspended; core pipeline path preserved

actions (e.g., DEGRADE), which in turn take precedence over quality-optimising substitutions. This ordering reflects the non-negotiability of compliance constraints relative to performance objectives. If two operators of equal priority conflict—for example, TUNECTX increasing context budget while DEGRADE suspends the reranker—the policy gate selects the action with the lower estimated quality impact score, computed from the affected services' descriptor quality indicators.

3.2 Prompt Construction and LLM Interaction

The planner prompt is assembled programmatically from four sections drawn from the Knowledge Base:

```
[SYSTEM]  Output ONLY a JSON array of operator calls from the catalogue.

[SERVICE DESCRIPTORS]  -- typed JSON per affected service
{"id":"retriever_A","grounding_rate":0.61,"cost_per_1k":0.002,
 "schema_out":{"chunks":"list[str]"},"data_residency":"AU"}, ...

[DIAGNOSIS]  Affected: retriever_A | Dimension: quality | Severity: HIGH
grounding_rate=0.61 (threshold 0.75), declining 0.04/hr over 3 windows

[OPERATOR CATALOGUE]  -- typed signatures with pre/post-conditions
Sub(s_i, s_j)  Pre: s_j in C, schemas compatible  Post: s_i replaced
TuneCtx(dc,dr) Pre: budget allows dc, dr in capacity  Post: budget adjusted
InsertVal(v,t) Pre: v in C, 0<t<=1  Post: validator active before delivery

[GOVERNANCE]  data_residency=="AU" required; provenance attestation active

[TASK]  Rank proposals by quality impact. Flag uncertainty explicitly.
```

This structure enforces three properties. *Output boundedness*: typed catalogue signatures constrain generation to parseable operator calls; outputs failing schema validation are rejected before reaching the policy gate. *Context completeness*: all required state—descriptors, metrics, alternatives, and governance rules—is present in the prompt, with no reliance on model memory. *Ranked uncertainty*: the explicit ranking instruction surfaces ambiguous cases as ordered alternatives for human review. In early deployment, before the reconfiguration log accumulates, this ranked mode also mitigates cold-start risk by defaulting uncertain top-ranked actions to human approval.

4 Illustrative Scenario and Evaluation Agenda

Document-Grounded Analytics. Consider an enterprise briefing pipeline with five services: document ingestion, dense passage retriever, reranker, GPT-class synthesis, and a citation validator plus report formatter. Three situations illustrate the operators. *Retrieval quality degradation*: rising citation-failure rates trigger TUNECTX$(+500, +3)$; if failures persist, the Planner chains INSERTVAL(cite-check, 0.85) or issues SUB$(\text{retriever}_A, \text{retriever}_B)$. *Cost-envelope pressure*: REROUTE(synth, 0.7) redirects routine requests to a cheaper model; under severe pressure, DEGRADE({reranker}) recovers budget headroom. *Governance tightening*: a new traceability policy triggers INSERTVAL(provenance-check, 1.0) before delivery.

These scenarios also illustrate *operator chaining*. In a combined degradation event—simultaneous quality drop and cost pressure—the Planner may propose first SUB$(\text{retriever}_A, \text{retriever}_B)$ to restore recall, then TUNECTX$(-200, 0)$ to reduce cost. Each step is independently verified, so partial plans can proceed when individual steps are rejected.

Evaluation Agenda and Expected Outcomes. We plan a controlled study comparing the proposed approach against (a) a static baseline and (b) a deterministic rule-based baseline. The study will inject three degradation scenarios into a six-service pipeline processing 1,000 document tasks: retriever recall reduction from 0.85 to 0.60, a 3× cost spike on the synthesis endpoint, and a mid-run policy change requiring provenance attestation. Metrics span four groups: **operational**—mean time to detect and recover (MTTR), false-positive reconfiguration rate; **economic**—cost per successful task, budget utilisation; **quality**—grounding rate, citation correctness; and **governance**—policy violations prevented, unsafe actions blocked.

Three research questions guide the study: (RQ1) under which degradation patterns does LLM planning outperform rule-only adaptation; (RQ2) which feedback signal combinations best predict reconfiguration safety; and (RQ3) how much benefit survives after policy gates and human approval are enforced.

Based on the architecture design and the motivating analysis of compound degradation in Sect. 1, we expect the following outcomes. For RQ1, we hypothesise that the LLM planner will show the largest advantage in *compound* events (e.g., simultaneous quality drop and cost spike), where cross-cutting conditions make deterministic rule enumeration impractical; for single-dimension degradations, the rule baseline may be competitive. For RQ2, we expect that combinations of quality and cost signals will be the strongest predictors of safe reconfigurations, while governance signals alone will be sufficient to unambiguously block non-compliant actions. For RQ3, we anticipate that policy gates will eliminate a meaningful fraction of LLM proposals—particularly in governance-tightening scenarios—but that the remaining accepted actions will still outperform the static baseline on overall task success rate. The cold-start period, during which the reconfiguration log is sparse, is an acknowledged risk: early planning cycles may require more conservative fallbacks or human approval until sufficient outcome history accumulates.

5 Related Work

Service Composition and Adaptation. Classical SOA composition focuses on constructing valid workflows with QoS modelling [3]. Dynamic QoS-aware adaptation [10] handles traditional web services at runtime but lacks mechanisms for the semantic signals inherent in LLM pipelines (e.g., grounding quality, task intent). Content-based service retrieval in federated environments [8] poses related routing challenges. Our work addresses how a deployed composition should evolve when operational conditions change, incorporating both QoS and semantic feedback.

Self-adaptive Systems and LLM Agents. MAPE-K [1] and Rainbow [2] demonstrated that explicit architectural models enable principled runtime repair. ReAct [4] shows LLMs can interleave reasoning with tool invocation; Pesl et al. [5] study LLM-assisted service composition at design time; PipeMind [7] demonstrates multi-agent feedback value for pipeline optimisation. Industrial LLMOps studies [9] document the immaturity of runtime management practices. AIOps research applies ML to operational tasks such as anomaly detection and root-cause analysis [11]. Our novelty is using an LLM as planner within a bounded operator catalogue over a typed service graph, enabling reasoning over semantic signals that resist deterministic encoding while remaining verifiable.

Limitations. The proposal depends on service descriptor quality—poorly specified descriptors may lead to operationally ill-suited substitutions. The planner itself introduces inference cost into the control loop, and the cold-start problem (planning before reconfiguration history accumulates) remains open. Empirical validation is the immediate next step.

6 Conclusion

Static service configurations are increasingly brittle in analytics pipelines where costs, provider quality, and governance requirements change during operation. This paper proposed a service-oriented architecture embedding a policy-bounded LLM planner inside a MAPE-K control loop—constrained by typed operators with explicit pre- and post-conditions—as a principled mechanism to adapt such pipelines without sacrificing inspectability or compliance. The architecture, operator catalogue, and evaluation agenda bridge LLM reasoning, runtime adaptation, and information systems governance. Future work will implement the architecture as an open-source prototype for reproducible evaluation, extend the operator catalogue with learned operators from reconfiguration logs, and investigate multi-pipeline coordination under shared governance constraints.

References

1. White, S.R., Hanson, J.E., Whalley, I., Chess, D.M., Kephart, J.O.: An architectural approach to autonomic computing. In: Proceedings of the 1st International Conference on Autonomic Computing (ICAC 2004), pp. 2–9. IEEE (2004)
2. Garlan, D., Cheng, S.-W., Huang, A.-C., Schmerl, B., Steenkiste, P.: Rainbow: architecture-based self-adaptation with reusable infrastructure. Computer **37**(10), 46–54 (2004)
3. Lemos, A.L., Daniel, F., Benatallah, B.: Web service composition: a survey of techniques and tools. ACM Comput. Surv. **48**(3), 33:1–33:41 (2016)
4. Yao, S., et al.: ReAct: synergizing reasoning and acting in language models. In: Proceedings of ICLR 2023 (2023)
5. Pesl, R.D., et al.: Compositio prompto: an architecture to employ LLMs in automated service computing. In: ICSOC 2025. LNCS, vol. 15405, pp. 276–286. Springer, Cham (2025)
6. Strehlow, R.K., Küster, T., Kupke, O.F., Llanque Kurps, B., Sivrikaya, F., Albayrak, S.: SAGE: tool-augmented LLM task solving in scalable multi-agent environments. arXiv preprint arXiv:2601.09750 (2026)
7. Rezaei, H., Rabhi, F., Beheshti, A.: PipeMind: toward a multi-agent framework for real-time feedback and continuous optimization in analytics pipelines. In: Companion Proceedings of the ACM Web Conference 2025 (WWW '25), pp. 2891–2894. ACM, New York (2025). https://doi.org/10.1145/3701716.3715193
8. Falconi, M., Plebani, P.: Improving content-based data product retrieval in federated environments with LLM and sampling. In: Snoeck, M., et al. (eds.) CAiSE 2025 Workshops. LNBIP, vol. 556, pp. 283–294. Springer, Cham (2025)
9. Borovits, N., Tamburri, D.A., van den Heuvel, W.-J.: On the maturity of LLMOps services computing: an industrial study. In: Snoeck, M., et al. (eds.) CAiSE 2025 Workshops. LNBIP, vol. 556, pp. 310–317. Springer, Cham (2025)
10. Cardellini, V., Casalicchio, E., Grassi, V., Iannucci, S., Lo Presti, F., Mirandola, R.: MOSES: a framework for QoS driven runtime adaptation of service-oriented systems. IEEE Trans. Softw. Eng. **38**(5), 1138–1159 (2012)
11. Notaro, P., Cardoso, J., Gerndt, M.: A survey of AIOps methods for failure management. ACM Trans. Intell. Syst. Technol. **12**(6), 81:1–81:45 (2021)

Towards LLM-Based RESTful Service Discovery

Antonios Smardas and Kyriakos Kritikos(✉)

Department of Information and Communication Systems Engineering, School of Engineering, University of the Aegean, Mitilini, Greece
icsdd22002@icsd.aegean.gr, kkritikos@aegean.gr

Abstract. This paper presents our approach towards LLM-based RESTful service discovery which involves two main methods. The first method utilises LLMs to compute any service's OpenAPI specification from its source code. The second method exploits LLMs in order to match textual service requests against the automatically generated OpenAPI specifications. The evaluation results produced according to a specific RESTful service dataset highlight the remarkable performance of LLMs in RESTful service discovery, reaching an F1 score of 89%, thus bypassing any other approach from the state-of-the-art.

Keywords: SOA · LLM · OpenAPI · RESTful services · functional discovery

1 Introduction

The Service-Oriented Architecture (SOA) is a very successful software development paradigm, widely adopted by many businesses due to the various advantages that it offers, including software re-use, interoperability and standards compliance [1]. Via SOA and service registries use, one can develop added-valued business applications and processes by composing existing services, which realise various business functions.

However, the vision of SOA has not been totally delivered as any attempt to offer a global registry has failed for various reasons. Initially, only lexical approaches [2], e.g., using common Information Retrieval (IR) techniques, were adopted το support service discovery in these registries, offering low accuracy performance. While machine learning (ML) techniques came to the rescue [3, 4], they suffered from insufficient service datasets for training, high computational costs for model training and inference, especially for the more specialised Deep Learning (DL) techniques, and the inability to transfer knowledge into new domains. Lastly, while ontology-based techniques were proposed [5–7], achieving high accuracy, they were never adopted by the market as: (a) it is hard to derive semantic information for services, requiring major expertise that was lacking; (b) automatic service I/O annotation tools were inaccurate; (c) organisations were reluctant to invest in adopting ontology-based techniques [8].

In result, due to the above situations, nowadays, organisational service registries still use inaccurate service discovery techniques. This creates frustration for application

R. Posenato and I. Vanderfeesten (Eds.): CAiSE 2026 Workshops, LNBIP 586, pp. 179–186, 2026.
https://doi.org/10.1007/978-3-032-28160-9_16

developers, who need to manually inspect the matched services and select those that satisfy the application requirements set. Further, this leads to increased effort and cost while delays the application development, even if it relies on modern methodologies.

Luckily, in the current era, the blowsome of Generative Artificial Intelligence (AI) can be observed. Indeed, the powerful computation and transformation abilities of Large Language Models (LLMs) create great opportunities in many areas, including software engineering [9] and BPM. As such, we believe that LLMs can really provide great support to service discovery. Inspired by this fact and the SOA vision, we have developed an LLM-based approach that can really boost service discovery accuracy. This approach comprises two methods that can be sequentially applied. The first method can automatically generate textually rich OpenAPI specifications from a RESTful service's source code. These rich specifications were shown in our previous work [10] to lead to better service discovery results when using a TFIDF service matcher.

This paper presents our approach's second method, mapping to an LLM-based functional service matcher. This method, by relying on a carefully-crafted prompt utilising well-known prompt patterns, instructs an LLM how to conduct the service matching based on the given input and the way it should rank its output matching results. While the supplied input corresponds to specific parts from the OpenAPI specifications of all registry's services as well as a simple textual functional service request from the user.

Our evaluation on a real service dataset shows that via the use of state-of-the-art LLMs, our matcher's accuracy is far greater than any other approach. Apart from this remarkable result, our matcher has the main benefits of flexibility in applying any LLM, producing both lexical and semantic match categories as well as of explainability, as it justifies per each service match why it satisfies the given request. Thus, it can potentially become the main ingredient of a global service registry to realise the SOA vision.

The rest of this paper is organized as follows. Section 2 analyzes our functional service publication and discovery approach. Section 3 explains the way our LLM-based service matcher was evaluated and supplies the respective evaluation results. Finally, Sect. 4 concludes this paper.

2 Proposed Approach

In the context of our work, we have developed a service management API [11] wraping a service registry, which supports RESTful service publication and discovery. In this section, we shortly present this registry's service publication capability, incorporating our approach's first method, as it enables richer service discovery but do not analyse it as it has been already published. The focus is rather on the registry's service functional discovery capability, which is innovative and maps to our approach's second method.

2.1 Service Publication – Approach First Method

When obtaining a request for the publication of a new RESTful service, our API attempts to automatically produce its rich OpenAPI specification based on its given source code repository URL. Figure 1 shows the overall OpenAPI specification generation process, realising our approach first method. Initially, once the service repository is cloned, its directories and files are filtered by a rule-based algorithm. Then, in an incremental manner, the OpenAPI specification is generated by processing each from the retained files. Finally, the specification is stored in the underlying registry.

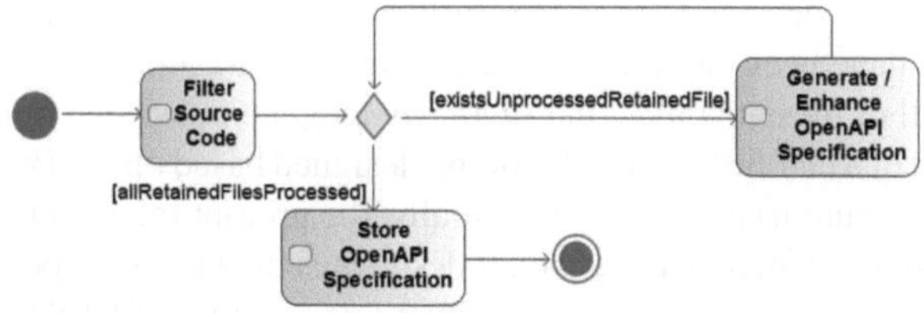

Fig. 1. The OpenAPI Specification Generation Process

More details about this method can be found in [10]. However, we must stress that the knowledge within each OpenAPI specification is rich as it enabled to increase service matching accuracy when TFIDF techniques were used from 42 to 92% in the context of natural language requests containing keywords partially included in the OpenAPI specifications [10]. While this signifies our work's potential in terms of enriched specifications generation, it still needs to be couplied with the right service matcher as lexicographic techniques like TFIDF are considered nowadays a baseline. This is where our new work comes in, analysed in the next sub-section.

2.2 Service Discovery – Approach Second Method

Our service management API incorporates an LLM-based functional service matcher. This matcher, implementing our approach's second method, relies on a process (see Fig. 2) comprising 5 main steps: (a) *service request receipt*; (b) *service document extraction*; (c) *LLM prompt generation*; (d) *LLM execution*; (e) *service results delivery*. As the first and last two steps are trivial, we explain the second and third only.

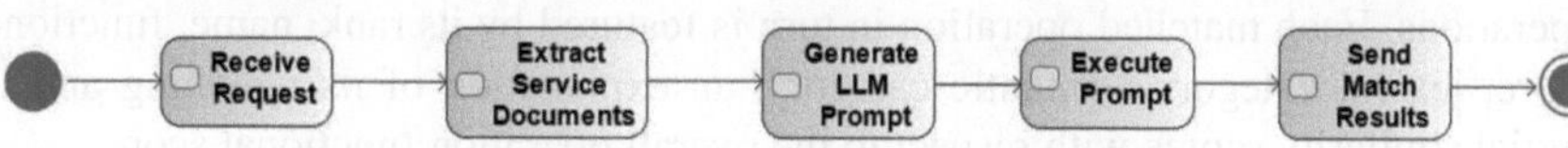

Fig. 2. The functional service matchmaking process

Service Document Extraction. The extraction of *service documents* relies on the retrieval of each OpenAPI specification from the registry and its subsequent processing in order to pull out only the necessary information for service matching purposes (see prompt analysis below). In result, a set of *service documents* is produced, which along with the service request, are passed to the *LLM prompt generation* step.

2.2.1 LLM Prompt Generation

Our matcher has been designed with features that distinguish it from other work. In particular, it is first able to categorise service matches in both lexical and semantic categories [7], thus covering different developer preferences and giving them different viewpoints to consider. Second, it hierarchically ranks both services and their operations. Lastly, it caters for explainability, justifying the inclusion of each service match in the results list. In the following, we first explain how the prompt leading to the realisation of these features was designed. Then, we further elaborate on the main ingredients of our matcher that have been carefully implanted in the LLM prompt.

To support all of these features, the *LLM prompt generation* step relies on the automatic production of a carefully-crafted prompt, designed based on the *Persona* (i.e., role) and *Template* (i.e., output) patterns [12]. Initially, the prompt requests from the LLM to act as an intelligent API matcher. Further, it designates the task to be performed, related to matching a plain request text with a structured description of RESTful services and their operations and producing a JSON-based structured, ranked output (of the matched services and operations). The prompt is then organised into five sections, which are now going to be analysed below. The whole prompt is available here: https://drive.google.com/drive/folders/1mLoD59j9t587vpqhfYFhTX3SX62NOa8s.

1. *Inputs*: This section designates the 2 main input sources for service matching: the *service documents* in the registry and the user's plain-language request. Each *service document* is confined to contain: (a) the service name and description with the latter covering the service summary and textual description in the *info* section of its OpenAPI specification; (b) each service's operation description including the operation's name, description (summary and textual description), input parameters and output.
2. *Matching Logic*: It dictates the exact logic for producing the (similarity) score for each service and its operations as well as for filtering and ranking them. It also explicates the lexical and semantic categories to consider for the matching and their meaning. Finally, it instructs the LLM to record: (a) each partial similarity score per service operation and (b) the justification for matching that operation along (c) with the rationale for its classification in specific lexical and semantic categories.
3. *Output format*: the LLM is prescribed to produce a specific JSON output format that includes the original request and the ranked set of matched services. Each matched service is featured by its rank, name and functional score as well as its matched operations. Each matched operation in turn is featured by its rank, name, functional score, lexical category, semantic category, an explanation of its matching and its partial similarity scores with respect to the overall operation functional score.
4. *Additional Instructions*: They demand to not consider historical usage in score calculation and to use normalised functional scores in the set [0.0, 1.0].
5. *Task*: This section just repeats the main LLM task. Further, it requests from the LLM to not include any external commentary or explanations in its output.

Matching Logic. The main matching logic designed relies on producing a similarity score for each service and its operations with respect to the given service request. The *service operation score* is calculated as the weighted sum of 4 partial similarity scores: (a) the *semantic score* between the service request and the operation's description and name; (b) the *intent score* between the request's action verb and the operation's intent; (c) the *parameter score* between the request's and operation's params; (d) the *domain context score* between the request and operation's inferred domain. Formally:

$$operationScore = 0.45 * semanticScore + 0.25 * intentScore + 0.20 * parameterScore + 0.10 * domainScore.$$

The weights given to the partial scores follow common sense as the semantic score should be the highest, the intention of both the request and operation follows, next the focus should be on how well their parameters align with each other and finally we must consider whether the same domain is designated by both the request and operation.

The *service score* is computed as follows: $serviceScore = 0.6 * serviceSim + 0.4 * max(operationScore)$, as the weighted sum of the (lexical) similarity score between the service description and request and of the maximum score across the service's operations. This is rational in the sense that the service should be similar to the request and include at least one operation that (best) matches it. Please note that our matching's focus is over service operations. As we expect that the user is seeking specific functions to re-use and not whole function groups. That is also the main reason we classify into two category types the service's operations and not the service itself.

Lexical Categories. Three main categories are involved: (a) *COMPLETE* mapping to full matching of all aspects between request and operation; (b) *PARTIAL*: lower than COMPLETE as there can be some intent or parameter gaps; (c) *POSSIBLE*: there is some topical match but it is incomplete.

Semantic Categories. We explain here the main intuition of the four categories formally defined in [7]: (a) *PERFECT*: the service operation is semantically equivalent to the request; (b) *PLUGIN*: service operation produces more specific output (a child concept) than that demanded by the request; (c) *SUBSUMES*: similar to *PLUGIN* but service operation output is a descending sub-concept of the request output; (d) *PARTIAL*: the service operation partially matches the request.

Filtering & Ranking. The LLM decides whether a service operation matches the request by applying thresholds over the *service operation score*. These thresholds are computed internally by the LLM and they influence where the service operation will be classified based on the aforementioned lexicographic categories. This is a rationale choice as the semantic categories require a different computation approach based on subsumption logic at least over the service operation and request I/O. Thus, if the service operation belongs to one of the three lexical categories, it is retained; otherwise, it is filtered. On the other hand, we only retain services with matched operations.

Once the filtering is performed, the LLM is instructed to conduct the ranking in a hierarchical manner: (a) first the retained services are ranked based on their overall score; (b) then each matched service operation is ranked based on its own score.

3 Experimental Evaluation

3.1 Experiment Structure

Experiment Datasets. To properly apply our approach, we have relied on the Evo Master Benchmark (EMB), produced in the context of a certain RESTful service testing framework [13]. This benchmark incorporates the source code of 19 RESTful services. So, it is a perfect dataset in our case, as the inclusion of source code enables to automatically produce the rich OpenAPI specification of the EMB services. Please note that there is no other RESTful service dataset that fits our needs. While greater (in size) datasets exist, they do not contain source code or even OpenAPI specifications [14].

Based on this dataset, we designed the EMBR request dataset. This dataset incorporates carefully crafted textual functional service requests that explicitly target the EMB services. This signifies that the ground truth of all requests is already known, thus facilitating service matching accuracy metrics computation. These requests map to small sentences that demand the supply of a specific function, typically including a verb and specific entities to formulate the requested function's intention. All such sentences have parts that have been named differently (i.e., via synonyms) to not exactly match with the words in the description of the EMB services.

Further, EMBR was cautiously separated into two subsets: (a) *single service results*: incorporating requests matching operations of a single service and (b) *multi-service results*: having requests that match operations from multiple services. This separation was conducted for multiple reasons. First, it covers two distinct cases in service matching so it simulates realistic situations. Second, the first subset "presses" matchers over precision while the second over "recall". Third, the first subset can be used for category-based threshold calibration of matchers, like the TFIDF one we implemented. You can find EMBR here: https://drive.google.com/drive/folders/1mLoD59j9t587vpqhf YFhTX3SX62NOa8s, while Table 1 provides some statistics over it:

Table 1. Statistics concerning the two subsets of EMBR.

EMBR Subset	Request Number	Avg./Min/Max Num of Matching Services	Avg./Min/Max Num of Matching Operations
Single-Service	15	1/1/1	2.4/1/4
Multi-Service	12	2.66/2/7	3.33/2/7

Evaluation Metrics. We compute three classical accuracy metrics in service matching: i.e., *average precision*, *average recall* and *average F1*. These metrics are easily computed as we already know the ground truth of the EMBR requests' matches. Please note that we consider as matching only service operations that map to the *COMPLETE* & *PARTIAL* lexical categories. This is proper common practice as POSSIBLE matches are partially satisfying the request so they do not match it.

TFIDF Matcher. We use this matcher as a baseline for the evaluation. This matcher relies on computing the TFIDF vectors of the service operation and request and then computes the cosine similarity between them. Then, it classifies the service operation in the lexical categories or filters it based on the use of three thresholds, computed based on a specific calibration algorithm [15]. The classification logic is as follows:

- If *operation score* $> = COMPLETE\_TH$, then *category* $= COMPLETE$
- Else if *operation score* $> = PARTIAL\_TH$, then *category* $= PARTIAL$
- Else if *operation score* $> = POSSIBLE\_TH$, then *category* $= POSSIBLE$
- Else discard

Experiment Process. We first inserted the EMB services in our registry to initiate the automatic generation of the OpenAPI specifications. Then, we created specific code to first calibrate the TFIDF matcher based on the 1st EMBR subset and then to use both our matchers, LLM and TFIDF, over the 2nd EMBR subset. Thus, the accuracy metrics were automatically computed over this second subset. As our LLM matcher can exploit any LLM, we evaluated 4 versions of it by utilising state-of-the-art LLMs: OpenAI's GPT 4.1, Anthropic's Claude Sonnet 4, Deep Seek's R1 and Mistral Large.

3.2 Experiment Results

Table 2 shows the produced experiment results. As can be seen, all different LLM-based matcher versions outperformed by far the TFIDF one. In fact, their service matching accuracy is greater than that of any other functional service matcher proposed. Further, as expected, the TFIDF has a hard time to accurately match the services operations as the requests in EMBR utilise a different terminology. However, these lexicographic differences do not seem to greatly impact the different versions of our LLM matcher.

Table 2. Service matching accuracy results over the second EMBR subset.

Matcher	Avg. Precision	Avg. Recall	Avg. F1
TFIDF	0.25	0.10	0.11
LLM (GPT 4.1)	0.86	0.68	0.67
LLM (Claude Sonnet 4)	0.91	0.91	0.89
LLM (DS R1)	0.96	0.60	0.69
LLM (Mistral Large)	0.86	0.70	0.72

From the different LLM matcher versions, we can discern the Anthropic's Claude Sonnet 4 one as it exhibits a balanced accuracy, with an average F1 score much higher than that of the other versions. Surprisingly, at the 2nd place, we find Mistral Large version with an F1 score of 0.72. The worst accuracy is exhibited by GPT 4.1 matcher version with an F1 score of 0.67. This signifies that while GPT 4.1 is an excellent LLM in terms of other tasks, it faces difficulties in terms of functional service matching, especially in recall, which is the second lowest across all LLM matcher versions.

By focusing on each distinct single accuracy metric, we can discern the LLM matcher's version with DS R1 as it achieves the highest average precision. On the other hand, the version with Claude Sonnet 4 achieves the best possible recall (0.91). In overall, we observe that LLMs behave well in terms of precision ($>= 0.86$) but have a harder time over recall ($>= 0.60$). Still, these results are much better than those exhibited by state-of-the-art service matchers. Please note that this recall behaviour (by all LLM matchers and TFIDF one) is expected based on the design of the EMBR second subset.

4 Conclusions

This paper presented a novel functional service matching approach that relies on using LLMs to both enrich service specifications and more accurately match them. This approach encompasses two methods. The first method automatically generates OpenAPI specifications from the services' source code. The second method takes as input the most important parts of these specifications and a functional request in natural language to generate a carefully crafted prompt that allows an LLM to optimally match them. The evaluation results against an existing RESTful service and request dataset showcase that our approach can attain a high accuracy level in service matching, well above the state-of-the-art functional matchers.

References

1. Georgakopoulos, D., Papazoglou, M.P.: Service-Oriented Computing. MIT Press (2008)
2. Dong, X., Halevy, A., Madhavan, J., Nemes, E., Zhang, J.: Similarity search for web services. In: VLDB '04. pp. 372–383. VLDB Endowment, Toronto, Canada (2004)
3. Lo, W., Yin, J., Wu, Z.: Accelerated sparse learning on tag annotation for web service discovery. In: ICWS, pp. 265–272. IEEE, New York, NY, USA (2015)
4. Yang, Y., et al.: ServeNet: a deep neural network for web services classification. In: ICWS, pp. 168–175. IEEE, Beijing, China (2020). https://doi.org/10.1109/ICWS49710.2020.00029
5. Baryannis, G., Kritikos, K., Plexousakis, D.: A specification-based QoS-aware design framework for service-based applications. SOCA **11**, 301–314 (2017)
6. Plebani, P., Pernici, B.: URBE: web service retrieval based on similarity evaluation. IEEE Trans. Knowl. Data Eng. **21**, 1629–1642 (2009)
7. Klusch, M., Fries, B., Sycara, K.: Automated semantic web service discovery with OWLS-MX. In: AAMAS, pp. 915–922. ACM Press, Hakodate, Japan (2006)
8. Hogan, A.: The semantic web: two decades on. SW **11**, 169–185 (2020). https://doi.org/10.3233/SW-190387
9. Hou, X., et al.: Large language models for software engineering: a systematic literature review. ACM Trans. Softw. Eng. Methodol. **33**, 1–79 (2024). https://doi.org/10.1145/3695988
10. Smardas, A., Kritikos, K.: Towards the automatic production of OpenAPI specifications from source code. In: FiCloud, pp. 342–349. IEEE, Istanbul, Turkiye (2025)
11. Smardas, A., Kritikos, K.: LLM-enhanced derivation of the maturity level of RESTful services. In: Grabis, J. and Wautelet, Y. (eds.) Advanced Information Systems Engineering Workshops, pp. 277–288. Springer Nature Switzerland, Cham (2025)
12. White, J., et al.: A Prompt Pattern Catalog to Enhance Prompt Engineering with ChatGPT. https://arxiv.org/abs/2302.11382 (2023). https://doi.org/10.48550/ARXIV.2302.11382
13. Arcuri, A.: RESTful API automated test case generation with EvoMaster. ACM Trans. Softw. Eng. Methodol. **28**, 1–37 (2019). https://doi.org/10.1145/3293455
14. Liu, M., Tu, Z., Zhu, Y., Xu, X., Wang, Z., Sheng, Q.Z.: Data correction and evolution analysis of the ProgrammableWeb service ecosystem. J. Syst. Softw. **182**, 111066 (2021). https://doi.org/10.1016/j.jss.2021.111066
15. Antonios Smardas: Semantic Service Discovery Supported by LLMs. University of the Aegean (2026)

Agent-Based Service Orchestration for Context-Aware Data Access in Industrial IoT

Monica Marconi Sciarroni and Emanuele Storti(✉)

DII, Marche Polytechnic University, Ancona, Italy
e.storti@univpm.it

Abstract. As the industrial paradigm is shifting toward human-centric collaboration, there is an increasing need for operators to interact seamlessly with complex intelligent systems. This transition, referred to as Industry 5.0, necessitates intuitive interfaces that empower workers to perform real-time analysis of heterogeneous devices and to explore data silos without specialized query expertise. This paper presents an agent-based orchestration framework designed to bridge unstructured natural language requests with structured industrial services for data streams monitoring and analytical queries. To address challenges in grounding and authorization, our approach implements a hybrid pipeline that decouples context-aware entity recognition from intent execution, ensuring the system operates only on contextually relevant resources. We evaluate the system across multiple LLMs, demonstrating high mapping accuracy and resilience to hallucinations.

Keywords: LLM · Agentic AI · Stream monitoring · IoT · Industry 5.0

1 Introduction

The transition to a more sustainable and human-centric enterprise, often referred to as Industry 5.0, requires intuitive interfaces to interact with complex Industrial IoT systems. While modern smart factories leverage robust Service-Oriented Architectures (SOA) to manage vast volumes of heterogeneous data, these systems often create a significant human-machine barrier: pre-configured applications or dashboards are indeed effective for routine monitoring, but lack the flexibility required for spontaneous troubleshooting or investigating unforeseen anomalies. Closing this gap requires industrial solutions that are not only data-driven, but also accessible and safe for operators to navigate without prior query expertise. The recent emergence of Large Language Models (LLMs) offers a solution to this usability challenge, since they can help to bridge the gap between natural language intent (e.g., "Extract the max vibration value in Assembly line 1 within the last 3 h") and technical execution, i.e., the identification of the services capable of responding to the request and the actual execution of the query

R. Posenato and I. Vanderfeesten (Eds.): CAiSE 2026 Workshops, LNBIP 586, pp. 187–194, 2026.
https://doi.org/10.1007/978-3-032-28160-9_17

[6]. This can be particularly valuable in Industry 5.0 to support monitoring, analyze sensor data, detect anomalies and produce human-readable reports, without needing expertise in multiple query languages or system protocols. Recent advancements in LLMs have introduced autonomous agents capable of reasoning about goals and decomposing complex tasks into logical actions. This progress is exemplified by the ReAct (Reasoning and Acting) paradigm [10], which enhances accuracy and transparency through iterative reasoning. Current research further highlights a hierarchical "Agent as a tool" strategy: frameworks like HuggingGPT [8] and AutoGen [9] leverage a central LLM to orchestrate specialized sub-models or sub-agents, treating their specific reasoning capabilities as encapsulated tools for higher-level execution. Despite their promise, deploying LLMs in an industrial context poses challenges related to their tendency to "hallucinate" non-existent sensors or data streams. Combined with a lack of grounding in the specific physical environment and access control policies, this makes LLMs unsuitable for an unsupervised use in critical settings. To address these limitations, researchers have begun to explore solutions to ground LLMs with factual data, including DBMS-based retrieval through RAG systems. While standard text-based RAG struggles with complex, multi-hop reasoning, Graph RAG solutions offer a structured alternative by integrating Knowledge Graphs (KG) to ensure retrieval is grounded in the actual functional logic and semantics of the ecosystem, e.g. supporting Named Entity Recognition, query decomposition, query answering [4], also in the industrial sector [3,5]. However, current Graph RAG approaches lack mechanisms for orchestrating subsequent actions, while existing multi-agent frameworks lack native integration with domain-specific KGs and the dynamic, role-based access controls essential for critical industrial operations.

This paper proposes a Service-Oriented AI Agent framework designed to fill this gap within an Industry 5.0 platform. Our approach integrates an LLM-based orchestrator with core industrial services providing environmental context, real-time monitoring for live stream consumption, and retrieval of historical data from federated storage systems. The approach employs a decoupled reasoning process where an entity recognition agent first grounds a natural language request in a Knowledge Graph, followed by an LLM-based orchestrator which identifies the user's intent and invokes the corresponding data access service. This creates a deterministic security layer that significantly reduces the risk of hallucinations and prevents unauthorized data access.

The rest of this work is structured as follows: Sect. 2 introduces the background to this work, namely a context-aware semantic platform for stream management. In Sect. 3 the agent-based framework is detailed, while its evaluation is discussed in Sect. 4. Finally, Sect. 5 concludes the paper and outlines future research directions.

2 Stream Management Platform

This section introduces a context-aware semantic platform for stream management, supporting technical and semantic interoperability in industrial scenarios.

The platform data model is based on a Knowledge Graph (KG) built on the Resource Description Framework (RDF), which serves as the industrial semantic backbone and provides an integrated view of the knowledge resources of the entire enterprise ecosystem: (1) *Device and topology*: details and relationships between human agents, smart objects and included sensors, their schemas, technical specifications and deployment in areas of the organization. (2) *Properties* define domain measures such as temperature, CO_2 or timestamp, which are used as global terminology to which specific attributes in stream schemas are mapped. (3) Role-based *access control* policies, including temporary roles related to delegation or collaboration relations among agents. The schema of the KG is based on SemIoE [2], a lightweight OWL2 ontology[1]. Logical reasoning is adopted to support automated knowledge derivation, e.g., to identify all accessible devices based on spatial containment (e.g., a right on the area "Assembly Line 1" extends to all resources contained within that domain), and dynamically expanding the set of accessible devices through delegation/collaboration relation. As such, since the domain-specific logic is encapsulated within the KG schema, the framework is inherently flexible for diverse industrial sectors without structural modifications.

On top of the KG, the platform [7] is organized into a set of independent microservices for stream gathering, management, processing, monitoring and storage, following a publisher/subscriber paradigm. Heterogeneous sources (MQTT, HTTP, etc.) are aggregated via gateways into an Apache Kafka cluster. This layer performs optional pre-processing (filtering, scaling) based on KG metadata, ensuring uniform stream management. The platform enables access to (meta)data through multiple services: (1) metadata on devices can be obtained through the *Resource Discovery Service*, which returns the list of contextually accessible devices for a user, along with their schema and relevant details, e.g. their location. Data access can regard real-time streams or historical data streams stored in persistent storage systems. In the first case, the platform includes (2) a semantic *Monitoring Service*, which enables the client to subscribe to incoming streams, using ontological terms rather than technical queue names. The service translates user constraints into SPARQL queries to resolve physical entities (e.g., sensors by location or property) and automates topic subscriptions. Furthermore, the system provides (3) a *Querying Service*, enabling federated analytical queries over historical data using Trino[2]. It leverages the KG to map global ontological terms to specific database schemas across a polyglot persistence layer, abstracting the complexity of the underlying storage from the user.

3 Context-Based Agentic Data Access

The approach is aimed to enable users (i.e., a human or an automated agent) to access data streams in a secure, contextually relevant way, based on natural language requests which may involve different types of intents. They include an

[1] Full specification is available at https://w3id.org/semioe.

[2] https://trino.io/.

informational intent, querying generic information regarding sensors and their associated metadata (e.g., "What temperature sensors are in Assembly station 01?", or "Extract the schema of sensor TMP-CYL-01-A"); a *real-time* intent, requesting access to live data streams for active monitoring (e.g., "What is the current vibration level for sensor OIL PUMP 2?"); finally, an *analytical* intent, executing analytical queries over the persistent storage systems to retrieve historical data (e.g., "What was the avg engine temperature in production plant 02 between yesterday and today at noon?").

All requests are subject to access control constraints that regulate a user agent's permission to interact with specific sensor metadata and data streams. These access policies are role-based and modeled within the Knowledge Graph. Specifically, access is granted if the user agent possesses a role with sufficient privileges or has been assigned temporary access through a delegation or collaboration relationship. To give an example, a senior technician can delegate a task to a junior colleague, temporarily enabling him/her to access an extended set of sensors, or two workers can temporarily collaborate to jointly solve a complex task. To this aim, the system architecture ensures that user requests are interpreted with high semantic fidelity, validated against dynamic, role-based access policies, and executed through a secure, context-aware pipeline. This process integrates agent-based orchestration with deterministic validation to strictly enforce access constraints across all data streams.

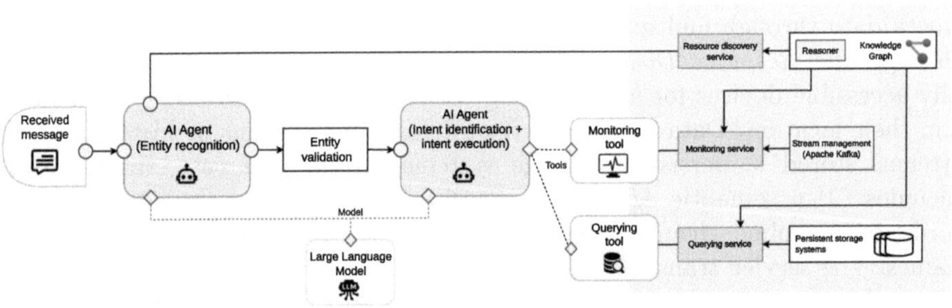

Fig. 1. Overview of the agent-based service orchestration for data access

The process, represented in Fig. 1, begins when the user submits a new request, which is then processed through the following transformations.

Entity Recognition. The goal of this module is identifying the entities (sensors, properties and location) expressed by the user in the natural language request. To this aim, the module queries the Resource Discovery Service, to obtain metadata on resources that are accessible to the specific user based on current context. The set of accessible resources, along with the user request, are used to enrich a prompt to an LLM, which is asked to perform the recognition task, mapping terms used in the request with globally defined terms. The output is a set of entities, each including the correct resource URI, the identified global properties requested by the user and the corresponding schema fields. Let us consider the following request: *"What was the average engine temperature between yesterday and today at noon?"*. Considering the user context, let us assume the accessible sensors are located in `http://homey/site/assembly_station-01`. Among them, there are `TMP-CYL-01-A`, measuring property `temperature_engine` and `Oil_Pump_2`, measuring property `vibration`.

The Entity Recognition module would output the following identified resource:

```
{"source_id": "http://homey/resource/TMP-CYL-01-A",
 "property": "http://homey/property/temperature_engine"}
```

Entity Validation. This stage validates extracted entities against the Resource Discovery Service, filtering out non-existent or unauthorized resources. By restricting subsequent operations to verified, accessible entities, the system mitigates hallucinations and prevents unauthorized access to restricted data streams.

Orchestration (Intent Identification and Execution). Once entities are validated, this stage is aimed to generate the response to the user request. This is realized through an AI Agent, in which the prompt is enriched with the original user request and the validated entities. The agent dynamically evaluates the validated context to identify the intent, i.e. determine the required operation and perform a tool call among the following:

- Informational: to directly respond using the available information.
- Real-time monitoring: a call to the *Monitoring Service* is performed to access a real-time data stream by subscribing to the corresponding topic, sending the continuous stream to the user.
- Analytical query: a call to the *Querying service* is performed to access the repositories where data streams are stored, for historical analysis. Parameters include the sensor URI, the URIs of the required properties, the aggregation function (optional), the time window, expressed by start and ending time.

As such, the Monitoring and Querying services are the agent's actuators within the platform. Considering the above-discussed example, and the set of validated entities, the identified intent would be *Analytical query*, and the service would be called with the following parameters:

```
{"source_id": "http://homey/resource/TMP-CYL-01-A",
 "property": "http://homey/property/temperature_engine",
 "aggregation": "avg",
 "start_time": "2026-03-04 12:00:00",
 "end_time": "2026-03-05 12:00:00"}
```

The prompting strategy enforces industrial rigor by decoupling entity extraction from intent execution. Each prompt defines a persona as an "Industrial IoT Support Specialist" to focus the model on a specific vocabulary. *Contextual grounding* uses authoritative data blocks and strict instructions to ensure alignment with physical reality. Finally, *Chain-of-Thought (CoT)* reasoning and *few-shot* examples guide the model through logical task decomposition and in-context learning, improving the interpretation of varied user requests. For what concerns the Entity recognition prompt, a *self-reflection* protocol is employed, requiring an internal review cycle to verify that extracted entities are permitted subsets of system resources before generating JSON output. On the other hand, the prompt for the Intent identification and execution is inspired by the *ReAct* paradigm, forcing the agent to analyze observations and verbalize reasoning through Thought-Action steps before executing tool calls. This process is vital to handle complex parameterization, such as translating relative time expressions (e.g., "since morning") into formal timestamps or reasoning on aggregation types, and significantly improves accuracy while reducing hallucinations [10].

4 Evaluation

To evaluate the proposed framework, a synthetic dataset was developed with four balanced intents: *informational*, *real-time monitoring*, *analytical querying*, and *out-of-scope*, each including 10 natural language requests[3]. The latter includes non-industrial and unsupported functional requests to test the agent's architectural boundaries and rejection capabilities. Testing involved three LLMs to assess the impact of scale and architecture: *Llama-3.1-8B-instant*, *Llama-3.3-70B-versatile*, and *Gemini-2.5-Flash-Lite*. The Llama models were selected for their balance of speed and privacy via on-premises deployment, while Gemini was chosen for cost-efficient, low-latency industrial performance through Google Cloud. For the evaluation, Llama models were deployed on Groq[4]. All models utilized a temperature of 0 to ensure factual consistency. The evaluation focuses on (1) end-to-end effectiveness, (2) response quality, and (3) entity recognition.

To assess (1) *end-to-end effectiveness*, we benchmarked the LLMs using a consistent environment of 5 accessible resources representing a typical mechanical assembly station. In Fig. 2, results show a strong correlation between parameter count and performance. Specifically, below a certain threshold, models struggle to adhere to structural instructions. Llama 3.1 achieved only 60% accuracy overall, with errors stemming from hallucinations (14 cases) or generation failures (2 cases). Conversely, larger models demonstrated superior reliability, with Gemini achieving the highest overall accuracy. A user study was conducted to evaluate (2) *response quality* for both informational and out-of-scope requests. Evaluators assigned scores from 0 to 5, assessing each response for understandability and coherence. The results indicate that Llama 3.3 achieved average scores of

[3] https://github.com/Homey-Prin22/agentic_data_access.

[4] https://groq.com/.

4.6 and 4.7 for informational and out-of-scope types, respectively. These results demonstrate a marginal improvement over Gemini 2.5 Flash-Lite, which received average scores of 4.6 and 4.5.

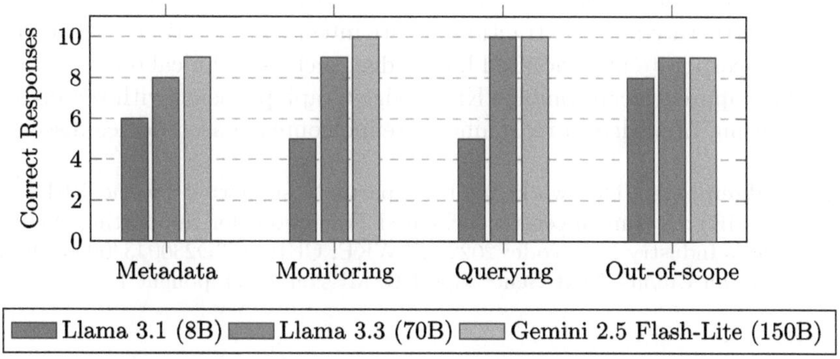

Fig. 2. End-to-end validation (40 requests).

Regarding *entity recognition* capabilities, we tested the two top performing models across scenarios with 5, 25, and 50 accessible devices. As shown in Table 1, Gemini 2.5 Flash-Lite remains remarkably robust, maintaining a consistent precision of 0.95 and near-optimal recall regardless of scale. Conversely, Llama 3.3 exhibited performance degradation as device count increased, with its F1 score dropping from 0.92 to 0.83, primarily due to precision errors in out-of-scope requests. Following standard conventions, precision and recall were set to 1 when the model correctly identified that no entities should be returned.

Table 1. Entity Recognition performance metrics (Precision, Recall, F1 score) across varying scales of accessible devices (5, 25, and 50).

	5 devices			25 devices			50 devices		
Model	P	R	F1	P	R	F1	P	R	F1
Llama 3.3	0.92	0.97	0.92	0.86	0.93	0.83	0.86	0.92	0.83
Gemini 2.5 Flash-Lite	0.95	1.00	0.95	0.95	1.00	0.95	0.95	0.99	0.95

5 Conclusion

The proposed architecture provides a secure, context-aware bridge between natural language and industrial data services by decoupling entity extraction from intent execution, ensuring only authorized, valid resources are accessed.

Future work will focus on two strategic horizons: standardization and knowledge fusion. Adopting the Model Context Protocol (MCP) represents an evolution towards a uniform communication among services: this would transform Monitoring and Querying into standardized MPC servers, enabling plug-and-play interoperability with further agents. Additionally, while the current system is focused on structured data extraction, we are integrating solutions such as RAG-IoE [1] to incorporate unstructured knowledge, such as technical documentation. This hybrid approach can combine Knowledge Graph precision with vector-based retrieval, using LLM-driven reasoning to refine context-based device discovery.

Acknowledgements. This work has been partially supported by the PRIN 2022 project "HOMEY: a Human-centric IoE-based Framework for Supporting the Transition Towards Industry 5.0" (code: 2022NX7WKE, CUP: F53D23004340006), funded by the European Union - Next Generation EU, Mission 4 Component 1.

References

1. Arazzi, M., Marconi Sciarroni, M., Nocera, A., Storti, E.: RAG-IoE: IoT context-aware information retrieval with large language models in industry 5.0. ACM Trans. Internet Things **6**(4), 1–31 (2025)
2. Arazzi, M., Nocera, A., Storti, E.: The SemioE ontology: a semantic model solution for an IoE-based industry. IEEE Internet Things J. **11**(24), 40376–40387 (2024)
3. Bahr, L., Wehner, C., Wewerka, J., Bittencourt, J., Schmid, U., Daub, R.: Knowledge graph enhanced retrieval-augmented generation for failure mode and effects analysis. J. Ind. Inf. Integr. **45**, 100807 (2025)
4. Han, H., et al.: Retrieval-augmented generation with graphs (GraphRAG). arXiv preprint arXiv:2501.00309 (2024)
5. Hussien, M.M., Melo, A.N., Ballardini, A.L., Maldonado, C.S., Izquierdo, R., Sotelo, M.Á.: Rag-based explainable prediction of road users behaviors for automated driving using knowledge graphs and large language models. Expert Syst. Appl. **265**, 125914 (2025)
6. Kumara, I., Kaplan, H., Owotogbe, J., Tamburri, D.A., van den Heuvel, W.J.: Large language models for service-oriented computing (LLM4SOC): review and research directions. In: Symposium and Summer School on Service-Oriented Computing, pp. 90–113. Springer (2025)
7. Sciarroni, M.M., Esposito, M., Pierleoni, P., Storti, E.: Monitoring data streams in industry 5.0: a knowledge graph approach. In: 2024 IEEE 8th Forum on Research and Technologies for Society and Industry Innovation (RTSI), pp. 566–571. IEEE (2024)
8. Shen, Y., Song, K., Tan, X., Li, D., Lu, W., Zhuang, Y.: HuggingGPT: solving AI tasks with ChatGPT and its friends in hugging face. In: Advances in Neural Information Processing Systems, vol. 36, pp. 38154–38180 (2023)
9. Wu, Q., et al.: AutoGen: enabling next-gen LLM applications via multi-agent conversations. In: First Conference on Language Modeling (2024)
10. Yao, S., et al.: ReAct: synergizing reasoning and acting in language models. In: The Eleventh International Conference on Learning Representations (2022)

BC4ISE

A Decentralized Architecture Integrating Non-Fungible Token (NFT) Based Digital Assets and DAO Governance for Real-World Information Systems

Asif Saeed[1,2(✉)], Marco Cipriani[1,2], and Massimiliano Nibid[1,2]

[1] Department of Information Engineering, Computer Science and Mathematics (DISIM), Università degli Studi dell'Aquila, L'Aquila, Italy
{c.priani,massimiliano}@bccstudio.biz
[2] BCC Studio S.r.l., 67100 L'Aquila, AQ, Italy
asif.saeed@graduate.univaq.it

Abstract. Blockchain technologies enable decentralized ownership, transparent governance, and secure management of digital assets. Within this ecosystem, Non-Fungible Tokens (NFTs) represent unique digital assets, while Decentralized Autonomous Organizations (DAOs) enable programmable governance. However, integrating these technologies into real-world information systems remains a challenge due to the lack of unified architectural frameworks. This paper proposes a layered architecture that integrates NFT-based asset management with DAO governance in enterprise-scale systems. The framework consists of five layers: user interaction, application services, governance, blockchain asset management, and distributed storage. This design enables seamless interaction between decentralized components and traditional infrastructures. The feasibility of the architecture is demonstrated through a digital credential management scenario, where certificates are issued as NFTs and governed through DAO-based mechanisms. The proposed framework enhances transparency, trust, and interoperability, while supporting scalable and practical deployment of decentralized technologies.

Keywords: Blockchain · Non-Fungible Tokens · Decentralized Autonomous Organizations · Digital Assets · Web3 Architecture · Decentralized Systems

1 Introduction

Blockchain technology enables the creation of transparent and decentralized digital infrastructures. Over the last decade, such systems have evolved from simple cryptocurrency platforms into entire ecosystems. They now include hosting applications that are decentralized, digital ownership and programmable governance models. This evolution is consistent with a larger vision of Web3 in which

R. Posenato and I. Vanderfeesten (Eds.): CAiSE 2026 Workshops, LNBIP 586, pp. 197–208, 2026.
https://doi.org/10.1007/978-3-032-28160-9_18

end users can own and have greater control over digital assets directly without central intermediaries [7,12,22,26]. In this ever-changing landscape, Non-Fungible Tokens (NFTs) are a key mechanism for representing unique items of digital nature on blockchain networks. Unlike fungible cryptocurrencies, NFTs model different objects, which may be an art, collectible, intellectual property or virtual goods, thus each token is one of a kind [7,16,20].

NFTs offer an attractive concept of controlling digital asset ownership and commercializing creative works due to their cryptographic backgrounds offering verifiable ownership, and provenance, which can be easily followed [1,4,15]. Recent research also shows that NFTs aid in new digital markets as well as increasing the trust in online ownership systems [10,11,18].

DAO has become one of the most significant changes in the way digital communities are governed. Decentralizing responsibility through blockchain-based voting and smart contracts will distribute decision-making strength throughout the stakeholders so that a single point of control that traditional governance depends on is eliminated [2,3,9]. The current model has already become successful in the world of decentralized finance, internet communities, and Web3 charts, providing a transparent and invariable structure on how online assets and resources can be managed [14,19,23].

In spite of the increased popularity of NFTs and DAOs, the scope of their implementation into the information systems of the real world is hardly attained. Current deployments are mostly focused on blockchain smart contracts or token transfers without much consideration of the more comprehensive architecture functionalities that are required to make a deployment viable. In the real world, systems consist of various layers such as user interfaces, back-end services, authentication system, and external storage systems and unless these components are considered, the decentralized technologies do not interact smoothly with the traditional software systems [8,24,25].

Recent studies in the area of the research on digital assets have shed some light on a conglomeration of architectural dilemmas facing modern NFT ecosystems a set of predicaments related to the dependability of data storage, the extensiveness of heterogeneous system integration and the capacity constraints of decentralized systems. Such empirical findings highlight the fact that there is an immediate need to work out systems-level architectural frameworks that may serve as a point of convergence between blockchain-based innovation and traditional information-systems paradigms [6,20,28]. They are, in fact, the problem of controlling the management of digital assets with the decentralized control in a single, unified architecture one of the most important focuses of interest. The need to do so is not an academic experiment only, but it can directly affect the practical feasibility of new DAOs, and their compatibility with pre-existing environment of applications [8,21,25].

Despite the rapid development of NFTs and DAO governance, their integration into real-world information systems remains limited. Existing solutions are often fragmented, focusing either on asset tokenization or governance mechanisms independently. However, practical systems require a unified architecture that combines ownership, governance, application logic, and storage. Without such integration, organizations face challenges in deploying decentralized technologies at scale, ensuring interoperability, and maintaining usability. This gap highlights the need for a structured architectural framework that bridges blockchain-based components with conventional information systems.

This paper proposes a conceptual architecture that integrate NFT-based digital assets and DAO governance within traditional application ecosystems. The architecture expresses a hierarchical model in which asset management runs on blockchain, user interfaces, application services, governance and hybrid storage is linked. It provides a structured and practical perspective, how decentralized technologies can be integrated into the preexisting software infrastructures to allow practical implementation.

2 Background and Related Work

The sphere of blockchain-based digital asset management has recently been receiving an increasingly academic interest, which can be explained mainly by the rapid adoption of the decentralized web technologies. The use of non-fungible tokens has become a central tool in the definition of a discrete digital asset in blockchain economies because of their uncontaminated provenance history and ontologically programmable metadata, which support the verification and transfer of assets without involving intermediary actors. Past empirical studies suggest that non-fungible tokens have the ability to rebrand the commercial spaces of digital artwork, intellectual property, and systems of digital identities [1,4,15,18].

NFT ecosystems still face several technical hurdles. High transaction fees, reliance on off-chain storage, and the challenge of proving long-term availability of digital assets are among them [5,27]. Researchers have explored decentralized storage solutions like IPFS and distributed content networks, aiming to separate asset storage from blockchain transaction records. Other studies emphasize the need to safeguard the uniqueness, authenticity, and persistence of digital assets in decentralized settings [4,10,15].

The other crucial attribute of the decentralized web is the decentralized autonomous organization (DAO) governance. DAO models enable communities to implement determinations through smart contracts and delegated ballots to enable collective organizations to control rules, propositions and treasuries resources without having a governing body [3,14,19]. Such governance can be supported by platforms like Aragon, DAO stack, Colony, Snapshot and Gnosis Safe. Empirical evidence shows that the structure of an architectural design of a DAO plays a huge role in how the architecture is viewed as legitimate, how many participate, how well it can be coordinated, and the accountability procedures [2,21,23].

While these technologies are studied separately, few works have examined how NFTs and DAO governance can be blended into larger software systems. Existing research typically focuses on token design or governance mechanisms, but rarely addresses the system-level integration of these components with application services [8,24,25]. This paper fills that gap by proposing an architecture that unifies NFTs, DAO governance frameworks, backend services, and hybrid storage infrastructures.

In addition to academic studies, several practical DAO platforms provide insights into real-world governance implementations. Aragon offers modular DAO creation with on-chain governance mechanisms, while Snapshot enables off-chain voting to reduce transaction costs. Colony focuses on reputation-based coordination, and Gnosis Safe provides secure multi-signature treasury management. Despite their capabilities, these platforms primarily address governance in isolation and do not provide integrated architectural solutions that combine governance with NFT-based asset management and backend system interoperability. This gap motivates the need for a unified system-level architecture as proposed in this work.

3 Problem Statement and Research Motivation

This paper addresses the gap between blockchain-centric solutions and the practical needs of real-world applications. While Decentralized Autonomous Organizations (DAOs) and Non-Fungible Tokens (NFTs) promise digital ownership, governance, and transparency, most existing work focuses narrowly on on-chain smart contracts, leaving out essential backend services, application interfaces, and reliable storage. Consequently, developers struggle to integrate blockchain components with traditional software, manage NFT metadata and ownership records, and employ DAO tools within existing architectures. We propose a simple, flexible architecture that unifies DAO governance, NFT infrastructure, and backend services, thereby enabling seamless deployment of blockchain technologies in practical, real-world systems.

4 Proposed Framework and Architecture

The proposed architecture follows a layered system design that integrates decentralized governance and NFT-based assets into real-world applications. Instead of treating application, protocol, governance, and storage independently, it follows a system-based perspective of blockchain [20,24,25].

The architecture is designed based on five main layers, ensuring consistency between the conceptual model and the system diagram.

These layers correspond to the conceptual grouping shown in Fig. 1, where Access represents user interaction, Orchestration corresponds to application and backend services, Governance/Assets represents DAO and NFT layers, and Persistence includes blockchain and storage components.

As shown in Fig. 1, the proposed system is organized into multiple layers that enable interaction between users, applications, governance mechanisms, and blockchain infrastructure.

4.1 Users and Organizations

This layer represents the users of the system, including the administrators, community, organizations, and normal users. The digital wallet is a point of interaction between them and the blockchain, managing cryptographic keys and identities. The identity model described further is based on wallet-mediated identity

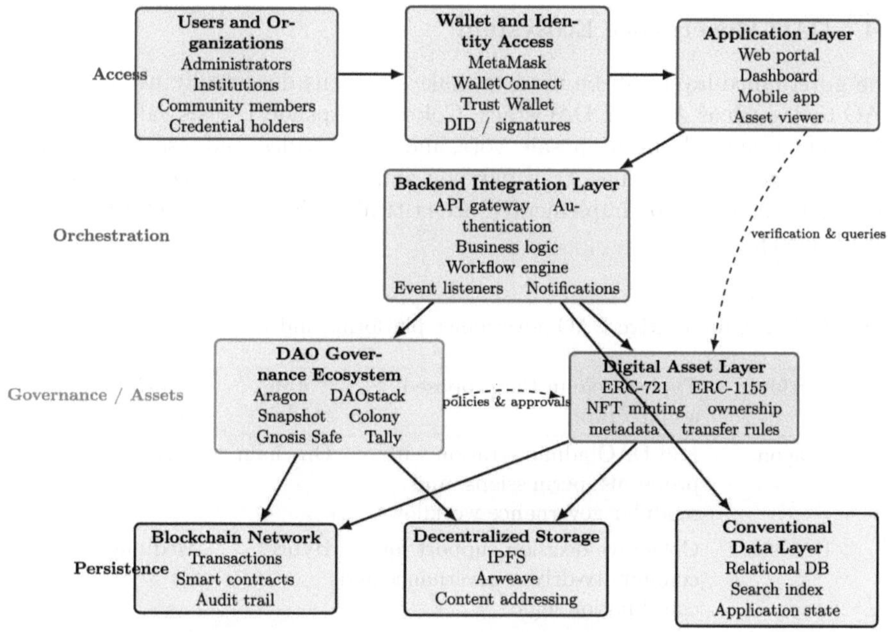

Fig. 1. Layered system architecture integrating users, wallets, application services, DAO governance components, NFT asset management, and hybrid storage infrastructures.

described in previous studies addressing decentralized identity and user-sovereign access in blockchain systems more broadly [13,16,29].

4.2 Application Layer

The uppermost portion of the system is the application layer. It provides web sites, mobile applications, dashboards and tools to manage digital assets for users. Using them, users will be able to view NFTs, verify their credentials or participate in governance. The significance of this layer is that it converts blockchain operations into easy-to-use services by individuals who are not technical [21,24,25].

4.3 Backend Integration Layer

The backend layer serves as the interface linking traditional software systems and blockchain networks. It offers APIs, authentication, and business rules as well as data-processing operations such that Web2 applications will communicate with Web3 technology not requiring users to see intricate blockchains at work. Investigations into decentralized apps reveal that they require the middleware and orchestration components in order to implement them [6,8,25].

4.4 DAO Governance Ecosystem

The governance layer can be used to make decisions decentrally using external DAO tools such as Aragon, DAOstack, Colony, Snapshot, Gnosis Safe, and Tally. These allow you to build proposals, vote, and impose rules, and research indicates that clear governance rules, transparency and, of course having clear methods that decisions are to be implemented are critical in the design of DAO [2,14,19, 23] (Table 1).

Table 1. Representative DAO governance platforms and their architectural roles

Platform	Typical role in the proposed architecture	Voting model	Integration fit
Aragon	Full DAO administration with proposals, permissions, and modular governance workflows	On-chain	High
DAOstack	Collective decision support for community-driven governance and coordination logic	Hybrid	Medium
Colony	Reputation-oriented coordination for distributed teams and task-centric operations	On-chain	Medium
Snapshot	Lightweight proposal management with gas-efficient off-chain voting	Off-chain	High
Gnosis Safe	Multi-signature treasury control and secure execution of approved actions	On-chain	High
Tally	Governance dashboards and proposal visibility for token-based organizations	Hybrid	Medium

4.5 NFT Digital Asset Layer

This layer processes the existence of digital property in the form of NFTs. It relies on new standards, including ERC -721 and ERC -1155 to demonstrate how these tokens are created, transferred, and kept on blockchain networks [1,4,18]. Also possible is fungible tokens, which can be exchanged interchangeably with other currencies or tokens of governance, whereas NFTs are unique items, and usually one-of-a-kind: certificates, identities, or digital works of art. The difference has been mentioned as one of the most important in the literature about the token economy and the research about digital ownership over blockchains [11,15,17].

Figure 2 illustrates the lifecycle of NFT-based assets within the proposed framework.

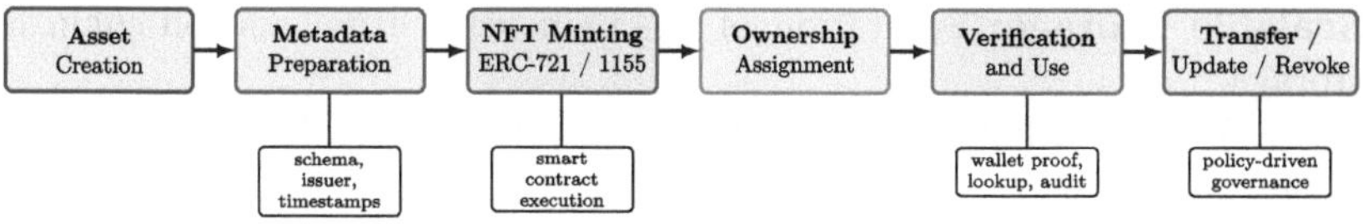

Fig. 2. Lifecycle of NFT-based digital assets in the proposed framework, showing how assets move from creation to governance-aware transfer, update, or revocation.

4.6 Hybrid Storage Infrastructure

The storage layer implies the following methods: blockchain records store the records of the transactions; decentralized networks like IPFS or Arweave store larger files; ordinary databases store the data in the app. This combination allows the system to scale, remain safe, and handle information and the distinction between on-chain verification and off-chain or decentralized storage has been a prevalent discussion in the research of blockchain [5,8,27,28].

5 Methodology

This section describes the systematic design approach used to develop the proposed NFT–DAO integrated architecture. Instead of presenting only a use-case description, the methodology is grounded in requirement analysis, literature synthesis, and architecture design principles.

5.1 Design Approach

The architecture is developed following a system-oriented design methodology, where decentralized components (blockchain, NFTs, DAO governance) are integrated with traditional information system layers. The goal is to ensure interoperability, scalability, and practical deployability.

The methodology is derived through a structured synthesis of existing literature, system requirements, and architectural design principles.

5.2 Requirement Identification

Based on existing literature and real-world system constraints, the following key requirements were identified:

- **Decentralized Ownership:** Ability to represent unique digital assets without reliance on central authorities.
- **Transparent Governance:** Support for distributed decision-making through DAO mechanisms.
- **System Integration:** Compatibility with existing backend services and application infrastructures.

- **Scalable Storage:** Separation of on-chain verification and off-chain data storage.
- **User Accessibility:** Simplified interaction through applications and digital wallets.

5.3 Architecture Design Process

The architecture was derived by mapping these requirements into functional layers. Each layer addresses a specific concern:

- User Interaction Layer enables access through applications and wallets
- Application and Service Layer manages business logic and workflows
- Governance Layer implements DAO-based decision-making
- Blockchain Asset Management Layer handles NFT creation and ownership
- Distributed Storage Layer ensures scalable and persistent data management

5.4 Justification of Layered Architecture

The five-layer architecture is justified by aligning system requirements with technological capabilities. Blockchain alone cannot handle user interfaces, storage, and orchestration; therefore, additional layers are necessary. The inclusion of a governance layer enables programmable decision-making, while hybrid storage resolves scalability limitations of blockchain systems.

5.5 Case Study Mapping

To validate the architecture, a digital credential management scenario is mapped onto the proposed framework. In this case:

- Credentials are represented as NFTs
- DAO governance manages issuance and revocation
- Blockchain ensures integrity and traceability
- IPFS stores credential metadata
- Applications enable user interaction and verification

Figure 3 illustrates the complete credential lifecycle, including proposal submission, DAO-based validation, smart contract execution, NFT minting, decentralized storage, wallet delivery, verification, and optional governance-driven updates.

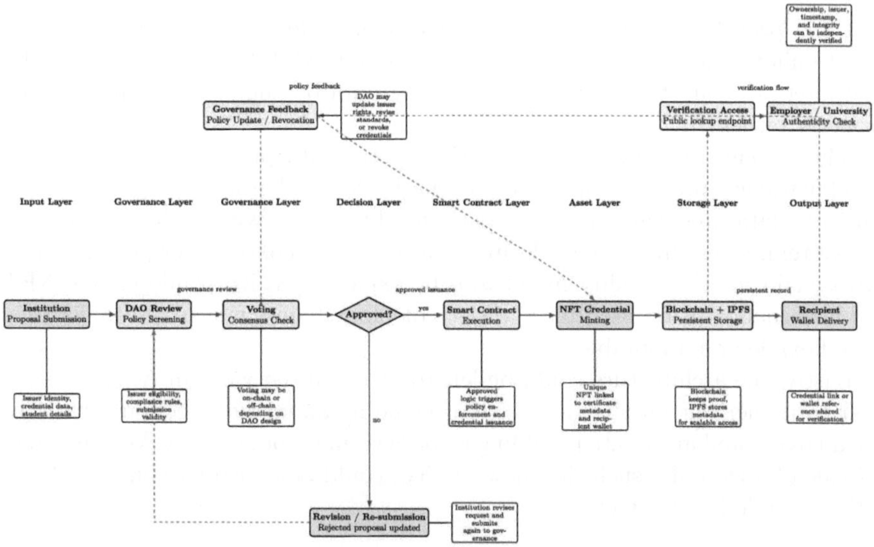

Fig. 3. Workflow for DAO-based academic credential management using blockchain and NFT technologies.

6 Discussion

The suggested architecture illustrates the way the decentralized technologies can be integrated into bigger information systems. It makes it more transparent and accountable by relating NFTs to the work of democratic autonomy organizations (DAO) [3,14,19]. It also emphasizes the relevance of backend integration layers to interface blockchain components with normal application services of an application without a layer, several blockchain applications cannot be usable in the real world [6,24,25].

The significance of digital wallets is that people can utilise blockchain networks as they allow them to identify themselves. We provide various and numerous wallet services thus making them easier to use by people. This is in line with studies that indicate that individuals appreciate the idea of decentralized identity, privacy, and control [13,16,29].

Although the proposed framework is promising, its practical implementation in the real world has to be planned in regard to the extent that it can scale, the cost of transactions, and security [8,10,28].

7 Future Work

The next steps in research will be creating the prototype platform that is planned to be built according to the suggested architecture in order to experiment with its functionality, usability, and performance. There are several main elements that the prototype will put in place, which include the use of a blockchain-based building dossier, representation of assets in NFT to create a system that guarantees the effective handling of building data by engineers, authorities and property owners.

The second direction is greater privacy and data protection. For example, zero-knowledge proofs allow users to check the credentials without exposing sensitive data, and this might be particularly helpful within the digital identity system, where individuals desire to have greater control over personal data. Cross-chain interoperability might also be explored, which would enable NFTs and governance to be used on a variety of blockchains, which will make them more flexible and adoptable.

Lastly, the architecture could be left to be enhanced with an AI-as-a-service layer to implement intelligent analysis, including anomaly detection, predictive risk analysis, and automated building records verification, and the AI layer would be scaled horizontally such that new services could be added without interfering with the underlying system.

8 Conclusion

This workshop paper presented a conceptual architecture for integrating NFT-based digital assets and DAO governance mechanisms into real-world information systems. The proposed framework emphasizes the importance of combining decentralized blockchain technologies with traditional backend services and application infrastructures.

By organizing system components into layered structures, the architecture provides a clear perspective on how NFTs, DAO governance frameworks, wallets, and storage systems can interact within a unified platform. The digital credential use case demonstrates how this architecture can support practical applications requiring trust, transparency, and verifiable ownership.

The proposed model aims to contribute to the ongoing discussion on how decentralized technologies can evolve from experimental prototypes into fully operational systems capable of supporting real-world digital ecosystems.

Acknowledgments. This work was carried out within the PNRR Doctoral Programme at the University of L'Aquila and is supported by the Italian Ministry of University and Research (MUR). The research is part of a project focused on data management for DAOs using artificial intelligence methods.

The authors would like to thank BCC Studio S.r.l. and its team for their collaboration and support during the research activities conducted at the company. Their practical insights into blockchain-based business networks and decentralized governance contributed to shaping the ideas presented in this work and highlight the impact of the PNRR programme in strengthening collaboration between academia and industry.

References

1. Ali, O., Momin, F., et al.: NFTS and the future of digital ownership: a review of technical, economic, and legal dimensions. IEEE Access **11**, 11245–11258 (2023)
2. Amhaz, R., Frey, S., et al.: Dao governance models and their applications: a systematic review. Blockchain Res. Appl. **5**(1), 100152 (2024)
3. Atzori, M.: Blockchain technology and decentralized governance: is the state still necessary? J. Gov. Regul. **6**(1), 45–62 (2017)
4. Bamakan, S.M.H., Nezhadsistani, N., Bodaghi, O., Qu, Q.: Patents and intellectual property assets as non-fungible tokens; key technologies and challenges. Sci. Rep. **12**(1), 2178 (2022)
5. Benet, J.: IPFS: content addressed, versioned, P2P file system (2014). arXiv preprint arXiv:1407.3561
6. Benisi, N., Aminian, M., Javadi, B.: Blockchain-based decentralized storage networks: a survey. J. Netw. Comput. Appl. **162**, 102656 (2020)
7. Buterin, V.: A next-generation smart contract and decentralized application platform (2014). Ethereum White Paper
8. Casino, F., Dasaklis, T.K., Patsakis, C.: A systematic literature review of blockchain-based applications: current status, classification and open issues. Telematics Inform. **36**, 55–81 (2019)
9. Christidis, K., Devetsikiotis, M.: Blockchains and smart contracts for the internet of things. IEEE Access **4**, 2292–2303 (2016)
10. Dowling, M.: Is non-fungible token pricing driven by cryptocurrencies? Financ. Res. Lett. **44**, 102097 (2022)
11. Liu, Y.: NFT market dynamics and digital ownership. Electron. Commer. Res. Appl. **46**, 101040 (2021)
12. Narayanan, A., Bonneau, J., Felten, E., Miller, A., Goldfeder, S.: Bitcoin and Cryptocurrency Technologies. Princeton University Press (2016)
13. Park, S., Park, S.: Decentralized identity systems and verifiable credentials: a review. IEEE Access **9**, 112334–112349 (2021)
14. Pérez, D., Livshits, B.: Decentralized autonomous organizations: a survey. arXiv preprint arXiv:2103.10098 (2021)
15. Regner, F., Schweizer, A., Urbach, N.: NFTs in practice – non-fungible tokens as core component of a blockchain-based event ticketing application. In: Proceedings of the 40th International Conference on Information Systems Workshop (2019)
16. Sun, J., Yan, J., Zhang, K.Z.K.: Web3: the future of the internet. IEEE Internet Comput. **26**(2), 6–11 (2022)
17. Voshmgir, S.: Token Economy: How the Web3 Reinvents the Internet. Token Kitchen (2020)
18. Wang, Q., Li, R., Wang, Q., Chen, S.: Non-fungible token (NFT): overview, evaluation, opportunities and challenges. arXiv preprint arXiv:2105.07447 (2021)
19. Wang, S., Ding, W., Li, J.: Decentralized autonomous organizations: concept, model, and applications. IEEE Access **10**, 117049–117062 (2022)
20. Wang, Y., Su, Z., Zhang, N., et al.: Web3 architecture and decentralized infrastructure: a survey. IEEE Internet Comput. **27**(3), 16–24 (2023)
21. Werbach, K.: The Blockchain and the New Architecture of Trust. MIT Press (2018)
22. Wood, G.: Ethereum: A secure decentralised generalised transaction ledger (2014). Ethereum Yellow Paper
23. Xu, J., Zhao, Y.: Governance of blockchain communities: decentralization, coordination, and institutional design. IEEE Trans. Eng. Manage. **69**(6), 3452–3464 (2022)

24. Xu, X., Weber, I., Staples, M.: Architecture design for blockchain-based systems. IEEE Softw. **37**(1), 46–61 (2020)
25. Xu, X., Weber, I., Staples, M., et al.: A taxonomy of blockchain-based systems for architecture design. IEEE Softw. **38**(1), 12–19 (2021)
26. Yaga, D., Mell, P., Roby, N., Scarfone, K.: Blockchain technology overview. Technical report, National Institute of Standards and Technology (2019)
27. Zhang, Q., Li, Y.: Research on distributed storage architecture based on IPFs. Future Internet **12**(7), 117 (2020)
28. Zheng, Z., Xie, S., Dai, H.N., Chen, X., Wang, H.: Blockchain challenges and opportunities: a survey. Int. J. Web Grid Serv. **14**(4), 352–375 (2018)
29. Zyskind, G., Nathan, O., Pentland, A.: Decentralizing privacy: Using blockchain to protect personal data. In: 2015 IEEE Security and Privacy Workshops, pp. 180–184 (2015)

Self-sovereign Identity Blockchain-Based Architecture for Personal Data Exchange

Silvio Langer(✉) and Fabiano Hessel

School of Technology, Pontifical Catholic University of Rio Grande do Sul (PUCRS), Porto Alegre, RS, Brazil
{silvio.langer,fabiano.hessel}@pucrs.br

Abstract. Personal data exchange systems currently depend on centralized intermediaries, creating systemic vulnerabilities and undermining data sovereignty. While Decentralized Identifiers (DIDs) have achieved adoption for identity resolution, no existing architecture uses DID Documents as governance layers for data exchange. This paper proposes a Self-Sovereign Identity (SSI) architecture leveraging W3C DIDs and Verifiable Credentials, positioning the DID Document as the primary governance artifact. The architecture employs three principles: DIDs as stable coordination anchors, consent as explicit on-chain agreement states managed through smart contracts, and governance commitments anchored on-chain with data artifacts maintained off-chain under identity control. DID Document service endpoints encode dataset availability, binding consent state transitions to identity changes for cryptographic non-repudiation of authorization events. This standards-compliant architecture provides a scalable foundation for sovereign, auditable personal data exchange.

Keywords: Blockchain · Self-Sovereign Identity · Decentralized Identifiers · Verifiable Credentials · Data Governance · IPFS

1 Introduction

The proliferation of digital services and data-driven applications has intensified concerns about user privacy, data sovereignty, and centralized control over personal information [4,15]. Traditional identity management systems, characterized by centralized authorities and federated trust models, have demonstrated significant vulnerabilities including single points of failure, data breaches, unauthorized access, and limited user control over personal data [11,13]. The increasing digitisation of personal data has exposed a fundamental architectural inadequacy in existing data sharing systems: centralized intermediaries remain the dominant mechanism through which personal data is published, accessed, and governed, undermining the foundational principles of data sovereignty and regulatory compliance [4,10,11,13]. These limitations have catalyzed the development of Self-Sovereign Identity (SSI) paradigms, which fundamentally shift control from centralized entities to individual users [5,11].

R. Posenato and I. Vanderfeesten (Eds.): CAiSE 2026 Workshops, LNBIP 586, pp. 209–221, 2026.
https://doi.org/10.1007/978-3-032-28160-9_19

The significance of this research is grounded in regulatory mandate and practical urgency. GDPR demands data confidentiality protection and allows owners to restrict and track data operations [9], while emphasizing transparency and privacy by design, principles SSI addresses through selective credential sharing [11]. The W3C standardization of DIDs and Verifiable Credentials has established decentralized identity as a recognized research direction [10]. Traditional centralized sharing depends on third parties, incurring risks of tampering, privacy leakage, and loss of user control [9], with users unable to control, revoke, or delete submitted identity data [11]. In the rapidly evolving data economy, the ability of stakeholders: individuals, organizations, and public institutions, to securely share data has become paramount [4]. Equally important is the assurance for data consumers that the information originates from trusted data owners [4,9].

This paper addresses the architectural challenge of developing an identity-centric coordination model that enables decentralized, user-centric personal data exchange while managing data ownership, data control, and dataset updates without relying on centralized mechanisms. The architecture is designed to remain scalable and privacy-preserving without introducing centralized dependencies. Building on these foundations, this work presents a decentralized personal data exchange architecture that embodies SSI principles by leveraging Decentralized Identifiers (DIDs) and Verifiable Credentials (VCs) as the primary identity and authorization layer.

The remainder of this paper is structured as follows: Sect. 2 defines the problem, identifies the gap in the literature, and states the guiding research questions. Section 3 presents the proposed architecture. Section 4 reports the results and discussion. Section 5 reviews related work. Section 6 concludes and identifies directions for future research.

2 Problem Statement

The literature reports advances in decentralized data sharing across four areas: blockchain-based access control [1,9,14], self-sovereign identity frameworks [5,11,13], decentralized storage [6,12], and data space governance [4,8]. DIDs and DID Documents have been consistently adopted as mechanisms for identity resolution and credential verification [4,10,11]. However, their role has remained strictly limited to answering the question of *who* a participant is, not *what* data they govern, *under what conditions* it may be accessed, or *how* their identity state evolves in response to exchange events.

This represents a precise and consequential gap. Existing approaches either address identity in isolation [11,13], focus narrowly on storage mechanisms [6,12], or propose access control schemes without grounding them in W3C identity standards [9,14]. Data owners do not retain direct control over their data and data access is regulated through intermediaries [4]. The result is a fragmented landscape in which no architecture simultaneously satisfies the requirements of persistent decentralized identity, verifiable data provenance, and enforceable consent.

To the best of our knowledge, no prior work has proposed using DID Documents as a governance layer for personal data exchange, a structure whose service endpoints encode dataset availability, controlled updates represent identity state transitions, and evolution is explicitly anchored to on-chain consent events. This architectural role for the DID Document constitutes the primary original contribution of this work.

While the separation of raw data from metadata is a recognized pattern in decentralized systems, no existing W3C-compliant architecture has demonstrated the use of the DID Document as the cryptographic coordination artifact that makes this separation verifiable, sovereign, and consent-coherent. In existing approaches, off-chain data management either lacks cryptographically verifiable bindings between identity, consent, and data references [4, 9, 10], or relies on centralized coordination to maintain coherence across layers. The proposed architecture uses the DID Document's service endpoints to bind the identity layer to the data layer, and its controlled updates to bind the consent layer to the identity layer, ensuring non-repudiation applies precisely to authorization events rather than data content, that data minimization is enforced as a regulatory constraint at the architectural level, and that no centralized intermediary is required to maintain coherence across the exchange lifecycle.

This work is guided by three interconnected research questions:

1. *How can DID Documents serve as a governance layer for personal data exchange, enabling data owners to publish, control, and evolve dataset availability through cryptographically verifiable identity artifacts without relying on a central authority?*
2. *How can exchange metadata be separated from raw personal data while preserving cryptographic provenance, a verifiable record of data origin, ownership, and authorization that cannot be silently altered and non-repudiation, ensuring that authorization events, rather than data content, are the subject of on-chain commitments?*
3. *How can consent be modelled as a verifiable, tamper-evident state machine in which permission lifecycle transitions are explicitly linked to DID Document updates, ensuring that identity state and consent state remain cryptographically coherent?*

The architecture is deployed on Polygon blockchain for the VDR and Agreement smart contract, with Ceramic as the mutable pointer layer. The identity layer is scoped to `did:ethr`, enabling a single keypair to handle blockchain transactions, DID ownership, and VC signing coherently. The architecture targets bilateral personal data exchange between owners and consumers; multi-party dataspace governance and cross-chain interoperability are identified as directions for future research.

3 Architecture Overview

The architecture is based on three premises:

1. Decentralized identifiers function as stable coordination anchors for participants and resources;
2. Consent is represented as an explicit, on-chain agreement state between a data owner and a data consumer, with access granted and governed through smart contract state transitions rather than informal application-level permissions. In this context, **Data owners** are individuals or organizations that make data available for exchange, while **Data consumers** are those seeking access to the data;
3. Governance commitments are anchored on-chain, while data artifacts and dataset references evolve off-chain under identity control, on a hybrid on-chain/off-chain state separation.

The proposed architecture extends the role of DID Documents beyond identity resolution toward active exchange governance, satisfying data minimization as a regulatory constraint, ensuring non-repudiation of authorization events, and eliminating dependence on centralized intermediaries at every layer of the exchange process, as illustrated in Fig. 1.

3.1 Requirements

This subsection derives the architectural requirements of the proposed architecture. Each requirement is classified as either a Functional Requirement (FR), specifying a discrete capability the system must provide, or a Non-Functional Requirement (NFR), specifying a systemic quality the system must uphold continuously across all architectural layers, based on Christopher Allen's ten foundational principles of Self-Sovereign Identity [3].

Functional Requirements

FR01 - Identity Existence (SSI Principle 1): The system must derive and anchor identity exclusively from cryptographic keypairs, without delegating identity creation or registration to any third-party provider. Identity must exist as an independent artifact whose validity is grounded in key ownership, not in provider authorization.

FR02 - Owner Control (SSI Principle 2): Data owners must be able to update, revoke, and manage their DID Documents and Verifiable Credentials at all times without requiring authorization from any intermediary.

FR03 - Data Access (SSI Principle 3): Data owners must always be able to retrieve all claims, credentials, and dataset references associated with their identity, with no component acting as a gatekeeper. Access to a specific data channel must be granted by presenting a Verifiable Credential issued by the data owner to the consumer, cryptographically binding the consumer's identity to a specific data channel, consent scope, and validity window, verified against the owner's DID Document resolved from the VDR.

FR04 - Consent (SSI Principle 8): The system must require explicit, cryptographically verifiable, and revocable user authorization before any data exchange transaction is permitted. Consent must be established and enforced through a smart contract that anchors the agreement on-chain as a tamper-evident commitment.

FR05 - Minimalization (SSI Principle 9): Raw personal data must be stored exclusively in decentralized off-chain storage, with only compact cryptographic references and content identifiers anchored on-chain or exposed through identity artifacts. This architectural separation enforces data minimization as a regulatory constraint at the structural level rather than as an optional feature.

Non-functional Requirements

NFR01 - Persistence (SSI Principle 5): Identity and dataset references must remain resolvable over time, independent of any single infrastructure component's lifecycle, with identity ownership maintained through key-rotation mechanisms so that continuity is not bound to a single cryptographic key.

NFR02 - Protection (SSI Principle 10): User rights must prevail across all architectural layers. No network participant, smart contract rule, or infrastructure component may override the data owner's sovereign control over their identity and data. This property is upheld by the collective design of the keypair ownership model, the consent state machine, the VC revocation registry, and the DID Document governance layer simultaneously.

NFR03 - Transparency (SSI Principle 4): All governance rules, consent state transitions, and DID Document updates must be publicly auditable through on-chain records, with no hidden coordination layer. The blockchain serves exclusively as trust and audit infrastructure while raw data content remains exclusively off-chain.

NFR04 - Interoperability (SSI Principle 7): The system must conform to W3C DID and Verifiable Credential standards, ensuring compatibility with any compliant identity resolution infrastructure [8].

NFR05 - Portability (SSI Principle 6): Identity must be transferable across any W3C-compliant DID resolution infrastructure using open, standardized identity methods, such that DID Documents, Verifiable Credentials, and service endpoint references can be resolved and verified by any conformant implementation without proprietary dependencies.

3.2 Architectural Layers

The proposed architecture enables decentralized personal data exchange by integrating decentralized identity mechanisms, smart contracts for consent management, and content-addressed off-chain storage deployed on Polygon. As illustrated in Fig. 1, participants are identified by DIDs, which provide persistent references for identity and authorization; DID Documents function as coordination artifacts, linking participants to datasets and consent relationships. A coordination actor operating as a VDR anchors DIDs and DID Document CIDs to the blockchain, ensuring identity state transitions and dataset references are cryptographically linked to immutable records, without transferring identity ownership or consent authority to the VDR. Consent relationships are established through smart contracts, where compact commitments record authorization state transitions and agreement metadata. Datasets are structured collections of personal data managed off-chain and referenced via content-addressed identifiers; updates result in new content identifiers, maintaining traceability through identity-bound coordination structures.

Identity Layer: establishes the cryptographic foundation for all participants, as illustrated in the upper band of Fig. 1. Both data owners and consumers generate a secp256k1 keypair from which a `did:ethr` identifier is deterministically derived by encoding the corresponding Ethereum address, satisfying FR01 by grounding identity exclusively in cryptographic key ownership without delegation to any third-party provider. This keypair signs both blockchain transactions and Verifiable Credential proofs, ensuring conformance with W3C DID and VC standards (NFR04). The DID Document, encoding the participant's public key and, for data owners, the service endpoints associated with each data channel, is serialised and stored on IPFS, yielding a content-addressed CID as a stable reference. The adoption of `did:ethr` eliminates the off-chain/on-chain consistency risk inherent in static key-derived identifiers: DID Document resolution is performed dynamically by replaying on-chain events rather than relying on a manually maintained registry entry, partially addressing NFR01 and NFR05.

Blockchain Layer: provides tamper-proof trust anchoring through two smart contracts deployed on the Polygon Amoy testnet, selected for its low transaction

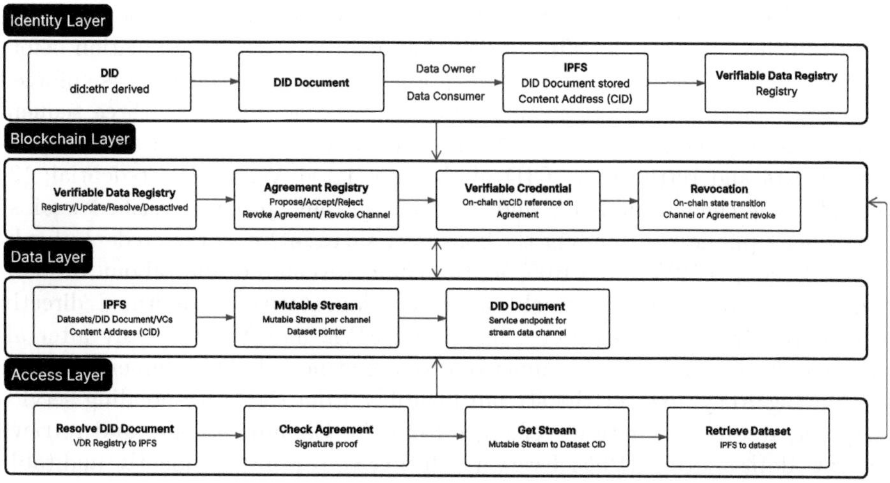

Fig. 1. High-level architecture overview for decentralized personal data exchange. The architecture is organized into Identity, Blockchain, Data, and Access layers.

cost and compatibility with the Ethereum tooling ecosystem. The `VDRRegistry` contract maintains a mapping from each participant's `did:ethr` identifier to the IPFS CID of their current DID Document, exposing functions to register, update, deactivate, and resolve DID identifiers, and emitting corresponding lifecycle events, thereby directly supporting FR01 and NFR03. The `AgreementRegistry` contract manages the full consent lifecycle between a data owner and a consumer, storing owner and consumer identifiers, a cryptographic digest of the off-chain terms document, the IPFS CID of the associated Verifiable Credential, a lifecycle status, a validity window, and a per-channel revocation mapping, implementing FR04 and FR02. Revocation is an on-chain state transition: dedicated functions move the full agreement or a specific channel to a revoked status, emitting immutable timestamped events that satisfy NFR02 and NFR03.

Data Layer: combines two complementary technologies for persistent storage of all content artifacts, as depicted in Fig. 1. IPFS serves as an immutable content store: DID Documents, raw dataset CSVs, and Verifiable Credentials are stored here and referenced by their content-addressed CIDs, enforcing FR05 by ensuring raw data content remains exclusively off-chain and supporting NFR03 by enabling independent integrity verification. IPFS data availability depends on active pinning by participating nodes; this dependency is acknowledged as a partial constraint on NFR01 and is identified as a direction for future infrastructure-resilience work in Sect. 6. The Channel/Stream component, implemented through Ceramic One, maintains mutable stream state by holding the current dataset pointer for each owner-channel pair, enabling dataset updates without modifying the service endpoint recorded in the DID Document, contributing to FR02 and partially addressing NFR01 within the constraints of the current prototype.

Access Layer: orchestrates the full data retrieval session by sequencing calls across all three layers in a defined order that enforces consent verification before granting dataset access, as illustrated in Fig. 1. Consent verification is enforced as a strict precondition before any data is accessible, following three sequential checks: (1) the `AgreementRegistry` is queried to confirm an active agreement exists and retrieve the CID of the associated Verifiable Credential; (2) the VC is fetched from IPFS and its cryptographic proof is verified against the owner's public key, binding the consumer's `did:ethr` as the credential subject, satisfying FR03 and FR05, as the chain reveals nothing about the credential's substance; (3) channel-level revocation status is confirmed directly against the `AgreementRegistry`, upholding FR02 and NFR02. Only after all three checks pass does the consumer resolve the owner's DID Document through the `VDRRegistry`, extract the stream identifier from the corresponding service endpoint, resolve the dataset reference from the Ceramic stream, and retrieve the raw dataset from IPFS. Every resolution step is independently auditable against on-chain records, satisfying NFR03.

4 Discussion

This section discusses three findings that address the architectural decisions underpinning the use of service endpoints, the stability of DID Documents, and the use of Verifiable Credentials as the primary authorization mechanism.

DID Document as Governance Layer: A DID encodes only cryptographic key material and provides no mechanism for locating associated resources. Without service endpoints, a consumer who resolves a DID obtains no actionable reference to the owner's datasets, rendering the identity anchor insufficient for data exchange. The service endpoint therefore transforms a self-sovereign identity into a complete, discoverable access point satisfying both authentication and resource resolution within a single decentralised artifact. The proposed architecture extends this role further by explicitly linking service endpoint updates to on-chain consent events, making the DID Document a living governance artifact rather than a static identity record.

DID Document Stability: Content-addressed systems such as IPFS generate unique identifiers from content hashes, ensuring integrity but creating a versioning challenge: when a publisher updates a dataset, the content hash changes, breaking all existing references. The architecture addresses this through Ceramic One, which maintains a mutable pointer to the current dataset CID for each owner channel pair, enabling updates without modifying the service endpoint recorded in the DID Document. When the DID Document itself requires updating, a new IPFS CID is generated and a corresponding re-anchoring in the `VDRRegistry` is required to preserve resolution consistency.

The use of Verifiable Credentials (VC): A DID establishes *who* a participant is but provides no mechanism for specifying *what* a consumer is authorised to access or *for how long*. Verifiable Credentials close this gap by cryptographically binding the consumer's identity to a specific data channel, consent scope, and validity window. The credential's proof is verified against the owner's public key before access is granted, ensuring authorization is grounded in the owner's current identity state, a security layer that the DID alone structurally cannot provide.

5 Related Work

The surveyed works were identified through a Scopus search targeting decentralized data sharing, self-sovereign identity, and blockchain-based access control, and selected based on direct relevance to the architectural requirements defined in Sect. 3.1. Table 1 presents a structured assessment of the twelve analyzed works against the ten requirements defined in Sect. 3.1, indicating the degree to which each work satisfies them based on evidence drawn from the authors' own contributions. Existing works address requirements individually; no surveyed work meets the complete set targeted by the proposed architecture.

Table 1. Comparison between surveyed works and derived requirements.● ● ● = Satisfied; ● ● ○ = Partially Satisfied; ● ○ ○ = Not Satisfied.

Paper	FR1	FR2	FR3	FR4	FR5	NFR1	NFR2	NFR3	NFR4	NFR5
[1]	●○○	●●○	●●○	●●○	●●●	●●○	●●○	●●○	●○○	●○○
[2]	●○○	●●○	●●○	●●○	●●○	●○○	●●○	●●○	●●○	●●○
[4]	●●○	●●●	●●○	●●○	●●●	●●○	●●○	●●●	●●●	●●○
[5]	●●○	●●○	●●○	●○○	●●●	●●○	●●●	●●○	●●●	●●●
[6]	●●○	●●○	●○○	●○○	●●○	●●○	●●○	●○○	●●○	●○○
[7]	●○○	●●○	●●○	●●○	●●○	●●○	●●○	●●○	●○○	●○○
[9]	●○○	●●○	●●○	●○○	●●○	●○○	●●○	●●○	●○○	●○○
[10]	●●○	●●○	●●●	●○○	●●○	●●○	●●○	●●○	●●●	●●○
[11]	●●○	●●○	●○○	●●○	●●●	●●○	●●○	●●○	●●●	●●○
[12]	●○○	●●○	●●○	●●○	●●○	●●○	●●○	●●○	●○○	●○○
[13]	●●○	●●○	●●○	●○○	●●○	●○○	●●○	●●○	●○○	●○○
[14]	●○○	●●○	●●○	●○○	●●○	●○○	●●○	●●○	●○○	●○○
This work	●●●	●●●	●●●	●●●	●●●	●●○	●●●	●●●	●●●	●●○

Identity Existence (FR01): The most discriminating requirement. Works without a W3C DID adoption score, as identity is registered through managed sidechains, certificate authorities, or platform accounts. DID-adopting works achieve partial satisfaction: each demonstrates DID-derived identity, but none implements the single keypair unification across blockchain transactions, DID ownership, and VC signing that FR01 requires.

Owner Control (FR02): Partially addressed across nearly all works, which provide mechanisms to grant or revoke access without a trusted intermediary. None, except [4], implements W3C-compliant DID Document service endpoint management alongside VC revocation as a unified control plane.

Data Access (FR03): VC-based access gating verified against a DID Document resolved from a VDR is rarely achieved. [10] is the only fully satisfied work; most others provide partial access control without binding consumer identity to a specific data channel, consent scope, and validity window through a W3C-compliant VC flow.

Consent (FR04): The least satisfied requirement across the corpus. Works that partially address it, [1,2,4,7,11,12], provide owner-controlled access mechanisms, but none anchor these as a verifiable state machine with cryptographically coherent state transitions explicitly linked to identity artifacts.

Minimalization (FR05): The on-chain/off-chain separation is broadly present, largely as a practical necessity of blockchain storage constraints. [1,4,5,11] achieve full satisfaction by framing it as a privacy and data minimisation design principle enforced at the architectural level. The remaining works implement the separation but frame it as a cost or performance optimisation rather than a regulatory constraint.

Persistence (NFR01): [6] offers the strongest mechanism, explicitly supporting key rotation without changing the DID. [5] and [10] imply resolvability through DID CRUD operations but describe no complete key rotation. Works relying on centralised identity registration score not satisfied, as resolvability is contingent on the managing authority rather than cryptographic key ownership.

Protection (NFR02): No surveyed work demonstrates sovereign protection of user rights enforced collectively across all architectural layers simultaneously. [5] comes closest, explicitly stating that no entity can override the owner's sovereign control, but does not describe the full multi-layer protection architecture NFR02 requires.

Transparency (NFR03): [4] achieves full satisfaction by providing an immutable audit trail for VCs, revocation lists, and data provenance, with explicit architectural separation of on-chain authorization records from off-chain raw data. Works with no blockchain layer [6] score is not satisfied; all others achieve partial satisfaction by recording on-chain interactions without explicitly separating authorization-event auditability from data content.

Interoperability (NFR04): [4,5,10,11] achieve full satisfaction through explicit W3C DID and VC conformance. [6] and [2] achieve partial satisfaction. Works relying on proprietary or platform-specific identity mechanisms score not satisfied.

Portability (NFR05): [5] is the only fully satisfied work, explicitly stating blockchain-platform-agnostic identity portability across any compliant DID resolution infrastructure. Works adopting W3C standards without explicitly discussing DID Document or VC portability achieve partial satisfaction; all others score not satisfied.

The analysis confirms that the landscape of decentralised data sharing is fragmented across orthogonal contributions: access control schemes without W3C-compliant identity standards [7,9,12,14]; SSI frameworks without verifiable consent lifecycles [5,11,13]; storage architectures without cryptographically verifiable identity bindings [6]; and data space governance approaches without complete sovereignty enforcement [1,2,4]. No surveyed work simultaneously satisfies FR01 through FR05 and NFR01 through NFR05. In particular, no existing architecture proposes the use of the DID Document as a governance layer for personal data exchange, a structure whose service endpoints encode dataset availability, controlled updates represent identity state transitions, and evolution is explicitly anchored to on-chain consent events, nor models consent as a verifiable state machine cryptographically linked to DID Document updates. These gaps define the original contribution of the proposed architecture, as detailed in Sect. 2.

6 Conclusion and Future Work

This paper proposes a Self-Sovereign Identity architecture for sovereign personal data exchange, in which the DID Document functions as the primary governance artifact, extending its role beyond identity resolution toward active exchange governance. To the best of the authors' knowledge, no prior work has proposed this architectural role for the DID Document. A working prototype demonstrates that the proposed architecture simultaneously satisfies all five functional requirements, a combination not achieved by any surveyed work, confirming the validity of the proposed approach.

Two systemic qualities are only partially addressed within the current prototype scope. Persistence (NFR01) depends on the sustained availability of the underlying blockchain, data channel, and storage layers; future work will design key-rotation and infrastructure-resilience strategies to ensure identity continuity. Portability (NFR05) has not been empirically demonstrated beyond the prototype; future work will conduct cross-platform interoperability testing to validate that identity artifacts remain resolvable by any conformant implementation.

Disclosure of Interests. The authors have no competing interests to declare that are relevant to the content of this article.

References

1. Alexandrescu, A., Bărbuţă, D.E., Buţincu, C.N.: Secure and decentralized data sharing using blockchain and cryptographic access control. In: 2025 7th International Conference on Blockchain Computing and Applications (BCCA), pp. 437–444. IEEE (2025). https://doi.org/10.1109/BCCA66705.2025.11229511

2. Chandran, L., Lundin, L., Padayatti, G.: Transforming personal data transactions with auditable, privacy-preserving data exchange agreements: fostering transparency and trust in digital wallet ecosystems. In: 2023 IEEE 28th International Conference on Emerging Technologies and Factory Automation (ETFA), pp. 1–9. IEEE (2023). https://doi.org/10.1109/ETFA54631.2023.10275546
3. Allen, C.: The path to self-sovereign identity. Life With Alacrity (blog) (2016). https://www.lifewithalacrity.com/article/the-path-to-self-soverereign-identity/. Accessed: 03-12-2026
4. Costagliola, A.R., Mazzocca, C., Bujari, A., Montanari, R., Bellavista, P.: Vespace: a verifiable blockchain-based data space solution to empower the data economy. Comput. Commun. **239**, 108180 (2025). https://doi.org/10.1016/j.comcom.2025.108180
5. Dixit, A., Zarpelao, B.B., Smith-Creasey, M., Rajarajan, M.: A privacy-aware authentication and usage-controlled access protocol for IIoT decentralized data marketplace. Comput. Secur. **146**, 104050 (2024). https://doi.org/10.1016/j.cose.2024.104050
6. Fotiou, N., Siris, V.A., Polyzos, G.C.: Enabling self-verifiable mutable content items in IPFS using decentralized identifiers. In: 2021 IFIP Networking Conference (IFIP Networking), pp. 1–6. (2021). https://doi.org/10.23919/IFIPNetworking52078.2021.9472820
7. Gazsi, J.S., Zafreen, S., Dagher, G.G., Long, M.: Vault: a scalable blockchain-based protocol for secure data access and collaboration. In: 2021 IEEE International Conference on Blockchain (Blockchain), pp. 376–381. IEEE (2021). https://doi.org/10.1109/Blockchain53845.2021.00059
8. Kernstock, P., Harms, C., Hein, A., Krcmar, H.: Establishing and governing data ecosystems at the crossroads of centralization and decentralization. Electron. Mark. **35**(1), 71 (2025). https://doi.org/10.1007/s12525-025-00810-x
9. Li, B., Yang, J., Wang, Y., Huang, X., Ren, J., Wang, L.: A blockchain-based privacy-preserving data sharing scheme with security-enhanced access control. In: 2023 26th International Conference on Computer Supported Cooperative Work in Design (CSCWD), pp. 825–830. IEEE (2023). https://doi.org/10.1109/CSCWD57460.2023.10152751
10. Lin, I.C., Yeh, I.L., Chang, C.C., Liu, J.C., Chang, C.C.: Designing a secure and scalable data sharing mechanism using decentralized identifiers (did). Comput. Model. Eng. Sci. **141**(1), 809–822 (2024). https://doi.org/10.32604/cmes.2024.051612
11. Lohar, S.N., Babar, S.D., Mahalle, P.N.: A self-sovereign identity framework for context-aware de-centralized identifier creation and credential verification. Eng. Sci. **36**, 1629 (2025)
12. Pincheira, M., Donini, E., Vecchio, M., Kanhere, S.: A decentralized architecture for trusted dataset sharing using smart contracts and distributed storage. Sensors **22**(23), 9118 (2022). https://doi.org/10.3390/s22239118
13. Thorve, A., Shirole, M., Jain, P., Santhumayor, C., Sarode, S.: Decentralized identity management using blockchain. In: 2022 4th International Conference on Advances in Computing, Communication Control and Networking (ICAC3N), pp. 1985–1991. IEEE (2022). https://doi.org/10.1109/ICAC3N56670.2022.10074477

14. Wang, S., Zhang, Y., Zhang, Y.: A blockchain-based framework for data sharing with fine-grained access control in decentralized storage systems. IEEE Access **6**, 38437–38450 (2018). https://doi.org/10.1109/ACCESS.2018.2851611
15. Zheng, Z., Xie, S., Dai, H., Chen, X., Wang, H.: An overview of blockchain technology: architecture, consensus, and future trends. In: 2017 IEEE International Congress on Big Data (BigData Congress), pp. 557–564. IEEE (2017). https://doi.org/10.1109/BigDataCongress.2017.85

Performance and Cost Trade-offs in Layer-2 Payment Channel Networks Using Real Raiden Nodes on Private Ethereum

Piotr Stolarski(✉), Szczepan Górtowski, and Elżbieta Lewańska

The Poznań University of Economics and Business, al. Niepodległości 10, 61-875 Poznań, Poland
{piotr.stolarski,szczepan.gortowski,elzbieta.lewanska}@ue.poznan.pl

Abstract. The paper investigates the performance and cost trade-offs of Layer-2 (L2) payment-channel networks for multi-vendor micromobility systems. Using a private Ethereum Layer-1, real Raiden nodes on L2, and a workload generator based on actual ride events, we evaluate how liquidity allocation, channel load, topology, and settlement strategies affect system reliability and operational expenditure. The results show that transaction success rate (TSR) improves with higher liquidity but is strongly constrained by channel congestion, while on-chain settlement cost scales with the number of channel closures and is significantly reduced by batched or lazy policies. The findings provide actionable guidance for designing economically sustainable L2 architectures for city-scale micromobility services.

Keywords: Layer-2 blockchain · Payment channel networks · Micromobility · Raiden Network · Scalability · Smart cities

1 Introduction

The Smart Cities development is closely linked to the evolution of transport systems, where micromobility plays a key role in solving the last-mile problem [12]. Traditional management systems for micromobility rely on centralized platforms. However, this creates some challenges, e.g., (i) limited transparency makes it difficult for users to verify how ride duration and pricing are calculated, which may leads to disputes; (ii) centralized control over operational data creates a risk that ride records can be modified or reinterpreted after the fact, complicating dispute resolution between users and operators; (iii) the absence of a shared and verifiable data source complicates coordination between competing operators and limits the ability of cities to perform fair audits and fleet-level regulation [8]. These limitations become more pronounced as micromobility systems scale, increasing transaction volume, operational complexity, and regulatory oversight requirements. The introduction of Distributed Ledger Technology (DLT) allows

R. Posenato and I. Vanderfeesten (Eds.): CAiSE 2026 Workshops, LNBIP 586, pp. 222–233, 2026.
https://doi.org/10.1007/978-3-032-28160-9_20

to create an immutable and secure audit trail that eliminates the need for a central authority of trust [11].

Most existing work on applying Blockchain to micromobility systems remains conceptual or focuses primarily on Layer-1 (L1) constraints and high-level architectural proposals. The implementation of these solutions on a city scale faces barriers related to the performance limitations of the main chain L1. This necessitates the adoption of off-chain scaling techniques, particularly Layer-2 (L2) solutions [3, 5], along with precise modeling of telemetry data pipelines to optimize network load and ensure efficient data processing.

Current literature generally relies on analytical abstractions or synthetic simulations, often ignoring practical limitations of real payment-channel implementations, such as liquidity fragmentation, asymmetric flows, routing instability, or the capital overhead required to sustain dependable service under heterogeneous demand. We identified a research gap: despite the relevance of L2 technologies for mobility-on-demand ecosystems, there is no systematic, empirically grounded evaluation of L2 payment-channel networks operating with real nodes and realistic micromobility workloads.

This study focuses on quantifying the operational behavior of a hybrid L1/L2 architecture under conditions representative of urban micromobility. We center our investigation around two research questions:

- RQ1 How do liquidity allocation, channel load, and network topology jointly affect the transaction success rate (TSR) in a payment-channel network (PCN) supporting high-frequency micromobility transactions?
- RQ2 How do different channel-closing and settlement strategies impact total operational cost and capital efficiency when periodic anchoring to an L1 network is required?

We aim to move beyond conceptual discussions and provide evidence-based insights into the risk-economics trade-offs inherent in L2 deployments for urban mobility. The contribution of this work lies in a combined prototype-and-simulation study leveraging a private Ethereum-based L1, a Raiden-style L2 network composed of real nodes, and a workload generator derived from real-world micromobility usage data. Specifically, the generator is parameterized using the publicly available Chicago e-scooter trip dataset[1], which captures temporal and spatial ride patterns in an urban setting. The assumptions, preprocessing steps, and event-generation methodology are described in detail in our prior work [11], which the present study builds upon.

The paper is structured as follows. Section 2 discussed related works. Architecture of the proposed system is describes in Sect. 3. In Sect. 4 we discussed the evaluation results and the paper concludes in Sect. 5.

[1] https://data.cityofchicago.org/Transportation/E-Scooter-Trips/2i5w-ykuw/about_data.

2 Background

Micromobility systems generate a stream of operational events, such as ride start, ride end, vehicle unlocking, and pricing updates. To ensure trust in a multi-vendor environment, the system must maintain an event log that records when and how each action occurred. It is needed for accountability, dispute resolution, and regulatory reporting. Micromobility platforms must also handle very high event frequency and low interaction latency.

Blockchain Constraints in Micromobility and Smart Cities.

The integration of Blockchain technology in urban ecosystems is the foundation for Mobility on Demand (MoD) services, where trust is built through cryptographic proofs rather than institutional authority [10,19]. This application goes beyond simple financial transactions, encompassing identity management, logistics, and process automation using smart contracts.

In a multi-vendor environment, where many operators use the same public space and compete for the same users, the key challenge is maintaining a consistent and reliable event log as it is a prerequisite for fair charging, transparent revenue sharing, and regulatory oversight. Traditional databases managed by single entities are prone to human error, reinterpretation of values, and intentional manipulation. DLT technology enables the creation of a shared ledger that is synchronized among all network participants ensuring near real-time transaction visibility [2,15].

Direct use of main L1 chains to handle mass microtransactions is inefficient due to the scalability trilemma [6]. It states that Blockchain systems can simultaneously achieve only two of three characteristics: decentralization, security, or scalability. Main L1 limitations include [1,5,8]:

- Low throughput. While systems like Visa process an average of 8 500 transactions per second (TPS)[2], Bitcoin handles about 5–7 TPS, and Ethereum 15–30 TPS[3]. This is insufficient for city scale.
- High Gas fees. The fee mechanism in L1 networks is based on auction-style access to limited block space. During high network load, gas fees can skyrocket, making the transaction cost higher than the service value itself (e.g., a $10 fee for a $2 scooter ride)[4].
- Latency. On-chain transaction finalization time can range from seconds to an hour, which is unacceptable for unlocking a vehicle where users expect an immediate response.

These constraints make L1 designs unsuitable for micromobility systems that generate continuous telemetry and mission-critical micro-transactions. Once ride execution is modelled as a stream of events, the challenge becomes how to economically anchor or settle these events without overwhelming the base layer.

[2] https://thebankingscene.com/opinions/visas-innovations-enhancing-travel-and-payment-experiences-worldwide.
[3] https://tokenterminal.com/explorer/metrics/transactions-per-second.
[4] https://etherscan.io/gastracker#chart_gasprice.

Layer-2 Scaling Through Payment Channels.

L2 solutions aim to increase throughput and lower costs by moving most transactions off-chain while maintaining L1 security guarantees [3]. In micromobility, where interactions are frequent and involve small amounts, state and payment channels are the most promising technology.

A Raiden-style Layer-2 network is a payment channel network on Ethereum that enables off-chain value exchange through bilateral channels with upfront locked funds and signed balance updates. Frequent, low-value micromobility events are settled off-chain, while only aggregated results and channel opening or closure are recorded on the main blockchain; here, "Raiden-style" denotes a general class of such architectures rather than a specific public implementation.

Payment channels networks, such as the Raiden Network or Lightning Network, allow two parties to conduct unlimited off-chain transactions after locking funds in a smart contract on L1 [14]. This protocol assumes that only two operations go to the main chain: opening the channel and closing it [13].

Key properties of payment channels are [13,14]: (i) transactions are limited only by the speed of data transfer between nodes and require no block confirmations; (ii) off-chain transactions are not publicly visible on the main chain, protecting user route data; (iii) Except for on-chain operations (opening/closing), microtransactions are free or have minimal fees for routing.

In a large network, it is impossible for every user to have a direct channel with every operator. Therefore, payments must be sent through intermediaries. The efficiency depends on the routing policy, which decides the path in the payment channel graph.

In the *simple approach* payment is possible only when a direct edge exists between sender and receiver. This has low complexity but also low utility. The *weighted approach* employs algorithms such as Dijkstra's algorithm to determine optimal paths based on dynamically assigned weights. These weights may represent factors such as fees, liquidity, and node reliability. However, such models require frequent updates, which may introduce communication overhead. *Trusted approach*, where network architecture is based on high-performance nodes (hubs) or Lightning Service Providers (LSP). Hubs maintain high-capacity channels with many participants, increasing the chance of finding a path. [4,9]

Micromobility systems require a reliable event log as a shared source of truth, while Layer-2 payment channel networks provide a scalable mechanism to settle the economic consequences of these events without overloading the base layer.

Benchmarking and Methodology.

Metrics for L2 Blockchain applications are mostly based on the evaluation metrics used in IT development [16–18]. We restricted our quantitative evaluation to metrics that are the most decision-relevant for cities and operators, i.e., cost, operational reliability, and channel-specific liquidity risk.

Transaction Success Rate (TSR) – the effectiveness of payment execution in the PCN network. TSR measures how often a transaction succeeds given a network topology.

Locked-Liquidity Ratio (LLR) – the efficiency of using locked capital. A high LLR means the system requires large frozen funds relative to transaction volume.

Dispute Probability (DP) – the probability of disputes requiring L1 intervention. Disputes can be a result of fraud attempts or node failures.

Effective Cost Reduction (ECR) – real reduction in operational costs by moving transactions to L2, after considering fees for opening channels and L1 cost amortization.

Existing benchmarking studies rarely examine L2 payment-channel networks under realistic micromobility workloads using real nodes and city-scale telemetry. This gap motivates the experimental framework developed in the present study.

Methodology. The proof of concept (PoC) was developed within the Design Science Research (DSR) paradigm [7], which emphasizes the creation of artifacts designed to address practical problems. We started by designing and implementing a prototype for multi-vendor micro-mobility management, leveraging smart contracts to ensure transparent data sharing and automated post-ride processing (Fig. 1). Then, we generalized the artifact into an experimentation simulator capable of exploring architectural and configuration alternatives under realistic workloads. As a last step, we document the PoC as the final artifact, operationalized through a standardized execution pipeline and evaluated using reproducible metrics that quantify routing success, capital efficiency, dispute likelihood, and settlement responsiveness.

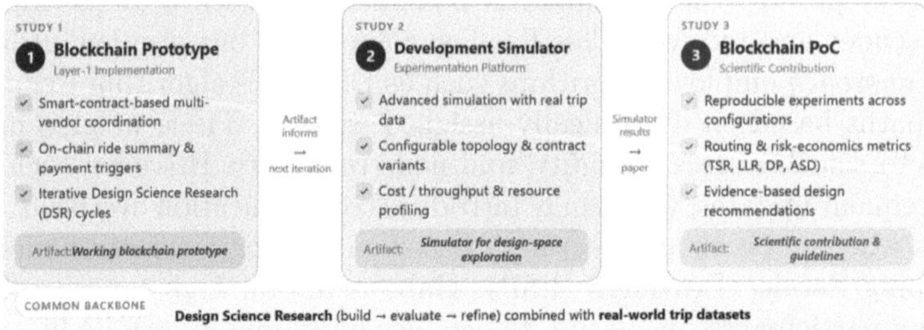

Fig. 1. Research Pipeline and Artifact Evolution. A three-stage Design Science Research (DSR) program progressing from a Blockchain prototype to PoC.

A key element of realism is the data pipeline, which maps vehicle activity to ledger operations. It follows the Entry → Event → Transaction sequence. The entry consists of a raw telemetry data (geolocation data, timestamp, etc.). Events are all processed logical units, such as “Ride Start” or “Ride End”. Transaction is a blockchain operation resulting from an event. For example, a “Minute of Ride” event generates an L2 balance update transaction.

This decomposition allows for effective load management: only high-value data (Events) become cryptographic operations (Transactions), reducing noise and costs.

3 Architecture

Actors and Interactions. The proposed architecture involves four main actors: users, scooter providers, city authorities, and the blockchain provider. Users use mobile applications to book rides, while scooter providers manage fleet operations and submit ride data to the blockchain. City authorities access aggregated data that are used in decision-making processes. The blockchain provider runs the underlying infrastructure, i.e., performs tasks like node management, contract deployment, and network configuration.

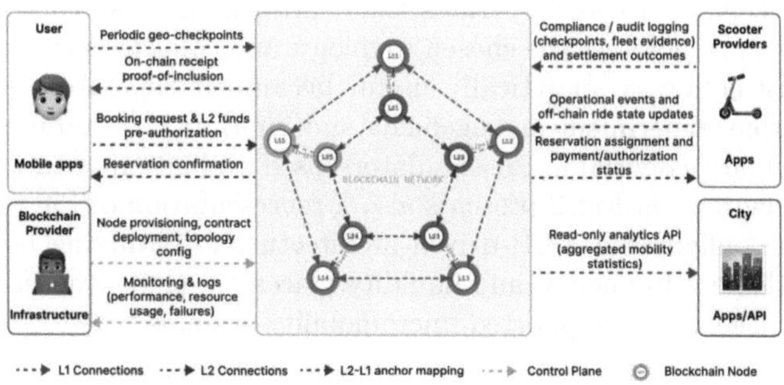

Fig. 2. Hybrid L1/L2 Blockchain architecture for multi-vendor e-scooter ride management

Figure 2 depicts a two-tier Blockchain architecture in which the outer L1 network acts as the canonical settlement, anchoring, and audit layer, whereas the inner L2 network absorbs high-frequency operational traffic through off-chain payment channels. This separation is consistent with the simulator architecture, where a private Ethereum-based L1 is coupled with a Raiden-style L2 network and a workload generator that replays events as micropayments routed off-chain and only periodically committed back to L1.

The visualized interaction model distinguishes stakeholder-specific interfaces: mobile application for users, applications for scooter providers that allows data input and access analytics dashboard, a read-only analytics interface for city authorities, and administration tool for the Blockchain provider.

The interaction architecture of the proposed solution embodies a strict functional stratification between the two Blockchain layers: L1 is reserved for settlement, state anchoring, contract execution, and audit logging, while L2 is tasked with processing the bulk of low-value, high-frequency operational interactions that would otherwise render a purely on-chain design economically inefficient. This layered separation is directly aligned with the simulator's architectural rationale, in which a configurable private Ethereum network is combined with a Raiden-style payment-channel layer in order to jointly observe on-chain behaviour, such as gas expenditure and settlement cost, and off-chain behaviour, such as routing success, liquidity utilisation, and dispute exposure, within one reproducible experimental environment.

There are three steps to manage a ride in the proposed system. The process starts when a mobile app (user) submits a booking request to L2, where channel deposits and off-chain balances can be checked and temporarily reserved before the ride begins. Then, during the ride execution, a L1 checkpointing is performed periodically. This gives the system an auditable on-chain trace without collapsing the entire operational workload back into the base layer. The last step is settlement. Instead of closing each ride independently, the architecture performs scheduled, batched L2-to-L1 anchoring and reconciliation, thus amortizing on-chain transaction cost across multiple ride events.

The Blockchain provider operates the control plane that configures nodes, deploys contracts, enforces the chosen topology, and collects operational telemetry. This distinction is analytically useful because it separates business-layer exchanges from experiment-management and runtime-observability functions, both of which are essential in the simulator-based evaluation of L1+L2 architectures. The diagram on Fig. 2 presents also a representation of the research artifact itself: a configurable, DSR-driven architecture for studying how topology, routing, settlement frequency, and liquidity placement shape the risk-economics trade-offs of Blockchain-supported micromobility systems.

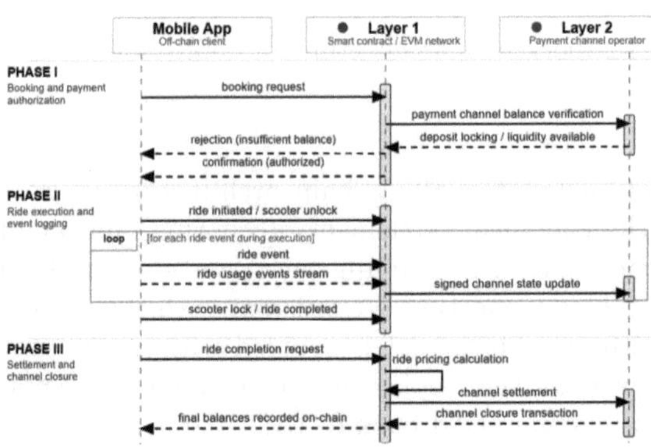

Fig. 3. Process view of the proposed hybrid L1/L2 ride-handling mechanism

Prototype and PoC Architecture. The prototype and PoC architecture is a direct instantiation of the conceptual design outlined in the previous section. The core components include: (i) a private Ethereum-based L1 network for settlement, anchoring, and audit functions; (ii) a Raiden-style L2 network for processing high-frequency, low-value transactions; and (iii) a workload generator for simulating ride events and micropayments.

The execution logic of a single e-scooter ride in the proposed layered Blockchain architecture (Fig. 3) is divided into three phases: (I) ride booking and payment authorization, (II) ride execution and event logging, and (III)

settlement and channel closure. This diagram explicates the temporal flow of responsibilities across the system's components.

In Phase I, the user submits a booking request through the mobile application. This request triggers a payment authorization procedure in which the availability of channel liquidity and deposit capacity is verified in L2. If funds are unavailable, the request is rejected. Otherwise, the system performs an off-chain hold by reserving part of the spending limit through a channel-state update.

Phase II covers ride execution. When the reservation is confirmed, the scooter unlocks and the ride is represented as a stream of operational events . These events are reflected in signed channel-state updates, thereby maintaining the dominant share of processing logic off-chain. This design increased scalability, as it avoids pushing every low-value event directly into the L1. At the same time, the process remains compatible with selective anchoring or checkpointing in L1 whenever auditability, compliance, or dispute preparedness requires it.

Phase III captures the transition from ride completion to final financial settlement. After the ride completion is issued, the system computes ride pricing and initiates channel settlement. Channel closure need not to occur immediately after each ride. Settlement may be synchronized with the closure of other channels, thus enabling deferred or batched on-chain finalization. This mechanism limits the frequency of expensive L1 transactions but at the same time provides possibility to verify data, because the final balances are recorded on-chain.

4 Results

This section reports the main findings from our hybrid L1/L2 experiments with real Raiden nodes, structured around the five analytic views. We explicitly connect the observations to RQ1 (TSR vs. liquidity, load, topology) and RQ2 (settlement strategies and cost/capital efficiency). Due to the high dimensionality of the configuration space, we augment the measurements collected from real prototype executions with a synthetic dataset generated under identical operational assumptions. The synthetic samples follow the empirical distributions extracted from the initial runs and are used solely to ensure statistical robustness across the full parameter grid.

TSR as a Function of Liquidity and Load (RQ1). Figure 4(a) shows that increasing the liquidity-to-demand ratio (LLR) improves transaction success rate (TSR), yet with diminishing returns once LLR reaches a moderate level. Under higher congestion (greater load per channel), the entire TSR-LLR curve shifts downward, indicating that congestion acts as a structural constraint on reliability even when additional liquidity is provisioned. This implies that "overfunding" channels is not an efficient path to reliability if load remains concentrated or poorly balanced across the topology.

This suggests that operators should target balanced liquidity placement and load distribution (e.g., through topology design or periodic rebalancing), rather than unconditional liquidity increases, to reach a high-TSR operating point without excessive capital lock-up.

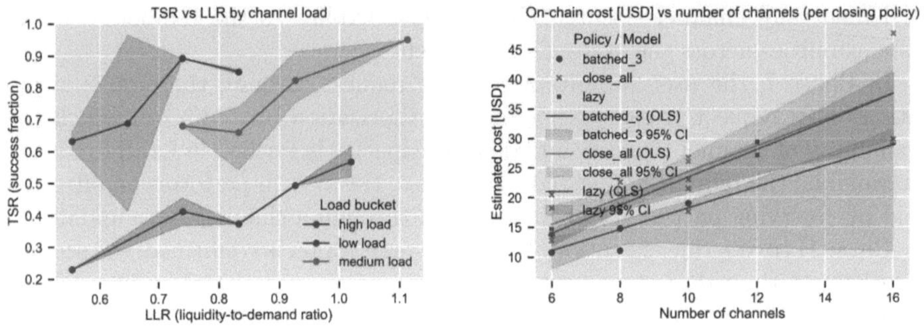

Fig. 4. (a) TSR vs. LLR (b) Cost vs. #channels

Settlement Cost Scaling and Channel-Closing Policies (RQ2). Figure 4(b) indicates that on-chain settlement cost grows approximately linearly with the number of channels that require closing during a settlement wave. Policies that batch or defer closures reduce total cost relative to close-all strategies. This pattern is robust across the reported configurations, underscoring that settlement policy is a first-order design lever for cost containment.

When periodic anchoring to L1 is mandatory due to the auditability andcompliance, batching settlements amortizes gas expenditure over multiple rides and channels, leading to a strictly better cost-reliability envelope than ride-by-ride closures.

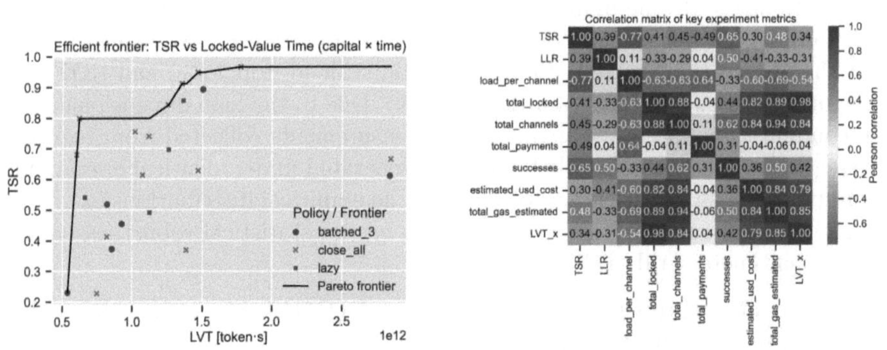

Fig. 5. (a) Pareto TSR–LVT frontier (b) Metrics correlation matrix.

Capital Efficiency and the Locked-Value-Time (LVT) Frontier (RQ1/RQ2). Figure 5(a) presents the Pareto frontier between TSR and LVT (the product of locked value and lock duration). Achieving higher TSR generally demands disproportionately more LVT, revealing a fundamental trade-off: beyond a certain TSR threshold, incremental reliability requires rapidly growing capital/time commitments. This effect is amplified when channel load is uneven, because more liquidity must be immobilized to absorb demand spikes and routing asymmetries.

For city-scale deployments, an economically sustainable operating region is indicated by the convex "knee" of the frontier: before it TSR improves meaningfully per unit LVT, and beyond it the marginal LVT cost per TSR gain rises sharply.

Correlation Structure Among Key Metrics (RQ1/RQ2). The correlation matrix in Fig. 5(b) consolidates the relationships observed across experiments. TSR correlates positively with LLR and negatively with channel load, while cost correlates strongly with the number of channels settled and with LVT.

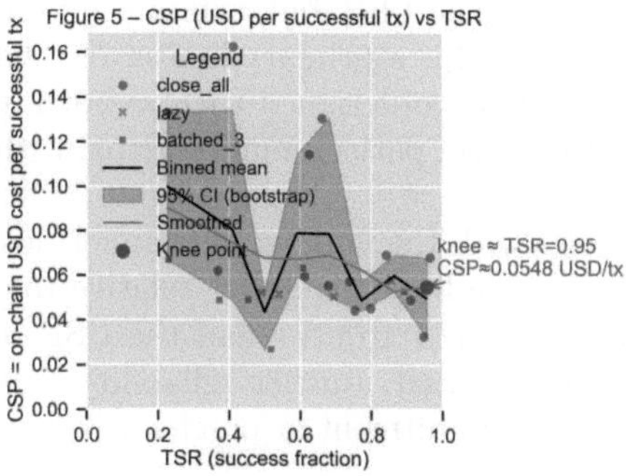

Fig. 6. CSP (USD per successful transaction) versus TSR.

Cost-Per-Success (CSP) vs. TSR and the Operational Knee (RQ2). Figure 6 plots CSP (USD per successful transaction) against TSR. The bootstrap-smoothed curve exhibits a distinct knee: initially, improving TSR is comparatively inexpensive; beyond the knee, the marginal cost of each additional percentage point of TSR rises steeply. This provides an actionable decision boundary for selecting an economically efficient operating point.

In deployment planning, we recommend locating the target TSR slightly before the knee and achieving further reliability through operational measures (e.g., monitoring-driven rebalancing and selective topology reinforcement) rather than pure liquidity or aggressive closure frequency, which push the system into the high-CSP regime.

5 Discussion and Conclusions

This study examined a hybrid L1/L2 payment architecture for multi-vendor micromobility using a private Ethereum L1, real Raiden nodes on L2, and workloads derived from ride events. The results clarify the interplay between reliability, liquidity, and settlement costs under realistic operating conditions.

Reliability, Liquidity, and Cost Trade-offs. Increasing the liquidity-to-load ratio (LLR) improves transaction success rate (TSR), but the gains diminish under congestion. Channel-level load, rather than aggregate liquidity, is the dominant factor limiting reliability, indicating that unbalanced demand concentrates failures on a subset of channels. On the cost side, settlement expenditure is driven primarily by the number of channel closures, not by transaction volume itself. Batched or lazy settlement strategies substantially reduce L1 costs compared to immediate close-all approaches, shifting operation toward more favorable regions of the cost–reliability space.

Answers to Research Questions. The experimental results provide clear answers to the posed research questions:

RQ1 TSR improves with higher LLR but exhibits diminishing returns under congestion; load per channel is a primary limiter of reliability. Consequently, liquidity allocation must be co-designed with network topology and routing so that traffic is balanced and paths remain feasible without excessive capital immobilization.

RQ2 Settlement cost scales with the number of channel closures; batched or lazy strategies materially reduce L1 expenditure relative to close-all policies. The joint analysis of the TSR–LVT frontier and the CSP–TSR knee shows that beyond a moderate TSR target, further reliability gains require disproportionately higher capital commitment or on-chain cost.

Implications and Limitations. From a practical perspective, designers should prioritize load-aware or hub-oriented topologies, batch anchoring and settlement operations, and minimize load variance across channels before increasing absolute liquidity levels. These measures position the system near the Pareto-efficient region identified in the experiments and keep operation on the favorable side of the CSP–TSR knee. While the evaluation on a configurable private L1 and a Raiden-style L2 captures essential operational dynamics, outcomes may vary under alternative fee markets, heterogeneous node implementations, or large-scale public network conditions. Future work will extend the framework to other L2 designs (e.g., rollups combined with payment channel networks), automated liquidity rebalancing mechanisms, larger topologies, and longer-horizon analyses of dispute behavior under adversarial or failure scenarios.

References

1. Abbas, K., Tawalbeh, L.A., Rafiq, A., Muthanna, A., Elgendy, I.A., Abd El-Latif, A.A.: Convergence of Blockchain and IoT for Secure Transportation Systems in Smart Cities. Secur. Commun. Netw. 1–13 (2021). https://doi.org/10.1155/2021/5597679
2. Chowdhury, A., Shafin, S.S., Masum, S., Kamruzzaman, J., Dong, S.: Secure electric vehicle charging infrastructure in smart cities: a blockchain-based smart contract approach. Smart Cities **8**(1), 33 (2025). https://doi.org/10.3390/smartcities8010033

3. De Rossi, L.M., Avital, M., Gleasure, R., Solcia, R.: The Impact of layer 2 technologies on the adoption and security of blockchain. In: Böhmann, T., Hui, K.L., Venkatesh, V. (eds.) Proceeding of the 43rd ICIS. AISeL (2022). https://icis2022.aisconferences.org/
4. Erdin, E., Cebe, M., Akkaya, K., Bulut, E., Uluagac, S.: A scalable private Bitcoin payment channel network with privacy guarantees. JNCAs **180**, 103021 (2021). https://doi.org/10.1016/j.jnca.2021.103021
5. Gangwal, A., Gangavalli, H.R., Thirupathi, A.: A survey of Layer-two blockchain protocols. JNCA **209**, 103539 (2023). https://doi.org/10.1016/j.jnca.2022.103539
6. Hafid, A., Hafid, A.S., Samih, M.: Scaling blockchains: a comprehensive survey. IEEE Access **8**, 125244–125262 (2020). https://doi.org/10.1109/ACCESS.2020.3007251
7. Hevner, A.R., March, S., Park, J., Ram, S.: Design Sci. Inf. Syst. Res. **28**(1), 75–105 (2004)
8. Karger, E., Jagals, M., Ahlemann, F.: Blockchain for smart mobility-literature review and future research agenda. Sustainability **13**(23), 13268 (2021). https://doi.org/10.3390/su132313268
9. Khojasteh, H., Tabatabaei, H.: A Survey and taxonomy of blockchain-based payment channel networks. In: 2021 IEEE HPEC, pp. 1–8. IEEE, Waltham, MA, USA (2021). https://doi.org/10.1109/HPEC49654.2021.9622868
10. Kummetha, V.C., Concas, S., Staes, L., Godfrey, J.: Mobility on demand in the united states - current state of integration and policy considerations for improved interoperability. Travel Behav. Soc. **37**, 100867 (2024). https://doi.org/10.1016/j.tbs.2024.100867
11. Lewańska, E., Stolarski, P.: Transparent e-scooter fleet management with blockchain. Proc. Comput. Sci. **270**, 3993–4002 (2025). https://doi.org/10.1016/j.procs.2025.09.524
12. Miron, R., Hulea, M., Muresan, V., Clitan, I., Rusu, A.: Integrating blockchain technology into mobility-as-a-service platforms for smart cities. Smart Cities **8**(1), 9 (2025). https://doi.org/10.3390/smartcities8010009
13. Negka, L.D., Spathoulas, G.P.: Blockchain state channels: a state of the art. IEEE Access **9**, 160277–160298 (2021). https://doi.org/10.1109/ACCESS.2021.3131419
14. Poon, J., Dryja, T.: The Bitcoin Lightning Network: Scalable Off-Chain Instant Payments (2023)
15. Rejeb, A., Rejeb, K., Simske, S.J., Keogh, J.G.: Blockchain technology in the smart city: a bibliometric review. Qual. Quant. **56**(5), 2875–2906 (2022). https://doi.org/10.1007/s11135-021-01251-2
16. Saif, M.B., Migliorini, S., Spoto, F.: A survey on data availability in layer 2 blockchain rollups: open challenges and future improvements. Future Internet **16**(9), 315 (2024). https://doi.org/10.3390/fi16090315
17. Singh, A., Click, K., Parizi, R.M., Zhang, Q., Dehghantanha, A., Choo, K.K.R.: Sidechain technologies in blockchain networks: an examination and state-of-the-art review. JNCA **149**, 102471 (2020). https://doi.org/10.1016/j.jnca.2019.102471
18. Touloupou, M., Themistocleous, M., Iosif, E., Christodoulou, K.: A systematic literature review toward a blockchain benchmarking framework. IEEE Access **10**, 70630–70644 (2022). https://doi.org/10.1109/ACCESS.2022.3188123
19. US Department of Transportation: Mobility on Demand (MOD). brief FHWA-JPO-18-739 (2019). https://www.itskrs.its.dot.gov/sites/default/files/2021-09/executive-briefing/EB11-Mobility_on_Demand_%2005_16_19_FINAL.pdf

Strategic Decision-Making in the Blockchain Era: The Blockchain Business Intelligence Framework

Marcel Bühlmann[1](✉), Hans-Georg Fill[1], and Florian Johannsen[2]

[1] University of Fribourg, Digitalization and Information Systems Group, Boulevard de Pérolles 90, 1700 Fribourg, Switzerland
{marcel.buhlmann,hans-georg.fill}@unifr.ch

[2] University of Applied Sciences Schmalkalden, Blechhammer 9, 98574 Schmalkalden, Germany
f.johannsen@hs-sm.de

https://www.unifr.ch/inf/digits/en/

Abstract. Although blockchain (BC) technologies are widely adopted, their integration with established Business Intelligence (BI) systems for strategic decision-making remains underexplored. This research-in-progress paper proposes the Blockchain Business Intelligence Framework, a multi-layered architecture that connects BC data analytics with enterprise BI systems and Six Sigma practices. The framework comprises four layers (Strategy, Steering, Intelligence, Data) supporting strategic alignment, operational monitoring, and continuous improvement. By embedding BC data into existing BI environments, it enables actionable insights, greater accountability, and stronger data-driven management. It also incorporates a Blockchain Balanced Scorecard to align strategic objectives, KPIs, and initiatives, providing a structured foundation for integrating decentralized application data into enterprise decision-making and future practical implementation.

Keywords: Blockchain Intelligence · Business Intelligence · Framework

1 Introduction

Blockchain has emerged as a transformative technology in academia and industry since the inception of Bitcoin [1]. Its core characteristics, distributed consensus, immutability, transparency, and traceability, combined with the programmable functionality of smart contract platforms like Ethereum, have enabled a wide array of innovative use cases across sectors [7,14].

At the same time, Business Intelligence (BI) systems have evolved from mere decision support tools to strategic assets enabling data-driven decision-making and organizational agility to gain a competitive advantage [9]. A competitive advantage is not gained once but must be continuously defended, for example by

R. Posenato and I. Vanderfeesten (Eds.): CAiSE 2026 Workshops, LNBIP 586, pp. 234–239, 2026.
https://doi.org/10.1007/978-3-032-28160-9_21

employing the Six Sigma methodology. Using BI tools in the Six Sigma structure enables continuous improvement in operations and decision making. The application of BI and Six Sigma to the field of blockchain (BC) is a promising, yet underexplored research and application domain [3]. For organizations engaging with BC, embedding BC data into BI systems can offer more insights. Despite existing BC data analytics approaches, there is, to the best of our knowledge, no comprehensive framework for integrating BC data into BI-systems and Six Sigma implementations to effectively support strategic management and continuous improvements. This paper addresses that gap by introducing the Blockchain Business Intelligence Framework (BBIF), a structured, multi-layered framework designed to integrate BC data analytics with BI-systems.

In Sects. 2 we introduce foundational concepts and previous work. Afterwards, we introduce our Framework in Sect. 3. The results are discussed in Sect. 4 and we conclude the paper in Sect. 5.

2 Foundations and Related Work

Business Intelligence and Data Analytics: BI emerged in the late 20th century alongside decision support systems. It integrates data from multiple sources with specialized tools, methodologies, and structured processes to improve decision-making and gain competitive advantage [15,16]. BI relies on advanced data analytics, the systematic examination of raw data to extract meaningful insights and actionable knowledge. Core processes include data collection, organization, preprocessing, modeling, and interpretation. Data analytics explains past phenomena (descriptive and diagnostic), monitors current conditions, predicts future outcomes, and evaluates potential scenarios using statistical and data mining techniques. It also supports prescriptive analytics, applying decision analysis tools such as optimization and simulation to recommend the most effective actions for achieving business objectives [12].

Quality Management - Six Sigma: Originating in the manufacturing industry, Six Sigma is a data-driven quality management methodology focused on systematic process and system improvement. Six Sigma follows the five-step DMAIC framework: Define, Measure, Analyze, Improve, and Control. In the Define phase, the performance goals, and stakeholder requirements are specified. Measure involves collecting data. In Analyze, data techniques are used to identify causes of deviations. Improve focuses on developing and implementing solutions, while Control ensures performance through continuous monitoring [10].

Related Work: The basic architecture of BI-systems has been discussed extensively in the scientific literature. [15, 12] presents a three-layer BI-system architecture consisting of data, analytics, and presentation layers. Data is integrated into a data warehouse and analytical results are then presented to stakeholders. [6] extend the framework with machine learning for predictive analytics, while [8] highlights that meaningful insights often require years of accumulated data. The integration of BC data isn't considered in any proposed framework.

QM and BI share similar goals: analyzing the current state and deriving improvements to reach a desired position. However, the integration of QM and BI remains underexplored. While existing research examines how QM can enhance BI systems, a framework combining QM practices with BI is missing.

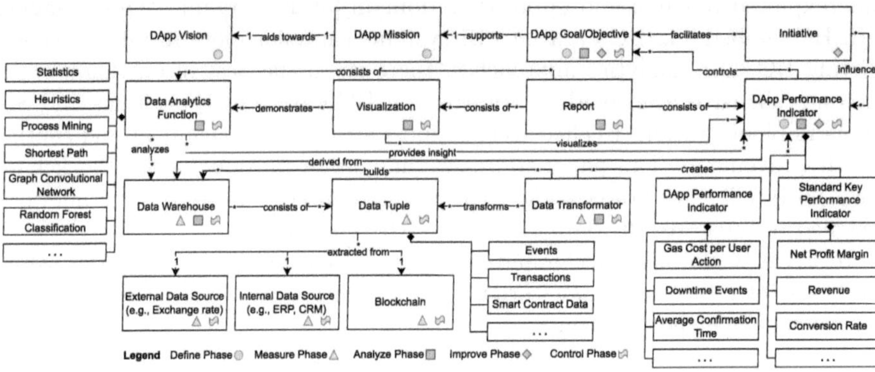

Fig. 1. Conceptual domain model of the Blockchain Business Intelligence Framework (BBIF) with the elements, relationships and cardinalities. The DMAIC-phases in which the elements are used are denoted by their respective icon-colour combination

The field of BC data analytics is fragmented and nascent, but is divided in focus areas such as financial analysis, illegal activity detection, or user behavior analysis [3]. Although frameworks and analysis methods exist, their application is limited to specific subtopics (e.g., forensics [11]). Many data analytics techniques analyze BC transactions [2], other use BC events [13]. As their work demonstrates, event-based BC analysis seems promising in the context BI.

Despite extensive research on BC data analytics, a holistic framework for integrating it into BI concepts remains lacking [3] and we aim to close the current research gap.

3 A Framework For Blockchain Business Intelligence

Guided by the Design Science Research methodology, the framework is derived by a synthesis of existing BI architectures and QM concepts (Six Sigma). The complete framework is illustrated as a domain model in Fig. 1. Leveraging the widely adopted architecture of traditional BI-systems [15] we propose the Blockchain Business Intelligence Framework.

The frameworks application process aligns with the Define âĂŞ Measure âĂŞ Analyze âĂŞ Improve âĂŞ Control (DMAIC) cycle from Six Sigma established in many organizations [10]. The elements used in specific DMAIC-Phases are illustrated in Fig. 1. Vision, mission and strategic goals and KPIs for the DApp environment are defined (Define), relevant BC and additional data is gathered (Measure), and insights are analyzed (Analyze). Based on these findings, improvements are implemented (Improve), and ongoing performance is continuously monitored (Control).

The Define-Phase elements serve as the primary mechanism for aligning DApp efforts. It encapsulates high-level decision-making processes that guide how organizations formulate, implement, and evaluate strategic objectives in the context of BC-related opportunities and challenges. The Strategy Layer includes the defined objectives based on the DApp's vision and mission statements, and identified relevant KPIs. These elements capture the relationships between business aspirations and measurable outcomes.

Objectives serve to translate the DApp's mission into actionable and clearly defined targets that are achievable through actions taken by the organization. The Strategy Layer must be both stable in vision and flexible in execution. DApp KPIs are critical in this context, as they provide the quantitative basis for monitoring progress. Effective KPIs must be stakeholder-relevant, context-specific, and directly linked to the goals they aim to measure. They are influenced by both internal variables and initiatives, such as organizational capabilities and external forces including market dynamics. Our framework defines initiatives as specific actions to achieve strategic goals, linking strategy to operational execution and assigning them during the Define phase. We use the BC Balanced Scorecard to combine goals, KPIs and initiatives [5] which enhance decision-making. The data used for building KPIs are gathered in the Measure-Phase. Blockchain-based systems present unique data characteristics, such as immutability, which require specialized handling [4]. The phase follows an ETL-like process (extract-transform-load) and stages the data in a data warehouse. To support multi-source analysis, the Measure-Phase introduces six core components: Data Sources, Data Tuples, Data Transformators, and the Data Warehouse. Data Sources may include BC networks, internal enterprise systems (e.g., ERP, CRM) or external services (e.g., exchange rates). The data that is stored on the BC can be extracted using different approaches, either an Application-Programming-Interface (API) or through a full node synchronization. We found that most data analytics techniques use either a pre-transformed dataset or full node synchronization [3]. For the internal systems and external services, the available approaches for data extraction might vary and depend on the systems deployed. The data extracted from data sources undergo aggregation and transformation operations to ensure data consistency and usability. The result is staged data in a data warehouse, with a BC-ready data schema. Building upon event-log mining [13] we suggest an event-oriented data-schema for the Ethereum BC extending the data-schema by [4].

During the Analyze-Phase the prepared data is transformed into actionable insights through analysis, visualization, and reporting and therefore bridges the gap between data and action. The phase is supported by six core components: the Data Warehouse, Data Transformators, Data Analytics Functions, Visualizations, KPIs, and Report. The data analytics function encompasses all forms of analysis functions (e.g., statistics, process mining, random forest classification etc.) excluding visualization, but including forecasting and AI-driven techniques. This flexibility supports descriptive-, diagnostic-, predictive-, and prescriptive-analysis, and allows the integration of auxiliary data staged in the data warehouse. Visualizations convert analytical results and KPIs into intuitive formats, such as charts or dashboards, improving data comprehension and stakeholder engagement. Reports combine analytical results and visualizations into customizable outputs tailored to different user roles. They may include performance dashboards, detailed analyses etc. depending on stakeholder needs. Reports may be supplemented by AI-enabled interpretation and proposals.

Following the Analyze-Phase, improvements are developed and implemented throughout the organization (Improve-Phase), represented by Initiatives. During this phase, the Blockchain Balanced Scorecard is used extensively. The effectiveness of these improvements is evaluated in the following Control-Phase.

During the Control-Phase the focus is on tracking the current status after implementing improvements, offering continuous operational control and decision support based on up-to-date performance data. This phase includes all elements except DApp Vision and DApp Mission, ensuring information flow and instant interpretation.

4 Discussion of Results

The proposed BBIF enables the systematic integration of BC data into BI processes and can be illustrated through a decentralized lodging use case. In this scenario, a decentralized lodging platform operates as a smart contract on the Ethereum BC, managing core functionalities such as listings, bookings, payments, and reviews while emitting events for traceable on-chain analytics. In the Define phase, DApp objectives and KPIs are derived from the corporate vision, mission, and financial goals. In the Measure phase, BC events, combined with off-chain data from, for example, a CRM system (e.g., customer surveys), are extracted, transformed, and staged in a data warehouse. In the Analyze phase, the data enables KPI calculations and stakeholder-specific insights, such as average booking length, campaign effectiveness, and Net Promoter Score, through statistical evaluation, forecasting, and AI-supported interpretation. The Improve phase converts these insights into targeted operational initiatives, while the Control phase ensures continuous KPI monitoring and organizational success. By integrating Six Sigma with BC-oriented BI, the framework provides a structured and measurable approach to evaluating DApp performance while transforming BC data into strategic intelligence for evidence-based decision-making.

5 Conclusion and Future Work

This paper proposed the BBIF, a multi-phase framework that integrates BC data into BI practices to support monitoring and informed decision-making. Addressing the gap between BC data analytics and traditional BI, the framework is oriented along the DMAIC-cycle.

The BBIF lays the foundation for integrating BC technologies with traditional BI but its effectiveness must be demonstrated in future work. Further, the application of the BBIF on a real-world use case in collaboration with industry experts or the implementation of the BBIF in a conceptual modeling toolsuite, that allows a low-code or no-code application of BC BI for domain-experts, are promising avenues.

Acknowledgments. This work was partially funded by the Swiss National Science Foundation project Domain-Specific Conceptual Modeling for Distributed Ledger Technologies [196889].

References

1. Banafa, A.: Introduction to Blockchain Technology. Taylor and Francies CRC Press River Publishers (2023)
2. Bartoletti, M., Pes, B., Serusi, S.: Data mining for detecting bitcoin ponzi schemes. In: 2018 Crypto Valley Conference on Blockchain Technology, pp. 75–84 (2018)
3. Bühlmann, M., Fill, H.G., Curty, S.: Blockchain Data Analytics: A Scoping Literature Review and Directions for Future Research (2025)
4. Camozzi, G., Härer, F., Fill, H.G.: Multidimensional analysis of blockchain data using an ETL-based approach. In: Proceedings Wirtschaftsinformatik 2022 (2022)
5. Curty, S., Bühlmann, M., Fill, H.G., Treiblmaier, H.: The blockchain balanced scorecard: an innovative approach to facilitate strategic management in enterprises. In: Proceedings of the 58th Hawaii International Conference on System Sciences (2025)
6. Davenport, T.: Competing on analytics. Harv. Bus. Rev. **84**, 98–107 (2006)
7. Fill, H.G., Meier, A.: Blockchain kompakt. Springer Vieweg Wiesbaden (2019)
8. Fraihat, S., Salameh, W.A., Elhassan, A., Tahoun, B.A., Asasfeh, M.: Business intelligence framework design and implementation: a real-estate market case study. J. Data Inform. Q.**13** (2021)
9. Jiménez-Partearroyo, M., Medina-López, A., Rana, S.: Business intelligence and business analytics in tourism: insights through Gioia methodology. Inter. Entrepreneurship Manag. J. **20**, 2287–2321 (2024)
10. Johannsen, F., Leist, S.: A six sigma approach for integrated solutions. Managing Service Quality: Inter. J. **19**(5), 558–580 (2009)
11. Mas'ud, M.Z., et al.: A review of digital forensics framework for blockchain in cryptocurrency technology. In: 2021 International Cyber Resilience Conference, pp. 1–6 (2021)
12. Moreira, J., Carvalho, A., Horvath, T.: A General Introduction to Data Analytics. Wiley, Berlin (2019)
13. Mühlberger, R., Bachhofner, S., Di Ciccio, C., García-Bañuelos, L., López-Pintado, O.: Extracting event logs for process mining from data stored on the blockchain. In: Business Process Management Workshops, pp. 690–703 (2019)
14. Singh, D., Malhotra, M.V.: A review on the capability and smart contract potential of block chain technology. In: 2023 3rd International Conference on Smart Data Intelligence, pp. 80–87 (2023)
15. Skyrius, R.: Business intelligence: a comprehensive approach to information needs, technologies and culture. Progress in IS (2021)
16. Wixom, B., Watson, H.: The BI-based organization. Inter. J. Bus. Intell. Res. **1**, 13–28 (2010)

EASI

Knowledge Graphs as a Semantic Layer for Understanding Robotic Video

Flavio Corradini, Barbara Re, Lorenzo Rossi, Massimiliano Sampaolo(✉), and Mattia Scattu

School of Science and Technology, University of Camerino, Camerino, Italy
{flavio.corradini,barbara.re,lorenzo.rossi,massimilian.sampaolo, mattia.scattu}@unicam.it

Abstract. Robotic systems are increasingly deployed in industrial environments, where understanding and analyzing their operations is essential for monitoring and optimizing automated processes. Techniques such as process mining offer powerful tools for analyzing operational workflows, but they require structured representations of activities that are difficult to extract from raw sensory data. Among available data sources, video streams capture the temporal evolution of robotic activities, yet interpreting robotic behavior directly from video remains challenging. In this paper, we propose the use of knowledge graphs as a semantic layer to support the interpretation of robotic video streams. The proposed approach separates visual perception from semantic reasoning through a modular architecture. A perception module extracts structured observations from video frames, while a knowledge graph encodes domain knowledge about the robotic environment, including objects, states, and possible interactions. This semantic layer supports the reasoning process used to interpret robot activities observed in the video. The resulting framework enables the extraction of structured representations of robotic activities from video streams, supporting event-based descriptions of robot behavior that can be used for process analysis.

Keywords: Knowledge Graphs · Robotics · Activity Recognition · Process Mining · Foundation Models

1 Introduction

Robotic systems are increasingly deployed in industrial and operational environments, where they perform repetitive, precise, and highly structured tasks [10,15]. As these systems become more integrated into production and service processes, understanding and analyzing their behavior becomes an important requirement for monitoring, optimization, and continuous improvement. In this context, process mining has emerged as a powerful set of techniques for analyzing operational processes based on event data, enabling the discovery, monitoring, and improvement of real-world processes [6]. In robotic systems, the

R. Posenato and I. Vanderfeesten (Eds.): CAiSE 2026 Workshops, LNBIP 586, pp. 243–253, 2026.
https://doi.org/10.1007/978-3-032-28160-9_22

application of process mining is particularly valuable in scenarios where robot behavior exhibits variability and depends on interactions with dynamic environments. This is especially evident in more autonomous robotic systems, where decisions are influenced by perception and contextual factors. However, even in traditionally programmed industrial robots, real-world executions may still deviate from predefined routines due to environmental and operational conditions, making process-oriented analysis useful for monitoring and optimization. However, applying process mining techniques to robotic systems requires structured event-based representations of robot activities. While traditional information systems naturally generate event logs, robotic platforms typically produce large volumes of fine-grained sensory data, such as video streams, images, or signals from embedded sensors. Transforming these raw observations into meaningful descriptions of robot activities remains a challenging task. In particular, video data contains rich information about the temporal evolution of robotic activities and interactions with objects and the environment, but extracting structured representations of these activities from visual data is far from trivial. Recent advances in computer vision and foundation models have significantly improved the ability of AI systems to interpret visual scenes [8]. Vision-language models and other generative architectures can identify objects, activities, and relationships in images and videos with impressive performance. Nevertheless, these models often rely on probabilistic reasoning and may produce ambiguous or logically inconsistent interpretations, especially when applied to structured operational environments such as robotic work cells. In these settings, reliable interpretation of robot behavior requires not only visual perception but also contextual knowledge about the domain, including objects, possible interactions, and operational constraints.

To address this challenge, this paper proposes the use of knowledge graphs as a semantic layer to support the interpretation of robotic video streams. Knowledge graphs provide a structured representation of domain knowledge, capturing entities, relationships, and constraints that characterize a given environment. By integrating such knowledge with visual observations extracted from video frames, it becomes possible to support a more informed reasoning process for interpreting robotic activities. The proposed approach separates **visual perception from semantic reasoning through a modular architecture**. A perception module processes video frames and extracts structured observations describing objects, activities, and contextual elements observed in the scene. These observations are then interpreted through a knowledge graph that encodes domain knowledge about the robotic environment, including objects, states, and possible interactions. Acting as a semantic layer, the knowledge graph provides contextual information that supports the interpretation of robot behavior and helps produce consistent representations of robotic activities. This interpretation step enables the generation of structured activity representations from robotic video streams. Such representations can serve **as a bridge between fine-grained sensory data and higher-level analytical techniques**, including the creation of event-based descriptions of robot behavior suitable for process analysis.

In particular, the proposed approach is designed to produce structured activity representations that can be directly mapped to event logs, enabling the application of process mining techniques such as process discovery, conformance checking, and performance analysis.

The remainder of the paper is structured as follows. Section 2 reviews relevant background on video understanding and knowledge graphs. Section 3 presents the proposed approach, while Sect. 4 discusses the obtained results. Finally, Sect. 5 concludes the paper and outlines future research directions.

2 Background and Related Work

Robotic systems operating in industrial environments continuously generate large volumes of sensory data describing their interactions with the physical world. These data sources include video streams, images, and signals produced by embedded sensors, which capture detailed observations of robot activities and object manipulations [5]. Such observations provide a fine-grained description of the system behavior but do not directly correspond to meaningful operational activities. Therefore, interpreting robotic behavior requires transforming raw sensory observations into structured representations that describe activities and interactions occurring in the environment [4]. Video data is particularly informative in this context, as it captures both the spatial configuration of the environment and the temporal evolution of robot movements. However, deriving meaningful descriptions of robotic activities from video streams remains a complex problem, especially in scenarios where they involve multiple objects, sequential manipulations, and interactions with dynamic environments. Recent advances in computer vision and foundation models have improved the ability of AI systems to analyze visual scenes and detect objects or activities in images and videos. Beyond traditional computer vision approaches, an increasing number of works leverage foundation models for activity recognition, highlighting their potential to handle fine-grained and heterogeneous data [9,16,17]. Despite these advances, interpreting robot activities reliably remains challenging. Generative models may produce plausible but inconsistent interpretations of observed scenes, particularly when reasoning about structured environments where activities follow well-defined operational constraints.

Understanding robotic behavior is particularly relevant when robotic systems are embedded within larger operational processes. In industrial settings, analyzing these processes is essential for monitoring system performance, detecting deviations, and identifying opportunities for optimization [10,15]. Process mining techniques provide powerful tools for analyzing operational workflows by extracting knowledge from event data [1]. However, these techniques require structured event-based representations of process executions. While traditional information systems naturally generate event logs, robotic platforms typically produce only fine-grained sensory observations rather than explicit descriptions of performed activities [5]. This gap between sensory data and structured events represents a major challenge for applying process-oriented analysis to robotic systems. Transforming observations derived from sensors or video streams into meaningful activity representations is, therefore, a crucial step for enabling process mining in robotic environments. Recent studies have also investigated the adoption of process mining techniques to video data [11,12,14]. However, these approaches primarily rely on activity recognition techniques applied directly to visual observations and typically lack an explicit semantic layer that can leverage domain knowledge to refine and contextualize the inferred activities.

Knowledge graphs provide structured representations of domain knowledge by modeling entities, relationships, and constraints. Their ability to capture and represent relationships among entities enables meaningful analysis and reasoning over complex data [13]. They have been widely used to support reasoning and contextual understanding in AI systems. Recent research in semantics-driven systems engineering emphasizes the role of explicit knowledge structures in supporting the interpretation and reasoning capabilities of AI systems, particularly when combined with machine learning approaches [3]. In complex environments such as robotic work cells, domain knowledge about objects, states, and possible interactions plays an important role in interpreting observed behaviors. Knowledge graphs can capture this knowledge in a structured form, providing contextual information that complements visual perception. When integrated with observations extracted from video streams, such knowledge can support more consistent and interpretable interpretations of robot activities. In this work, we leverage knowledge graphs as a semantic layer that connects visual observations derived from robotic video streams with structured domain knowledge. This layer supports the interpretation of observed activities and enables the generation of structured representations of robotic activities for further analysis.

The problem of interpreting robotic activities from sensory data is inherently affected by uncertainty, as multiple plausible interpretations may arise from the same observations. Recent work has addressed uncertainty in process data from different perspectives. [2] introduces SKTR, a framework for recovering deterministic traces from stochastically known logs, where each event is associated with a probability distribution over possible activities. Their approach combines probabilistic event information with process models to identify the most plausible execution trace. In parallel, [7] extends Event Knowledge Graphs with ambiguity to explicitly represent multiple interpretations of high-level events derived from IoT-based monitoring. Their work focuses on ambiguity-aware event representation, especially for uncertain event-entity correlations and role assignments in object-centric settings. Our work addresses a complementary problem. Rather than starting from probabilistic event logs or from high-level events already abstracted from low-level sensor streams, we focus on deriving semantically consistent robotic activities directly from raw video data. In this setting, the knowledge graph is not only used as a representational layer but as a semantic constraint mechanism that guides generative video interpretation and reduces implausible activity assignments.

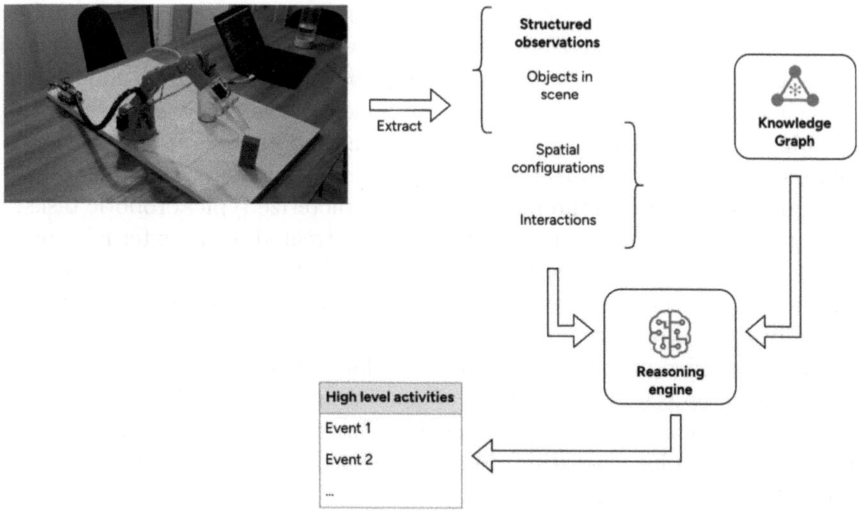

Fig. 1. Overview of the approach

3 Approach

The proposed approach aims to support the interpretation of robotic activities from video streams by integrating visual perception with domain knowledge. The central idea is to introduce a knowledge graph acting as a semantic layer that contextualizes observations extracted from video frames and supports the reasoning process used to infer robot activities. By combining visual information with structured domain knowledge, the system produces consistent interpretations of robotic behavior. Figure 1 illustrates the overall workflow of the proposed approach.

The approach follows a pipeline in which robotic video streams are first analyzed to extract structured observations describing the state of the environment. To capture the temporal evolution of robot activities, the video stream is segmented into fixed-length temporal windows, with consecutive windows partially overlapping. This sliding-window strategy allows the system to preserve temporal continuity between observations while reducing the risk of missing relevant transitions between activities. Video frames within each temporal window are processed using computer vision models capable of detecting objects and describing elements of the observed scene. In our implementation, visual observations are extracted using the Gemini-2.5-Flash model, which generates structured descriptions of the scene for each temporal segment. The output of this stage consists of fine-grained observations, such as detected objects, spatial configurations, and potential interactions occurring within the scene. While these observations provide detailed information about the visual context, they still *do not directly correspond to meaningful robotic activities.*

To interpret these observations within the operational context of the robotic system, the proposed approach leverages a knowledge graph representing domain knowledge about the robotic environment. The knowledge graph models entities such as objects, tools, and robot components, together with relationships describing how these entities can interact during robotic operations. This structured representation captures relevant aspects of the domain, including possible object manipulations and interactions that characterize typical robotic tasks. In the proposed approach, the knowledge graph is treated as an external input to the system, rather than as a fixed component of the architecture. This design choice allows the semantic layer to be adapted depending on the analyzed scenario. Given the strong generalization capabilities of recent foundation models, different knowledge graphs can be provided for different video analyses, focusing on specific objects, relationships, or operational details relevant to the task under investigation. This flexibility enables the system to refine the interpretation process by incorporating domain knowledge tailored to the particular robotic activity being analyzed.

Observations extracted from the video stream are mapped to corresponding entities and relationships in the knowledge graph. This mapping enables the system to contextualize the detected objects and interactions within the domain model describing the robotic environment. In particular, the structured observations produced by the visual perception component are combined with the topological information encoded in the knowledge graph, allowing the system to reason about which activities are theoretically compatible with the objects present in the scene. A logical reasoning component orchestrates this interpretation process. The module receives the structured observations generated by the perception layer and queries the knowledge graph to retrieve the set of activities that can be associated with the detected objects according to the operational domain, based on the relationships encoded in the knowledge graph. The retrieved contextual information is then combined with the visual description of the current scene and evaluated by a generative reasoning component based on a language model. Concretely, the visual observations and the set of candidate activities retrieved from the knowledge graph are encoded into a structured prompt, which is provided as input to the model. In this stage, the model operates as a textual evaluator whose task is to identify the most coherent activity given the observed configuration of objects and interactions. Since generative models may produce verbose or syntactically inconsistent outputs, the generated description is not directly accepted by the system. Instead, a deterministic parsing step converts the generated text into a structured command following a predefined representation of the form activityâĂŞobject. During this step, a visual grounding mechanism ensures consistency between the inferred activity and the objects actually detected in the scene. If discrepancies arise between the generated output and the visual observations, priority is given to the objects identified by the perception module. Through this interpretation process, the system produces structured representations of robotic activities describing the operations performed by the robot and the involved objects. These representations provide a higher-level description of robot behavior compared to the original visual observations. In addition, activities can be associated with temporal information derived from the video stream, enabling the creation of event-based descriptions of robot behavior that can subsequently support process-oriented analyses.

Such event-based representations provide a bridge between fine-grained sensory observations and higher-level analytical techniques. In particular, they enable the generation of structured event data that can support process-oriented analyses of robotic operations, including the application of process mining techniques for understanding and improving robotic processes.

4 Evaluation

To evaluate the proposed approach, we conducted experiments using publicly available videos depicting robotic manipulators performing object manipulation tasks. The selected videos show robotic arms executing typical activities such as grasping, moving, and placing objects within a workspace. These videos were collected from online sources and represent common robotic manipulation scenarios. The goal of the evaluation is to assess the ability of the proposed approach to interpret robot behavior from video observations and to generate structured representations of the corresponding activities. The experiments focus in particular on analyzing how the integration of the knowledge graph as a semantic layer supports the interpretation of activities inferred from visual observations. For each experiment, a dedicated knowledge graph was created to model the objects, tools, and possible interactions relevant to the specific scenario depicted in the analyzed video. This design allows the semantic layer to capture the operational context of each experiment and support the interpretation of the observed activities.

Figure 2 shows an example of the activity recognition results obtained in one experimental scenario. The video depicts a robotic manipulator interacting with a square object placed on a workspace. The sequence illustrates the activities inferred by the proposed approach over consecutive temporal windows. Initially, the system identifies an IDLE state, indicating that no manipulation activity is occurring. In the following window, the system detects the GRASP activity performed by the robot on the object identified as black square. The next temporal segment is interpreted as a MOVE activity, where the robot transports the object across the workspace. The activity is then classified as DROP, corresponding to the release of the object. Finally, the system returns to an IDLE state once the manipulation task is completed.

To support the interpretation of the activities observed in the first experiment, a dedicated knowledge graph was constructed to represent the objects and possible interactions present in the scene. The graph models the manipulated object, the surrounding elements in the environment, and the set of activities that can be associated with the manipulated object. Figure 3 shows the knowledge graph used in this scenario. The manipulated object is connected to

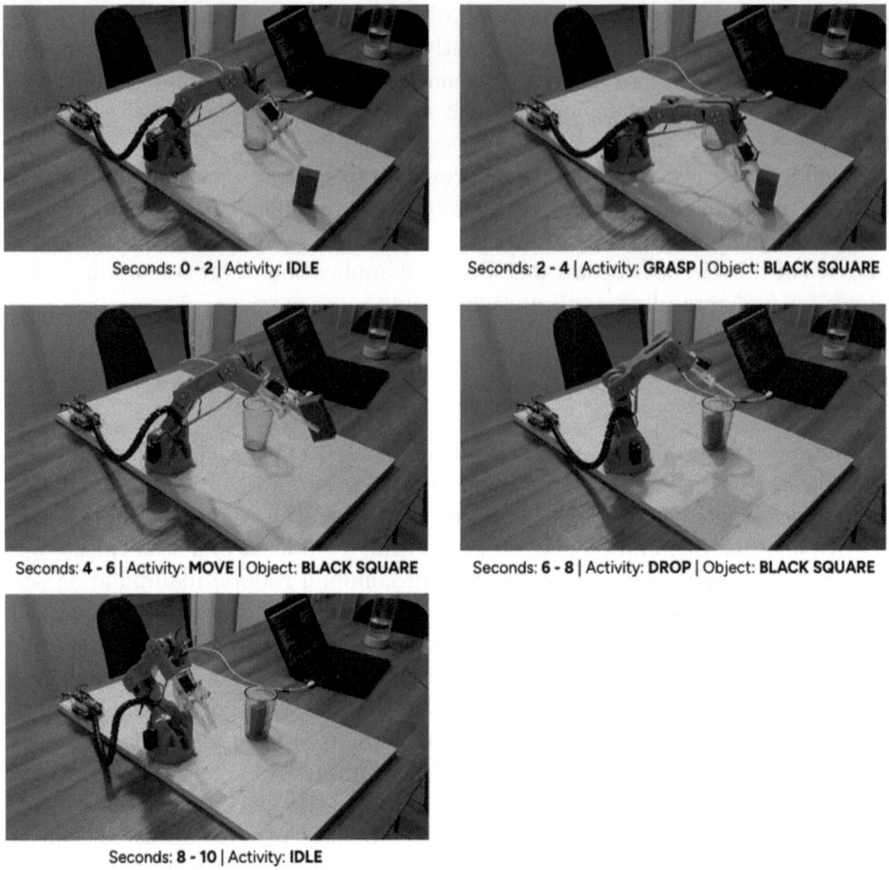

Fig. 2. Activity recognition results for a robotic manipulation task

the possible robot activities through affords_action relationships, indicating that the object can be grasped, moved, and dropped. Additional relationships capture contextual information about the environment, such as the surface from which the object is picked (picked_from) and the intended destination (intended_for). By encoding these relationships, the knowledge graph constrains and contextualizes the interpretation of visual observations. When the perception module detects the presence of the black square, the reasoning component queries the graph to retrieve the set of activities that are compatible with the detected object, allowing the system to infer the most coherent activity from the observed scene dynamics.

The proposed approach was evaluated on three different robotic manipulation videos. For each scenario, a dedicated knowledge graph was constructed to model the objects and interactions relevant to the specific task. Due to space

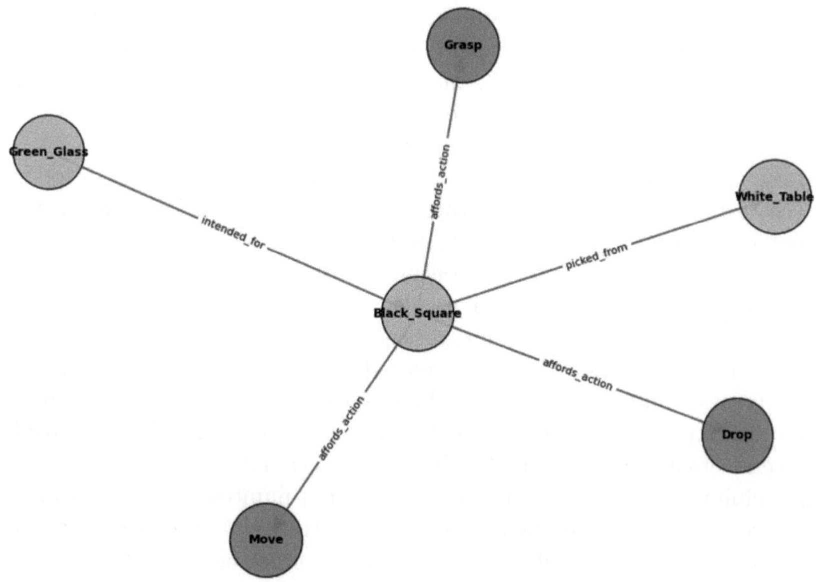

Fig. 3. Knowledge graph used in the experimental scenario

limitations, only one representative example is reported in this paper, while additional experimental materials are available in the public repository[1].

This result shows how the proposed semantic layer enables the system to interpret the sequence of robot activities in a consistent way, transforming visual observations into structured activity descriptions. Moreover, the extracted activity sequences provide structured descriptions of robotic behavior that can be further transformed into event-based representations, enabling the application of process mining techniques for analyzing robotic operations.

5 Conclusions

This paper presented an approach for the semantic interpretation of robotic activities from video streams, leveraging the synergy between visual perception and domain knowledge encoded in a knowledge graph. The core of our approach lies in the introduction of a semantic abstraction layer that contextualizes visual observations and supports the reasoning process used to infer robot activities. By integrating structured domain knowledge with observations extracted from video frames, the system generates consistent representations of robotic activities.

The experimental evaluation on robotic manipulation videos showed how the proposed approach can transform fine-grained visual observations into structured activity descriptions associated with manipulated objects. The use of dedicated knowledge graphs for each scenario allows the system to adapt the interpretation

[1] https://bitbucket.org/proslabteam/rag_robot/src/main/.

process to different operational contexts. The structured activity representations generated by the system provide a bridge between raw sensory observations and higher-level analytical techniques, enabling the potential application of process mining methods to analyze robotic operations.

Limitations. Despite the promising results, several challenges remain for future research. First, the evaluation operates under the assumption that each video segment corresponds to a single, isolated execution of a robotic task. In real-world scenarios, video streams are continuous; therefore, a robust temporal segmentation logic is needed to automatically detect case boundaries and partition the stream into distinct process instances. Second, the approach relies on manually constructed knowledge graphs tailored to each scenario. While this design enables precise modeling of domain knowledge, building such representations may require expert knowledge and may limit scalability when dealing with large and diverse environments. Finally, the current evaluation focuses on relatively simple manipulation scenarios involving a limited number of objects and activities. More complex environments involving multiple actors, concurrent interactions, or ambiguous visual observations may introduce additional challenges for both perception and reasoning.

Future Work. Moving forward, we aim to extend this approach to collaborative scenarios involving multiple actors, where knowledge graphs must evolve to represent interactions and coordination between robots, humans, and other entities present in the scene. We also plan to investigate automated knowledge acquisition strategies, exploring how large language models and ontological learning can be used to bootstrap knowledge graphs directly from technical manuals or unlabelled video demonstrations, reducing the need for human experts. Lastly, we intend to integrate a probabilistic reasoning layer to better handle the inherent uncertainty of visual perception, ensuring robust activity recognition even in noisy environments. In particular, future work will investigate the integration of probabilistic trace inference techniques, such as those proposed for stochastically known logs [2], to complement the semantic constraints introduced by the knowledge graph.

References

1. van der Aalst, W.: Process Mining: Data Science in Action. Springer (2016)
2. Bogdanov, E., Cohen, I., Gal, A.: Sktr: Trace recovery from stochastically known logs. In: International Conference on Process Mining, pp. 49–56 (2023)
3. Buchmann, R., et al.: Large language models: expectations for semantics-driven systems engineering. Data Knowl. Eng. **152** (2024)
4. Corradini, F., Pettinari, S., Re, B., Rossi, L., Sampaolo, M.: Enabling process mining on multimodal robotic data. In: Advanced Information Systems Engineering Workshops. LNBIP, vol. 556, pp. 257–269. Springer (2025). https://doi.org/10.1007/978-3-031-94931-9_21

5. Corradini, F., Pettinari, S., Re, B., Rossi, L., Sampaolo, M.: Robotic datasets for process mining. In: Intelligent Information Systems. LNBIP, vol. 557, pp. 53–61. Springer (2025) https://doi.org/10.1007/978-3-031-94590-8_7
6. Corradini, F., Pettinari, S., Re, B., Rossi, L., Sampaolo, M.: Multimodal zero-shot activity recognition for process mining of robotic systems. In: Business Process Management: Responsible BPM Forum, Process Technology Forum, Educators Forum, pp. 263–275. Springer (2026). https://doi.org/10.1007/978-3-032-02936-2_19
7. Franceschetti, M., Buchegger, D.M., Seiger, R., Weber, B.: Toward iot-based process analytics: extending event knowledge graphs with ambiguity. In: Enterprise, Business-Process and Information Systems Modeling. pp. 176–192. Springer Nature Switzerland, Cham (2025). https://doi.org/10.1007/978-3-031-95397-2_11
8. Jang, D.S., et al.: Unlocking robotic autonomy: a survey on the applications of foundation models. Int. J. Control Autom. Syst. **22**, 2341–2671 (2024)
9. Ji, S., Zheng, X., Wu, C.: Hargpt: are llms zero-shot human activity recognizers? In: 2024 IEEE International Workshop on Foundation Models for Cyber-Physical Systems & Internet of Things (FMSys), pp. 38–43 (2024)
10. Keith, R., La, H.M.: Review of Autonomous Mobile Robots for the Warehouse Environment. arXiv e-prints (2024)
11. Knoch, S., Ponpathirkoottam, S., Schwartz, T.: Video-to-model: unsupervised trace extraction from videos for process discovery and conformance checking in manual assembly. In: Fahland, D., Ghidini, C., Becker, J., Dumas, M. (eds.) BPM 2020. LNCS, vol. 12168, pp. 291–308. Springer, Cham (2020). https://doi.org/10.1007/978-3-030-58666-9_17
12. Kratsch, W., König, F., Röglinger, M.: Shedding light on blind spots – developing a reference architecture to leverage video data for process mining. Dec. Support Syst. **158** (2022)
13. Laurenzi, E., Mathys, A., Martin, A.: An llm-aided enterprise knowledge graph (ekg) engineering process. In: Proceedings of the AAAI Symposium Series, vol. 3(1), pp, 148–156 (2024)
14. Melfsen, A., Lepsien, A., Bosselmann, J., Koschmider, A., Hartung, E.: Describing behavior sequences of fattening pigs using process mining on video data and automated pig behavior recognition. Agriculture **13**(8), 1639 (2023)
15. Weckenborg, C., Thies, C., Spengler, T.S.: Harmonizing ergonomics and economics of assembly lines using collaborative robots and exoskeletons. J. Manuf. Syst. **62**, 681–702 (2022)
16. Weng, Y., Wu, G., Zheng, T., Yang, Y., Luo, J.: Large model for small data: Foundation model for cross-modal rf human activity recognition. In: Conference on Embedded Networked Sensor Systems, pp. 436–449. ACM (2024)
17. Zhou, Y., Yang, J., Zou, H., Xie, L.: Tent: connect language models with iot sensors for zero-shot activity recognition. IEEE Trans. Mob. Comput. **01**, 1–12 (2023)

Towards a Cyber Threat Operationalization Engine

Ofir Manor[1], Ortal Lavi[1], Ahmed M. Elmesiry[1], Igor Podoski[2], Ewa Seroczynska[2], and Andrés Murillo[1](✉)

[1] Fujitsu Research of Europe, Slough, UK
{ofir.manor,ortal.lavi,ahmed.elmesiry,andres.murillo}@fujitsu.com
[2] Fujitsu Technology Solutions, Munich, Germany
{igor.podoski,ewa.seroczynska}@fujitsu.com

Abstract. New adversarial threats being reported every day, make it imperative to hardening existing systems against them as fast as possible. Cyber Threat Intelligence (CTI) reports describe adversarial behaviour in narrative form, but operationalizing these reports into network-specific, executable emulations remains labour-intensive and slow, delaying validation and mitigation. Nevertheless, existing tooling rarely provides a direct path from narrative CTI to runnable, topology-aware emulation artefacts, forcing experts to manually translate reports into environment-specific actions; which delays vulnerability mitigation and exposes organizations to cyber threat actors. We present a work-in-progress Cyber Threat Operationalization Engine that transforms a CTI report into (i) ATT&CK-labelled behaviours, (ii) a network-constrained representation of a feasible attack path derived via logic-based attack-graph reasoning, and (iii) an executable emulation plan instantiated in MITRE CALDERA and executed safely inside an isolated, emulated "CyberTwin" network. Our design leverages established components: ATT&CK, CALDERA, Multi-host, Multi-stage Vulnerability Analysis Language (MulVAL), and Graphical Network Simulator 3 (GNS3)—while using an agentic orchestration layer to connect CTI-derived intent to concrete actions on a specific topology. We focus on the representation and compilation of adversarial behaviour into attack-graph form and discuss practical challenges toward autonomy, including topology uncertainty, and the gap between abstract techniques and runnable emulation artefacts. A case study based on the Cutting Edge campaign was also introduced to demonstrate the feasibility of the proposed framework.

1 Introduction

Public vulnerability disclosures have grown dramatically in volume in recent years, from 6487 in 2015 to 48172 in 2025[1]. This trend creates a porous environment by increasing the opportunity for adversaries to weaponize newly exposed weaknesses before organizations can deploy mitigations. Security Operations

[1] https://nvd.nist.gov/vuln/search#/nvd/home?resultType=statistics.

R. Posenato and I. Vanderfeesten (Eds.): CAiSE 2026 Workshops, LNBIP 586, pp. 254–266, 2026.
https://doi.org/10.1007/978-3-032-28160-9_23

Centers (SOCs) struggle to manually validate which threats are feasible in their specific infrastructure, a process that may require days to weeks of expert effort and leaves systems exposed during this validation window. When attacks are detected, organizations can collect data and may share indicators of compromise, but it may still take weeks before some global solutions (i.e. patches) are created to plug the vulnerability [4]. The organizations' collected information about cybersecurity threats, which can be reported in CTI reports, describe many of the attackers' steps and targets.

When exploitation is observed, defenders and vendors publish CTI describing the intrusion's tactics and techniques. SOC teams must then determine whether the reported behaviour is feasible in their own environment, what assets are exposed, and what mitigations reduce risk—all under strict constraints on operational disruption. Testing these hypotheses directly on production networks is high risk and often unacceptable.

This work targets the operationalization gap: given a CTI report and an enterprise topology, how can we, semi-automatically, produce a safe and environment specific adversary emulation that helps defenders understand plausible attack progress and defensive priorities without touching production. Furthermore, we aim to explore how to accomplish this using open and trusted tools.

Our work leverages the recent developments of Natural Language Processing (NLP) and Large Language Model (LLM) as interface layers between unstructured reporting and structured representations (e.g. technique identifiers, prerequisites, and action parameters). In our design, we use an LLM primarily as a normalization layer between narrative CTI and structured representations. Concretely, an LLM-based agent extracts candidate ATT&CK techniques and relevant context from CTI text, which are then consumed by the attack-graph and emulation stages. We intentionally scope the LLM's role to structured extraction and orchestration, while topology grounding and execution semantics are handled by deterministic components.

In this paper, we propose a threat operationalization engine that combines (i) CTI-to-ATT&CK extraction, (ii) topology-aware feasibility reasoning via attack-graph construction, and (iii) execution of an emulation plan in an isolated "CyberTwin" environment using established tooling. The generated information can then be used by security professionals to secure the network. The core technical challenge is not extracting ATT&CK IDs, but operationalizing them: binding abstract techniques to concrete, topology-specific preconditions, targets, and parameters, and emitting runnable emulation artefacts. Our engine contributes to this bridge by translating CTI-derived behaviours into attack-graph semantics grounded in a specific network model and compiling feasible, parameterized steps into CALDERA-ready artefacts (adversary profile + fact source) that an operator can execute without manual re-authoring.

This paper makes four contributions: (i) We define threat operationalization as the conversion of narrative CTI into a network-grounded, executable emulation plan. (ii) We present an end-to-end architecture that converts CTI into ATT&CK-labelled behaviours, constrains them via logic-based attack-graph feasibility (Multi-host, multi-stage Vulnerability Analysis Language (MulVAL)), and compiles feasible paths into CALDERA-ready artefacts. (iii) We introduce a safety-by-design execution model using an isolated CyberTwin network emulator (GNS3) to enable rapid validation without production risk. (iv) We report an initial case study to operationalize a real-world APT campaign (Cutting Edge) that exploited zero-day vulnerabilities in enterprise VPN infrastructure against a realistic enterprise topology with limited manual intervention in the case study. Additionally, we outlined the challenges of achieving a fully autonomous threat-operationalization system.

2 Frameworks and Tools

We start by presenting the existing frameworks and tools which make up our engine. These components provide the behavioural, emulation, and reasoning substrate for our engine. For the most part, these are open-source and widely used in practice and research.

MITRE ATT&CK and CALDERA: MITRE ATT&CK provides a standardised representation of adversarial tactics and techniques grounded in real-world observations [12]. We use ATT&CK as the behavioural vocabulary for CTI extraction and for linking extracted behaviours to executable emulation steps. MITRE CALDERA [8] is an adversary-emulation framework built around ATT&CK that executes abilities through adversary profiles and fact sources on real or virtual networks.

GNS3: GNS3 is a network emulation platform that allows for risk-free building, designing, and testing of a network[2]. We use GNS3 with Docker and QEMU virtual images of network and host devices to emulate the behaviour of a customer network. This emulation, called CyberTwin, is used to safely evaluate the impact of cybersecurity threats.

MulVAL: The framework [9] is a Datalog-based modelling language, used for modelling the interaction of software bugs/vulnerabilities and network configurations. An Attack Graph (AG) is constructed with vertices that represent two types of entities:

- Facts: network topologies and configurations, security policies, and known vulnerabilities.
- Rules (also known as Interaction Rules (IRs)): possible interactions between components in the network.

Facts are *partially* collected using existing tools and services such as Nessus [2] and OVAL [1] along with custom scripts. The edges between them display the interactions between components of a network and the possible malicious behaviours that can be taken on it, culminating in a logical AG.

[2] https://www.gns3.com/.

3 Related Work

Similar works have processed CTI reports and the Adversarial Tactics, Techniques, and Common Knowledge (ATT&CK) knowledge database to automatically extract intelligence from the reports. TTPHunter [10] and TTPXHunter [11] both use BERT [3] to extract from each sentence of an unstructured CTI report a fitting technique (if one is present). Two more are AttacKG [5] and AttacKG+ [15]. Both extract Tactics, Techniques, and Procedures (TTPs) from an unstructured CTI report and then create an AG from it. The former uses what were, at the time, top-of-the-line NLP models, while the latter uses LLMs for the extraction. This final graph represents not only the techniques but also provides information on their order or dependencies. And in [14], the researchers create an attack based solely on the report.

Prior CTI-to-graph approaches primarily focus on extraction and relationship modeling, whereas our goal is to produce operator-ready emulation artefacts grounded in a specific topology. Conversely, LLM-assisted emulation authoring improves convenience but often lacks explicit, logic-based feasibility grounding; our design places topology constraints at the center of operationalization.

In the work of [13], the authors give a detailed description of MulVAL, and address adding new IRs from MITRE IRs TTPs. Their work provides a comprehensive synthesis of IRs extensions contributed across the literature, cataloguing their attack-scenario coverage and the corresponding ATT&CK mappings.

Finally, in automatic adversary emulation, the CALDERA MCP plugin uses LLMs to assist in the generation of CALDERA abilities [7]. This allows the user to pick their own LLM and have it produce an adversary, along with all the fitting abilities, from a *human-text* like request. It also provides the functions to run an operation. These do not take any topology into account outside the LLM input, but provide good indicators for future artificial intelligence (AI) assisted threat emulation.

Table 1 positions prior CTI-to-emulation approaches along three axes: (i) the type of output artefact produced, (ii) whether the system applies topology constraints during reasoning, and (iii) whether the output is an operator-ready, executable emulation artefact.

Table 1. Comparison of CTI-to-Emulation Approaches

System	Output Artefact	Topology	Executable
TTPHunter [10]	Technique list	✗	✗
TTPXHunter [11]	Technique list	✗	✗
AttacKG [5]	ATT&CK graph	✗	✗
AttacKG+ [15]	ATT&CK graph	✗	✗
Wang et al. [14]	Scripted attack plan	Partial	Partial
CALDERA MCP [7]	CALDERA operation	✗	✓
Our Engine	CALDERA profile + facts	✓	✓

The table reveals that our system is the only approach that *simultaneously* produces topology-grounded *and* operator-ready CALDERA artefacts from narrative CTI input.

4 Design

To make each design stage concrete, we introduce the *Cutting Edge* campaign (MITRE ATT&CK C0029) as a running example. Cutting Edge targeted Ivanti Connect Secure VPN appliances by exploiting CVE-2023-46805 (authentication bypass), CVE-2024-21887 (command injection), and CVE-2024-21893 (SSRF bypass), and combined initial access with follow-on defence evasion and lateral movement. We will trace how the engine (1) extracts ATT&CK techniques from the Cutting Edge CTI report, (2) instantiates the corresponding CyberTwin topology, (3) grounds the techniques against the topology via logic-based attack-graph construction, and (4) compiles the resulting path into a CALDERA adversary profile. The full case study appears in Sect. 5; the running-example annotations in this section reference the same artefacts (Fig. 1).

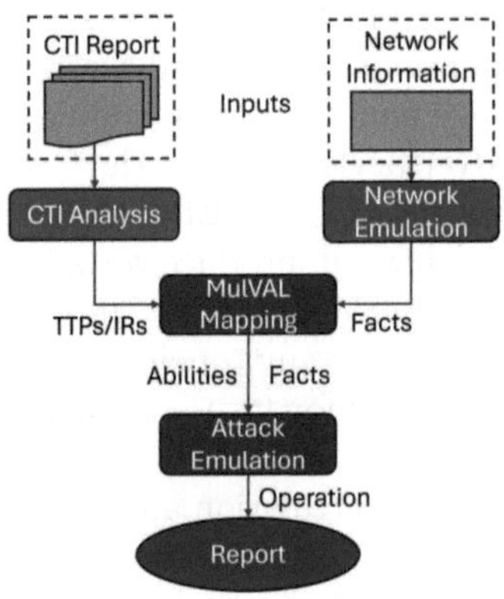

Fig. 1. Engine Framework.

4.1 Technique Extraction

The first stage extracts candidate ATT&CK techniques and sub-techniques from a CTI report. These techniques and sub-techniques form the basis for our threat emulation, as they describe the adversarial behaviour in a generic language that is not tied to a specific network or system, which allows us to use them dynamically. In our work, we use a simple mechanism; we input the entire report to a SOTA LLM and request it to list out for us all the relevant TTPs. We also provide it with a list of all current TTPs to assist in avoiding a hallucination that would create a novel technique or return one that has been deprecated.

Extraction Evaluation (Cutting Edge Case Study) . The MITRE ATT&CK campaign page for Cutting Edge (C0029)[3] lists eleven associated techniques as ground truth. Table 2 reports extraction performance.

Table 2. LLM Technique Extraction Results—Cutting Edge Campaign

Metric	Value	Notes
Ground-truth techniques	11	MITRE C0029 page
Extracted (correct)	9	Precision = 100%
Missed	2	Recall = 81.8%
Hallucinated (not in list)	0	Grounding effective
Precision	**100%**	9/9 returned
Recall	**81.8%**	9/11 recovered

The two missed techniques, T1036.005 (*Masquerading: Match Legitimate Name*) and T1070.004 (*File Deletion*), were described implicitly in the CTI report without explicit procedural language, representing a known limitation of surface-level extraction. No hallucinated techniques were returned, confirming that grounding the LLM against the canonical technique list effectively prevents out-of-vocabulary output. These error modes motivate future integration of STIX parsing and keyword-pattern matching as complementary deterministic extraction channels.

4.2 Network Emulation

One of the goals of our engine is to provide a safe environment for testing a novel threat. For this, we use an emulated network, disconnected from the enterprise environment, so that attacks can be validated without affecting live services. We use the network emulation tool GNS3.

The current prototype is scoped to environments where a network and system inventory already exists, such as organisations that maintain a Configuration Management Database (CMDB), an asset management platform, or a prior network digital twin—where asset inventories are mandated by compliance frameworks (e.g., NIS2, CIS Controls).

In the current implementation, we assume access to the information required to instantiate the CyberTwin, including host inventory, software images, network links, and relevant configuration commands. At least one machine also runs a CALDERA agent so that the generated adversary can be executed in the emulated environment. When inventory or configuration facts are incomplete, the system may fail to ground or compile a feasible path rather than infer unsupported bindings.

[3] https://attack.mitre.org/campaigns/C0029/.

4.3 Topology-Constrained Adaptation to Network

At this step, our system has the two main elements to emulate the attack and these are combined to evaluate the impact of the analysed attack. MulVAL is used in this step, by using the acquired information to generate an attack graph that provides a full description of how this attack would be executed on the target network. As for MulVAL facts, representing network and system information required to configure the elements in the CyberTwin, these are gathered along with the rest of the information from the enterprise network. This includes information that can be analysed from the topology, such as which components make up the network and which devices are connected to each other, but also information from the configuration of the machines themselves, such as which vulnerabilities they possess and what level of user access they require. Each piece of information that is relevant is turned into a fact and stored. Then, we use the work mapping ATT&CK TTPs to MulVAL IRs[4] and run eXtended Stony Brook (XSB), the program that builds MulVAL AGs, to create a simple AG that includes only machines from the network and uses only attacks related to the original CTI report we started from. We determine if the AG created was successful if: i) it contains only IRs that are related to TTPs from the report (and no more); ii) there is a feasible path from the attacker to their goal, and iii) the vulnerabilities mentioned in the CTI report are found in corresponding places in the AG.

If so, we choose a path that reaches the bottom node of the graph, representing the final goal of the attack. And if the graph creation fails (assuming all the components are correct), then we assume that the attack is irrelevant for the network. This'attack path' provides us with the information we need to understand which action in the attack is directed at what machine in the network and in what order. Finally, notice that if multiple paths reaching the bottom node of the graph are identified, testing them all, one by one, with our system is trivial.

4.4 Attack Emulation

Once MulVAL identifies a feasible attack path, the system compiles each step into a corresponding CALDERA ability, from the IRs, together with the execution facts needed to run it, including the source host, target host, and relevant parameters such as ports and protocols. The selected abilities are then ordered according to the chosen path and combined with a fact source to create an adversary profile. This makes the output not only an analytical attack graph, but an executable emulation package grounded in the target topology. **Formal Compilation Pipeline Specification.** Let $\mathcal{E} = \{e_i\}_{i=1}^{n}$ denote the set of CTI-extracted behaviours, where each $e_i = (\tau_i, \sigma_i)$ contains an ATT&CK technique or sub-technique τ_i and the supporting context span σ_i. Let the network model be $\mathcal{N} = (H, S, R, V, C)$, where H is the set of hosts, S the set of running services, $R \subseteq H \times H$ the reachability relation, V the vulnerability facts, and C the

[4] https://github.com/dtayouri/MulVAL-MITRE/tree/main.

set of credential and configuration facts. Define two mappings:

$$M_{\mathrm{IR}} : \tau \rightarrow \mathcal{I} \quad \text{(ATT\&CK technique} \mapsto \text{MulVAL IR set)}, \qquad (1)$$

$$M_{\mathrm{AB}} : \tau \rightarrow \mathcal{A} \quad \text{(ATT\&CK technique} \mapsto \text{CALDERA ability set)}, \qquad (2)$$

where $\mathcal{I}$ is the set of MulVAL Interaction Rules and $\mathcal{A}$ is the CALDERA ability repository.

The MulVAL reasoning engine accepts $\mathcal{N}$ and $\{M_{\mathrm{IR}}(\tau_i)\}_{i=1}^{n}$ and produces an Attack Graph $G = (V_G, E_G)$, where each vertex $v \in V_G$ represents either a fact (a ground atom from $\mathcal{N}$) or a derived rule node, and each directed edge $(u, v) \in E_G$ represents a logical inference step. A *feasible path* is a directed path $P = (p_1, \ldots, p_m)$, $p_j \in V_G$, from the designated attacker node to the goal node in G, such that: (i) every rule node on P corresponds to an IR in $\{M_{\mathrm{IR}}(\tau_i)\}_{i=1}^{n}$; (ii) the goal node is reachable; and (iii) every CVE mentioned in the CTI report appears as a fact node on the path. If no feasible path exists, the engine concludes that the described campaign is not reachable in the target network under the supplied facts. For each step p_j on the feasible path, the compiler produces a parameterised execution tuple $x_j = (a_j, \theta_j)$, where $a_j \in \mathcal{A}$ is the selected CALDERA ability and θ_j is the variable binding derived from $\mathcal{N}$. The compiler emits two artefacts: a CALDERA adversary profile whose ability sequence follows the topological order of P, and a fact source containing the seed facts required by the selected abilities. Algorithm 1 summarises the procedure.

Algorithm 1. TTP-to-CALDERA Compilation

Require: Feasible path $P = (p_1, \ldots, p_m) \subseteq V_G$, network model $\mathcal{N}$, mapping M_{AB}, fact base $\mathcal{F}$
Ensure: Adversary profile $\mathcal{O}$, fact source $\mathcal{FS}$

$\mathcal{O} \leftarrow \langle\rangle$; $\mathcal{FS} \leftarrow \{\}$
for $j = 1$ **to** m **do**
  $\tau_j \leftarrow$ GetTechnique(p_j)
  $A_j \leftarrow M_{\mathrm{AB}}(\tau_j)$
  if $A_j = \emptyset$ **then**
    MarkUnsupported(p_j)
    continue ▷ requires analyst delegation
  end if
  $a_j \leftarrow$ SelectByPlatform(A_j, p_j)
  $h_{\mathrm{src}}, h_{\mathrm{tgt}} \leftarrow$ ExtractHosts(p_j)
  $\theta_j \leftarrow$ BindParams(a_j, h_{src}, h_{tgt}, $\mathcal{N}$, $\mathcal{F}$)
  $\mathcal{O}$.append(a_j)
  $\mathcal{FS} \leftarrow \mathcal{FS} \cup \theta_j$
end for
return $\mathcal{O}$, $\mathcal{FS}$

The current prototype automates the CTI-to-ATT&CK extraction, MulVAL fact population from a topology inventory, attack-graph construction, and compilation of supported abilities into a CALDERA adversary profile and fact source.

Three steps remain *semi-automated* and require analyst involvement in the current implementation: (a) provision of the host inventory and configuration files required to instantiate the CyberTwin; (b) authoring of CALDERA abilities for techniques that lack an existing implementation in the ability repository (one of five TTPs in the Cutting Edge case study); and (c) selection among multiple feasible paths when the attack graph contains more than one path to the goal node. Future work targets full automation of (a) via network discovery integration and (b) via LLM-generated ability synthesis. All automation decisions are logged and exposed to the operator to support audit and review.

5 Prototype Implementation and Case Study

The case study was performed on a Standard D16s v3 Azure VM, with an Ubuntu 24.04 OS. Our prototype was developed mostly in Python (3.12.3), with some additional MulVAL auxiliary rules created. The only LLM resource used was a GPT-4o model accessed through Azure. Our prototype is executed using a Docker stack.

To show the feasibility of our approach, we conducted a case based on a real-world adversarial campaign, MITRE ATT&CK's Cutting Edge campaign[5], which targeted Ivanti Connect Secure VPN appliances.

CTI Analysis: The use case starts by inputting Cutting Edge's CTI report in our system. The report documented an intrusion chain that included exploitation of CVE-2023-46805 and CVE-2024-21887, with CVE-2024-21893 later used to bypass mitigations. The campaign combines initial access through VPN appliance exploitation with follow-on defence evasion and living-off-the-land activity, making it a representative end-to-end operationalization target. Several reports have been written based on this attack, including those by Google [6] and CISA[6]. The Ivanti vulnerabilities created a 3-week exposure window between disclosure and patch availability. During this period, organizations faced a critical question:"Is our network vulnerable to this specific attack chain, and what defensive measures can we implement immediately?"

Network Emulation: In our CyberTwin, we emulated an enterprise-style topology with user subnets, servers, routing/firewall boundaries, and a VPN gateway reachable from a simulated Internet. The topology captures the campaign logic using a role-equivalent VPN gateway stand-in rather than a byte-faithful reproduction of the vendor-specific appliance exploit chain. The environment was instantiated automatically in GNS3 from topology and configuration files, producing the testbed shown in Fig. 2

MITRE TTP Extraction: We apply the technique-extraction step described in 4.1 to produce a set of candidate ATT&CK techniques and sub-techniques associated with the campaign described in the CTI report. The extractor returned nine techniques/sub-techniques, which were then used as inputs to

[5] https://attack.mitre.org/campaigns/C0029/.

[6] https://www.cisa.gov/news-events/cybersecurity-advisories/aa24-060b.

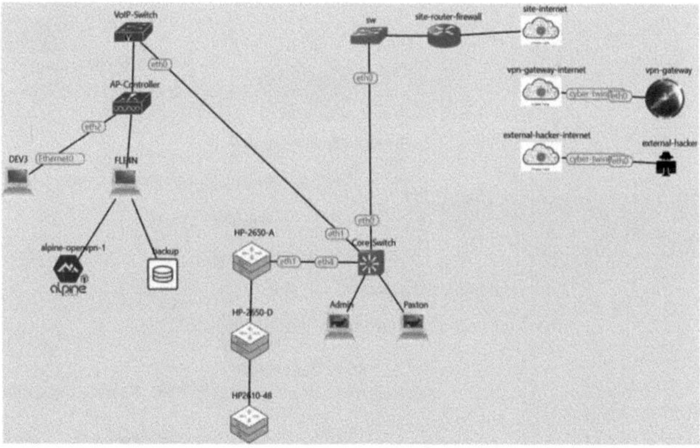

Fig. 2. The Enterprise case study topology created on GNS3 and presented through the GUI

the topology-constrained reasoning and emulation stages that were later used to determine the MulVAL IRs and the CALDERA abilities.

MulVAL Mapping: Our technology assists MulVAL in performing two processes: i) mapping extracted techniques to defined MulVAL IRs, and ii) using the network and system information from the test topology to populate MulVAL facts. We derive part of the MulVAL facts using a script that goes over the topology. The rest are pre-mapped by our knowledge of the emulated network. After these two steps are done, MulVAL generates an attack graph that is grounded to the test network topology. Figure 3 shows the attack graph.

Attack Emulation: From a feasible path in the AG, we selected the techniques for emulation. In this case, the system determined that 5 TTPs were needed for the attack. Of those, four had at least one implemented ability on CALDERA. The remaining step had no suitable CALDERA ability in the current prototype and would require analyst-authored support. The system also extracts the information to populate the CALDERA facts required to execute the CALDERA abilities, such as ports, transmission protocols, from where the attack is coming, and who the target is. We created an adversary we called *Caldera Cutting Edge Adversary* and ran the attack (a CALDERA operation) on the topology. CALDERA reported successful completion of the configured operation objectives in the emulated environment.

In summary, the extractor returned nine candidate ATT&CK techniques and sub-techniques. Topology-constrained grounding reduced these to a feasible path requiring five TTPs, four of which had implemented CALDERA abilities. The resulting adversary profile executed successfully in the CyberTwin, providing initial evidence of end-to-end feasibility while leaving broader evaluation of extraction accuracy, scalability, and robustness to future work.

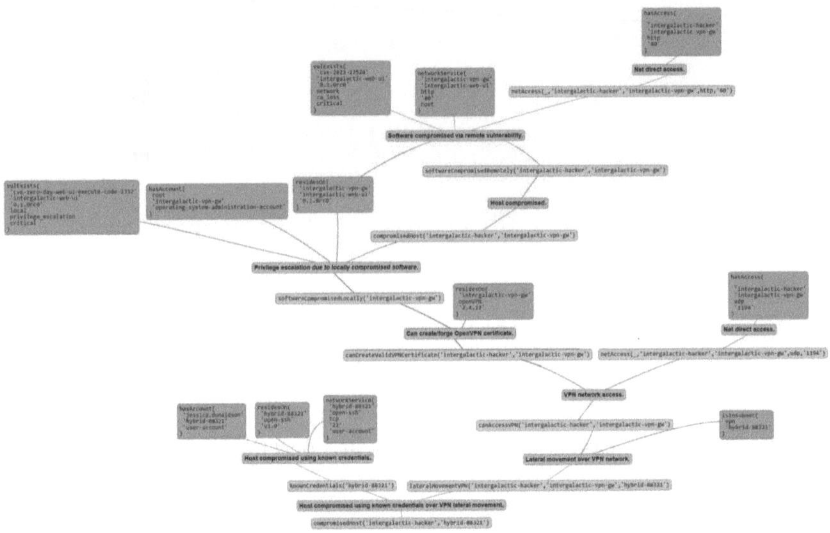

Fig. 3. The MulVAL attack graph generated from the topology and the techniques extracted from the CTI report

5.1 Case Study Discussion and Future Work

This case study demonstrates end-to-end feasibility in a controlled environment and illustrates the intended practitioner workflow. Starting from a CTI report, the engine extracts ATT&CK-labelled behaviours, constrains them using topology-aware attack-graph reasoning, compiles the resulting feasible steps into a CALDERA adversary profile plus fact source, and executes the operation inside the CyberTwin. The result is not only a feasibility assessment, but a reusable emulation package that can support regression testing, control validation, and analyst review. However, the current prototype still depends on sufficiently accurate inventory data and on the availability of suitable CALDERA abilities.

Technique Extraction and Hybrid Approaches: CTI report analysis using LLMs is still a work in progress. In this paper, we used a simple SOTA LLM to demonstrate initial capabilities and a simple RAG system. Nevertheless, future work could also include combining the LLMs with STIX parsing and other deterministic methods to improve the extraction of techniques. This can be especially useful for intelligence reports that are not formally written.

Semi-Automatic Abilities Generation: In this paper, we relied only on techniques that already had a CALDERA ability implemented. This limits the scope of our framework, because for other attacks, a human analyst would have to develop a CALDERA ability grounded in the specific network or system being analysed. Nevertheless, AI Agents could be used to automatically or semi-automatically generate these abilities, either by modifying base abilities or creating tailored abilities for the specific test system.

CyberTwin Generation: Building an accurate CyberTwin remains a substantial engineering task. Future work will focus on creating and maintaining network and system inventories and on semi-automatic CyberTwin deployment from those inventories.

Threat Mitigation: Our framework could be extended to incorporate existing countermeasures within the targets and propose updates to those countermeasures to mitigate the evaluated threats.

Other Applications: Finally, although we initially focused this work on traditional IT networks, we can extend the presented framework to address cybersecurity threats in other systems, such as industrial control systems, robotics, and autonomous systems. One requirement for such an extension is that an attack taxonomy similar to MITRE ATT&CK is available for those systems.

6 Conclusion

This paper presented a work-in-progress threat operationalization engine that converts narrative CTI into topology-grounded, executable adversary-emulation artefacts. The main contribution is the compilation layer that bridges CTI-derived ATT&CK behaviours, logic-based feasibility reasoning in MulVAL, and execution in CALDERA within an isolated CyberTwin. The Cutting Edge case study demonstrated end-to-end feasibility.

References

1. Baker, J., Hansbury, M., Haynes, D.: The oval® language specification. The MITRE Corporation (2011)
2. Deraison, R.: The nessus project (nd). https://www.tenable.com/
3. Devlin, J., Chang, M.W., Lee, K., Toutanova, K.: BERT: pre-training of Deep Bidirectional Transformers for Language Understanding (2019). https://arxiv.org/abs/1810.04805
4. Jones, D.: Delayed Ivanti Patch Arrives After Weeks of Exploitation (January 2024). https://www.cybersecuritydive.com/news/delayed-ivanti-patch-arrives/706157/, Accessed 21 Nov 2025
5. Li, Z., Zeng, J., Chen, Y., Liang, Z.: AttacKG: Constructing Technique Knowledge Graph from Cyber Threat Intelligence Reports (2022). https://arxiv.org/abs/2111.07093
6. McLellan, T., Wolfram, J., Roncone, G., Lin, M., Wallace, R., Andonov, D.: Cutting Edge: Suspected APT Targets Ivanti Connect Secure VPN in New Zero-Day Exploitation (2024). https://cloud.google.com/blog/topics/threat-intelligence/suspected-apt-targets-ivanti-zero-day/
7. Michalak, E., Perry, M.: Connecting LLMs to CALDERA with the MCP Plugin. Medium (November 2025). https://medium.com/@mitrecaldera/connecting-llms-to-caldera-with-the-mcp-plugin-da1450254827, Accessed 24 Nov 2025
8. Miller, D., Alford, R., Applebaum, A., Foster, H., Little, C., Strom, B.E.: automated adversary emulation: a case for planning and acting with unknowns. Tech. rep., MITRE Corporation (2018). https://api.semanticscholar.org/CorpusID:145814722

9. Ou, X., Govindavajhala, S., Appel, A.W.: MulVAL: a logic-based network security analyzer. In: USENIX security symposium, Baltimore, MD, vol. 8, pp. 113–128 (2005)
10. Rani, N., Saha, B., Maurya, V., Shukla, S.K.: TTPHunter: automated extraction of actionable intelligence as TTPs from narrative threat reports. In: Proceedings of the 2023 Australasian Computer Science Week, ACSW 2023, pp. 126–134. Association for Computing Machinery, New York (2023). https://doi.org/10.1145/3579375.3579391
11. Rani, N., Saha, B., Maurya, V., Shukla, S.K.: TTPXHunter: actionable threat intelligence extraction as TTPs from finished cyber threat reports. Digital Threats: Res. Pract. **5**(4), 1–19 (2024). https://doi.org/10.1145/3696427
12. Strom, B.E., Applebaum, A., Miller, D.P., Nickels, K.C., Pennington, A.G., Thomas, C.B.: Mitre att&ck: Design and Philosophy. Technical report (2018)
13. Tayouri, D., Baum, N., Shabtai, A., Puzis, R.: A survey of MulVAL extensions and their attack scenarios coverage. IEEE Access **11**, 27974–27991 (2023)
14. Wang, L., et al.: From Sands to Mansions: Towards Automated Cyberattack Emulation with Classical Planning and Large Language Models (2025). https://arxiv.org/abs/2407.16928
15. Zhang, Y., et al.: AttacKG+:Boosting Attack Knowledge Graph Construction with Large Language Models (2024). https://arxiv.org/abs/2405.04753

Towards a Domain-Agnostic Safety-by-Design AI Engineering Pipeline

Elena Hoemann(✉), Akshay Anilkumar Girija, Johann Maximilian Christensen, Yannick Kees, Florian Krone, Thomas Liebert, Ryan Mut, Gerald Sauter, Thomas Stefani, Frank Köster, and Sven Hallerbach

Institute for AI Safety and Security, German Aerospace Center (DLR), Sankt Augustin and Ulm, Germany
elena.hoemann@dlr.de

Abstract. AI-based applications already revolutionize our everyday lives; however, it remains unclear how to assess their safety given their black-box nature. Certifying them for safety-critical applications is thus still under current research. Therefore, we developed the Safe AI Pipeline (SAIPi) as an example of a safety-by-design approach to the engineering of AI systems. The pipeline contains several tools for data, model, and monitoring design, fulfilling requirements such as data completeness and model accuracy. We use MNIST as an exemplary showcase and proof of concept for developing deep learning models. We completed an entire iteration of the pipeline, which demonstrates how to engineer an AI system in a safe, iterative way. Future work will improve the tool and pipeline and increase the complexity of use cases.

Keywords: AI Engineering · AI Safety · Engineering Methodology · Safety-by-Design · AI Certification

1 Introduction

Artificial Intelligence (AI) is shaping our everyday lives, though we are still scratching the surface of its potential applications. Especially in safety-critical applications, such as automated driving or pilot assistance systems, the potential benefits for the economy and society are enormous [21]. However, applications like this need to comply with stringent safety and security standards and regulations, which AI systems are still struggling to meet [16]. Due to the black-box nature of AI, common methods and processes, such as ISO 26262 [9], for ensuring the safety of classical systems are not directly transferable. Therefore, new methods, tools, and processes are required to assess their safety. Although norms such as ISO/PAS 8800 [11] and guidelines published by the European Union

A. A. Girija, J. M. Christensen, Y. Kees, F. Krone, T. Liebert, R. Mut, G. Sauter and T. Stefani—These authors contributed equally and are ordered alphabetically

R. Posenato and I. Vanderfeesten (Eds.): CAiSE 2026 Workshops, LNBIP 586, pp. 267–273, 2026.
https://doi.org/10.1007/978-3-032-28160-9_24

Aviation Safety Agency (EASA) [8] already exist, their implementation is not yet fully defined [6]. Data-driven approaches [3], run-time monitors [17], and other explainability methods [1] are used, for example, to understand AI functions and fulfill certain requirements. This paper presents the Safe AI Pipeline (SAIPi), a safety-by-design approach to developing AI systems. We constrained our pipeline to engineering deep learning models as a first step towards a holistic approach that will also feature other forms of machine learning and AI in the future. As an exemplary requirement, we set an accuracy threshold and implemented tools to meet it. The pipeline is therefore a hands-on example of how requirements-driven engineering could shape future AI development. To showcase the pipeline, we built a Streamlit application that visualizes each step for the MNIST dataset [14]. The paper is organized as follows. The safety-by-design approach is introduced in Sect. 2. Afterwards SAIPi will be described in Sect. 3. Finally, shortcomings of this approach are discussed, and conclusions are drawn in Sect. 4.

2 Safety-by-Design Approach

Several approaches to engineering an AI system already exist, such as DevOps and the W-shaped process [8]; however, a consistent safety-by-design methodology, including the development of a safety argumentation, remains under active research. Since safety can only be assessed at the system level, the engineering process must be embedded in the system's overall development. Therefore, the AI system's requirements can be derived from the system-level requirements. An AI system consists of at least one AI component exhibiting black-box behavior. However, the AI system may also include other rule-based components, such as monitors, normalizations, or post-processing. Therefore, system-level requirements need to be broken down into requirements for the individual components. Their fulfillment needs to be traced during the AI system's engineering phase. Each fulfilled requirement then produces evidence which is part of the safety argumentation, a structured argumentation for the safety assurance of the AI system, as suggested by ISO/PAS 8800 [11]. The engineering process for AI systems is highly iterative. This begins during development, as the choice of data and training parameters does not always have foreseeable effects on the AI system. Even small changes can lead to unpredictable shifts in model behavior. To track these changes systematically, the requirements are continuously verified and redefined throughout the entire development process. From these updated requirements, derived specifications cascade down to other AI system components. But also in operation, iterations can return to the development phase through triggered updates, similar to the DevOps cycle in classical software development. A methodology for engineering AI systems, therefore, needs to provide a link between the continuous engineering process and a safety argumentation, built up during development and continuously assessed during operation.

The tools of the process deliver the evidence on which the safety argumentation is built and connect it to the development process. During operation, the safety argumentation, especially its assumptions, is assessed. If the safety argumentation is found to be no longer valid, this would trigger an update, if necessary, and hence a new iteration of the development cycle.

3 Safe AI Pipeline

To evaluate the previously proposed safety-by-design approach, we translated it into an exhaustive pipeline, called the Safe AI Pipeline (SAIPi), depicted in Fig. 1 and available on GitHub[1]. We chose the MNIST dataset [14] as a straightforward example to show a proof of concept for a deep learning use case. For training and validation, the dataset with digits 1 through 9 was used. The test dataset also included the digit 0, to provide the monitor with out-of-distribution data. The input to the process is the requirements for the AI system, bro-

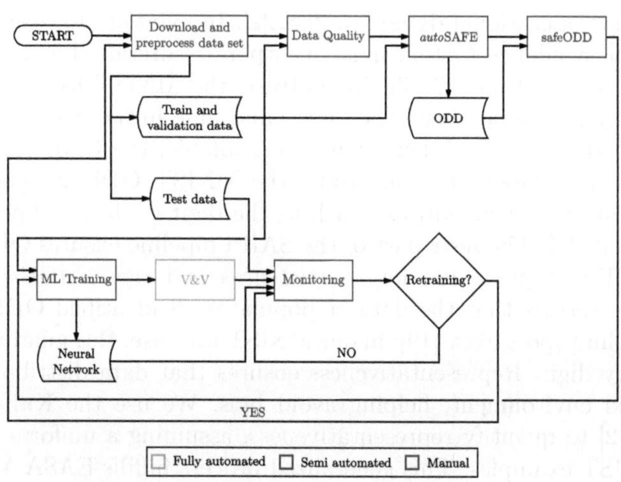

Fig. 1. High-level flowchart of the Safe AI Pipeline.

ken down at the system level. Each requirement is specified and verified to be measurable and testable during the Verification & Validation (V&V) step. The fulfillment of requirements is directly linked to a structured safety argumentation in accordance with ISO/PAS 8800 [11]. The requirements are assigned to the corresponding V&V process, and evidence is produced, e.g., by test results, validation reports, dataset analyses, or monitoring statistics. The tool chain starts by downloading the data and splitting it into training, validation, and test sets. Data is the essential basis of all machine learning systems; therefore, a rigorous

[1] https://github.com/DLR-KI/saipi.

analysis of its information content and quality is a prerequisite. This consideration begins with the sensor technology's basic properties, allowing for an assessment of which real-world information is lost during sensing. The acquired sensor data can be further analyzed with respect to its structural properties, e.g., at the pixel level for image data. The results of these tests allow the identification of characteristic properties of the data set—particularly gaps, correlations, or systematic distortions, also known as bias. These findings can then be used to regenerate specific data, control model training behavior, or derive specific requirements for the monitoring systems used. After assessing the data quality, a data-driven Operational Design Domain (ODD) is derived. Although slightly different definitions for the ODD exist throughout the domains, in general, the ODD is the set of specific conditions, including environmental, geographical, and time-of-day restrictions, under which an AI system has to function [8,10]. Thus, the ODD plays a critical role in the development of AI systems. While expert knowledge theoretically suffices to define an ODD, real-world applications usually rely on empirical data [5]. Modern frameworks even require specific distributions for each ODD parameter, making expert-only definitions difficult in the face of complex operational dynamics [6,8,22]. In aviation, for example, ODDs for a collision avoidance system must incorporate aircraft dynamics, weather, and human reaction times [7,13]. In contrast, the MNIST use case is elementary; with only one parameter—the digit—and nine initial classes, the ODD is easily described. If a formal definition is unavailable, the ODD can be derived directly from data labels. In this study, the MNIST ODD is generated from these labels, allowing new entries—such as the digit 0—to be appended as the dataset expands [5]. The next part of the SAIPi pipeline ensures ODD coverage by adopting EASA guidelines for *completeness* and *representativeness* [8,18]. Completeness verifies that the dataset populates all identified ODD scenarios, ensuring no blind spots exist [19]; in our MNIST use case, this guarantees entries exist for every digit. Representativeness ensures that data distributions reflect the real-world environment, helping avoid bias. We use the Kullback-Leibler divergence [12] to quantify representativeness, assuming a uniform distribution over the MNIST examples. This generalized process fulfills EASA MOC DM-08 requirements for safe-by-design AI. After data engineering, we train the model. Here, the supervised learning problem is solved using deep learning, where performance depends primarily on the architecture and the loss function. The loss function—the network's learning goal—allows the prioritization of safety properties, e.g., by assigning higher weights to avoid confusion between two specific digits or to focus on generalizability at the expense of test-set performance. For a well-founded safety argument, all of these design decisions—including the hyperparameter choices—should be justified empirically through repeated, documented, and thus traceable training runs. The V&V step concludes the development of the AI system; during this step, the requirements are checked. Although the process is depicted linearly, it should be understood as highly iterative. If issues arise, e.g., bad image quality is detected, the dataset is adjusted, or requirements are adapted. We mimic the AI system's operational phase by monitoring for anomalies during testing. Many AI models are trained on massive amounts of data that match the real-world distribution. However, real-world environments can change over time, leading to a distribution shift and necessitating model adaptation to maintain performance and safety compliance. Anomaly detection can indicate when a model requires adaptation. To approximate the in-distribution data, we map features to distinct regions using a set of learnable vectors that serve as representative cluster centers in the latent space [4]. During inference, Euclidean distance is used to measure the proximity between input features and learned cluster centers, thereby determining whether a sample is an anomaly [20]. Detected anomalies are then cropped and saved to form a curated dataset. For retraining in our MNIST use case, the model is expected also to learn the anomaly class, resulting in a class-incremental learning scenario. Given the widespread use of large-scale foundation and pre-trained open-source models, we assume that the original data may no longer be available and that full retraining may be computationally infeasible. We therefore expand the classifier head, use the Learning without Forgetting loss [15] together with a replay-based buffer [2], and evaluate the model's safety compliance by measuring accuracy across all classes and comparing it with a threshold set by the safety requirement.

4 Discussion and Conclusion

With the Safe AI Pipeline we show how an engineering pipeline for safety-critical AI systems could be established. To provide a proof of concept for our safety-by-design approach, exemplary tools for all key process steps are presented and applied to the MNIST dataset to demonstrate their functionality for a deep learning model. The next step is to build a safety argumentation based on the evidence generated by the pipeline's individual steps. Afterward, the pipeline and the safety argumentation can be validated on a more complex example, extending its use to object detection or segmentation, as well as to other AI methods such as unsupervised/self-supervised learning. Additionally, the methodology does not yet account for the AI system's security, leaving it vulnerable to attacks, thereby undermining its safety.

Author contributions. Akshay Anilkumar Girija, Johann Maximilian Christensen, Yannick Kees, Florian Krone, Thomas Liebert, Ryan Mut, Gerald Sauter and Thomas Stefani–These authors contributed equally and are ordered alphabetically.

References

1. Ali, S., Abuhmed, T., El-Sappagh, S., et al.: Explainable artificial intelligence (xai): What we know and what is left to attain trustworthy artificial intelligence. Inform. Fusion **99**, 101805 (2023). https://doi.org/10.1016/j.inffus.2023.101805
2. Bagus, B., Gepperth, A.: An investigation of replay-based approaches for continual learning. In: 2021 International Joint Conference on Neural Networks (IJCNN), pp. 1–9 (2021). https://doi.org/10.1109/IJCNN52387.2021.9533862

3. Bhatt, N., Bhatt, N., Prajapati, P., et al.: A data-centric approach to improve performance of deep learning models. Sci. Rep. **14**(1) (2024). https://doi.org/10.1038/s41598-024-73643-x
4. Chen, C., Li, O., Tao, D., et al.: This looks like that: deep learning for interpretable image recognition. Adv. Neural Inform. Process. Syst. **32** (2019)
5. Christensen, J., Hoemann, E., Köster, F., Hallerbach, S.: Defining operational conditions for safety-critical ai-based systems from data (Jan 2026). https://doi.org/10.48550/ARXIV.2601.22118
6. Christensen, J.M., Stefani, T., Anilkumar Girija, A., et al.: Formulating an engineering framework for future ai certification in aviation. Aerospace **12**(6) (2025). https://doi.org/10.3390/aerospace12060482
7. Christensen, J.M., Zaeske, W., Beck, J., et al.: Towards certifiable ai in aviation: a framework for neural network assurance using advanced visualization and safety nets. In: 2024 AIAA DATC/IEEE 43rd Digital Avionics Systems Conference (DASC). IEEE (Sep 2024). https://doi.org/10.1109/dasc62030.2024.10749321
8. European Union Aviation Safety Agency (EASA): Easa concept paper: guidance for level 1 & 2 machine learning applications. techreport, European Union Aviation Safety Agency (EASA) (April 2024). https://www.easa.europa.eu/en/document-library/general-publications/easa-artificial-intelligence-concept-paper-issue-2
9. ISO: Road vehicles – functional safety. Standard ISO 26262-1:2018(E), International Organization for Standardization (2018)
10. ISO: Road vehicles — test scenarios for automated driving systems — specification for operational design domain. Tech. Rep. ISO 34503:2023(E), International Organization for Standardization (2023)
11. ISO: Road vehicles — safety and artificial intelligence. Standard ISO/PAS 8800:2024, International Organization for Standardization (2024)
12. Joyce, J.M.: Kullback-Leibler Divergence, pp. 720–722. Springer Berlin Heidelberg (2011). https://doi.org/10.1007/978-3-642-04898-2_327
13. Julian, K.D., Kochenderfer, M.J.: Guaranteeing safety for neural network-based aircraft collision avoidance systems. In: 2019 IEEE/AIAA 38th Digital Avionics Systems Conference (DASC). IEEE (Sep 2019). https://doi.org/10.1109/dasc43569.2019.9081748
14. Lecun, Y., Bottou, L., Bengio, Y., Haffner, P.: Gradient-based learning applied to document recognition. Proc. IEEE **86**(11), 2278–2324 (1998). https://doi.org/10.1109/5.726791
15. Li, Z., Hoiem, D.: Learning without forgetting. In: Leibe, B., Matas, J., Sebe, N., Welling, M. (eds.) Computer Vision - ECCV 2016, pp. 614–629. Springer International Publishing, Cham (2016)
16. Perez-Cerrolaza, J., Abella, J., Borg, M.: Artificial intelligence for safety-critical systems in industrial and transportation domains: a survey. ACM Comput. Surv. **56**(7), (2024). https://doi.org/10.1145/3626314
17. Rahman, Q.M., Corke, P., Dayoub, F.: Run-time monitoring of machine learning for robotic perception: a survey of emerging trends. IEEE Access **9**, 20067–20075 (2021). https://doi.org/10.1109/ACCESS.2021.3055015
18. Stefani, T., Christensen, J.M., Anilkumar Girija, A., et al.: Automated scenario generation from operational design domain model for testing ai-based systems in aviation. CEAS Aeronaut. J. **16**(1), 197–212 (2024). https://doi.org/10.1007/s13272-024-00772-4
19. Stefani, T., Christensen, J.M., Hoemann, E., et al.: From high-dimensional spaces to verifiable odd coverage for safety-critical ai-based systems (2026). https://arxiv.org/abs/2604.02198

20. Tayeh, T., Aburakhia, S., Myers, R., Shami, A.: Distance-based anomaly detection for industrial surfaces using triplet networks. In: 2020 11th IEEE Annual Information Technology, Electronics and Mobile Communication Conference (IEMCON), pp. 0372–0377. IEEE (2020)
21. Wang, Y., Chung, S.H.: Artificial intelligence in safety-critical systems: a systematic review. Indust. Manag. Data Syst. **122**(2), 442–470 (2021). https://doi.org/10.1108/IMDS-07-2021-0419
22. Werner, F., Christensen, J.M., Stefani, T., et al.: Formulating a learning assurance-based framework for ai-based systems in aviation. Aerospace **13**(2) (2026). https://doi.org/10.3390/aerospace13020200

CAI

A Neuro-symbolic Framework for Compliance Management with Declarative Models

Konstantinos Varvoutas(✉), Julian Neuberger, and Hugo A. López

Technical University of Denmark, Kongens Lyngby, Denmark
{konva,jtone,hulo}@dtu.dk

Abstract. Ensuring regulatory compliance is a central concern for organizations operating under complex legal frameworks. Translating regulatory texts into formal process models is a time-consuming task, complicated by the discretionary and obligation-driven nature of legal language. We propose a neuro-symbolic framework for compliance management using Multi-Perspective Dynamic Condition Response (MP-DCR) graphs as a formal backbone. We illustrate the framework through a case study showing how a normative model can be elicited, refined, and used to check compliance of existing cases with the law. Furthermore, violations can be verbalized to different stakeholders in natural language.

Keywords: Compliance Management · Conformance Checking · Neuro-Symbolic AI · Large Language Models

1 Introduction

Ensuring that business processes comply with applicable laws and regulations has become a central concern across both public and private sectors, where non-compliance carries significant legal, financial, and reputational consequences. Checking processes for compliance is usually carried out by auditors, who create process models of the process under audit based on sources, such as regulatory texts or guidelines. Among others, the auditor's task then involves assessing if deviations from the process model are acceptable, or evidence of control failure [12]. An auditor therefore, performs after-the-fact compliance checking [21]. Properly supporting auditors in this task means highlighting discrepancies and letting them judge their severity.

This is different from existing compliance-by-design systems. These systems assume that a process is designed in such a way that it can never be executed without complying to law. However, this requires having a model of law relevant to a given business process, *before* executing it the first time. In the real world this assumption usually does not hold. Instead, the process is run, and an auditor checks compliance with laws and regulations at regular intervals. To this end, they transform norms and guidelines into a formal specification of compliance

R. Posenato and I. Vanderfeesten (Eds.): CAiSE 2026 Workshops, LNBIP 586, pp. 277–290, 2026.
https://doi.org/10.1007/978-3-032-28160-9_25

rules (so-called *normative process*). These are refined iteratively in a collaboration between modelers, auditors, and legal experts. The normative process is then used to check conformance of existing cases. Figure 1 depicts this workflow.

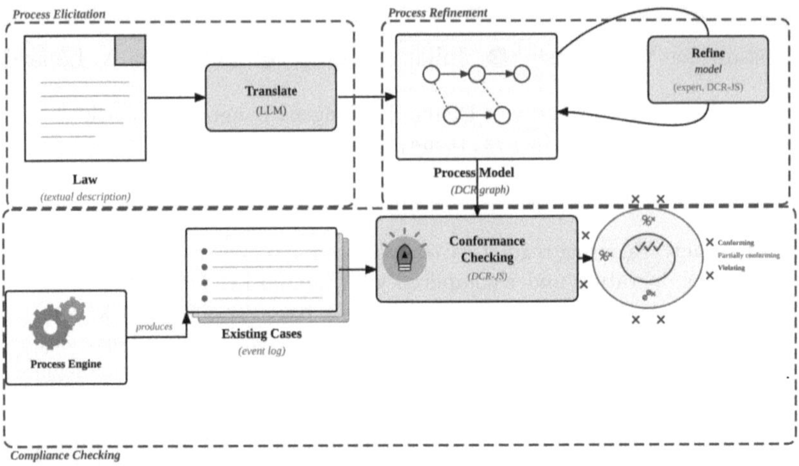

Fig. 1. After-the-fact compliance management.

Effectively supporting a process analyst means expediting the creation and refinement of formal process representations and making it as easy as possible to focus on assessing the severity of deviations. We envisage a neuro-symbolic framework for compliance management using DCR graphs, implemented in the open source tool DCR-JS available at https://kmvarvou.github.io/dcr-js/. Our system combines neural aspects in elicitation, modeling, and explainability of laws, while compliance is formalized in rule-based systems based on DCR graphs.

Our Contributions. We propose a neuro-symbolic framework for after-the-fact compliance management combining LLM-based process elicitation with a formal symbolic backbone for conformance checking. To this end, we extend the term-based DCR formalism of [19] with data values and guards, and define a three-way trace classification into conforming, partially violating, and violating. We demonstrate the framework with an example case study.

The remainder of this paper is structured as follows. Section 2 introduces a running example and identifies key challenges and opportunities for Artificial Intelligence (AI) in compliance management. Section 3 presents a formalism for symbolic conformance checking. In Sect. 4 we use our framework in a case study end-to-end. Section 5 discusses related work, and we conclude in Sect. 6 along with directions for future work.

2 AI in Compliance Management

Consider the following fragment of the Consolidation Act for Social Services (CASS) §50 [8], which regulates child protection examinations in Denmark. This fragment motivates the framework, we present in Sect. 2.1. It also highlights opportunities and challenges for AI in compliance management (see Sect. 2.2).

CASS §50 (7)

The examination must be completed within four (4) months after the municipal council has become aware that a child or young person may be in need of special support. Where, exceptionally, an examination cannot be completed within 4 months, the municipal council shall prepare a provisional assessment and complete the examination as soon as possible thereafter.

2.1 Compliance Management Framework

The above example fragment of law serves as the pivotal element in checking compliance of an organization with the law. The pipeline, presented in Fig. 1 integrates a set of coordinated components designed to support this in three steps: **(1)** a model of a law is built from regulatory text, **(2)** the model is refined with legal experts, **(3)** executions are checked for conformance with that model.

Thus, the first stage in our proposed framework is **process elicitation**. Transforming a regulatory text into a process model involves identifying all events in it, here "*the examination must be completed*", "*the municipal council has become aware that a child or young person may be in need of special support*", and "*prepare a provisional assessment*". Next, permissions and obligations are extracted, which are usually marked by modal verbs, such as "*must*", "*shall*", or "*may*". Specifications of deadlines and delays are identified here, for example "*withing four (4) months*".

Once an initial draft is produced, it is iteratively **refined**. To this end a process analyst collaborates with legal experts to verify model correctness. This step may require refining high-level goals into observable activities [5]. This loop reflects that initial elicitation may not produce a fully accurate model of law. Refinement can also be rerun at a later time to incorporate amendments and repeals of parts of the law, thus enabling continuous curation of models of law.

Finally, executions of the process can now be checked for **conformance** against the refined model, resulting in a list of conforming and non-conforming executions. We assume that previous process executions were recorded by a *Process Engine* in the organization and are available as event logs to the auditor. In scenarios, where this assumption does not hold, we also see the option of manually modeling the as-is process with employees of the organization, or automatically extracting it from textual process descriptions using existing techniques [23]. The event log, along with a model of the law, is fed as input to the conformance checking component, evaluating the conformance of executions with the constraints encoded in the model. The output is a classification of executions into conforming, partially violating, and violating cases, providing the basis for an assessment of non-compliance.

The proposed framework follows a neuro-symbolic paradigm, combining learning-based and symbolic components, as described in Kautz's taxonomy [13], which defines six types of neuro-symbolic AI systems. A textual description of a law is converted by an LLM into a formal MP-DCR model, corresponding to Kautz's Type 3 definition, where a neural system generates symbolic representations that are then processed by symbolic reasoning to verify compliance.

2.2 Opportunities and Challenges of AI

We see several opportunities and challenges of using AI to support the management of compliance at each stage of this pipeline.

Process Elicitation. This is a time-consuming task that takes up to 60% of the time allotted to business process management projects [10]. The use of AI can free up valuable time of process analysts and domain experts in several ways. First, AI can be used to automatically transform regulatory text into formal representations, however they struggle with correctly extracting constraints (permissions, obligations) [18]. Addressing this challenge would require special fine-tuned or neuro-symbolic extraction tools. Next, the data and time perspectives are highly relevant for compliance checking. Extracting these aspects is challenging as deadlines might be expressed in various formats, and data may be implicit. While Large Language Models (LLMs) could address this challenge, they introduce new issues, e.g., hallucinations. Finally, ambiguous statements in text need additional context to be resolved. This context can be common sense (world knowledge), or an external source (domain knowledge). Recent work studied the detection of ambiguities [9,20] and their resolution [1]. Knowledge of ambiguous statements is valuable for formulating the right questions in interviews with legal experts.

Process Refinement. Given an initial draft of the formal representation of a regulation, the process analyst has to iteratively refine it and verify its correctness in collaboration with legal experts. Recent research explored AI chatbots as a more intuitive interface to process modeling and refinement [15,16]. However, supporting the right set of commands is challenging. Syntax-level commands, like "insert a new event", do not help a user unfamiliar with the exact notation of DCR. Instead, commands should address the semantics of the model, e.g., "this event should never be executed, if these two events were executed previously". Ideally, the chatbot would support realizing desired pragmatics, e.g., "the event should only be required, if the child is underage". Correctly identifying user intent and applying the correct changes is an open challenge [14]. Beyond that, laws and regulations are updated, amended, and repealed regularly, e.g., when the government and its policies change and warrant the constant curation of existing models. AI tools could find changes in different versions of laws and regulations, highlight parts in the model that require changes, or help during comparing different versions of the model. Similar to conversational model refinement, automatically applying the correct changes is an open challenge.

Compliance Checking. This step goes beyond classifying executions as conformant or non-conformant with a given formal model of a law. Instead, it also involves the analysis of common characteristics of non-conformant executions and the reporting to affected parties. Explanations for non-compliance need to address the specific stakeholder, as it is not the same explanation for an auditor as for a regular citizen. For instance, an auditor might prefer a precise formal explanation, while citizens might find a natural description more useful. Understanding common patterns in non-compliant cases is key to providing useful feedback to organizations. To this end, we see an opportunity for AI in variant analysis, to summarize classes of non-compliant cases into succinct rules. However, finding patterns involving time and data is challenging, akin to temporal association rule mining [2].

3 Multi-perspective DCR Processes

In this section, we present the syntax and semantics of Multi-Perspective (MP) Dynamic Condition Response (DCR). In this work, we are building upon the term-based presentation in [19] by extending it with data [11] and guards. We assume fixed universes of *events* $\mathcal{E}$, *labels* $\mathcal{L}$, and variables V, ranged over by e, f, l, and v, respectively, with a special tick symbol $(\mathsf{tick}) \notin \mathcal{E}$.

3.1 Syntax

An MP-DCR process $P = [M, V, C]\ \lambda T$ is a term comprising a *marking* M, a set of variables V, a labeling function λ, a list of computations C, and a composition of constraint *terms* T. The syntax is presented in Fig. 2.

A process *term* P represents a process model, consisting of a finite set of events (nodes) and their relations (arcs). The global state of a process is its *marking* M, a finite map from events to local states. Each event e carries a state $\Phi = (\langle t_h, v\rangle, i, p)$, where $h = \langle t_h, v\rangle$ describes whether the event e has *(h)appened*, and if so, t_h describes how many time steps ago; $t_h = \mathsf{f}$ means never happened. At the same time, the value v records the data value produced in execution, and $v = \mathtt{null}$ means no value has been produced. i in the marking describes whether e is currently *(i)ncluded* in the process. Finally, p in the marking describes whether e is *(p)ending*, and how many time units are missing until its deadline. We write $p = \omega$ to denote that e needs to be executed *eventually*. The guard definition is adopted from [11], with v_b and v_i ranging over variables of Boolean and integer type respectively.

Relations between events take one of the following forms: **Condition** $e \blacktriangleright\!\!\xrightarrow[{[g]}]{t_0}\!\!\odot\, f$. A *guarded timed condition* defines a *prohibition* for f: f is only allowed to occur, when g is true, after e has happened and at least t_0 time units

$P, Q ::= [M, V, C]\ \lambda T$	process
$M, N ::= M, e : \Phi \mid \epsilon$	marking
$V ::= V, \mathsf{v} : e \mid \epsilon$	variables
$C ::= C, e : g \mid \epsilon$	computations
$\lambda ::= \lambda, e : l \mid \epsilon$	labelling
$\Phi ::= (h, i, p)$	event state
$h ::= \langle t_h, dv \rangle$	(h)appened
$t_h ::= \mathsf{f} \mid t_0$	time since execution $t_0 \in \mathbb{N} \cup \{0\}$ 0-time
$dv ::= \mathtt{null} \mid d : D$	data value
$D ::= \mathtt{bool} \mid \mathtt{int} \mid \cdots$	data type
$i ::= \mathsf{f} \mid \mathsf{t}$	(i)ncluded
$p ::= \mathsf{f} \mid 0 \mid t_\omega$	(p)ending deadline $t_\omega \in \mathbb{N} \cup \{\omega\}$ ω-time
$g ::= BExp \mid IExp$	guard
$BExp ::= \mathsf{v}_b \mid b \mid IExp\ IBOp\ IExp \mid BExp\ BOp\ BExp \mid \neg BExp$	bool expression
$IExp ::= \mathsf{v}_i \mid n \mid IExp\ IOp\ IExp$	int expression
$IBOp ::= = \mid < \mid > \mid \leq \mid \geq \quad IOp ::= + \mid - \mid * \quad BOp ::= and \mid or$	operators

$T, U ::= e \blacktriangleright\!\xrightarrow[[g]]{t_0}\!\circledcirc f$	condition	$\mid e \blacktriangleright\!\xrightarrow[[g]]{t_\omega}\!\odot f$	response
$\mid e \blacktriangleright\!\xrightarrow[[g]]{}\!\oplus f$	inclusion	$\mid e \blacktriangleright\!\xrightarrow[[g]]{}\!\ominus f$	exclusion
$\mid T \parallel U$	parallel composition	$\mid 0$	unit

Fig. 2. DCR Processes Syntax.

ago, or e must be excluded. If the guard g is true, we omit it, and the condition applies as if unguarded. $t_0 = 0$ the constraint is untimed; we write $e \blacktriangleright\!\!\longrightarrow\!\circledcirc f$. **Response** $e \blacktriangleright\!\xrightarrow[[g]]{t_\omega}\!\odot f$. A *guarded timed response* defines an *obligation*: once e has occurred, and g is true, f must occur within t_ω time units or be excluded. Once again, the guard g may be omitted when it is true. Setting $t_\omega = \omega$ gives the untimed response $e \blacktriangleright\!\!\longrightarrow\!\odot f$, interpreted as *eventually* (no finite bound). **Inclusion** $e \blacktriangleright\!\xrightarrow[[g]]{}\!\oplus f$. After e is executed, if g is true, f is added to the set of included events. Inclusion renders f executable without imposing any obligation. **Exclusion** $e \blacktriangleright\!\xrightarrow[[g]]{}\!\ominus f$. After e is executed, if g is true, f is removed from the set of included events. Conditions originating from f are ignored until f is re-included. A self-exclusion $e \blacktriangleright\!\!\longrightarrow\!\ominus e$ ensures e executes at most once.

3.2 Semantics

In this section, we define the enabledness of an event and the effects of its execution. Again, we built upon the work introduced in [19] by extending it to account for the presence of data and guards. Figure 3 relies on the judgment $[M]\ T \vdash e : (Exc, Inc, Pen)$, which expresses that in marking M, event e is enabled by term T, producing the effects of excluding the events in Exc, including those in Inc, and setting those in Pen as pending.

The rules in Fig. 3 are described from left to right, top to bottom. **Condition:** f is enabled if it included, and if e is included, then it e must have occurred at least k time steps ago. **Response:** If e is included, e may fire, upon which f becomes pending with deadline k. **Inclusion:** If e is included, e may fire with the effect of adding f to the included events. **Exclusion:** Converse of

$$\frac{i \Rightarrow t_e \geq k \quad g \Downarrow \mathtt{tt}}{[M, e : ((\langle t_e, dv_e \rangle, i, \_), f : (\_, \mathsf{t}, \_)]\ e \xrightarrow[{[g]}]{k}\!\circledcirc\ f \vdash f : (\emptyset, \emptyset, \emptyset)} \qquad \frac{g \Downarrow \mathtt{tt}}{[M, e : (\_, \mathsf{t}, \_)]\ e \xrightarrow[{[g]}]{k}\!\text{(!)}\ f \vdash e : (\emptyset, \emptyset, \{f : k\})}$$

$$\frac{g \Downarrow \mathtt{tt}}{[M, e : (\_, \mathsf{t}, \_)]\ e \xrightarrow[{[g]}]{}\!\oplus\ f \vdash e : (\emptyset, \{f\}, \emptyset)} \qquad \frac{g \Downarrow \mathtt{tt}}{[M, e : (\_, \mathsf{t}, \_)]\ e \xrightarrow[{[g]}]{}\!\ominus\ f \vdash e : (\{f\}, \emptyset, \emptyset)}$$

$$\frac{}{[M, e : (\_, \mathsf{t}, \_)]\ 0 \vdash e : (\emptyset, \emptyset, \emptyset)} \qquad \frac{e \neq f \quad \mathcal{R} \in \{\xrightarrow[{[g]}]{k}\!\text{(!)}, \xrightarrow[{[g]}]{}\!\oplus, \xrightarrow[{[g]}]{}\!\ominus\} \quad g \Downarrow \mathtt{tt}}{[M, e : (\_, \mathsf{t}, \_)]\ f\, \mathcal{R}\, f' \vdash e : (\emptyset, \emptyset, \emptyset)}$$

$$\frac{[M]\ T_i \vdash e : (\mathsf{Ex}_i, \mathsf{In}_i, \mathsf{Pe}_i) \quad i = \{1, 2\}}{[M]\ T_1 \parallel T_2 \vdash e : (\mathsf{Ex}_1 \cup \mathsf{Ex}_2, \mathsf{In}_1 \cup \mathsf{In}_2, \mathsf{Pe}_1 \cup \mathsf{Pe}_2)}$$

Fig. 3. Enabling & effects. "_" means either true t or false f.

inclusion—if e is included, e may fire with the effect of removing f from the included events. **Unit:** Events in a graph with no constraints can be fired if they are included. **Non-consequent:** An event e appearing as the source but not the target of a relation does not have its enabledness affected by that relation. **Parallel composition:** The enabledness and effects of e in $T_1 \parallel T_2$ are obtained by combining the contributions of each constituent term.

For guarded relations to be included, their expressions must evaluate to true. Moving on, the *action* of respectively an *event* e and an *effect* $\delta = (\mathsf{Ex}, \mathsf{In}, \mathsf{Pe})$ on a marking M pointwise by the action on individual event state $f : (\langle t_f, dv_f \rangle, i, r)$ is defined as follows. Assume e is enabled in the process $[M, V, C]\ \lambda T$ with effect $\delta = (\mathsf{Ex}, \mathsf{In}, \mathsf{Pe})$. The state of e reflects that the event has happened now, updating its executed flag to $\langle 0, dv_e \rangle$. Similarly, it is no longer pending. The effect of executing e in a marking M, written $e < .M. >$, is inductively defined as follows:

$$e < .M. > = \begin{cases} \epsilon & \text{if } M = \epsilon \\ e < .N. >, f : (\langle 0, dv_f \rangle, i, \mathsf{f}) & \text{if } M = N, f : (\_, i, \_) \wedge e = f \\ e < .N. >, f : (\langle t, dv \rangle, i, r) & \text{if } M = N, f : (\langle t, dv \rangle, i, r) \wedge e \neq f. \end{cases} \tag{1}$$

where dv_f is the result of evaluating the computation associated with e in C.

The application of effect $\delta = (\mathsf{Ex}, \mathsf{In}, \mathsf{Pe})$ over a marking M, denoted $\delta < .M. >$, follows the definition in [19] extended to carry data values $\langle t_f, dv_f \rangle$ in place of the plain happened flag. Concretely, executing e resets its state to $\langle 0, dv_e \rangle$ and clears its pending flag; the effect δ then updates inclusion and deadlines as before. Here, r' is defined as $\min\{d \mid (f, d) \in \mathsf{Pe}\}$ if $(f, d) \in \mathsf{Pe}$, and $r' = r$ otherwise. That is, the pending flag takes the minimal deadline for which $f : d \in \mathsf{Pe}$, otherwise it is unchanged. The data value dv'_f may be updated by the computation associated with f in C, if any: $dv'_f = g$ if $(f : g) \in C$ and $f \in Pe$, and $dv'_f = dv_f$ otherwise.

$$\delta < .M. >= \begin{cases} \epsilon & \text{if } M = \epsilon \\ \delta < .N. >, f : (\langle t_f, dv'_f \rangle, \underbrace{(i \land f \notin \mathsf{Ex}) \lor f \in \mathsf{In},}_{\text{included?}}\ r') & \text{if } M = N, f : (\langle t_f, dv_f \rangle, i, r) \end{cases} \tag{2}$$

Additionally, we extend the deadline and tick functions from [19] to account for the data component of the marking:

$$\mathsf{deadline} < .M. >= \begin{cases} \omega & \text{if } M = \epsilon \\ \min(\mathsf{deadline} < .M'. >, p') & \text{if } M = M', e\colon (\langle t_e, dv_e \rangle, i, p) \end{cases} \tag{3}$$

$$\mathsf{tick} < .M. >= \begin{cases} \epsilon & \text{if } M = \epsilon \\ \mathsf{tick} < .M'. >, e\colon (\langle t_e + 1, dv_e \rangle, i, p-1) & \text{if } M = M', e\colon (\langle t_e, dv_e \rangle, i, p) \land t_e < k \\ \mathsf{tick} < .M'. >, e\colon (\langle t_e, dv_e \rangle, i, p-1) & \text{if } M = M', e\colon (\langle t_e, dv_e \rangle, i, p) \land t_e \geq k \end{cases} \tag{4}$$

$$\frac{[M]\, T \vdash e : \delta}{T \vdash M, V \xrightarrow{e} \delta\langle e\langle M \rangle\rangle}\ [\text{EVENT}] \qquad \frac{\mathsf{deadline}\langle M \rangle > 0}{T \vdash M \xrightarrow{\mathsf{tick}} \mathsf{tick}\langle M \rangle}\ [\text{TIME}]$$

Fig. 4. Transition semantics. $T \vdash M \xrightarrow{\alpha} M'$

Figure 4 presents the transition semantics [19], extended to the data-enriched marking. Rule [EVENT] fires an enabled event e, updating the marking with the produced data value dv_e; rule [TIME] advances the marking by one time unit. As customary, $\xrightarrow{\alpha}^*$ denotes the transitive closure of $\xrightarrow{\alpha}$, and the state space of $[M, V, C]\ \lambda T$ is $\mathcal{P}([M, V, C]\ \lambda T) = \{[M', V, C']\ \lambda T \mid T \vdash M \xrightarrow{\alpha}^* M'\}$. Event transitions give rise to a labelled transition system:

Definition 1 (LTS). *Given a MP-DCR process $[M, V, C]\ \lambda T$, its Labeled Transition System is $lts([M, V, C]\ \lambda T) = \langle \mathcal{P}(M),\ [M, V, C]\ \lambda T,\ \mathcal{E}',\ \longrightarrow,\ \Sigma,\ \lambda'. >$, where*

- *$[M, V, C]\ \lambda T \in \mathcal{P}([M, V, C]\ \lambda T)$ is the initial state,*
- *$\mathcal{E}' = \mathcal{E} \cup \{\mathsf{tick}\}$ is the set of labels,*
- *Σ is an alphabet,*
- *$-- >\subseteq \mathcal{P}([M, V, C]\ \lambda T) \times \mathcal{E}' \times \mathcal{P}([M, V, C]\ \lambda T)$ iff $T \vdash M \xrightarrow{\alpha} M'$, and*
- *$\lambda' \subseteq \mathcal{E} \times \Sigma$ is defined by $\lambda'(e) = \lambda(e)$ for $e \in \mathcal{E}$, and $\lambda'(\mathsf{tick}) = \mathsf{tick}$.*

The LTS is equipped with the notion of *accepting runs*, incorporating similar notions defined for DCR Graphs [6,22] to their timed setting:

Definition 2 (Runs, Accepting Runs). *A run of* $[M, V, C]\ T$ *is a finite or infinite sequence of transitions* $[M, V, C]\ T = [M_0, V, C_0]\ T_0 \xrightarrow{e_0} \cdots$. *A run is* accepting *iff for every state* $[M_i, V, C_i]\ T_i$, *when* $M_i(e) = (\_, \mathsf{t}, \mathsf{t})$ *then there exists* $j \geq i$ *s.t. either* $M_j(e) = (\_, \mathsf{f}, \_)$ *or* $[M_j]\ T_j \xrightarrow{e} [M_{j+1}]\ T_{j+1}$.

In essence, an accepting run considers transitions that either execute pending events or exclude them. Also, because it is possible for the same event e to happen more than once, even processes with finite events may have infinite runs. Having defined those, the language of a DCR process is the set of all its accepting runs.

Definition 3 (Traces). *Assume a set of events* $\mathcal{E}$. *A* trace *in* $\mathcal{E}$ *is a (possibly infinite) string* $s = (s_i)_{i \in I}$ *where each* $s_i \in \mathcal{E}$. *A* trace *of a DCR process* $[M, V, C]\ \lambda T$ *is a (possibly infinite) string* $s = (s_i)_{i \in I}$ *s.t.* $[M, V, C]\ \lambda T$ *has a run* $[M_i, V, C_i]\ \lambda T \xrightarrow{e_i} [M_{i+1}, V, C_{i+1}]\ \lambda T$ *with* $s_i = \lambda(e_i)$. *Such a trace is accepting if the run is accepting. Finally, the process* $[M, V, C]\ \lambda T$ *has the* language $\mathsf{lang}([M, V, C]\ \lambda T) = \{s \mid s \text{ is an accepting trace of } [M]\ \lambda T\}$.

Definition 4 (Conforming Trace). *A trace* s *is* conforming *with a MP-DCR process* $[M, V, C]\ \lambda T$ *if* $\forall s_i \in s$ *s.t.* $0 \leq i \leq |s|$, *then* $[M_i, V, C_i]\ \lambda T \xrightarrow{s_i} [M_{i+1}, V, C_{i+1}]\ \lambda T$, *and for every event* e_j *in* $[M_n, V, C_n]\ \lambda T$, $e_j : (\_, \mathsf{f}, \_)$ *or* $e_j : (\_, \mathsf{t}, \mathsf{f})$.

Based on the notion of accepting runs, we define three classes of traces that arise during conformance checking. Intuitively, a trace is *conforming* if it corresponds to an accepting run of the process, meaning all obligations are fulfilled. A trace is *partially violating* if it can be replayed on the process and reaches an accepting final state, but passes through a non-accepting intermediate state along the way—meaning obligations were temporarily unfulfilled but eventually resolved. Finally, a trace is *violating* if no run that produces it is accepting.

Definition 5 (Partially Violating Trace). *A trace* $s = (s_j)_{j \in J}$ *is* partially violating *with a MP-DCR process* $[M, V, C]\ \lambda T$ *if*
$[M_0, V, C_0]\ \lambda T \xrightarrow{s_0} \cdots [M_{n-1}, V, C_{n-1}]\ \lambda T \xrightarrow{s_n} [M_n, V, C_n]\ \lambda T$ *such that:*

1. *there exists* $i \in \{0, \ldots, n-1\}$ *such that* s_j *is not an enabled event for* $[M_i, V_i, C_i]\ \lambda T\ [M_i, V, C_i]\ \lambda T \xrightarrow{s_j} [M_{i+1}, V, C_{i+1}]\ \lambda T$, *and*
2. *the final state* $[M_n, V_n, C_n]\ \lambda T$ *is accepting. A state is accepting if there are no included pending events.*

Definition 6 (Violating Trace). *If a trace* s *is neither conforming nor a partially violation, then* s *is a* violating trace.

3.3 Trace Classification

Conformance is evaluated by replaying each trace event-by-event against the MP-DCR process, tracking enabledness, temporal constraints, and guard conditions at each step. At the log level, a trace is classified as *conforming* if a replay sequence exists that leads to an accepting state without violating any control-flow or temporal constraint. When perfect replay is not possible, a second pass quantifies deviations by selecting, for each observed event, the enabled model event with the fewest constraint violations; after replay, any unfulfilled pending responses are counted as additional violations. This yields the number of control-flow violations (e.g. executing an event whose condition is unsatisfied) and temporal violations (e.g. missing a response deadline), which together determine whether a trace is *partially violating* or *violating* per Definitions 3–5.

This differs from the alignment-based conformance checking of [7], where a trace is reconciled with a DCR model by computing the minimum-cost sequence of insertions and deletions needed to make the trace an accepting run. This approach yields a globally optimal deviation measure, that is defined for the untimed and unguarded DCR formalism.

4 Case Study

We illustrate the proposed framework using the CASS §50(7) fragment introduced in Sect. 2. To elicit a draft DCR model from the legal text, we use the prompting strategy of [18], adopted to handle timed and guarded constraints. The extraction is divided into five stages: (1) extract roles, (2) extract activities and assign them to roles, (3) extract DCR constraints, (4) extract deadlines and delays and assign them to conditions and responses, and (5) extract guards and assign them to constraints. There is a separate prompt for each phase, and phases are linked sequentially. We then show how the model is refined and used as a reference model for conformance checking of existing cases.

4.1 Model Refinement

In Fig. 5, we present the elicited model and its refined version. The elicited model contains a timed response from *Become aware of child in need* to *Complete examination*, and a condition and response from *Prepare provisional assessment* to *Complete examination.* On the other hand, the refined model follows the logic: upon becoming aware of a case (*Become aware of child in need*), the *Age* of the person under consideration is recorded. Based on this value, two response obligations may be triggered, which are mutually triggered. If $Age > 18$, the examination must be rejected (*Reject examination*), modelled as a guarded response. If $Age \leq 18$, the examination must eventually be completed (*Complete examination*), also modelled as a guarded response. The two outcomes are mutually exclusive via bidirectional exclusion edges: completing the examination excludes the rejection, and vice versa. To handle the special case of provisional assessments, the model combines a timed response and an exclusion: a provisional

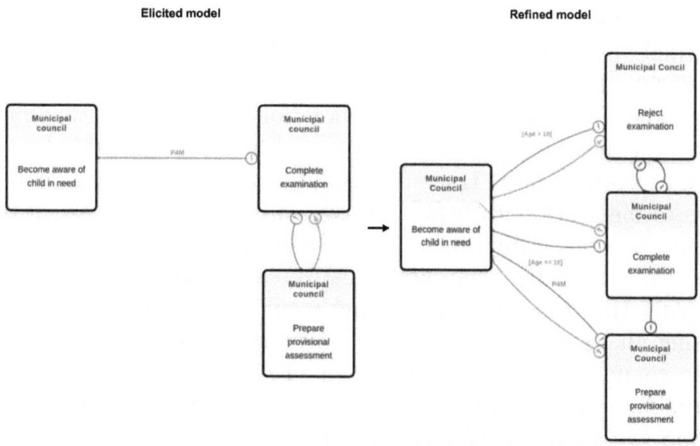

Fig. 5. Elicited (left) and refined (right) DCR models for CASS §50 fragment.

Table 1. Conformance classification for example traces in CASS §50 event log

Trace	Event	Data	Date	Classification
	Become aware of child in need	Age: 12	02/04/2026	
Trace 1	Prepare provisional assessment	null	01/07/2026	⊘ Conforming
	Complete examination	null	11/07/2026	
	Become aware of child in need	Age: 17	11/07/2026	
Trace 2	Prepare provisional assessment	null	09/11/2026	%× Part. Violating
	Complete examination	null	14/11/2026	
	Complete examination	null	14/11/2026	
Trace 3	Prepare provisional assessment	null	14/11/2026	⊗ Violating
	Become aware of child in need	Age: 10	14/11/2026	

assessment must be produced within 4 months of receiving the report, but this obligation is lifted via an exclusion edge once the examination is completed. In other words, if the examination is concluded within the deadline, the provisional assessment is never required.

4.2 Conformance Checking

We evaluate existing cases by replaying their traces in Table 1 against the refined model using the conformance checking component of DCR-JS. Trace 1 represents the standard compliant case: first, the council becomes aware, then a provisional assessment is prepared within the 4-month deadline, and the examination is completed shortly after. All obligations are fulfilled in time, and the trace is classified as *conforming* (✓). Trace 2 is classified as *potentially violating* (%×): while the final marking is accepting, the provisional assessment is only prepared on 09/11/2026—121 days after the council became aware on 11/07/2026, just past the 4-month deadline. A temporal violation is detected at the intermediate marking, as the deadline for *Complete examination* has elapsed before the trace reaches its accepting state. Trace 3 is *violating* (⊗): the examination and provisional assessment are both before the council has become aware of the child's situation on the same date. Since *Become aware of child in need* is a condition for both events, executing them first constitutes a violation.

To explain the conformance checking results, we verbalize the compliance results using an LLM. For instance, the temporal violation detected in Trace 2 could be communicated to a *citizen* as: *"Your case was eventually resolved, but the provisional assessment was completed later than required by law. According to CASS §50(7), it should have been prepared within 4 months of the council becoming aware of your situation."* The same violation would be reported to a *caseworker* in more operational terms: *"Trace 2 contains a deadline violation related to the provisional assessment, which was prepared 121 days after the awareness event, exceeding the 120-day limit. The case reached an acceptable state but passed through a non-accepting intermediate marking."* This illustrates how the symbolic output of conformance checking—violation type, affected constraint, and elapsed time—provides a structured basis for an LLM to generate audience-appropriate explanations without sacrificing formal grounding.

5 Related Work

Compliance management in business processes can be approached at three different stages [21]: at *design time*, where processes are evaluated against compliance rules before deployment; at *runtime*, where executions are monitored as they unfold; or *after-the-fact*, where recorded event logs are audited against a normative model. Our work falls in the latter category, as we check existing cases against a refined DCR model derived from regulatory text.

LLMs have been used to elicit business process models from textual descriptions [3,23], although their application to DCR is a recent line of research [18]. LLMs were also applied to model refinement. On the syntactic level several chatbots have been proposed [15,16], while work studying the recognition and application of change patterns is more recent [14]. Beyond these two stages, the use of LLM has also been explored in conformance checking. [17] applies LLMs to conformance checking in medical processes, utilizing them to extract normative rules from textual guidelines, which are then used to assess the conformance of event logs. [4] proposes prompt abstractions and scenario definitions for structuring LLM interactions focused on event logs and process models in a broader process mining context, which includes among others outlier detection.

6 Conclusions and Future Work

This work presents a neuro-symbolic framework for compliance management using MP-DCR processes, integrating LLM-based elicitation and explainability with a formal symbolic backbone. We show the framework on a fragment of the Danish Child Assessment Support Services Act, showing how a normative model can be elicited, refined, and used to check for the compliance of existing cases, and how the resulting violations can be verbalized to different stakeholders using an LLM. Several directions remain open for future work. Supporting model refinement through chatbots would reduce reliance on manual expert intervention. Further, we see an opportunity for AI in variant analysis, to summarize classes of non-compliant cases into rules, providing actionable feedback to organizations.

Acknowledgements. This work has been supported by the grant "Center for Digital CompliancE (DICE)" (VIL57420) from VILLUM FONDEN, and by the Innovation Foundation project "Explainable Hybrid-AI for Computational Law and Accurate Legal Chatbots" 4355-00018B XHAILe.

References

1. van der Aa, H., Leopold, H., Reijers, H.A.: Dealing with behavioral ambiguity in textual process descriptions. In: La Rosa, M., Loos, P., Pastor, O. (eds.) BPM 2016. LNCS, vol. 9850, pp. 271–288. Springer, Cham (2016). https://doi.org/10.1007/978-3-319-45348-4_16
2. Ale, J.M., Rossi, G.H.: An approach to discovering temporal association rules. In: ACM SAC (2000)
3. Bellan, P., Dragoni, M., Ghidini, C.: Extracting business process entities and relations from text using pre-trained language models and in-context learning. In: EDOC (2022)
4. Berti, A., Schuster, D., van der Aalst, W.M.P.: Abstractions, scenarios, and prompt definitions for process mining with LLMs: a case study. In: BPM Workshops (2024)
5. Caballero-Villalobos, J., Burattin, A., López, H.A.: High-level requirements-driven business process compliance. In: BPM Forum (2025)
6. Carbone, M., Hildebrandt, T.T., Perrone, G., Wasowski, A.: Refinement for transition systems with responses. In: FIT (2012)
7. Christfort, A.K.F., Slaats, T.: Efficient optimal alignment between dynamic condition response graphs and traces. In: Di Francescomarino, C., Burattin, A., Janiesch, C., Sadiq, S. (eds.) BPM 2023. LNCS, vol. 14159, pp. 3–19. Springer, Cham (2023). https://doi.org/10.1007/978-3-031-41620-0_1
8. Debois, S., López, H.A., Slaats, T., Andaloussi, A.A., Hildebrandt, T.T.: Chain of events: modular process models for the law. In: iFM (2020)
9. Franceschetti, M., Seiger, R., López, H.A., Burattin, A., García-Bañuelos, L., Weber, B.: A characterisation of ambiguity in BPM. In: ER (2023)
10. Herbst, J., Karagiannis, D.: An inductive approach to the acquisition and adaptation of workflow models. In: IJCAI (1999)

11. Hildebrandt, T.T., Normann, H., Marquard, M., Debois, S., Slaats, T.: Decision modelling in timed dynamic condition response graphs with data. In: Marrella, A., Weber, B. (eds.) BPM 2021. LNCS, vol. 436, pp. 362–374. Springer, Cham (2021). https://doi.org/10.1007/978-3-030-94343-1_28
12. Jans, M., Alles, M.G., Vasarhelyi, M.A.: A field study on the use of process mining of event logs as an analytical procedure in auditing. Account. Rev. (2014)
13. Kautz, H.A.: The third AI summer: Aaai robert s. engelmore memorial lecture. AI Mag. **43**(1), 105–125 (2022). https://doi.org/10.1002/aaai.12036, https://onlinelibrary.wiley.com/doi/abs/10.1002/aaai.12036
14. Klievtsova, N., Kampik, T., Mangler, J., Rinderle-Ma, S.: Conversational process model redesign. arXiv preprint arXiv:2505.05453 (2025)
15. Köpke, J., Safan, A.: Efficient LLM-based conversational process modeling. In: BPM (2024)
16. Kourani, H., Berti, A., Schuster, D., van der Aalst, W.M.: Process modeling with large language models. arXiv:2403.07541 (2024)
17. Leonardi, G., Montani, S., Striani, M.: Checking medical process conformance by exploiting LLMs. Appl. Sci. (2025)
18. Lindner, J., López, H.A.: Discovering declarative processes in textual descriptions using large language models. In: ICPM Workshops (2025)
19. López, H., Debois, S., Slaats, T., Hildebrandt, T.: Business process compliance using reference models of law. In: FASE (2020)
20. López, H.A., Feng, B., Lindner, J., Franceschetti, M., Abbad-Andaloussi, A.: Ambiguity detection in business process descriptions: an evidence and an automated approach. In: BPM (2025)
21. López, H.A., Hildebrandt, T.T.: Three decades of formal methods in business process compliance: a systematic literature review. arXiv (2024)
22. Mukkamala, R.R., Hildebrandt, T.T., Slaats, T.: Towards trustworthy adaptive case management with dynamic condition response graphs. In: EDOC (2013)
23. Neuberger, J., Ackermann, L., van der Aa, H., Jablonski, S.: A universal prompting strategy for extracting process model information from natural language text using large language models. In: ER (2024)

From Architecture to Compliance: A Model-Driven Assessment of AI Systems

Ijeoma Faustina Ekeh(✉), Raimundas Matulevičius, Abasi-amefon Affia-Jomants, and Mihhail Karagjaur

Institute of Computer Science, University of Tartu, 51009 Tartu, Estonia
{ijeomafa,rma,amefon.affia}@ut.ee

Abstract. Artificial intelligence systems (hereafter, AI systems) are subject to regulatory scrutiny under frameworks such as the EU AI Act, ISO/IEC 24001, and the NIST AI Risk Management Framework. While these regulatory initiatives define obligations related to security, risk management, and trustworthiness, they are intentionally specified at a high level of abstraction to remain broadly applicable. As a result, organisations must translate these requirements into concrete architecture-level controls within AI systems, a process that is often non-trivial in practice.

Keywords: Artificial Intelligence Systems · Security · EU AI Act · Compliance · AI governance

1 Introduction

Regulatory compliance for AI systems is increasingly effective in providing legal grounds and controls for deployment in operational environments. AI systems are no longer experimental artefacts but are embedded in business processes, decision-support environments, public administration, and critical infrastructures such as healthcare. In line with Article 3 of the EU AI Act [4], an AI system is defined as a machine-based system designed to operate with varying levels of autonomy and capable of generating outputs, such as predictions or decisions, that influence physical or virtual environments. In this work, we focus on AI systems based on machine learning models, particularly large language models (LLMs) deployed within structured architectural environments. Due to deployments and use of these AI systems, regulatory frameworks such as the EU AI Act [4] and ISO/IEC 42001:2023 [5] are driving growing demand for auditability and traceability, which require demonstrable evidence of risk management, security, and governance for AI systems. For instance, the EU AI Act [4] introduces and mandates compliance with a comprehensive set of technical and organisational obligations, including stringent requirements for technical documentation (Articles 11 and Annex IV) and for accuracy, robustness, and cybersecurity (Article 15).

However, for organisations, there is a structural disconnect in determining whether an AI system is truly compliant or trustworthy between regulatory

R. Posenato and I. Vanderfeesten (Eds.): CAiSE 2026 Workshops, LNBIP 586, pp. 291–303, 2026.
https://doi.org/10.1007/978-3-032-28160-9_26

requirements and the AI system's architectural composition. Also, the connection between functional design decisions and security implications in AI systems remains a gap in organisations [12], leading to security being treated as an afterthought in AI development rather than an integral component of system design. To address this challenge, this paper stresses the need for AI systems' compliance to be grounded in their architecture. Accordingly, this paper is guided by the following research question: **"How can AI system architecture enable identifying requirement gaps towards compliance"**

To answer this research question, this paper proposes a model-driven approach that enables the systematic mapping of regulatory requirements to architectural components and the identification of requirement gaps. To operationalise this approach, we apply a model-driven assessment that bridges the architectural composition of AI systems and security requirements. We propose an AI system asset model that models the architecture into business and system assets across the machine learning lifecycle, enabling a systemic evaluation of functional and security requirements. These requirements represent the operational controls through which regulatory obligations are fulfilled – e.g., the EU AI Act's obligation to provide technical documentation (Article 11; Annex IV) and its security and robustness requirements (Article 15). We define measurable compliance coverage indicators that quantify the extent to which architectural components satisfy the derived functional and security requirements.

The rest of the paper is as follows: Sect. 2 presents the background and related work on regulations and the AI security threat landscape. Section 3 presents the AI asset model and the derivation of requirements. Section 4 presents the approach, its assessment, and demonstration. Section 5 discusses and concludes the paper.

2 Background and Related Works

This section outlines regulatory obligations and the technical foundations necessary for AI compliance, and examines prior work on AI compliance and security assessments.

2.1 Background

Regulations. The governance of AI systems has evolved from ethical guidance (such as the European Union's Level Expert Group on Trustworthiness) to enforceable regulatory obligations (EU AI Act). The European Union's Level Expert Group presents trustworthiness principles as a prerequisite for organisations that develop, deploy and use AI systems [3]. The group highlights technical robustness and safety as a dimension of achieving trustworthiness. The EU AI Act [4] introduces a risk-based classification and imposes obligations on high-risk systems to implement risk management procedures, ensure robustness against manipulation, maintain cybersecurity safeguards and document technical measures. Also, ISO/IEC 42001:2023 [5] establishes requirements for AI systems, emphasising lifecycle governance, security integration and documented evidence of control implementation. Across these obligations and frameworks, their characteristics remain consistent, meaning that regulation is risk-based. Compliance requires technical documentation and traceability of how risks are mitigated and of how models are developed and validated. However, while these regulatory frameworks define what must be achieved, they rarely specify how organisations should map compliance with these regulations to a concrete AI system architecture.

AI Security. AI systems introduce security risks that surface from conventional systems. These risks include data poisoning, model extraction, adversarial manipulation, prompt injection, and unauthorised access to model assets. Security controls are defined at the policy level, with limited traceability to specific architectural composition, such as embedding repositories, preprocessing pipelines, model storage mechanisms, or inference APIs. Under Article 15 of the EU AI Act, the obligations establish robustness, accuracy, and cybersecurity requirements for AI systems. It requires that AI systems be designed and developed to be resilient to security attacks and errors. In particular, the obligation emphasised the implementation of technical measures to protect system integrity and prevent unauthorised attacks. To achieve this, several frameworks provide structured guidance for identifying and mitigating security risks. MITRE ATLAS [6] provides a knowledge base of adversarial machine learning tactics and techniques, documenting real-world attacks and patterns against AI systems. While these frameworks provide comprehensive taxonomies of AI-specific threats and mitigation strategies, they do not prescribe how organisations should systematically map these security obligations to concrete architectural assets.

2.2 Related Works

In [7], the authors proposed the Databricks AI security framework (DASF), a defence-in-depth approach to securing AI by mapping to standards. The approach focuses on governance, AI threats, and controls, with limited lifecycle coverage of AI systems (deployment phases), resulting in less emphasis on other phases. Similarly, [16] proposed the Compliance Agentic Model (CAM) framework to support compliance for generative AI and machine learning systems. The framework establishes a thin line of trustworthiness by ensuring alignment with organisational values and regulatory obligations. The authors [12] investigate an AI system that integrates large language models with knowledge graphs to support security decision-making. The approach targets compliance with IEC 62443-3-3 and alignment with the EU AI Act. [13] analyses provisions of the EU AI Act, emphasising the compliance requirements applicable to high-risk AI systems. The study maps known AI security threats to the regulation's technical requirements and evaluates the extent to which security measures mitigate the risk. Based on this analysis, there is a need for an integrated framework to assess AI systems. To address the challenge of evaluating AI across regulatory frameworks, [2] introduces the CAVe framework, which maps controls from the NIST

AI RMF, the EU AI Act, and standards into a common indicator set used to compute the compliance coverage index, enabling evaluation across multiple AI governance frameworks. Additionally, in [17], the authors present a framework combining ontologies, assurance cases, and fact sheets to support compliance and security documentation for AI systems, helping engineers and stakeholders ensure that LLM-based systems align with regulatory requirements and are resilient to potential security threats.

Despite these contributions, existing approaches address only parts of the compliance assessment problem. Governance-oriented frameworks focus on aligning organisational processes with regulatory requirements but provide limited support for linking these requirements to system architecture. Security-oriented approaches emphasise threat identification and mitigation but do not explicitly connect these controls to regulatory obligations. Compliance mapping frameworks translate regulatory requirements into control sets or indicators; however, they often lack an explicit representation of the underlying AI system architecture as a unit of compliance assessment. In contrast, this work integrates these perspectives by combining architecture-based modelling, threat-informed requirement derivation, and coverage-based assessment. This integration enables explicit traceability between regulatory requirements, architectural components, and security controls, allowing the systematic identification and quantification of compliance gaps within AI systems.

3 A Model for Architecting AI Security Compliance

3.1 Methodology

The proposed AI system asset model was developed by synthesising existing research and frameworks. A systematic literature review (SLR) [11], building on earlier work in [14], was conducted to identify the architectural composition of AI systems and their lifecycle elements, along with associated threats and mitigation patterns. The SLR [11,14] identified recurring AI system assets (e.g., training data, model artefacts, embeddings, and infrastructure), lifecycle-specific threat patterns, and corresponding mitigation strategies. These findings informed both the structuring of business and system assets in the proposed model and the derivation of functional and security requirements. To structure these elements and support artefact development, we adopt the established Information Systems Security Risk Management (ISSRM) model [15], which distinguishes among assets, threats, requirements, and mitigation. Additionally, we used a UML class diagram to depict the static structure of the proposed model.

3.2 Model Development

To develop the AI system asset model (Fig. 1), based on the SLR synthesis and ISSRM approach[1], the model is organised into two main asset layers, represented

[1] Technical report containing review and abstractions of the model [11].

as classes throughout the AI lifecycle, each with operations. The model distinguishes between business assets and system assets [11,14]. Business assets are high-value information elements that determine the AI's functional behaviour and logic, including training and test data, the machine learning model, model parameters, query input data, input embeddings, and associated intellectual property. These assets represent the primary objects of protection from a compliance and security perspective.

In contrast, system assets refer to the technical components and infrastructure of an AI system that process, store, or facilitate the business asset. These include the machine learning (ML) model, which appears as a business asset and represents the informational value. In contrast, as a system asset, it functions as a technical component with the system architecture, the ML system input API, the training system, the enabling system components, and the supporting IT infrastructure. Article 11 and Annex IV of the EU AI Act [4] require providers of AI systems to provide and maintain technical documentation describing system architecture; consequently, systems and business assets as defined in the model correspond directly to the architectural composition under regulatory obligations.

In practice, the identification of these assets is grounded in the technical documentation of the AI system under assessment, as required by the Act. The anchor of asset identification in formal technical documentation, such as system design specifications, API documentation, deployment configurations, and infrastructural descriptions, establishes a traceability chain from architectural components to derived security requirements and implemented controls, enabling evidence evaluation at the AI system level.

3.3 Derivation of Functional and Security Requirements

The derivation of requirements is grounded in the SLR synthesis and the AI system asset model. The transformation proceeds in three stages: (1) Identification of relevant architectural assets from the SLR, (2) Extraction of threats and mitigation associated with the identified assets, and (3) Formalisation of identified mitigations into implementable security requirements aligned with Article 15 of the EU AI Act

Functional and Security Requirements. In Sect. 3.2, the AI asset system model is presented, from which the functional requirements are derived. The functional requirements represent the core operational capabilities necessary for an AI system. These capabilities include traceable mechanisms embedded within the system and business asset and lifecycle components. The functional requirements enable accountability and operational robustness of the AI system. Security requirements, in contrast, represent the protective measures imposed on the architectural assets to preserve confidentiality, integrity, availability and resilience against security attacks. These methods include access control [9], model hardening [8], encryption [10]. Also, Article 15 of the EU AI Act requires

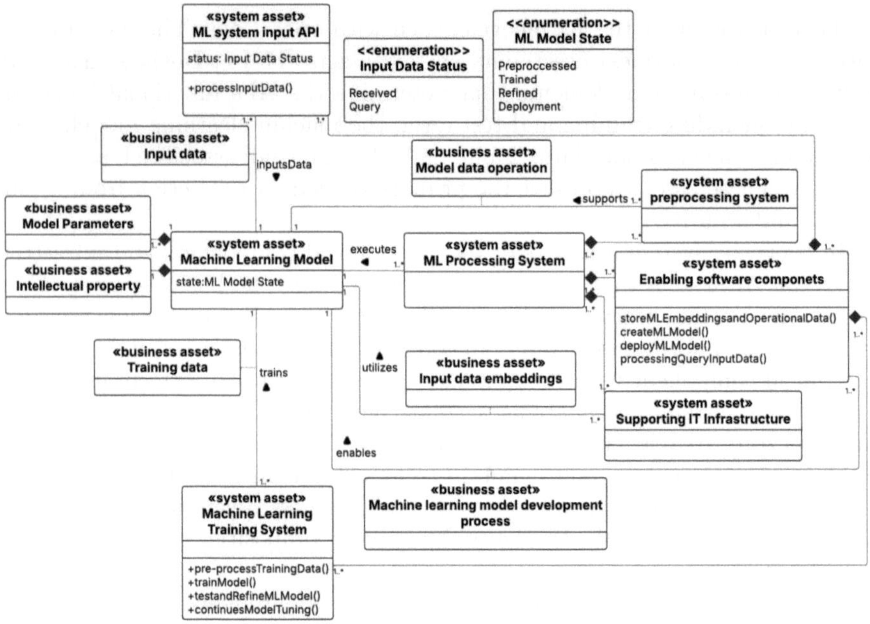

Fig. 1. AI System Asset Model

AI systems to achieve appropriate levels of robustness, accuracy and cybersecurity. through technical and organisational measures. The derived security requirements apply these obligations at the architectural level.

From Threat to Security Requirement. Building on the security threat abstraction synthesised from the SLR [11], identified threat vectors are systematically mapped to architectural assets defined in Sect. 3.2. This synthesis highlights recurring threats that affect AI systems across multiple lifecycle stages. The consolidated threats include, but are not limited to,

1. Inference Time Manipulation – prompt injection and adversarial inputs.
2. Unauthorised access and Model Extraction
3. Data manipulation and poisoning such as corruption of training data and adversarial modification of the model.

Due to the evolving nature of AI, constraints on exhaustive representation of threats are limited. Yet, they reflect recurring risk patterns across the reviewed literature and threat intelligence sources such as the MITRE ATLAS [6]. Thus, this enables flexible adaptation to new threats and mitigation, resulting in actionable security requirements. The security requirements were then derived as implementable mitigation constraints for protecting the assets against mapped threats. We mapped the derived security requirements to the robustness and cybersecurity obligations under Article 15. This mapping establishes a regulatory reference for interpreting the architectural controls assessed in the coverage analysis. For example, an asset ML system's input API is affected by inference-time manipulation, such as prompt injection. Expected mitigation would be contextual analysis (automated guardrail), from which the derived requirement is that the ML system input API should perform analysis on Input data. Tables 1 and 2 present derived functional and security requirements, along with mappings to EU regulations, intended to enhance compliance.

Table 1. Functional Requirements of the AI Systems

ID	Functional Requirements
REQ1.1	Preprocess training data
REQ1.2	Train the model
REQ1.3	Test and refine the ML model
REQ1.4	Continous tune the model
REQ2.1	Store ML embeddings and operational data
REQ2.2	Create an ML Model
REQ2.3	Deploy the ML model
REQ2.4	Process the query input data
REQ3.1	Model states (preprocessed, trained, refined and deployed)
REQ4.1	Process the user input data

4 The Model-Driven Assessment Approach

This section addresses the component of the research question by defining how the implementation of the derived functional and security requirements is measured and aggregated into compliance indicators.

4.1 Assessment of AI System

The assessment of an AI system is evaluated at the level of architectural compositions identified in the Sect. 3.2. Each asset is associated with a set of functional requirements. Each security requirement represents an implementable solution derived from a threat and its mitigation in accordance with the EU regulation. The assessment is conducted in a two-phase approach: the AS-IS phase identifies the baseline functions, revealing architectural deficiencies in the AI system, and the TO-BE phase proposes the architecture configuration of requirements. The scoring guideline for every requirement – functional (REQ1.1–REQ4.2) and security (SRQ1-SRQ14) follows a Likert scale of 1–5. Scores of 4–5 indicate fully

Table 2. Security Requirements mapping of Article 15 of the EU AI Act

ID	Security Requirements	EU Article 15 Obligation
SRQ1	Maintain and monitor training data	Protect pre-trained components used in training from poisoning
SRQ2	Sanitise Training data	Prevent, detect, respond to attacks manipulating training datasets
SRQ3	Training data and ML model should be limited to only approved users	Resilient against unauthorised third-party attempts to alter use, outputs or performance
SRQ4	The ML model parameters should be protected against an attacker attempting access	Protect against confidentiality attacks on the model
SRQ5	Monitor and limit the number of abnormally large inputs performed in a given amount of time	robustness may be achieved through technical redundancy solutions
SRQ6	The ML model should be monitored for concept and training data drift	Address and control for model flaws
SRQ7	Cross-validate to detect performance inconsistencies of the model	Achieve an appropriate level of accuracy for the intended purpose and context through validated models, calibration, performance testing
SRQ8	Different ML models should be combined to reduce model redundancy	include backup or fail-safe plans
SRQ9	Maintain integrity by permitting pruning of model parameters that do not degrade the performance of the model	Resilient against unauthorised third-party attempts to alter use, outputs or performance
SRQ10	Perform analysis on user prompts/inputs.	Protect against inputs designed to cause model mistakes (evasion)
SRQ11	Obscure sensitive information	Protect against confidentiality attacks on the model.
SRQ12	Noise should be added to training data	Protect against confidentiality attacks on the model.
SRQ13	The AI artefacts should be verified before usage	Protect pre-trained components used in training from poisoning
SRQ14	Harden model to increase the Robustness	Achieve an appropriate level of robustness throughout the lifecycle

explicit fulfilment (technically verifiable), scores of 2–3 indicate partial fulfilment (limited operational coverage), and scores of 0–1 indicate the absence of the requirement, thus not implemented or conceptually addressed. Based on the scoring guideline above, the coverage of requirements is calculated using the following formulas: n = number of requirements (functional or security); m = number of assessors; $s_{\max}$ = maximum evaluation score (5 on Likert scale); and E_{ij} = evaluation score given by the assessor i for requirement j. The scoring process is guided by the presence and clarity of architectural evidence for each requirement, ensuring evaluations are grounded in documented system artefacts rather than subjective assumptions.

Requirement coverage (RC): quantifies the degree to which functional and security requirements are implemented to comply with regulatory requirements. It is a composite indicator for gap identification in AI systems.

$$RC = \frac{\sum_{j=1}^{n} \sum_{i=1}^{m} E_{ij}}{m \times s_{\max} \times n} \times 100\% \tag{1}$$

This guideline ensures consistency across assessor(s) by linking the given score to observable architectural evidence specific to the AI system.

Interpretation of Assessment Coverage Indicators. To support the interpretability and govern decision-making for analysis between the AS-IS and TO-BE states, the coverage indicators are grouped into three thresholds: (1) Low Coverage (0%-39.99%), (2) Moderate Coverage (40% -60.99%) and (3) High Coverage (61%-100%). The thresholds were selected to differentiate between limited and broadly implemented requirements clearly. High implementation coverage indices indicate a stronger alignment with Articles 11 and 15 obligations, whereas low implementation coverage signals structural compliance gaps requiring remediation.

4.2 Use Case: Approach Demonstration on Mistral AI

This section presents a preliminary demonstration of the assessment approach discussed in previous sections. We present an instantiation of Mistral AI [1], a large language model (LLM) designed for text generation and reasoning tasks. The objective is to map the core components of Mistral, including model artefacts, embedding representations, inference APIS, and supporting infrastructure.

Asset Identification from Technical Documentation. The instantiation of Mistral populates the AI asset system model (see Fig. 1) grounded on technical documentation, including the system architecture description, API specifications, and deployment and infrastructure details. The Mistral Small model was categorised as a machine learning model asset: the request-handling module, mistral-common/protocol/instruction/request. Py was mapped to the ML system input API, while the Mistral common library was categorised as an enabling software component. The local development environment was categorised as supporting IT infrastructure and preprocessing systems. For business assets, the element included the training data, test data, model parameters, tokenisers, embeddings and intellectual property. Other lifecycle phases, such as processUserQueryInput(), storeEmbeddingAndTokeniser(), deployMLModel(), and trainMistralSmall(), were mapped to corresponding system assets (Fig. 2).

Assessment of Mistral. Following the architectural instantiation of the model, the Mistral system is assessed against the requirements. The assessment is conducted using evaluations described in the section. 4.1, based on the system's

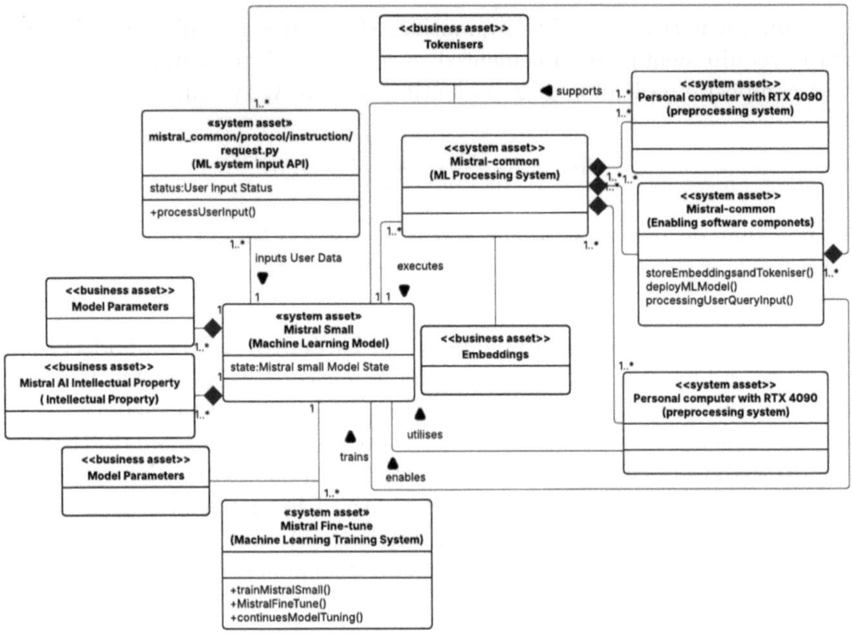

Fig. 2. Instantiated Architecture of Mistral AI LLM-based system

architectural documentation and composition. Figure 3 presents the resulting coverage indicators (*RC*) for both AS-IS and TO-BE assessment phases. The AS-IS assessment produced functional and security coverage values at 65.5% and 24.3%, respectively. These results indicate moderate functional implementation maturity but limited security coverage within the assessed architecture. The evaluation examined how each requirement is reflected in the documented architectural components. This process revealed gaps in functional mechanisms supporting system operation, such as the training process, and missing or underspecified security controls aligned with Article 15 expectations.

Based on the gaps identified in the as-IS assessment, including the security analysis of the Mistral system, a To-BE architectural configuration addresses missing or weakly implemented security requirements. The mitigation strategy is based on requirements aligned with Article 5 obligations on robustness and cybersecurity. These changes included strengthening protections against inference manipulation and model parameter compromise, as well as improving architectural representation of security controls in the documentation. The functional architecture remained unchanged; however, missing or insufficiently described components were assigned low scores to indicate incomplete compliance representation under Article 11 documentation requirements. The TO-BE evaluation demonstrates a substantial increase in security coverage, reflecting improved alignment between the system architecture and the derived requirements.

	AS-IS Estimations		TO-BE Estimations	
	Expl		Expl	
REQ1.1	5	5.0	5	5.0
REQ1.2	1	1.0	1	1.0
REQ1.3	1	1.0	1	1.0
REQ1.4	5	5.0	5	5.0
REQ2.1	4	4.0	4	4.0
REQ2.2	1	1.0	1	1.0
REQ2.3	5	5.0	5	5.0
REQ2.4	5	5.0	5	5.0
REQ3.1	3	3.0	3	3.0
REQ4.1	5	5.0	5	5.0
REQ4.2	1	1.0	1	1.0
Functionality Coverage (FC)	65.5%	65.5%	65.5%	65.5%

	AS-IS Estimations		TO-BE Estimations	
SRQ1	1	1.0	5	5.0
SRQ2	2	2.0	1	1.0
SRQ3	1	1.0	1	1.0
SRQ4	1	1.0	5	5.0
SRQ5	1	1.0	5	5.0
SRQ6	1	1.0	1	1.0
SRQ7	1	1.0	1	1.0
SRQ8	1	1.0	1	1.0
SRQ9	1	1.0	1	1.0
SRQ10	1	1.0	5	5.0
SRQ11	1	1.0	5	5.0
SRQ12	1	1.0	1	1.0
SRQ13	3	3.0	5	5.0
SRQ14	1	1.0	1	1.0
Security Coverage (SC)	24.3%	24.3%	54.3%	54.3%

Fig. 3. Functionality and Security coverage of Mistral AI Model

5 Discussion and Conclusion

To drive discussions on AI systems towards security compliance, AI system architecture assessments provide a foundation for implementing compliance requirements. The EU AI Act imposes mandatory requirements for comprehensive technical documentation, as well as robustness and cybersecurity provisions in Articles 11 and 15. Thus, the AI asset model provides a blueprint for the AI system, supporting an explicit definition of its architecture, including components, and the identification of requirements gaps. A key contribution of the approach is its ability to translate regulatory expectations into architectural controls. From a usability perspective, the approach drives organisations to assess their compliance with regulations by ensuring that the interpretation of technical documentation is informed by a compliance lens applied to their asset composition. By mapping assets, organisations can identify implementation gaps and prioritise mitigation efforts. Importantly, the coverage indicators are not intended to provide a formal determination of regulatory compliance; instead, they function as a tool to highlight the implementation gaps and support remediation compliance plans for the organisation.

The use case illustrates how the approach moves from architectural mapping to reveal core functional and security gaps. It quantifies the improvements through the AS-IS and TO-BE assessments of the system. Several limitations remain, such as coverage scores that rely on the assessor's interpretation of the technical documentation for architecture mapping, which introduces an element of subjectivity. The derived requirements are grounded in the analysed threat landscape and aligned with the EU AI Act's regulatory obligations. However, they are not exhaustive; additional requirements may emerge as AI systems, threat patterns and regulatory interpretations evolve. The framework is therefore designed to remain extensible, enabling organisations to incorporate new requirements within the ongoing compliance and risk management process.

In conclusion, this paper introduced an AI asset system model and an architectural approach to assess compliance coverage in AI systems. By mapping derived security requirements to regulatory obligations, such as Article 15 of the EU AI Act, the approach helps identify compliance gaps in AI systems. Future work will focus on extending the approach's validation across a broader range of AI systems. Regarding generalisability, the case study demonstrates applicability to a single AI system; however, the proposed method is not limited to this context[2]. The approach can be applied to other AI systems with sufficient architectural documentation. Nevertheless, broader empirical validation is required across diverse system configurations.

To limit bias in the assessor's judgement, the approach will include independent validation through practitioner-based evaluations and empirical studies in organisational settings. Although structured requirements and scoring criteria improve consistency, future work will focus on refining evaluation guidelines and providing concrete scoring examples to enhance the reliability of evaluation results. Also, future research would explore automation mechanisms to streamline the model instantiation and assessment process.

Acknowledgments. The European Union funds this research under Grant Agreement No. 101087529. However, views and opinions expressed are those of the author(s) only and do not necessarily reflect those of the European Union or European Research Executive Agency. Neither the European Union nor the granting authority can be held responsible.

Disclosure of Interests. The authors have no competing interests to declare that are relevant to the content of this article.

References

1. Bienvenue to Mistral AI Documentation — Mistral AI. https://docs.mistral.ai/
2. Cross-Assessment & Verification for Evaluation (CAVe) Framework for AI Risk and Compliance Assessment Using a Cross-Compliance Index (CCI) — MDPI. https://www.mdpi.com/2079-9292/15/2/307#Introduction
3. Ethics guidelines for trustworthy AI — Shaping Europe's digital future. https://digital-strategy.ec.europa.eu/en/library/ethics-guidelines-trustworthy-ai
4. High-level summary of the AI Act — EU Artificial Intelligence Act. https://artificialintelligenceact.eu/high-level-summary/
5. ISO/IEC 42001:2023. https://www.iso.org/standard/42001
6. MITRE ATLAS™. https://atlas.mitre.org/
7. Introducing the Databricks AI Security Framework (DASF) (2024). https://www.databricks.com/blog/introducing-databricks-ai-security-framework-dasf
8. Almagrabi, A.O., Khan, R.A.: Optimizing secure AI lifecycle model management with innovative generative AI strategies. IEEE Access pp. 1–1 (2024). https://doi.org/10.1109/ACCESS.2024.3491373, https://ieeexplore.ieee.org/document/10742321/?arnumber=10742321&tag=1, conference Name: IEEE Access

[2] An extensive demonstration of the Mistral and other LLM systems can be found in the technical report [11].

9. Altun, I., Emre Ozkok, A.: Securing artificial intelligence: exploring attack scenarios and defense. Strategies (2024). https://doi.org/10.1109/ISDFS60797.2024.10527288
10. Bogdanov, D., Etti, P., Kamm, L., Stomakhin, F.: Artificial intelligence system risk management methodology based on generalized blueprints. In: 2024 16th International Conference on Cyber Conflict: Over the Horizon (CyCon), pp. 123–140 (2024). https://doi.org/10.23919/CyCon62501.2024.10685644, https://ieeexplore.ieee.org/document/10685644/?arnumber=10685644&tag=1
11. Ekeh, I.F., Matulevicius, R.: Systematic technical report for model-driven elicitation of functional and security requirements in AI-supported systems. Technical report, Zenodo (2025). https://doi.org/10.5281/zenodo.17878604
12. Hosseini, A.M., Sauter, T., Kastner, W.: Trustworthy AI for security decision-making in ICSs: towards compliance with the EU AI act. In: 2025 IEEE 30th International Conference on Emerging Technologies and Factory Automation (ETFA), pp. 1–4 (2025). https://doi.org/10.1109/ETFA65518.2025.11205756, iSSN 1946-0759
13. Kalodanis, K., Rizomiliotis, P., Anagnostopoulos, D.: European artificial intelligence act: an AI security approach. Inf. Comput. Secur. **32**(3), 265–281 (2023). https://doi.org/10.1108/ICS-10-2022-0165
14. Karagjaur, M.: Asset-oriented threat analysis for large language model systems. Master's thesis, University of Tartu, Tartu, Estonia (2025). https://thesis.cs.ut.ee/fa0d6ab8-fff5-45bf-9e07-5ece225171fd
15. Mayer, N.: Model-Based Management of Information System Security Risk (2012). https://www.semanticscholar.org/paper/Model-based-Management-of-Information-System-Risk-Mayer/66c31937f0a8734842ff115bc0e38d90ff2b833a
16. Menezes, V.P., Chowdhury, M.J.M., Mahmood, A.: An agentic framework for compliant, ethical and trustworthy GenAI applications in healthcare. In: Proceedings of the 2025 Australasian Computer Science Week. ACSW '25, pp. 48–54. Association for Computing Machinery, New York, NY, USA (2025). https://doi.org/10.1145/3727166.3727191
17. Momcilovic, T.B., Buesser, B., Zizzo, G., Purcell, M., Balta, D.: Towards assuring EU AI act compliance and adversarial robustness of LLMs (2024). https://doi.org/10.48550/arXiv.2410.05306, arXiv:2410.05306 [cs] version: 1

Trustworthy Robotic Process Automation: Challenges and Emerging Research Directions

Simone Agostinelli[1](✉), Glenda Hannibal[2], Aleksandre Asatiani[3], and Artur Modlinski[4]

[1] Universitas Mercatorum, Rome, Italy
simone.agostinelli@unimercatorum.it
[2] University of Salzburg, Salzburg, Austria
glenda.hannibal@plus.ac.at
[3] University of Gothenburg, Gothenburg, Sweden
aleksandre.asatiani@ait.gu.se
[4] University of Lodz, Lodz, Poland
artur.modlinski@uni.lodz.pl

Abstract. Although many studies have investigated trust in automation broadly, little is known about trust in Robotic Process Automation (RPA). Unlike general automation, RPA presents unique trust challenges, as it operates at the intersection of human decision-making and rule-based digital labor. Existing research often conflates trust with trustworthiness and fails to distinguish between trusting attitudes and the actual attributes that make RPA systems trustworthy. Furthermore, the current body of research is predominantly qualitative and lacks empirical studies examining the design features that drive RPA trustworthiness, experiments focused on trust formation, or longitudinal investigations of trust dynamics. Addressing these gaps, this paper identifies five key research challenges and directions that must be overcome to enable a new wave of trustworthy RPA systems.

Keywords: Robotic Process Automation · Trust · Trustworthiness

1 Introduction

Robotic Process Automation (RPA) has emerged over the last decade as a distinct and rapidly maturing technology. RPA represents only a narrow and specific subset of automation technologies, focusing exclusively on software (SW) robots that automate repetitive, rule-based tasks executed on user interfaces of existing systems [25]. Since RPA excels in handling rule-based, well-structured, and repetitive tasks, their uptake by organizations rest on the promises of rapid deployment, high return on investment, and inexpensive and non-invasive system integration [7,10]. However, as RPA adoption increased, so did the rate of failed RPA projects. Research suggests that anywhere between 50% and 75%

R. Posenato and I. Vanderfeesten (Eds.): CAiSE 2026 Workshops, LNBIP 586, pp. 304–310, 2026.
https://doi.org/10.1007/978-3-032-28160-9_27

of RPA projects fail to achieve set objectives [11,27]. Failures often stem from poor planning at the early implementation stages, and inability to scale the RPA initiatives beyond proof-of-concept [2,15].

Although there are many ingredients for successful RPA projects [1,14], one important and often overlooked factor is the `trustworthiness` of and `trust` in RPA [22]. In the current literature, these terms are often used interchangeably, creating theoretical and practical ambiguity. In this paper, we define trust as a user's subjective willingness to rely on an RPA system under uncertainty, driven by their perceptions of its reliability and intentions. In contrast, trustworthiness refers to the objective, system-centered properties—such as transparency, predictability, and compliance—that justify such reliance.

There is currently no systematic understanding of how trust and trustworthiness are conceptualized, operationalized, and interrelated in the context of RPA, nor how deficiencies in these constructs contribute to implementation challenges and failures. As a result, organizations lack clear guidance on how to design, deploy, and govern RPA systems in a way that fosters appropriate trust. For instance, organizations wanting to implement RPA may seek reassurances before making a decision to adopt the technology [28]. Managers often establish trustworthiness of technology through external validation for RPA tools from technical specifications, industry peers, RPA consultants, and the broader community [11]. The anthropomorphism of RPA could lead users to put undue trust in the capabilities of the technology, leading to overblown expectations [11,23]. Alternatively, belief in advance capabilities could lead to psychological resistance caused by fear of job loss or concerns about the capabilities and maturity of technology [11,13]. Conflating these concepts in research design could lead to unjustified generalizations in how trust in RPA is established and how it impacts the implementation and use of the technology.

Furthermore, trust research often treats automation as a monolith, failing to distinguish between technologies as diverse as self-driving cars and RPA. RPA requires a nuanced approach because its role is unique: it is embedded directly into human workflows to perform tasks formerly handled by people. Although traditional RPA is deterministic and rule-based, its human-like framing creates a perception of intelligence that must be managed carefully. This challenge is further intensified by the integration of Artificial Intelligence (AI) and machine learning, which introduces non-deterministic behaviors and opaque decision-making into previously transparent processes.

Just as trust in AI is studied through specific applications like chatbots or autonomous vehicles, trust in RPA must be examined as a distinct phenomenon shaped by its unique organizational role. Consequently, this paper aims to provide a research agenda for trustworthy RPA. The authors of this paper—who have backgrounds in RPA-related fields and Human-Centered AI—identified and discussed challenges and emerging research directions during the Dagstuhl Seminar 24292, "Improving Trust between Humans and Software Robots in Robotic Process Automation"[1], as well as in follow-up discussions.

[1] https://www.dagstuhl.de/24292.

2 Research Agenda on Trustworthy RPA

This section outlines five research challenges and directions that should be pursued to advance the state of the art in trust and trustworthiness of RPA. It is important to emphasize that these challenges do not constitute an exhaustive list, as the discipline is dynamically evolving. Rather, they illustrate problems that are currently substantially underexplored and that emerged from the Dagstuhl discussion group. While grounded in these seminar discussions, the challenges are not purely anecdotal, indeed they reflect recurring themes identified in prior literature on RPA, automation, and human – AI interaction. Each challenge is systematically related to existing research streams, including technology adoption, human – automation trust, and information systems implementation.

C1: The Need for Calibration Between Trust and Trustworthiness in RPA. RPA technology may be highly trustworthy due to the technical proficiency and reliability of SW robots. Yet, users might not trust RPA if they lack an understanding of such technology or if past interaction experiences have been negative. Alternatively, users might trust RPA technology that appears efficient but lacks underlying robustness, leading to potential errors or failures. This divergence often leads to a mismatch in expectations, resulting in disillusionment and a growing sense of mistrust.

Therefore, it is important to reduce the gap between the pre-implementation expectations (trustworthiness of RPA technology) and post-implementation reality (trust placed in RPA technology) to ensure continued trust in the technology. By calibrating the trustworthiness of the RPA technology with the trust of its users, businesses can facilitate smoother integration, higher adoption rates, and more effective utilization of automation within their processes.

Since existing approaches primarily use qualitative methods to measure trust [21] and tend to conceptualize trust and trustworthiness calibration outcomes using a categorical model [19], the next step in effectively calibrating trust and trustworthiness is the development of a quantitative framework. For example, this could involve developing a *gradient trust scale*, which positions possible outcomes on a continuum range. The scale should be defined based on a set of properties derived from empirical findings [3,4], such as expert interviews and/or surveys. The following overarching question is proposed for future research: (**RQ1**) *What are the key factors influencing trust calibration between RPA technology trustworthiness and user trust?*

C2: The Need to Describe the Profiles of Users with the Lowest and Highest Levels of Trust in RPA. While researchers investigating trust towards other technologies (i.e., AI, autonomous vehicles, or virtual reality) have identified several factors that stand behind high or low trust, the profile of people using RPA in view of their subjective trust in SW robots is still scarce. It was found that high subjective trust is observable among people having experience with RPA, understanding the work of SW robots, having low level of anxiety and need of control [2,3,21,26], while it remains unknown how age, gender, education background, work engagement and ethical values influence such trust.

Interestingly, research on subjective trust towards one technology is not simply transferable to another. It is shown, for instance, that while females have higher trust in online shopping than males [24], males have higher trust in autonomous vehicles than females [12]. As such differences in subjective trust among different technologies exists, researchers should devote more time to consider variables related to the user profile and determining their level of trust in RPA. The following research question is proposed: (**RQ2**) *How do demographic factors such as age, gender, and educational background influence higher or lower levels of subjective trust in RPA technology?*

C3: The Need to Conduct Experimental Studies to Investigate Trust in RPA. Experimental studies offer an insight into people's behavior while surveys and interviews collect their attitude that may not be fully translatable to behavioral indicators of trust. While studies investigating, for instance, trust in AI [5] or virtual reality [9] use experiments to check whether people really trust such systems, no experimental research has been conducted in the context of RPA to verify who trusts SW robots and under what conditions. This is a shortcoming that should be investigated in future research to better analyze and describe trust of employees using RPA. As a starting point future research should investigate: (**RQ3**) *How can experimental methods be designed to accurately measure real behavioral trust in RPA systems among employees?*

C4: The Need to Describe the Features that Foster Trustworthiness in RPA. Similarly, although a plethora of research has investigated factors influencing the trustworthiness of various technologies, there is a need to focus on the impact of their design [16], interaction style [6], country of origin, and safety certifications [17]. A list of factors influencing the trustworthiness of RPA is lacking although researchers found that low transparency [20] and little capabilities [20,21] decrease the trustworthiness of SW robots. As such, little is known about when actual users perceive RPA as being transparent and capable of performing the tasks. The following research question is proposed: (**RQ4**) *What are the key design elements that influence the perceived trustworthiness of RPA technology?*

C5: The Need to Research How to Restore Trust in RPA After Failures Occur. Research on trust in new technologies is divided into trust acquisition, trust loss, and trust restoration [8]. While current research on trust in RPA investigates how trust is built (trust acquisition) and lost, no research investigates how trust in RPA can be restored after violation. Insight into trust repair is important because research reports that the effect of disappointment with SW robots and low trust may result in the retirement of RPA and financial loss [18]. Therefore, future research should collect best practices of companies that have experience with lost trust in RPA and that have successfully restored it. The following research question has been formulated: (**RQ5**) *What strategies can organizations use to successfully restore trust in RPA after a trust violation?*

3 Conclusion

RPA is increasingly adopted by organizations to automate routine business processes and improve operational efficiency. Despite its technological maturity, the successful integration and sustained use of RPA strongly depend on the alignment between the trustworthiness of SW robots and the trust placed in them by users. To address this gap, this paper identifies five research challenges and directions that should be pursued to advance the understanding of trustworthy RPA systems. The identified challenges, summarized below, should not be viewed as isolated issues but as interdependent components of a broader socio-technical system (e.g., insufficient system transparency may lead to miscalibrated user trust, which in turn affects adoption and long-term system performance).

First, there is a need to calibrate the relationship between technological trustworthiness and user trust, potentially through the development of quantitative frameworks capable of measuring trust on a continuum. Second, the characteristics of users who exhibit high or low levels of trust in RPA remain insufficiently understood, particularly with respect to demographic and psychological factors. Third, existing studies rely largely on qualitative methods, highlighting the need for experimental approaches capable of capturing behavioral indicators of trust during human – RPA interaction. Fourth, the design features that contribute to the perceived trustworthiness of RPA systems—such as transparency, capability, and interaction design—require systematic investigation. Finally, little is known about how organizations can effectively restore trust after failures or trust violations in automated systems.

By outlining these five research directions and associated research questions, this work provides a foundation for future empirical and conceptual studies aimed at strengthening trust and trustworthiness in RPA adoption and use.

Acknowledgments. This work has benefitted from Dagstuhl Seminar 24292 "Improving Trust between Humans and Software Robots in Robotic Process Automation" (https://www.dagstuhl.de/24292) and supported by the Excellence in Digital Sciences and Interdisciplinary Technologies (EXDIGIT) project, funded by Land Salzburg under grant number 20204-WISS/263/6-6022.

References

1. Aguirre, S., Rodriguez, A.: Automation of a business process using robotic process automation (RPA): a case study. In: Applying Computing Science in Engineering, pp. 65–71. Springer (2017). https://doi.org/10.1007/978-3-319-66963-2_7
2. Asatiani, A., Copeland, O., Penttinen, E.: Deciding on the robotic process automation operating model: a checklist for RPA managers. Bus. Horiz. **66**(1), 109–121 (2023)
3. Asatiani, A., Penttinen, E., Ruissalo, J., Salovaara, A.: Knowledge workers' reactions to a planned introduction of robotic process automation—Empirical evidence from an accounting firm. Inf. Syst. Outsourcing: Era Digit. Transf. 413–452 (2020)

4. Axmann, B., Harmoko, H.: The assessment model of robotic process automation (RPA) project using benefit study and balanced scorecard (BSC) approach. Tehnički glasnik **18**(2), 246–253 (2024)
5. Bartosiak, M.L., Modlinski, A.: Fired by an algorithm? Exploration of conformism with biased intelligent decision support systems in the context of workplace discipline. Career Dev. Int. **27**(6/7), 601–615 (2022)
6. Cai, N., Gao, S., Yan, J.: How the communication style of chatbots influences consumers' satisfaction, trust, and engagement in the context of service failure. Human. Soc. Sci. Commun. **11**(1), 1–11 (2024)
7. Capgemini, C.: Robotic process automation—Robots conquer business processes in back offices (2017)
8. Di Dio, C., et al.: Shall I trust you? From child-robot interaction to trusting relationships. Front. Psychol. **11**, 469 (2020)
9. Hale, J., Hamilton, A.F.D.C.: Testing the relationship between mimicry, trust and rapport in virtual reality conversations. Sci. Rep. **6**(1), 35295 (2016)
10. Hallikainen, P., Bekkhus, R., Pan, S.L.: How OpusCapita Used Internal RPA Capabilities to Offer Services to Clients. MIS Q. Exec. 17(1) (2018)
11. Herm, L.V., Janiesch, C., Helm, A., Imgrund, F., Hofmann, A., Winkelmann, A.: A framework for implementing robotic process automation projects. IseB **21**(1), 1–35 (2023)
12. Hulse, L.M., Xie, H., Galea, E.R.: Perceptions of autonomous vehicles: relationships with road users, risk, gender and age. Saf. Sci. **102**, 1–13 (2018)
13. Kraus, P., Fißler, E., Schlegel, D.: A typology of challenges in the context of robotic process automation implementation projects. Int. J. Organ. Anal. **32**(11), 60–73 (2024)
14. Lacity, M., Willcocks, L.P., Craig, A.: RPA at Telefonica O2. The London School of. Economics and Political Science (2015)
15. Lindgren, I., Johansson, B., Söderström, F., Toll, D.: Why is it difficult to implement robotic process automation? Empirical cases from Swedish municipalities. In: International Conference on Electronic Government, pp. 353–368. Springer (2022)
16. Modliński, A.: The psychological and ethological antecedents of human consent to techno-empowerment of autonomous office assistants. AI Soc. **38**(2), 647–663 (2023)
17. Modliński, A., Gladden, M.: Applying ethology to design human-oriented technology. Experimental study on the signalling role of the labelling effect in technology's empowerment. Hum. Technol. **17**(2), 164–189 (2021)
18. Modliński, A., Kedziora, D., Jiménez Ramírez, A., del Río-Ortega, A.: Rolling back to manual work: an exploratory research on robotic process re-manualization. In: International Conference on Business Process Management, pp. 154–169. Springer (2022)
19. Razin, Y., Feigh, K.: Toward Interactional trust for humans and automation: extending interdependence. In: 2019 IEEE SmartWorld (SmartWorld/SCALCOM/UIC/ATC/CBDCom/IOP/SCI), pp. 1348–1355 (2019)
20. Sarilo-Kankaanranta, H., Frank, L.: Managing is adoption challenges in emerging technologies: a longitudinal case study of financial management services automation in a medium-sized enterprise. In: Information Systems - 20th European, Mediterranean, and Middle Eastern Conference, EMCIS 2023, vol. 502, pp. 183–203. Springer (2023)
21. Syed, R., et al.: Robotic Process Automation: Contemporary themes and challenges. Comp. Industries **115** (2020)

22. Syed, R., Wynn, M.T.: How to Trust a Bot: An RPA User Perspective. In: Asatiani, A., et al. (eds.) BPM 2020. LNBIP, vol. 393, pp. 147–160. Springer, Cham (2020). https://doi.org/10.1007/978-3-030-58779-6_10
23. Toll, D., Booth, M., Lindgren, I.: Robot colleagues in Swedish municipalities: how RPA affects the work situation of employees. In: International Conference on Electronic Government, pp. 160–173. Springer (2023)
24. Tutar, G., Küçükoğlu, H., Özdemir, A., Alkan, Ö., Ipekten, O.B.: An investigation of gender differences in E-commerce shopping frequency during COVID-19: evidence from Türkiye. SAGE Open **14**(4), 21582440241287630 (2024)
25. van der Aalst, W., Bichler, M., Heinzl, A.: Robotic process automation. Bus. Inf. Syst. Eng. **60**(4), 269–272 (2018)
26. Waizenegger, L., Techatassanasoontorn, A.A.: You have no idea how much we love Casper - Developing configurations of employees' RPA implementation experiences. In: Australasian Conference on Information Systems, ACIS 2020, Wellington, New Zealand, 1–4 December 2020, p. 21 (2020)
27. Willcocks, L., Hindle, J., Lacity, M.: Keys to RPA success. Executive Res. Rep., Knowl. Capital Partners, USA, Technical report (2018)
28. Zefreh, M.M., Edries, B., Esztergar-Kiss, D., Torok, A.: Intention to use private autonomous vehicles in developed and developing countries: what are the differences among the influential factors, mediators, and moderators? Travel Behav. Soc. **32**, 100592 (2023)

Detecting Gender Patterns in Programming Datasets: Towards Compliance and AI Governance

Giulia Ricci(✉), Francesca De Luzi, Flavia Monti, and Massimo Mecella

Sapienza Università di Roma, Roma, Italy
{ricci,deluzi,monti,mecella}@diag.uniroma1.it

Abstract. The present study investigates whether Python source code produced in an academic examination setting exhibits gender-related stylistic patterns using structural metrics such as Lines of Code, control structures, and cyclomatic complexity. The analysis finds no statistically significant differences, suggesting that structural stylistic variation may be limited in controlled educational contexts. Based on these findings, the paper proposes a Design Science framework for detecting and auditing potential gender-related bias in programming datasets, supporting dataset governance and bias-aware analysis.

Keywords: Gender Bias · Fairness Compliance · Programming Style · Design Science Research · Educational Information Systems

1 Introduction

Modern information systems are progressively being shaped by data that are continuously produced, reused, and repurposed in different contexts. In such settings, datasets do not have to be considered as just passive inputs but as evolving components that actively influence the system's behavior over time. This is particularly evident in AI-driven environments, where even subtle patterns in training data can have vast effects on systems and tools that rely on it. According to this perspective, datasets must be treated as part of the system design space, requiring systematic analysis and governance. In line with CAiSE's call for new approaches to address the complexity of modern systems, this work proposes a pipeline to identify and analyze gender-related patterns in programming data, extending traditional concerns of correctness to fairness-aware engineering and supporting the development of adaptive and responsible systems that can be monitored and refined over time, in line with emerging ethical and regulatory expectations. In doing so, the work exemplifies how information system engineering must evolve to incorporate social sustainability and technical accountability as a fundamental concern.

R. Posenato and I. Vanderfeesten (Eds.): CAiSE 2026 Workshops, LNBIP 586, pp. 311–317, 2026.
https://doi.org/10.1007/978-3-032-28160-9_28

Prior studies document male dominance and structural barriers limiting women's participation in SE [5,7], while implicit stereotypes and biases further contribute to persistent gender gaps [2]. When embedded in AI models, such socio-technical biases can be reproduced or amplified [4,8], affecting how development practices and roles are represented. LLMs, leveraging large-scale datasets for code generation and automated reasoning, thus pose both fairness and compliance challenges under emerging ethical and regulatory frameworks. To address this issue, this study adopts a Design Science Research perspective [11] highlighting how the detection of gender bias in educational programming datasets has implications beyond data analysis, raising crucial challenges related to transparency and responsible data governance.

2 Related Work

Research on gender bias in software and AI spans empirical studies on representation in software engineering, bias in language models, and fairness-aware analysis techniques. SE studies document persistent gender imbalances in developer communities and task allocation. In AI and NLP, substantial work investigates bias in training data and model outputs. Domain-specific studies highlight that code-generating LLMs may produce biased outputs for gender-related tasks [10], to address this kind of issues, mitigation approaches such as fine-tuning and model editing have been proposed [12]. Existing governance frameworks for trustworthy AI explicitly emphasize the need to ensure data quality, representativeness, and bias mitigation throughout the system lifecycle[1]. Within this perspective, bias is a data governance concern that must be addressed systematically. Despite these guidelines, there is still limited methodological support for operationalizing such requirements in the context of programming datasets. This makes it difficult to assess how existing approaches align with governance expectations and highlights the need for solutions, such as the pipeline proposed in this work, that explicitly target bias detection and mitigation at the dataset level.

At the intersection of SE and AI fairness, research shows that algorithmic systems may reproduce gendered structures in software artifacts. Bai provides evidence of code-level features embedding gendered assumptions and proposes methods for systemic bias detection [1]. Despite these advances, limited work investigates structural programming style patterns in educational code datasets as a source of representational imbalance for code-oriented LLMs, motivating methodologies that link structural metrics with fairness-aware dataset construction, the focus of this study.

3 Research Approach

Our research follows Design Science principles [11], structured in four phases: Problem Explication, Requirements and Use Case Definition, Design and Development, and Demonstration and Evaluation. The study begins by framing the

[1] https://www.europarl.europa.eu/topics/en/article/20230601STO93804/eu-ai-act-first-regulation-on-artificial-intelligence.

ethical and methodological challenges of gender bias in AI-enabled code analysis, highlighting how LLMs and automated tools may internalize biases from unbalanced educational datasets and formulating research questions to guide the investigation. Building on this, we define methodological and ethical requirements for the artifact, emphasizing robustness to superficial code variations and practical applicability. University programming exams serve as the use case, providing authentic student code and reference solutions for systematic comparison.

The feasibility of the proposed methodology is demonstrated through its application to the exam dataset, systematically comparing student implementations against instructor-provided reference solutions. The approach is evaluated with respect to its robustness, interpretability, and practical applicability, highlighting its potential for supporting bias-aware analysis of educational programming datasets and informing fairness-conscious AI practices in learning environments (Fig. 1).

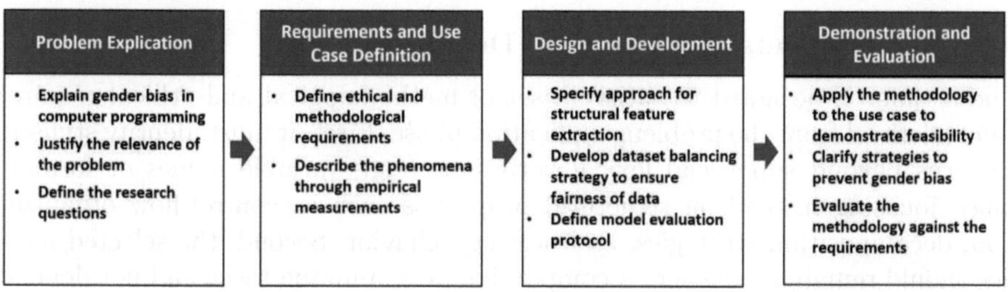

Fig. 1. Research approach based on Design Science principles by [11].

3.1 Problem Explication

Detecting gender bias in programming assignment datasets is not only a data analysis problem but turns out to be a governance issue for educational information systems, as biased datasets can propagate unfairness through learning analytics, automated assessments, and data-driven decision processes. In many data-driven systems the governance of training data remains insufficiently examined, particularly with respect to representational balance and potential biases embedded in the datasets [3]. Building on this, the present study follows three research directions which correspond to three fundamental questions to investigate:

- *RQ1: Are there measurable differences in code style or structure between genders?* Prior work shows gender-related differences may appear without affecting code quality [6].
- *RQ2: Can these patterns be used to construct balanced training datasets, and does this mitigate bias in code-LLM outputs?* Balanced datasets can help reduce the risk that models reproduce partial or skewed representations of programming behavior.

- *RQ3: How can the findings of the present research be used to build a new idea of governance in order to guarantee AI systems compliance especially in educational contexts?*

The three proposed research questions are designed to assess complementary aspects of the proposed pipeline. RQ1 focuses on the empirical detection of potential gender-related differences in programming style and structure, while RQ2 evaluates whether the proposed feature-based representation can support subsequent steps such as dataset balancing in a methodological and fairness-aware perspective. RQ3, in turn, addresses the role of the overall pipeline as a governance-oriented artifact to support compliance in AI-enabled educational systems. Therefore, even in cases where RQ1 does not reveal significant differences, RQ2 and RQ3 remain meaningful as they assess the applicability, robustness, and governance value of the proposed framework beyond specific outcomes of statistical analysis.

3.2 Requirements and Use Case Definition

The artifact is designed to satisfy a set of methodological and ethical requirements derived from the problem explication phase. First, it must identify stylistic patterns beyond superficial lexical variations (e.g., variable names or formatting), focusing instead on structural properties such as control-flow organization, decomposition strategies, and nesting behavior. Second, the selected metrics should remain stable across comparable programming tasks and not depend heavily on specific problem statements or minor syntactic differences. Additionally, deterministic interpretations of gender must be avoided; any observed stylistic differences are treated as contextual patterns rather than intrinsic traits. Finally, the artifact should be applicable to existing datasets without requiring invasive data collection procedures or complex tooling, supporting practical adoption.

The artifact is evaluated in an educational setting based on introductory programming exams from a university-level Foundations of Computer Science course. The assignments are written in Python and involve structured problem-solving tasks using control structures, conditionals, and basic functions. For each exercise, an instructor-provided reference solution enables systematic comparison between student implementations and a canonical version.

Students provided informed consent for the use of their submissions for research purposes, and data handling follows institutional ethical guidelines. The dataset offers several advantages: it reflects authentic programming behavior under comparable constraints, allows systematic comparison with reference solutions, and provides a controlled environment for analyzing structural stylistic variation.

3.3 Design and Development

The proposed artifact is a methodological pipeline designed to detect structural programming patterns potentially related to gender in educational datasets, supporting fairness-aware auditing and compliance in AI-enabled learning systems. It combines software components and analytical procedures to enable systematic evaluation of student code while respecting ethical and methodological requirements. The pipeline is organized into three main stages: (1) Feature Extraction, (2) Dataset Balancing, and (3) Model Evaluation Protocol. The first stage focuses on extracting structural stylistic features from programming exam solutions, allowing the identification of potential gender-related coding patterns. The second stage addresses dataset imbalance through balancing strategies, including classical oversampling techniques and LLM-based approaches [9]. These interventions aim to ensure a more balanced representation of coding styles, reducing the risk that AI models learn or amplify biased patterns. Finally, the evaluation stage defines a preliminary protocol combining quantitative and qualitative analyses. Quantitative evaluation examines changes in the distribution of structural features after balancing interventions, while qualitative inspection assesses diversity of control strategies, interpretability of patterns, and the absence of homogenization effects in generated outputs. While the motivation for this work is grounded in fairness and bias-awareness in AI systems, we acknowledge that large-scale LLM training scenarios are often guided by the assumption that increasing the amount of training data improves model performance. Nevertheless, our focus is better aligned with settings where models are trained, adapted, or fine-tuned on datasets that are not necessarily large-scale, such as domain-specific, educational, or organizational datasets. In such settings, the composition and structure of the data can have a more direct and observable impact on system behavior, making systematic auditing and mitigation of dataset-level biases particularly relevant.

3.4 Demonstration and Preliminary Evaluation

We conducted an exploratory quantitative analysis on 50 students (25 female, 25 male) during the Fundamentals of Computer Science exam in the Management Engineering program. Structural metrics were selected to capture complementary aspects of coding style and solution complexity, while remaining language-independent and commonly adopted in software engineering analysis. In particular, Lines of Code (LOC) provides a proxy for solution size, the number of conditionals (IF) and loops (FOR) reflects control-flow structuring choices, and cyclomatic complexity (CC) captures the overall logical complexity of the code. Table 1 reports the means and standard deviations by gender. For reproducibility, the dataset is available online[2].

Female students had mean LOC = 59.4 (SD = 8.25) and CC = 21.8 (SD = 4.11); male students had LOC = 57.04 (SD = 11.32) and CC = 23.88 (SD = 4.91). Conditionals and loops were slightly higher for males (IF = 11.72, FOR = 8.40) than females (IF = 10.28, FOR = 7.6).

Welch's t-test did not show statistically significant differences ($t \approx 0.84$ $p = 0.40$), indicating that the mean differences are consistent with the variability of

[2] https://tinyurl.com/uda5dwae.

the sample. However, subtle structural asymmetries may influence LLM outputs when overrepresented in larger corpora, justifying the use of dataset balancing as a precautionary strategy. A direct comparison to reference solutions would not be appropriate in this context, as programming tasks do not have a unique correct answer. As a preliminary analysis, it focuses only on structural and distributional metrics of code features, rather than correctness-based or solution-level comparisons.

Table 1. Results of the exploratory analysis.

Metric	Women (μ + std)	Men (μ + std)
Lines of Code	59.4 ± 8.25	57.04 ± 11.32
If	10.28 ± 2.32	11.72 ± 2.94
For	7.6 ± 2.33	8.40 ± 2.45
Cyclomatic complexity	21.8 ± 4.11	23.88 ± 4.91

4 Conclusion, Limitations and Future Works

Empirical analysis primarily focuses on the first stage of the proposed pipeline, feature extraction and the identification of structural programming patterns. While the full pipeline also includes dataset balancing strategies and an evaluation protocol, these components are currently presented at a methodological level and are not yet fully applied in the case study. This design choice reflects the preliminary nature of the study, which aims to validate the feasibility of the feature-based analysis step before extending the empirical evaluation to the subsequent stages. The outcome of the present research proposal lies in how the proposed multi-stage pipeline contributes to mitigating gender bias and stereotype amplification by adopting a relational perspective on ethics. In this view, ethics is not only a theoretical framework but also a practice guiding how data-driven systems are designed and evaluated, emphasizing contextual understanding and treating concepts such as bias, fairness, and responsibility as evolving and open to refinement [3]. The artifact demonstrates how a Design Science Research approach can operationalize fairness and compliance by supporting dataset governance, algorithmic auditing, and bias-aware system design. Future work will expand evaluations to larger and more diverse datasets, additional programming tasks and languages, and integration with learning analytics platforms to enable continuous monitoring and regulatory alignment.

Acknowledgments. The work of Giulia Ricci has been partly supported through the PhD scholarship *Metodi e tecniche di Intelligenza Artificiale per la gestione dei dati sulle acque* by Istituto Superiore di Sanità. The work has also been partly supported by the EU Projects GAINAfrica (ID 101298559).

References

1. Bai, H.: Algorithmic bias and the power of code: investigating the reproduction of gender structures in the development of computer technologies. Appl. Comput. Eng. **173**, 50–56 (07 2025). https://doi.org/10.54254/2755-2721/2025.25254
2. Bartels, R., Marín, G., Fonseca, R.: Attacking the gender gap in technology: a triple helix case study. In: Proceedings of the Int. Conf. on Gender Research ICGR, pp. 52–60. Academic Conf. and Publishing International Limited, Reading, UK (2018)
3. Birhane, A.: Algorithmic injustice: a relational ethics approach. Patterns **2**(2), 100205 (2021)
4. Borsotti, V.: Barriers to gender diversity in software development education: actionable insights from a Danish case study. In: Lago, P., Young, M. (eds.) Proceedings of the 40th Int. Conf. on Software Engineering: Software Engineering Education and Training, ICSE (SEET) 2018. pp. 146–152. ACM (2018). https://doi.org/10.1145/3183377.3183390. https://doi.org/10.1145/3183377.3183390
5. Brinkman, B., Diekman, A.: Applying the communal goal congruity perspective to enhance diversity and inclusion in undergraduate computing degrees
6. Brooke, S.: Programmed differently? Testing for gender differences in Python programming style and quality on GitHub. J. Comput. Mediat. Commun. **29**(1) (2023). https://doi.org/10.1093/JCMC/ZMAD049
7. Carver, J.C., Serebrenik, A.: Gender in software engineering. IEEE Softw. **36**(6), 76–78 (2019)
8. Dagan, E., Sarma, A., Chang, A., D'Angelo, S., Dicker, J., Murphy-Hill, E.R.: Building and sustaining ethnically, racially, and gender diverse software engineering teams: a study at Google. In: Chandra, S., Blincoe, K., Tonella, P. (eds.) Proceedings of the 31st ACM Joint European Software Engineering Conf. and Symposium on the Foundations of Software Engineering, ESEC/FSE 2023, pp. 631–643. ACM (2023). https://doi.org/10.1145/3611643.3616273. https://doi.org/10.1145/3611643.3616273
9. Gao, X., et al.: A Comprehensive Survey on Imbalanced Data Learning. CoRR **abs/2502.08960** (2025https://doi.org/10.48550/ARXIV.2502.08960. https://doi.org/10.48550/arXiv.2502.08960
10. Huang, D., Zhang, J.M., Bu, Q., Xie, X., Chen, J., Cui, H.: Bias Testing and Mitigation in LLM-based Code Generation (2025). https://arxiv.org/abs/2309.14345
11. Johannesson, P., Perjons, E.: An introduction to design science. Springer (2014). https://doi.org/10.1007/978-3-319-10632-8
12. Zhao, J., Wang, T., Yatskar, M., Ordonez, V., Chang, K.W.: Gender bias in coreference resolution: evaluation and debiasing methods. In: Proceedings of the 2018 Conference of the North American Chapter of the Association for Computational Linguistics: Human Language Technologies, Volume 2, pp. 15–20 (2018)

HybridAIMS

Interpretable Execution State Abstraction from Object-Centric Event Logs for Process-Aware Decision Support: Linking Execution States to Stock and Policy Regimes

Alessandro Berti[1(✉)], Dina Kretzschmann[1], and Wil M. P. van der Aalst[1,2]

[1] Process and Data Science (PADS), RWTH Aachen University, Aachen, Germany
{a.berti,dina.kretzschmann,wvdaalst}@pads.rwth-aachen.de
[2] Celonis, Munich, Germany

Abstract. Object-Centric Event Logs (OCELs) capture business events that may refer to multiple objects at once. For long-lived objects with recurring behavior, the resulting event sequences interleave phases that matter for different operational decisions, making it difficult to obtain a clear *state view*. In domains such as inventory management, practitioners often reason in terms of regimes (e.g., *understock*, *normal*, *overstock*) and apply different policies per regime, while the log records fine-grained activities and attributes. We present an unsupervised method to derive an interpretable execution-state abstraction from OCELs and to relate the discovered states to such regimes. The method encodes each sliding window of an object's event sequence as a numeric vector capturing activities, object participation, and selected attributes, compresses the window vectors with principal component analysis, and maps them to a self-organizing map (SOM), treating each SOM cell as an execution state. A transition is detected when consecutive windows map to different cells. To explain transitions, we contrast windows observed at state changes with windows observed while the object remains in the same cell, yielding *boundary conditions* described by characteristic activity patterns and contextual signals. We apply the approach to an inventory management OCEL and show that appending stock level to the encoding connects learned states to post-hoc stock regimes and supports a policy matrix that links states to issues and candidate actions.

Keywords: Object-Centric Process Mining · Execution State Abstraction · Decision Support · Self-Organizing Maps · Inventory Management

1 Introduction

Process-aware information systems record business events and their attributes. Process mining uses this data to analyze behavior, performance, and compliance.

R. Posenato and I. Vanderfeesten (Eds.): CAiSE 2026 Workshops, LNBIP 586, pp. 321–333, 2026.
https://doi.org/10.1007/978-3-032-28160-9_29

Many techniques assume a case-centric event log, where each event belongs to one case. In many settings, events refer to multiple business objects at once, such as orders, deliveries, tickets, assets, or resources. Converting such data into a case-centric log often duplicates events or removes relations between objects. Object-centric process mining addresses this by using Object-Centric Event Logs (OCELs), where each event can relate to multiple objects.

Decision support often requires a *state view* of an object. A state view summarizes what happens around an object at a point in time and supports questions such as what the object is currently undergoing, whether it is stable, and which situations tend to precede changes. This is hard for objects with long lifetimes and recurring activities. If one model covers the full event history of an object, it mixes phases that matter for different decisions. In addition, operational rules and policies are usually expressed in terms of states or regimes, while event data is recorded at the level of activities and attributes. This creates a gap between event-level behavior and state-level reasoning.

This paper proposes a method to derive *execution states* from OCELs. An execution state is a recurring local configuration of events and context for a given object. The method is unsupervised and does not assume domain labels. It has three phases. First, we encode events as numeric vectors that capture activities, object participation, and selected attributes, and we aggregate per-object sequences into sliding windows to represent local context. Second, we compress window vectors with principal component analysis and map them to a self-organizing map (SOM), treating each SOM cell as a discrete state. A state change is detected when consecutive windows of an object map to different cells. Third, we explain state changes by collecting windows at transitions and contrasting them with windows observed when the object stays in the same cell. These contrasts yield *boundary conditions* expressed as activity patterns and contextual signals.

The resulting state space supports analysis of object trajectories and state transitions, and the boundary conditions provide explanations that can be used in monitoring, dashboards, and rule-based interventions. Sections 3 and 4 describe the method in a setting-independent way. Section 5 instantiates it for inventory management by adding stock level as one contextual feature and by using stock-regime labels only for post-hoc interpretation and evaluation. This illustrates how learned execution states can be related to domain regimes and how boundary conditions can be mapped to a policy matrix that links states to issues and candidate actions.

The rest of the paper is organized as follows. Section 2 reviews related work. Section 3 introduces preliminaries. Section 4 presents the approach. Section 5 reports the case study. Section 6 concludes the paper and outlines future work.

2 Related Work

Prior work on inventory analysis with OCELs makes states explicit or reduces lifecycle length before analysis. State-aware object-centric process mining extends OCELs with state transition events and associates activity occurrences with a state, so behavior can be analyzed with respect to state changes [2]. Segmentation methods split long object lifecycles into segments based on relations, event types, and time, so that analysis and optimization can be applied on fragments and their order [1]. These approaches rely on a state definition or a segmentation rule, while we infer states from event patterns in short windows and derive transition conditions from observed state changes.

State-based abstractions are also studied in process mining beyond inventory settings. Composite State Machines discover state-based models for multi-perspective processes and support exploration and performance analysis across interacting artifacts [8]. Artifact-centric process mining formalizes processes around business entities, their lifecycles, and their relations, and provides concepts for discovery and conformance at the artifact level [4]. Our work follows this line by analyzing object evolution, but it does not assume predefined lifecycles and it characterizes transitions through boundary windows extracted from the log.

A second line of work studies how to represent event sequences as vectors. Surveys and benchmarks compare trace encoding methods used in prediction and classification, including prefix encodings, aggregation features, and embeddings [7]. Representation learning adapts embedding techniques to activities, traces, and logs to obtain vector encodings for analysis tasks [3]. In this paper, we use a window-based encoding and PCA to obtain vectors that support mapping to states and comparison of windows that stay within a state with windows observed at transitions. Window and n-gram representations connect to time-series mining, where shapelets use subsequences as units for mining and classification [9].

Our method combines an unsupervised discretization step with a transition explanation step. Self-organizing maps map vectors to a low-dimensional grid using prototype vectors and preserve neighborhood relations [5]. We use a SOM to discretize window embeddings into a state space where nearby cells correspond to similar windows, which supports analysis of object trajectories on the grid. To explain state changes, we contrast windows observed at transitions with windows observed within the same state to obtain boundary conditions expressed as activity patterns and contextual signals.

3 Preliminaries

We introduce key concepts and techniques that enable the transformation of raw object-centric event data into interpretable state representations.

3.1 Object-Centric Event Logs and Event-Level Vectorization

We use object-centric event logs as defined in [6]. Let $\mathcal{U}\sigma$ denote the universe of strings and let $\mathcal{P}(\cdot)$ denote the power set. An object-centric event log (OCEL) provides a finite set of events E, a finite set of objects O, a finite set of activities A, and a finite set of object types OT, together with the following mappings:

- $\pi_{act} : E \to A$, which assigns an activity to each event,
- $\pi_{time} : E \to \mathbb{R}$, which assigns a timestamp to each event,
- $\pi_{ot} : O \to OT$, which assigns an object type to each object,
- $\pi_{omap} : E \to \mathcal{P}(O)$, which assigns related objects to each event,
- $\pi_{vmap} : E \times \mathcal{U}\sigma \nrightarrow \mathcal{U}\sigma \cup \mathbb{R}$, which assigns values to event attribute names when defined,
- $\pi_{ovmap} : O \times \mathcal{U}\sigma \times \mathbb{R} \nrightarrow \mathcal{U}\sigma \cup \mathbb{R}$, which assigns values to object attribute names at a time when defined.

We use π_{time} to induce a total order $\leq$ on events, defined by $e_1 \leq e_2 \iff \pi_{time}(e_1) \leq \pi_{time}(e_2)$, with tie-breaking for equal timestamps.

For a given object $o \in O$, we denote its related events by $E(o) := \{e \in E \mid o \in \pi_{omap}(e)\}$. Sorting $E(o)$ by $\leq$ yields an event sequence $(e_1^{(o)}, \ldots, e_{T(o)}^{(o)})$. The approach in Sect. 4 encodes each event e as a numeric vector $x(e)$ and then constructs window representations from these per-object sequences.

3.2 Principal Component Analysis (PCA)

Principal Component Analysis (PCA) maps vectors in $\mathbb{R}^D$ to vectors in $\mathbb{R}^d$ with $d < D$ using a linear projection learned from data. Given a set of vectors $x \in \mathbb{R}^D$, PCA estimates a mean $\mu \in \mathbb{R}^D$ and a projection matrix $W \in \mathbb{R}^{D\times d}$. Each vector is represented as $z := W^\top(x - \mu) \in \mathbb{R}^d$.

We choose d using an elbow heuristic on explained variance or reconstruction error. In this paper, PCA is used only to compress encodings before training the self-organizing map.

3.3 Self-Organizing Maps (SOM)

Self-organizing maps are networks trained without labels that map input vectors in $\mathbb{R}^d$ to cells of a 2D grid [5]. Let $\mathcal{G} := \{1, \ldots, M_x\} \times \{1, \ldots, M_y\}$ be the grid. Each cell $(p, q) \in \mathcal{G}$ has a prototype vector $m_{p,q} \in \mathbb{R}^d$. For an input $z \in \mathbb{R}^d$, the best-matching unit is $(p^*, q^*) := \arg\min_{(p,q)\in\mathcal{G}} \|z - m_{p,q}\|_2$, and the mapping is $f(z) := (p^*, q^*)$.

Training initializes the prototypes and then repeats the following for iterations $t = 0, \ldots, T-1$: sample an input z, compute its best-matching unit (p^*, q^*), and update prototypes with $m_{p,q}(t+1) = m_{p,q}(t) + \eta(t) \cdot h_{(p^*,q^*),(p,q)}(t) \cdot (z - m_{p,q}(t))$. The learning rate $\eta(t)$ decreases over time. The neighborhood weight $h_{(p^*,q^*),(p,q)}(t)$ depends on the grid distance between (p^*, q^*) and (p, q), for example $h_{(p^*,q^*),(p,q)}(t) = \exp\left(-\frac{\|(p,q)-(p^*,q^*)\|_2^2}{2\sigma(t)^2}\right)$ with a radius $\sigma(t)$ that decreases over time.

After training, each input vector is assigned to its mapped cell $f(z)$. In this paper, we treat each grid cell as a state. SOM training uses only the input vectors. Any labels shown on cells are assigned after training and are used only for interpretation.

We compress the window vectors using PCA (Sect. 3.2). PCA estimates a mean $\mu \in \mathbb{R}^{Ln}$ and a projection matrix $W \in \mathbb{R}^{Ln \times d}$. Each window is projected to

$$z_t^{(o)} := W^\top (g_t^{(o)} - \mu) \in \mathbb{R}^d.$$

We align each projection to the window end index t, yielding $(z_t^{(o)})_{t=L}^{T^{(o)}}$. These vectors are used to train the SOM in Sect. 3.3. The window length L and the PCA dimension d are hyperparameters. Section 5 reports values for the case study.

4.3 From Window Representations to States

We take the PCA vectors from Sect. 4.2, denoted $z_t^{(o)} \in \mathbb{R}^d$, and train a self-organizing map (SOM) (Sect. 3.3) on $Z = \{z_t^{(o)}\}$. Let the SOM grid be $\mathcal{G} = \{1, \ldots, M_x\} \times \{1, \ldots, M_y\}$ with prototype vectors $m_{p,q} \in \mathbb{R}^d$ for $(p, q) \in \mathcal{G}$. After training, each vector z is mapped to the best-matching unit

$$(p^*, q^*) := \arg \min_{(p,q) \in \mathcal{G}} \|z - m_{p,q}\|_2,$$

and we define the state mapping $f(z) := (p^*, q^*)$.

For each object o, the sequence $s_t^{(o)} := f(z_t^{(o)})$ defines a path on the grid. We treat each grid cell as an execution state and detect a state change when consecutive cells differ, that is, when $s_{t-1}^{(o)} \neq s_t^{(o)}$. The grid size (M_x, M_y) is a hyperparameter. In practice, it can be chosen to trade off cell occupancy and temporal continuity of object paths. Section 5 reports the choice for the case study.

4.4 From States to Boundary Conditions

After training the SOM, we map each window representation $z_t^{(o)}$ for $t = L, \ldots, T^{(o)}$ to a grid cell $s_t^{(o)} := f(z_t^{(o)}) \in \mathcal{G}$. We interpret each cell as an execution state.

Let $(e_1^{(o)}, \ldots, e_{T^{(o)}}^{(o)})$ be the events of o sorted by the total order $\leq$. For the fixed window length L, we denote the corresponding event window ending at index t by

$$\gamma_t^{(o)} := (e_{t-L+1}^{(o)}, \ldots, e_t^{(o)}), \qquad t \geq L.$$

A transition occurs at (o, t) if $s_{t-1}^{(o)} \neq s_t^{(o)}$ (hence $t > L$). For a transition with $s_{t-1}^{(o)} = c$ and $s_t^{(o)} = c' \neq c$, we collect boundary windows in multisets for exits and entries:

$$\mathcal{B}_c^{\text{exit}} \leftarrow \mathcal{B}_c^{\text{exit}} \uplus \{\gamma_{t-1}^{(o)}\}, \qquad \mathcal{B}_{c'}^{\text{enter}} \leftarrow \mathcal{B}_{c'}^{\text{enter}} \uplus \{\gamma_t^{(o)}\}.$$

For analyses of ordered state pairs, we also store interface windows,

$$\mathcal{B}_{c \to c'} := \{\gamma_t^{(o)} \mid s_{t-1}^{(o)} = c,\ s_t^{(o)} = c'\}.$$

To summarize behavior without a state change, we collect in-state windows for each cell $c \in \mathcal{G}$,

$$\mathcal{C}_c := \{\gamma_t^{(o)} \mid t > L,\ s_{t-1}^{(o)} = c,\ s_t^{(o)} = c\}.$$

The multisets $\mathcal{C}_c$, $\mathcal{B}_c^{\text{exit}}$, and $\mathcal{B}_c^{\text{enter}}$ allow contrasts between windows observed while staying in c and windows observed when leaving or entering c. We define boundary conditions as differences between summaries computed on these multisets.

Summarizing Windows as Activity Patterns. We project an event sequence $\xi = (e_1, \ldots, e_\ell)$ to an activity sequence $\alpha(\xi) = (a_1, \ldots, a_\ell)$ with $a_t = \pi_{\text{act}}(e_t)$. For a multiset $\mathcal{S} \subseteq E^\star$ (such as $\mathcal{C}_c$, $\mathcal{B}_c^{\text{exit}}$, or $\mathcal{B}_c^{\text{enter}}$), we compute four summaries.

First, directly follows counts

$$C_{a \to b}^{\mathcal{S}} := \sum_{\xi \in \mathcal{S}} \sum_{t=1}^{|\alpha(\xi)|-1} \mathbf{1}\{\alpha(\xi)_t = a,\ \alpha(\xi)_{t+1} = b\}$$

define a directly follows graph over A. Second, start counts $S_a^{\mathcal{S}} := \sum_{\xi \in \mathcal{S}} \mathbf{1}\{\alpha(\xi)_1 = a\}$ and end counts $E_a^{\mathcal{S}} := \sum_{\xi \in \mathcal{S}} \mathbf{1}\{\alpha(\xi)_{|\alpha(\xi)|} = a\}$ describe window boundaries. Third, variant counts aggregate identical activity strings: for $v \in A^\star$,

$$F^{\mathcal{S}}(v) := \#\{\xi \in \mathcal{S} \mid \alpha(\xi) = v\}, \qquad \text{supp}^{\mathcal{S}}(v) := F^{\mathcal{S}}(v)/|\mathcal{S}|.$$

For a given cell c, we compute the summaries on $\mathcal{C}_c$, $\mathcal{B}_c^{\text{exit}}$, and $\mathcal{B}_c^{\text{enter}}$. Boundary conditions for exits of c are defined by differences between $\mathcal{B}_c^{\text{exit}}$ and $\mathcal{C}_c$, and boundary conditions for entries are defined by differences between $\mathcal{B}_c^{\text{enter}}$ and $\mathcal{C}_c$. For a transition $c \to c'$, we use $\mathcal{B}_{c \to c'}$ to obtain patterns at that interface.

5 Case Study

This case study applies the pipeline from Sects. 3 and 4 to a real retail inventory dataset, explicitly tracing the transformation from raw operational records to actionable execution states. Inventory postings and planning records become an object-centric event log (OCEL). Per-material event sequences are extracted, encoded as sliding windows, compressed via PCA, mapped to SOM states and transitions, and used to derive boundary conditions that form a policy matrix.While Fig. 1 outlines the generic method, we highlight the inventory-specific inputs and outputs.

Input: transactional inventory and planning records. We start from an object-centric inventory log extracted from the information system of a major European pet retailer[1]. The raw records describe recurring outbound movements (*GI*), inbound movements (*GR*), and planning-related events (e.g., *PS→PO*, *SOI*).

[1] Key traits: observation window *December 2022–April 2024*; *9,648 materials* tracked.

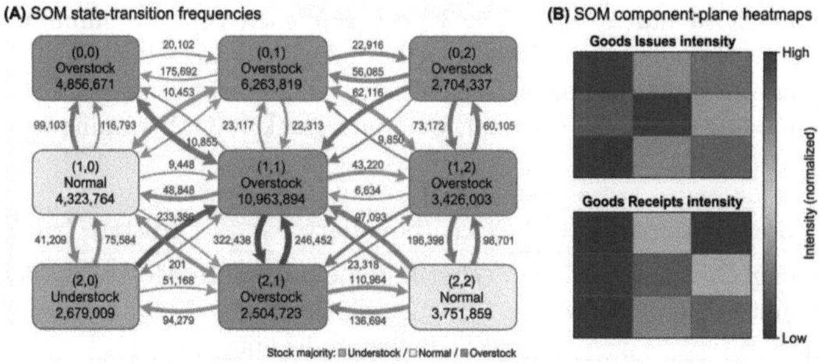

Fig. 2. Overview of the 3 × 3 self-organizing map (SOM) trained on window embeddings. **(A)** State-transition graph: nodes are grid cells annotated with window counts and a post hoc stock-regime label; directed edges represent transitions between consecutive windows and are scaled by frequency. **(B)** Component planes: per-cell averages of selected input dimensions shown as heatmaps. Regime labels are used only for interpretation and evaluation.

Importantly, these records are *not* interpreted as separate case traces; instead, they are kept as a multi-object history in which a single event can refer to multiple entities (e.g., a receipt that touches both a material and a purchase document).

Enrichment: building an object-centric inventory event log. We represent the dataset as an OCEL where events are standardized into a small set of interpretable activity labels (*GI, GR, PS, PO, SOI*), each with a timestamp and selected attributes, and where the domain entities that appear in those records (most importantly, *materials*) are modeled as objects. Each event is linked to *all* objects it refers to, so that downstream analysis can follow the evolution of a material while still preserving its interaction with planning and execution artifacts. In addition to the event-level information, we enrich the OCEL with a contextual signal that decision makers explicitly reason about: the *stock level* of a material. We attach the on-hand stock level as an object attribute aligned to event time (via π_{ovmap}), so that every local event context can be interpreted not only by *what happened* (activities), but also by *under which inventory conditions* (stock).

Output: per-material state trajectories and transition explanations. We then choose *materials* as the focal object type and transform each material's time-ordered event history into short, local windows that capture what has happened *recently* around the material. These windows are encoded (Sect. 4.2), compressed with PCA, and mapped to a 3 × 3 SOM, yielding (i) a discrete execution-state trajectory for each material, (ii) detected transitions when consecutive windows map to different cells, and (iii) boundary-condition windows summarizing which activity patterns and signals are characteristic when entering or leaving a state. These outputs are the basis for the state characterization (Table 1, Fig. 2) and

Table 1. Nine SOM states on a 3 × 3 grid. For each cell, we summarize activity patterns for entry boundary windows, exit boundary windows, and in-state windows. The Stock column reports the most frequent stock-regime label assigned post hoc from stock bands (O=Overstock, N=Normal, U=Understock). SOM training uses no regime labels.

State	Stock	Enter (boundary)	Exit (boundary)	In-state (runs)
(0,0)	O	Long *GI* runs; *SOI* bursts; *PS*→*PO*; few *GR*.	*GI* still dominant; more *SOI*; occasional *PS*/*PO*before leaving.	Mostly *GI*→*GI*; rare *GR*; steady *PS*→*PO*.
(0,1)	O	*GI*→*GI*, some *GR*→*GI* or *PO*→*GI*; little *PS*.	Leave under continued *GI* runs; very low diversity.	Near-pure *GI*→*GI* (steady outbound).
(0,2)	O	Outbound + planning: *GI*→*PS*, *PS*→*PO*; *GR*→*GI*present.	*SOI*→*SOI*rises; small *GR*persists.	*GI* with *PS*→*PO*and *SOI* bursts (replenishment-aware).
(1,0)	N	*GI* runs with *GR*→*GI*; moderate *SOI* and *PS*→*PO*.	*GI* stays high; more *SOI* starts; *PS*→*PO*persists.	Mixed: *GI*-dominant, with visible *SOI* and *PS*→*PO*.
(1,1)	O	*GI*→*GI*; *GR*↔*GI*; *SOI*→*GI*visible.	Boundary under *GI* continuation; little else.	Almost only *GI*→*GI*.
(1,2)	O	*SOI*↔*GI*; *PS*→*PO*; *PO*→*GI*.	Exits after long *GI* runs; limited diversification.	*GI*-centric with *SOI*↔*GI*and *PS*→*PO*(balancing).
(2,0)	U	*SOI*→*SOI*backlog; *GI* follows; light *GR*.	*SOI* runs remain; *PS*→*PO*signals persist.	*SOI*-dominant; *GI* and *PS*→*PO*secondary.
(2,1)	O	High-volume mix: *GI*, *SOI*↔*GI*, *PS*→*PO*; many *GR*.	Still diverse (*GI*/*SOI*/*GR*/*PS*); shifts resemble rebalancing.	Busy hub: outbound + inbound + planning all active.
(2,2)	N	Hybrid: *GI* with *GI*→*PS*, *PS*→*PO*; moderate *GR*; *SOI*↔*GI*.	Similar hybrid flows; no single driver dominates.	Hybrid: *GI* + *SOI*/*PS*loops; moderate *GR*sustained.

for operationalization via the policy matrix (Table 2).

Encodings and Evaluation Reference. To isolate the value of contextual enrichment, we consider two encodings: *activities only* and *activities + stock level* (stock appended as a numeric feature). As an external reference concept for interpretation (not used for training), we derive the stock-state triad *understock/normal/overstock* from stock-level bands and assign these regime labels post hoc. SOM training remains fully unsupervised. Prior analysis of the same log reports weak coupling between goods receipts and issues and these stock states [2]. We therefore ask whether execution states inferred from short windows, using *activities only* or *activities + stock*, better capture how materials are handled, and we evaluate stability, interpretability, and agreement with the stock labels. The implementation is available in an open source repository[2].

Parameter Selection. For this case study, we select hyperparameters on the stock-aware encoding (activities + stock) using only unlabeled windows. For the sliding window, we sweep $L \in [2, 20]$ and, at a fixed probe dimension, compute the weighted mean PCA reconstruction error across materials; the elbow of the $E(L)$ curve occurs at $L^\star = 8$ (e.g., $E(8) \approx 1.15 \times 10^{-3}$). With $L^\star$ fixed, we select the PCA dimension by the elbow of $E(d)$ versus the number of components, yielding $d^\star = 10$. For the SOM grid, we evaluate square sizes $M \times M$ and maximize $J(M) = \alpha R(M) + (1-\alpha)\tilde{H}(M)$ with $\alpha = 0.7$, where $R(M)$ measures continuity of object paths on the grid (fraction of consecutive assignments that stay in the same cell or a neighbor) and $\tilde{H}(M)$ is the normalized entropy of cell occupancy; we use quantization error as a tie-breaker. The best grid was 3×3 for 70% of the materials (vs. 21% for 4×4 and 9% for 5×5), balancing continuity and cell utilization without fragmentation. We therefore fix $M = 3$ globally and use $(L^\star, d^\star, M) = (8, 10, 3)$ for the analyses below.

Why activities + stock? We compare *activities only* vs. *activities + stock* on a 3×3 SOM, evaluating micro/balanced accuracy for stock-state alignment, Adjacency (neighbor-preservation), and η^2 (stock variance explained). Activities alone yield coherent clusters (Adjacency=0.91) but poor alignment: micro accuracy 0.66, balanced 0.33 (chance), $\eta^2 = 0.03$, with scattered Understock. Adding stock preserves smoothness (Adjacency=0.92) and boosts alignment: micro 0.74, balanced 0.44, $\eta^2 = 0.43$, concentrating Understock distinctly. Thus, stock enhances state interpretability without losing coherence, confirming its value as a contextual signal.

Identified States. Table 1 shows that the SOM discovers *distinctive, interpretable regimes.* Two cells, **(0,1)** and **(1,1)**, are "pure issuing" states dominated by *Goods Issue→Goods Issue*, offering a clean baseline. Others mix outbound with planning and/or inbound: **(0,2)** and **(1,2)** consistently exhibit *Purchase Suggestion→Purchase Order* alongside sales-order couplings; **(2,1)** is a high-volume hub where outbound, inbound, and planning co-exist at scale. The cell **(2,0)** stands out for *Create Sales Order Item* runs (order build-up), which also explains why it concentrates the largest share of *Understock* among all cells. Finally, Normal-majority cells **(1,0)** and **(2,2)** differ in kind; **(1,0)** is more throughput-oriented, while **(2,2)** is a hybrid with persistent planning. Overall, these patterns are interpretable, while also revealing finer structure (e.g., order build-up vs. replenishment-aware outbound) that stock alone does not distinguish. Figure 2 combines the SOM transition structure (left) with component-plane heatmaps (right) that color-code key operational dimensions (blue=low, red=high), supporting a joint interpretation of movement across states and the signals that

[2] https://github.com/fit-alessandro-berti/states-detection-understanding.

Table 2. Policy matrix per SOM cell (3×3 grid). A cross (×) means the issue is observed for that state or the recommendation applies.

State		Issues in current state						Stay suggestions (if favorable)				Leave suggestions (if not favorable)					
	Favorable (N)?	Overstock (accumulated)	Understock or backlog	GI monoculture	Cancelled receipts	GI lag versus SO	Weak PS→PO	Maintain PO cadence and lot size	Cross-dock or fast receiving	Balance slots or storage	Drift alerts (GI-only)	Expedite POs or higher reorder (U→N)	Reserve stock or throttle GI (U→N)	Substitutes or transfer-in (U→N)	Reduce receipts or lot size (O→N)	Promote demand or transfer-out (O→N)	Suppress new suggestions (GI-only O)
(0,0)		×			×										×	×	
(0,1)		×		×			×								×	×	×
(0,2)		×			×										×	×	
(1,0)	×				×			×	×	×	×						
(1,1)		×		×			×								×	×	×
(1,2)		×			×		×								×	×	
(2,0)			×		×	×						×	×	×			
(2,1)		×			×										×	×	
(2,2)	×				×			×	×	×	×						

characterize them.

Operational Suggestions. We operationalize the learned state space using the policy matrix in Table 2. For each SOM cell c, we compute issue indicators from (i) in-state windows $\mathcal{C}_c$ and (ii) entry and exit boundary windows $\mathcal{B}_c^{\text{enter}}$ and $\mathcal{B}_c^{\text{exit}}$. Indicators are derived from the window summaries used for boundary conditions, for example concentration of *GI*-only variants, frequency of *PS*→*PO* conversions, receipt cancellation signals, and lag proxies between *SOI* and subsequent *GI*, plus the stock signal when included in the encoding. In the matrix, an issue is marked when its indicator is higher in that cell than in the full population, or when it appears among the top contrasts for entering or leaving the cell. The suggested actions are not learned by the SOM. They are inventory responses mapped to these issue indicators, such as reducing inbound when overstock indicators dominate, expediting replenishment when backlog indicators dominate, or checking planning and receiving when *PS*→*PO* conversion or receipt execution is low. In use, a material is monitored by mapping its latest window to a cell and checking the cell indicators; when a transition occurs, the boundary conditions provide the activity patterns and signals used to trigger an alert and to select candidate actions.

6 Conclusion and Future Work

We presented an unsupervised pipeline (sliding windows, PCA, SOM) that derives execution states and boundary conditions from object-centric event logs. The method is setting-independent and applies to long-lived objects with recurring events, where local event context is relevant for decision support. Execution states are obtained by mapping window embeddings to SOM cells, and boundary conditions are obtained by contrasting windows observed at transitions with windows observed during in-state behavior. We instantiated the pipeline on an inventory management OCEL by adding stock level as a contextual feature and by using stock-regime labels only for post-hoc interpretation and evaluation. In this instantiation, activity-only states formed coherent clusters but showed limited agreement with stock regimes, while adding stock improved agreement and supported a policy matrix that links states to issue indicators and candidate actions. Next, we will study alternative window representations, additional temporal and object attributes, and procedures for selecting hyperparameters.

Acknowledgments. Funded by the European Union. This work has received funding from the European High Performance Computing Joint Undertaking (JU) and from the German Federal Ministry of Research, Technology and Space (BMFTR), the Ministry of Culture and Science of North Rhine-Westphalia (MKW NRW) and the Hessian Ministry of Science and Research, Arts and Culture (HMWK) under grant agreement No 101250682.

References

1. Berti, A., Kretzschmann, D., van der Aalst, W.: Segmentation for optimizing long-lifecycle processes in object-centric process Mining. TechRxiv (2025)
2. Berti, A., Kretzschmann, D., van der Aalst, W.: State-aware object-centric process mining: enhancing OCEL 2.0 with explicit state transitions. TechRxiv (2025)
3. De Koninck, P., vanden Broucke, S., De Weerdt, J.: act2vec, trace2vec, log2vec, and model2vec: representation learning for business processes. In: BPM. Lecture Notes in Computer Science, vol. 11080, pp. 305–321. Springer (2018)
4. Fahland, D.: Artifact-centric process mining. In: Encyclopedia of Big Data Technologies. Springer (2019)
5. Kohonen, T.: Self-Organizing Maps, 3rd (edn.). Springer Series in Information Sciences, Springer (2001)
6. Koren, I., Adams, J., Berti, A., van der Aalst, W.: OCEL 2.0 resources - www.ocel-standard.org In: ICPM Doctoral Consortium / Demo. CEUR Workshop Proceedings, vol. 3648. CEUR-WS.org (2023)
7. Tavares, G., Oyamada, R., Barbon, S., Paolo Ceravolo: trace encoding in process mining: a survey and benchmarking. Eng. Appl. Artif. Intell. **126**(Part D), 107028 (2023)
8. van Eck, M., Sidorova, N., van der Aalst, W.: Guided interaction exploration and performance analysis in artifact-centric process models. Bus. Inf. Syst. Eng. **61**(6), 649–663 (2019)
9. Ye, L., Keogh, E.: Time series shapelets: a new primitive for data mining. In: KDD, pp. 947–956. ACM (2009)

A Knowledge Graph-Grounded Low-Code Application for Educational Chatbots in the Railway Domain

Eveline Walker, Emanuele Laurenzi(✉), Charuta Pande, and Terry Inglese

FHNW University of Applied Sciences and Arts Northwestern Switzerland, Basel, Switzerland
eveline_heidy.walker@sbb.ch,
{emanuele.laurenzi,charuta.pande,terry.inglese}@fhnw.ch

Abstract. The development of educational chatbots is often hindered by the technical expertise required. This paper addresses this challenge by investigating how a low-code application for language teachers can be grounded with a knowledge graph to serve in the development and maintenance of educational chatbots for language teachers, specifically those working in the railway sector.

Using a Design Science Research (DSR) approach, we developed a method where language teachers can use intuitive low-code interfaces to input teaching content. This content is then automatically structured into a knowledge graph, which serves as a basis for educational chatbots for train drivers to learn the railway-specific Italian language used in Switzerland. In this sense, our proposed approach contributes to democratizing the development and maintenance of educational chatbots for language teachers.

Keywords: Educational Chatbot · Low-Code Application · Knowledge Graph · Teaching Ontology · Chatbot Ontology

1 Introduction

The increasing integration of technology into language education offers new possibilities for personalised learning. Educational chatbots are proving to be a significant support for both teachers in creating lectures and students in learning. However, developing and maintaining educational chatbots is still highly challenging as they require expertise in two specific areas: (1) technical expertise in chatbot development and (2) pedagogical expertise in a given domain. In highly specialised fields such as language education for train drivers, this challenge is exacerbated by the need to integrate unique terminology into a machine-readable format.

Although teachers possess the required subject matter knowledge, they often lack the technical skills to develop and maintain chatbots independently. This makes the development and maintenance of educational chatbots even more time-consuming and expensive, as back-and-forth between two roles is required.

R. Posenato and I. Vanderfeesten (Eds.): CAiSE 2026 Workshops, LNBIP 586, pp. 334–346, 2026.
https://doi.org/10.1007/978-3-032-28160-9_30

Recently, LLM-based agents have made it easier to create educational chatbots as one can provide instructions and required knowledge in natural language [3]. However, such agents are limited when it comes to domain-specific teaching content and feedback [4]. Additionally, LLMs lack the structure required to maintain teaching material and guided learning paths.

By grounding the teaching materials in a knowledge graph, the application captures relevant vocabulary and semantics formally, making it ready for powerful query-answering and logical reasoning services.

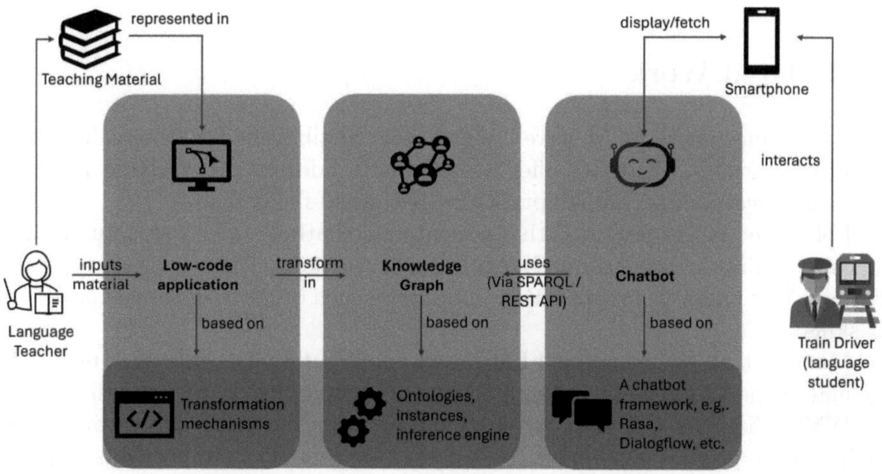

Fig. 1. Overview of the proposed solution.

Figure 1 illustrates an overview of our proposed system. It begins with a language teacher who uses a low-code interface to enter or adapt teaching materials. This input is then converted into a data graph that follows an ontology structure. Hence, the knowledge graph, comprising instance and schema layers, serves as a structured knowledge base for an educational chatbot.

The chatbot can then be accessed by language students via a web or mobile application, enabling them to engage in conversational learning.

In doing so, our proposal has the ultimate goal of enabling language teachers in developing and maintaining educational chatbots without the need of chatbot and AI expertise. Thereby, the main research question guiding this study is the following:

How can a low-code application that is grounded in a knowledge graph support language teachers in the development and maintenance of a chatbot in the railway sector?

To address this question, this research follows a Design Science Research (DSR) [9] methodology. The methodology follows five phases: Problem Awareness, Suggestion, Development, Evaluation, and Conclusion. To ensure rigor during the artifact's construction, particularly for the ontologies, the DSR approach was supplemented with established Ontology 101 [19] guidelines.

The remainder of this paper is as follows. Section 2 outlines the relevant literature review, which establishes the theoretical foundation and identifies the existing research gap. As part of the *Awareness of Problem* phase, Sect. 3 describes the domain analysis and requirements. To ground this research in the real world, we considered the case of the Swiss railway company SOB (Schweizerische Südostbahn AG). Next, 4 introduces the suggested artifact, which addresses the listed requirements. Section 5 describes the implementation in a technical prototype, and finally Sect. 7 concludes the paper and outlines future work.

2 Related Work

Rapid advancements in AI have opened new possibilities for personalised and adaptive learning. Chatbots offer a solution to address the evolving needs of modern education and are adaptable in specialised fields [7].

Følstad et al. [8] described that educational chatbots offer a structured approach to guiding learners through regular, short sessions. These sessions, typically lasting a few minutes, progressively build upon each other to enhance knowledge or skills.

Martin et al. [5] proposed LLM-based conversational agents as a means to simulate expert interviews, integrated into a simulational learning environment.

While chatbots can improve learning experiences, their development and maintenance present significant challenges. Creating effective chatbots requires a deep understanding of technical details and domain-specific knowledge [1]. In highly specialised domains, such as language education for train drivers in the Swiss public transportation sector, this challenge is enforced by the need to integrate unique terminology and complex operational scenarios (e.g., [15]) into a machine-readable format.

The challenges of developing and maintaining educational chatbots can be mitigated using no- and low-code applications, which offer a promising solution for democratising AI development [2]. By simplifying the process of creating and managing AI products and services, these platforms empower professionals without a deep understanding of IT or AI, such as language teachers, to contribute to AI initiatives. This increased accessibility enables faster solution deployment and lower development costs. New ideas can be implemented without following the traditional development cycle, accelerating time-to-market—thus accelerating innovation [16]. The agile and innovative use of no- and low-code applications mentioned by Luo et al. [17] is also valuable to language teachers in the Swiss railway sector.

Moreover, the education domain is characterised by diverse and heterogeneous structured data, making it a suitable candidate for knowledge graph representation. Chen et al. [6] introduced KnowEdu, a system designed to construct educational knowledge graphs that can be used to enhance teaching and learning experiences. In a related vein, Pande et al. [14] employed an ontology-based knowledge representation to structure domain content and drive a conversational agent aimed at supporting individual student reflection in group assignments.

Additionally, Peng et al. [18] emphasise the growing significance of knowledge graphs in the education sector. Knowledge graphs enable efficient data processing and dissemination by structuring educational data. They also propose using knowledge graphs to support educational activities, including course allocation, teaching, and learning.

While knowledge graph technology offers the potential for enhancing education, its engineering remains a grand challenge. Yang et al. [21] have demonstrated the feasibility of using knowledge graphs to power intelligent Question and Answer systems. However, these systems often require significant technical expertise to develop and maintain. This technical barrier directly conflicts with the capabilities of domain experts, such as language teachers, who typically lack programming skills.

The adoption of this technology can be accelerated by simplifying the knowledge graph creation and integration into a no- or low-code application.

Grounding low-code approaches with knowledge graphs allows applications to capture semantic models, reason over complex data, automate tasks, and provide intelligent insights [20]. Chis et al. [12] proposed a modeling method for low-code knowledge graph building. Laurenzi [10] suggested an agile and ontology-based meta-modelling approach that ensures semantic alignment between graphical enterprise models and knowledge graphs, where the former can serve as a low-code editor for knowledge graphs [11].

Hutzli and Leoncio [13] explored the potential of knowledge graphs to support low-code applications. Using metaphactory, a low-code platform, they developed an interface that enables stakeholders to access and visualise knowledge graph data without programming expertise. This approach promotes knwoledge accessibility and consistency while allowing the rapid creation and customisation of user interfaces grounded in an ontological knowledge model. Among the reviewed works, this approach most closely aligns with our research objective and therefore serves as a foundation for our work.

In summary, while existing approaches have explored the integration of knowledge graphs and low-code platforms, none of them addresses their combined application for language learning support in the railway domain. In this work, we address this gap by applying knowledge graphs to semantically ground a low-code application for language teachers, who target train drivers.

This represents a foundational step towards an AI platform capable of automatically maintaining educational chatbots for train drivers, given structured learning content as input.

3 Gathering Teacher Requirements

Based on semi-structured interviews with two language teachers (the interview questions are available on GitHub[1]) and an analysis of existing teaching materi-

[1] https://github.com/Knowledge-basedAI/KnowledgeGraphGroundedLowCode Application4ducationalChatbotsInTheRailwaySector.

als, a set of requirements was identified for the low-code application. The requirements are categorized into four key areas:

Learning Needs: Personalised teaching materials; efficient management of digital resources; chatbot as supplementary learning tool.
Challenges: Infrequent in-person lessons; difficulty adapting physical materials for digital use; bridging theory and practice.
Opportunities: Enhanced learning experience through low-code integration; efficient content management and adaptable learning paths.
Data Construction Needs: User-friendly content input interface; support for structured data, contextual texts, and multilingual content; audio and voice capabilities.

3.1 Analysing the Teaching Content

The language course is distinguished by its contextualised, modular structure of twelve lessons, designed specifically for Swiss train drivers. The curriculum integrates traditional self-study with audio-visual materials and simulator training, which blends technical and linguistic instruction for professional relevance. This approach uses a "golden thread" scenario based on real service situations to ensure the application of learned material.

Each lesson follows a fixed progression:

1. **Introduction:** Familiarisation with the Italian language begins with a reading text accompanied by an audio file and German/Italian translations.
2. **Reinforcement:** New vocabulary and grammar rules are introduced, often with German explanations for clarity.
3. **Contextualisation:** The course incorporates essential technical terminology and phrases (like signal examples) specific to the railway domain.
4. **Conclusion:** Lessons end with various language training exercises and homework.

The analysis of existing teaching materials defines five task categories that the low-code application must support, as summarised in Table 1.

The Written Production and Communication category mandates the highest level of system flexibility and integration, as these tasks require learners to actively generate original, extended content. The two main subtypes are general writing tasks and dialogue translation tasks.

While general writing tasks prompt learners to produce free-form written content (e.g. reports, descriptions, responses) that must typically be submitted to the instructor for evaluation and feedback, dialogue translation tasks require learners to convert German dialogue text directly into Italian, often focusing on practical, service-related conversations. Like general writing tasks, the resulting translation is usually reviewed by the instructor.

These production-focused tasks are crucial for assessing the student's ability to apply grammar and vocabulary in context, meaning the application must support the capture, submission, and subsequent display of rich, qualitative feedback from the language teacher.

Table 1. Task types identified in the teaching materials.

Task Category	Key Characteristics
Reading and Listening Comprehension	Introductory tasks using parallel texts and audio to build familiarity; includes comprehension checks.
Grammar Tables	Structured data format (tables) used to teach and test linguistic rules (e.g. conjugation) that requires structured input/output.
Visual Tasks	Integration of visual and linguistic elements where learners describe images or match labels to visual features.
Fill-in-the-Blank	Focuses on vocabulary and contextual understanding using gap-text exercises or word-to-definition matching.
Written Production and Communication	Requires active, expressive written output for communicative purposes.

4 Knowledge Graph-Grounded Low-Code Application Design

A low-code application was chosen as the primary technological means to address the need for accessible tools for language teachers, who may lack significant technical expertise. The purpose of this approach is to abstract the complexities of knowledge management, enabling teachers to create, manage, and adapt digital learning content through a visual interface. This empowers non-technical users to build and maintain educational resources, bridging the gap between pedagogical expertise and technological implementation.

The application's underlying structure is a purpose-built ontology, developed using the "Ontology Development 101" framework [19]. This ontology's domain is language teaching for train drivers, and its purpose is to serve as a structured knowledge model for teachers to input data into the application.

By serving as a structured knowledge model for teacher input, the knowledge graph captures rich information about teaching practices, materials, and learning interactions, which is essential for a chatbot to function effectively.

The first step was to define the ontology's domain as language teaching for train drivers in the Swiss public transportation sector. This focused the effort on the pedagogical practices, curriculum content, and professional context required by the end-users. The purpose was to create a structured framework for teachers to input data, which would then be used to facilitate the development of a chatbot.

By analysing the teaching materials and interview findings, the methodology helped identify core terms for the two main components of the application:

1. **Teaching Ontology** with the key terms included being "Task" and "Lesson".
2. **Chatbot Ontology** with the key terms included being "Question", "Answer", "User", "Bot", and "Intent".
3. **Combined Ontology**, which was created to combine the teaching and chatbot ontology.

The framework guided the organisation of these terms into a logical hierarchy. For instance, in the teaching ontology, the overarching class of "Task" was created, with specific task types (e.g. `GrammarTables`, `VisualTask`) defined as subclasses.

The next step involved detailing the relationships and attributes of each class. The framework helped define both datatype properties (e.g. `taskTitle`, `difficultyLevel`) and object properties (e.g. `isPartOfLesson`, `hasAnswer`). These properties allowed for the semantic linking of information. For example, `isPartOfLesson` explicitly connects a "Task" to a "Lesson", capturing the structural relationship of the teaching material. The result of this is shown in Fig. 2 (a).

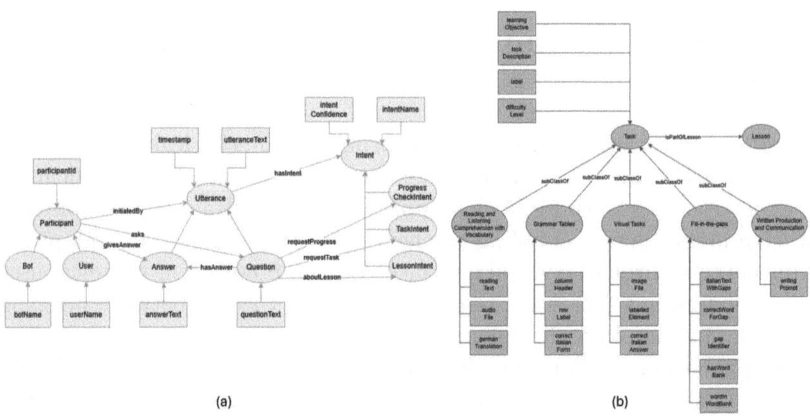

Fig. 2. An excerpt of the Teaching Ontology (a) and of the Chatbot Ontology (b).

To finalise the ontology, the framework required the specification of cardinalities for each property. This ensured data integrity by defining the number of values a property could have (e.g. a "Task" must have a `taskTitle`, so the cardinality is one). This step guaranteed that the knowledge graph's structure was complete and consistent, which is essential for accurate data storage and retrieval.

The methodology similarly guided the definition and structuring of the chatbot's dedicated ontology. This development focused on organising the chatbot components into a logical hierarchy. The resulting structure established *Intent*, *Utterance*, and *Participant* as the core, overarching classes. Specific functional types, such as *Question* and *Answer*, were then precisely classified as subclasses under the *Utterance* class.

The subsequent step involved detailing the inherent relationships and attributes for each core class. The framework supported the definition of both datatype properties (e.g. `intentName`) and object properties (e.g. `hasIntent`). These properties are semantically linking the interaction elements. For instance, the `hasIntent` property connects a user's Utterance to a specific Intent, thereby capturing the behavioural relationship within the conversation flow. This ontology is visually represented in Fig. 2 (b).

The process of merging the two existing ontologies required the creation of new relational connections to ensure functional coherence. The core of this integration lies in explicitly linking the user's Task Intent (what the user wants to achieve) with the appropriate system Task required to achieve it. This ensures a comprehensive coverage, guaranteeing that all possible task intents map to a specific Task Type, and that every defined task type can be triggered by a valid task intent. Ultimately, questions submitted by the user are formalized as tasks within the system, and the correctness of the generated responses is validated by checking the task against the expected answers.

When looking at the running case, the connection between the teaching ontology and the chatbot ontology is done using the `isFormOf` connection from Task to Question. This allows for the mapping of the writing prompt of the written production task to the question text in the chatbot ontology.

5 Implementation of the Knowledge Graph-Grounded Low-Code Application

The prototype was built using metaphactory [22], a platform that facilitated the construction and management of knowledge graphs. This environment allowed for the definition of classes, properties, hierarchies, and instances, alongside visualisation capabilities. The low-code teacher interface was developed using HTML and CSS, ensuring seamless integration with the knowledge graph and providing a simple, visual way for teachers to interact with the data.

The development process focused on creating a functional prototype with three main components: a knowledge graph to store content, a teacher interface to manage the content, and a chatbot interface for student interaction.

Within metaphactory, three distinct ontologies were defined: a teaching ontology, a chatbot ontology, and a combined ontology, which integrates them. This combined knowledge graph displays the connections between the two logical groupings (ontologies), while hiding the inputs of the two ontologies and omitting those that are unnecessary for representing the combined structure. While the low-code application is designed for teachers to handle day-to-day content creation, the initial setup of its underlying structure, the ontology, still requires a technical expert. This is a one-time effort that establishes the foundational framework for all future content. Once this is complete, teachers are empowered to use the intuitive low-code interface independently. This allows them to focus on what they do best: creating and managing pedagogical content, rather than on complex data modelling or programming. The technical complexity is thus abstracted away, enabling the teachers to become citizen developers who can independently build and evolve their own specialised learning tools.

Figure 3 illustrates the prototype of the low-code application. The teacher first selects the lesson to which the task belongs and then defines the corresponding writing prompt, both of which are subsequently stored in the knowledge graph.

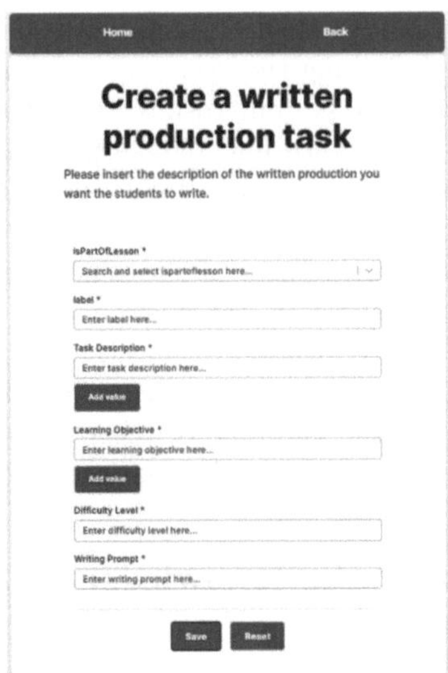

Fig. 3. Written Production Task in the Low-Code Application.

Upon saving, a new knowledge graph instance representing the writing task is created, preserving the relationship to its corresponding lesson as defined in the ontological schema. The integration with metaphactory enables this process to occur automatically, without requiring additional implementation effort beyond the low-code configuration.

At the end the teacher is able to click on a button to create a chatbot out of the content that was entered into the knowledge graph. The chatbot leverages the structured data within the knowledge graph to provide personalised feedback and offer on-the-go learning experiences. By enabling a flexible learning schedule and real-time interaction, the chatbot serves as a supplementary tool that reinforces learning beyond the classroom.

The technical prototype is available for download from GitHub[2].

6 Evaluation and Key Findings

The evaluation phase centered on the evaluation of the developed artifact to confirm its utility in achieving the predefined design objectives and addressing the identified practical problem. The evaluation proceeded in two main parts: an analysis of the technical fidelity and generalisability of the application, followed by a usability assessment.

The application's accuracy and operational fidelity were tested by integrating teaching materials sourced from a new, independent dataset (Lessons 4–9). The success rate of this integration process served as the direct measure for evaluating the knowledge graph schema's structure and its ability to handle content outside its initial development scope.

To check the application's capacity for generalisation, a match assessment was performed. This validation step confirmed the feasibility of inputting and mapping various information structures from the new materials into the application, thereby ensuring the artifact could accommodate and process a diversity of learning task types.

To address the concern regarding limited teacher adoption, a user-focused usability assessment was conducted via an informal, qualitative interview with a teacher. This individual was specifically chosen as a representative partner due to their domain expertise and direct connection to the intended user group.

This qualitative review of the prototype provided stakeholder feedback on the user experience. The session focused on several key criteria to guide the assessment:

- **Input Clarity:** Was the logic for entering new content intuitive and easily understood?
- **Ease of Navigation:** Was the application simple to operate and move through?
- **Feature Gaps:** Which functionalities or updates are necessary to improve the application's practical utility?

The teacher was asked to provide detailed, qualitative input on both positive and negative aspects, alongside identifying functional priorities for future iterations.

Accuracy and Generalisation of the System. The first evaluation assessed the system's low-code application and knowledge graph. The goal was to measure the success rate of ingesting new teaching materials to validate the system's generalisation capabilities. Lessons 4 through 9 were used for this, as the system was developed initially using content from Lessons 1–3 and 10–12. To assess the accuracy, the "match accuracy" formula was used:

[2] https://github.com/Knowledge-basedAI/KnowledgeGraphGroundedLowCodeApplication4ducationalChatbotsInTheRailwaySector.

$$\text{Match Accuracy} = \frac{\text{Total Matched Tasks}}{\text{Total Tasks in Lesson}} \tag{1}$$

This formula compares the tasks that were possible to be integrated into the knowledge graph to the total tasks within the lesson. Table 2 shows the number of exercises, segmented by task type, that were successfully integrated into the knowledge graph using the teacher interface. Only a few specific, complex task types—such as form-completion tasks and multiple-choice questions—were not directly supported by the existing interface.

Table 2. Accuracy assessment of knowledge graph integration.

Lesson	Total Matched	No Match	Total Tasks	Match Accuracy
4	116	1	117	99.15%
5	129	1	130	99.23%
6	80	0	80	100.00%
7	131	2	133	98.50%
8	108	1	109	99.08%
9	77	1	78	98.72%

User-Focused Usability Assessment. A second user-focused evaluation was conducted to assess a teacher's perspective. A teacher who is part of the primary user group at SOB (the Schweizerische Südostbahn AG) was interviewed while using the prototype with example teaching materials. The questions asked were answered and the results were that the logic is understandable but needs some improvement mostly in the way cardinalities were described. The navigation was mentioned to be good and understandable, and there are still some functionalities that need to be included for the solution to be used in a practical way. In general, this qualitative feedback was positive, with the teacher expressing an intention to use the application in future teaching. The evaluation highlighted specific areas for improvement, such as clarifying input fields and adding better explanations for difficulty levels.

7 Conclusion and Future Work

In this work, we proposed a knowledge graph-grounded low-code approach for language teachers to create and maintain chatbot-ready learning content in the Swiss railway domain. The ontologies make the approach technology-agnostic, i.e., one can choose an appropriate platform or technology–can be traditional chatbot development platforms or LLM-based implementation. A limitation of the approach lies in its generalization. Both the knowledge graph and the low-code application addresse the requirements of current assignments used for language teaching at SOB. The design may have to be adapted for other teaching or assignment requirements.

In future work, we intend to employ LLMs to automate the integration of knowledge graph-based educational content into a chatbot platform such as Rasa, enabling the chatbot to be continuously updated and grounded in factual knowledge over time.

Acknowledgments. This work was supported by Innosuisse under grant no. 71922.1 INNO-ICT, in collaboration with FHNW School of Business and Suter Bahnkompetenz GmbH.

References

1. Adamopoulou, E., Moussiades, L.: An overview of chatbot technology. In: Artificial Intelligence Applications and Innovations, pp. 373–383. Springer International Publishing (2020). https://doi.org/10.1007/978-3-030-49186-4_31
2. Cabot, J., Clarisó, R.: Low code for smart software development. IEEE Softw. **40**(1), 89–93 (2023). https://doi.org/10.1109/MS.2022.3211352
3. Fraiwan, M., Khasawneh, N.: A review of ChatGPT applications in education, marketing, software engineering, and healthcare: benefits, drawbacks, and research directions. arXiv preprint arXiv:2305.00237 (2023). https://arxiv.org/abs/2305.00237
4. Rawte, V., Sheth, A., Das, A.: A survey of hallucination in large foundation models. arXiv preprint arXiv:2309.05922 (2023). https://arxiv.org/abs/2309.05922
5. Martin, A., Pande, C., Witschel, H.F., Mathez, J.: ChEdBot: designing a domain-specific conversational agent in a simulational learning environment using LLMs. In: Proceedings of the AAAI Spring Symposium on Empowering Machine Learning and Large Language Models with Domain and Commonsense Knowledge (AAAI-MAKE 2024). AAAI Press (2024). https://proceedings.aaai-make.info/AAAI-MAKE-PREPRINTS-2024/07292-MartinA.pdf
6. Chen, P., Lu, Y., Zheng, V., Chen, X., Yang, B.: KnowEdu: a system to construct knowledge graph for education. IEEE Access **6**, 31553–31563 (2018). https://doi.org/10.1109/ACCESS.2018.2839607
7. Chen, Y.: An intelligent question-answering system for course learning based on knowledge graph. https://lutpub.lut.fi/handle/10024/167427 (2024)
8. Følstad, A., Skjuve, M., Brandtzaeg, P.: Different Chatbots for different purposes: towards a typology of chatbots to understand interaction design. In: Internet Science, pp. 145–156. Springer International Publishing (2019). https://doi.org/10.1007/978-3-030-17705-8_13
9. Hevner, A., March, S., Park, J., Ram, S.: Design science in information systems research. MIS Q. **28**(1), 75–105 (2004). https://doi.org/10.2307/25148625
10. Laurenzi, E.: An agile and ontology-based meta-modelling approach for the design and maintenance of enterprise knowledge graph schemas. Enterprise Model. Inf. Syst. Architect. (EMISAJ) – Int. J. Concept. Model. **19** (2024). https://doi.org/10.18417/emisa.19.6, Special Issue on Enterprise Modeling and Knowledge Graphs.

11. Laurenzi, E.: AOAME: an enterprise knowledge graphs editor for domain experts. In: Pufahl, L., Rosenthal, K., España, S., Nurcan, S. (eds.) Intelligent Information Systems. CAiSE 2025. LNBIP, vol. 557, pp. 181–188. Springer, Cham (2025). https://doi.org/10.1007/978-3-031-94590-8_22
12. Chiş, A., Buchmann, R.A., Ghiran, A.M.: Towards a modeling method for low-code knowledge graph building. In: Companion Proceedings of the 16th IFIP WG 8.1 Working Conference on the Practice of Enterprise Modeling and the 13th Enterprise Design and Engineering Working Conference (PoEM-EDEWC 2023). CEUR Workshop Proceedings, vol. 3645. CEUR-WS.org, Vienna, Austria (2023). https://ceur-ws.org/Vol-3645/forum4.pdf
13. Hutzli, P., Leoncio, P.: How BKW Energie resolved smart meter choke points with a knowledge graph. https://blog.metaphacts.com/how-bkw-resolved-smart-meter-choke-points-with-a-knowledge-graph (2024)
14. Pande, C., Witschel, H.F., Martin, A., Montecchiari, D.: Hybrid conversational AI for intelligent tutoring systems. In: Martin, A., Hinkelmann, K., Fill, H.-G., Gerber, A., Lenat, D., Stolle, R., van Harmelen, F. (eds.) Proceedings of the AAAI 2021 Spring Symposium on Combining Machine Learning and Knowledge Engineering (AAAI-MAKE 2021). CEUR Workshop Proceedings, vol. 2846. CEUR-WS.org, Stanford University, Palo Alto, CA, USA (2021). https://ceur-ws.org/Vol-2846/paper23.pdf
15. Inglese, T., Korkut, S.: Modellierung des Unterrichtsdesigns eines Sprachtrainings für berufliche Zwecke unter Verwendung von Augmented Reality. In: Neue Trends in Wirtschaftsinformatik und eingesetzte Technologien, pp. 219–237. Springer International Publishing (2023). https://doi.org/10.1007/978-3-031-32538-0_14
16. Leible, S., Simic, D., Gücük, G.-L., von Brackel-Schmidt, C.: Citizen Developer als Katalysatoren für die Entwicklung mitarbeitergetriebener Innovationen. HMD Praxis der Wirtschaftsinformatik **61**(5), 1088–1114 (2024). https://doi.org/10.1365/s40702-024-01102-2
17. Luo, Y., Liang, P., Wang, C., Shahin, M., Zhan, J.: Characteristics and challenges of low-code development: the practitioners' perspective. In: Proceedings of the 15th ACM/IEEE International Symposium on Empirical Software Engineering and Measurement (ESEM), pp. 1–11 (2021). https://doi.org/10.1145/3475716.3475782
18. Peng, C., Xia, F., Naseriparsa, M., Osborne, F.: Knowledge graphs: opportunities and challenges. Artif. Intell. Rev. **56**(11), 13071–13102 (2023). https://doi.org/10.1007/s10462-023-10465-9
19. Noy, N.F., McGuinness, D.L.: Ontology development 101: a guide to creating your first ontology. Stanford University, Stanford, CA (2001)
20. Trame, J.: Building a knowledge graph application is easier than ever with metaphactory's intuitive wizards. https://blog.metaphacts.com/building-a-knowledge-graph-application-is-easier-than-ever-with-metaphactory-s-intuitive-wizard (2021)
21. Yang, Z., Wang, Y., Gan, J., Li, H., Lei, N.: Design and research of intelligent question-answering (Q&A) system based on high school course knowledge graph. Mobile Netw. Appl. **26**(5), 1884–1890 (2021). https://doi.org/10.1007/s11036-020-01726-w
22. metaphacts GmbH: Metaphactory (Version 4.x) - A Low-Code Knowledge Graph Platform. https://metaphacts.com (2024). Accessed 10 Mar 2026

Multi-step Schema-Aware RAG for ArchiMate Model-Based Answering of Natural Language Queries

Aritha Kumarasinghe(✉) and Marite Kirikova

Institute of Applied Computer Systems, Riga Technical University, 6A Kipsalas Street, Riga 1048, Latvia
{balasuriyage-aritha-dewnith.kumarasinghe, marite.kirikova}@rtu.lv

Abstract. Enterprise Architecture Models (EAMs) represent a key source of knowledge about an organization, which could potentially serve as an external knowledge source that can be utilized by a Large Language Model. This work seeks to propose a Multi-Step Schema-Aware Retrieval Augmented Generation (RAG) approach where EAM (specifically ArchiMate) elements are retrieved from an XML-serialization of the model through a multi-step prompting process. The proposed approach is evaluated using an ArchiMate model defined to represent the ArchiSurance business case, through RAGAs metrics, retrieved element-specific metrics, and the token usage, when compared to a benchmark that consists of using a single prompt that includes all model elements. The evaluation results indicate that there is no significant variation (>10%) between the proposed approach and the baseline in terms of the quality of the responses generated and the model elements retrieved; however, there is a 4 to 6 (depending on the LLM used) fold difference in input tokens utilized to generate a response.

Keywords: Enterprise Architecture Models · Large Language Models · ArchiMate · Retrieval Augmented Generation

1 Introduction

Since the introduction of Large Language Models (LLMs), improving their performance has been a highly researched topic, with approaches like Retrieval Augmented Generation (RAG) [1] being used to supplement the tasks carried out by LLMs using knowledge from external sources such as documents or knowledge graphs, through GraphRAG [2]. The use of RAG has been shown to address limitations of LLMs, such as a limited context window and hallucinations [1]. Subsequent research in the domain of RAG-based systems has explored how, instead of retrieving relevant knowledge only once during the generation process, retrieval in multiple steps can improve performance in the contexts where queries are more complex [3].

Similar to knowledge graphs, formal conceptual models (e.g., BPMN models) can act as external knowledge sources that can be utilized during the response generation process

R. Posenato and I. Vanderfeesten (Eds.): CAiSE 2026 Workshops, LNBIP 586, pp. 347–358, 2026.
https://doi.org/10.1007/978-3-032-28160-9_31

of LLMs, with previous research concluding that the models, such as BPMN models, can be used as external knowledge sources to ground the responses that are generated by large language models [4]. The experiments done in [4] consist of transforming BPMN models into an RDF serialization-based knowledge graph, which in turn is used for RAG. This decision was made based on the results of previous research that showcased how RDF-serialized BPMN models perform better than XML-serialized BPMN models when used to respond to natural language queries using LLMs [5].

Unlike BPMN models, which focus mainly on representing business processes that are carried out within an organization, Enterprise Architecture Models (EAMs) seek to represent a more holistic view of organizations [6]. EAMs are applied within the context of digitalization, given their ability to align the business and IT landscape of organizations. They allow a model developer to represent the structure of a company, including their business processes, information systems, and IT infrastructure; therefore, they have richer semantics compared to other conceptual models, such as BPMN that are specialized for a specific aspect, such as business processes. ArchiMate is an enterprise architecture modelling language that can be used to develop EAMs that are aligned with the TOGAF standard (an enterprise architecture standard) and has been presented as the de facto standard for representing enterprise architectures [7].

While previous research has presented theoretical reasoning as to why RDF/OWL must be used when representing EAMs that can be utilized during retrieval based generation, i.e., RAG or Retrieval Interleaved Generation (where unlike traditional RAG knowledge retrieval is done in several steps instead of only once before generating the query response) [8], experimentation on whether the results shown in BPMN specific research [5] are generalizable for semantically richer modelling languages, such as ArchiMate, when retrieval is done in several steps is yet to be explored.

In order to further explore this topic, in this work, we seek to investigate the influence of multi-step retrieval of XML-serialized ArchiMate-based EAM elements for responding to natural language queries. To do this, we propose Multi-step Schema-Aware RAG, a Multi-step RAG approach that retrieves ArchiMate model elements (entities and relationships) that are relevant to the user query in several steps, with the retrieval of entities being guided by the entity and relationship types that have been defined in the ArchiMate model. This approach can be used by stakeholders or other IT systems to interact with a defined ArchiMate EAM through natural language queries based solely on the default XML-serialization that is created by the Archi tool [9]. For the sake of comparison, the proposed approach is compared with the baseline of using prompts that include formatted versions of all the entities and relations. The evaluation of the proposed solution is done using the Retrieval Augmented Generation Assessment (RAGAs) framework, which provide a multidimensional evaluation of the RAG-based query response using "faithfulness (i.e., is the answer grounded in the retrieved context), answer relevance (i.e., does the answer address the question), and context relevance (i.e., is the retrieved context sufficiently focused)" [10], and some additional metrics that relate to the model elements used to generate the response. By doing so, we seek to answer the following research question: 'How does using Multi-step Schema-Aware RAG compare to single prompt based generation of natural language query responses based on XML-serialized

ArchiMate models using LLMs in terms of response relevance, factual correctness, semantic similarity, faithfulness, and LLM token utility?'.

The remainder of this paper is organized as follows. In Sect. 2, we introduce the background knowledge that is relevant to this research and detail how the current work builds upon it. This is followed by an overview of the proposed Multi-step Schema-Aware RAG in Sect. 3. The proposed solution is then evaluated, using the RAGAs framework, the results for which are presented in Sect. 4. The conclusion drawn from the results of the evaluation and possible direction for future research are presented in Sect. 5.

2 Background

While several previous works have discussed the role of LLMs within EAMs, they solely focus on how LLMs can be utilized in the modelling activities related to generating/maintaining EAMs [11, 13]. One such work presents how the knowledge graph-based Enterprise Modelling can be used to automate the generation of the enterprise models by utilizing the type semantics of ArchiMate in combination with the formal semantic representation capabilities of knowledge graphs and ontologies [13]. This work seeks to demonstrates how the type semantics that are inherent to Enterprise Modelling Languages like ArchiMate can support tasks that utilize LLMs, and while it cannot be argued that the symbolic reasoning can be achieved through OWL/RDF based knowledge representations [14], more research must be done on how it can be leveraged in the context of the LLM-supported Enterprise Modelling. The topic of RDF/OWL- based representation of EAM is discussed in more detail in [8], describing how RDF can result in easier integration with other RDF-based tools, although at the time of writing this article the benefits remain hypothetical. Additionally, it can be argued that while XML-serialized ArchiMate model does not utilize the full capabilities of RDF/OWL, it can already be considered as a knowledge graph based on an underlying ontology (the underlying ArchiMate metamodel) as presented in [15].

While, to the best of the authors' knowledge, very limited prior research on utilizing EAMs as a knowledge source for LLMs has been conducted, there is a growing body of knowledge on the use of business process models as an external knowledge source for LLMs. An overview of how LLMs can be incorporated into the business process management lifecycle is presented in [16], with process model querying being explicitly considered, and with possible benefits of LLMs being able to improve the quality of the model, but it is recognized that this would entail the LLM being able to understand an XML-serialized process model. The ability of LLMs to "understand" business process models was discussed in several works [5, 17, 18], and [4]. The first three works ([5, 17, 18]) explicitly compare the influence of the XML versus RDF serialization of BPMN models, demonstrating how RDF serialization allows for better understanding of models in relation to user queries. However, within the experimentation, RDF serialization allows for semantics-based querying functionality, thereby enabling the LLM to consider only a specific subset of model elements. The current research seeks to better understand if implementing the retrieval of XML-based model data based on the underlying ArchiMate metamodel (entity types and relationship types) can influence the performance of LLMs in responding to user queries based on the EA model elements.

The retrieval of specific data to support the LLM-based query response generation was proposed as the RAG framework in [19], which demonstrated how the responses that are generated were made more factual and specific, by retrieving relevant knowledge from an external knowledge source (e.g., a document) and then augmenting that knowledge into the prompt that is used to generate the query response. A review conducted on the RAG presents the concept of a modular RAG framework that takes a more flexible approach to RAG [20], by using specific modules to carry out RAG in many different ways, such as iteratively retrieving and reading retrieved entities until the relevant data is retrieved. A more recent term that is used to describe such an approach is referred to as the multi-step RAG in several works [21–23]. In this paper, such an approach is utilized for the retrieval of ArchiMate Process Model elements. In addition, we also utilize the underlying schema of ArchiMate (the ArchiMate Metamodel) to inform retrieval, drawing inspiration from the results that were achieved in [24], which proposed the anchoring of the knowledge retrieval process on a dynamically defined ontology based on domain specific ontologies and the external knowledge source that is used for RAG; since entity types are already defined within the ArchiMate metamodel as well as the XML-serialized ArchiMate model (through "xsi:type").

3 Multi-step Schema-Aware RAG

In order to allow an LLM to utilize XML-serialized ArchiMate models, the proposed solution must be able to parse an XML file to access the underlying model element representations. Within.archimate files saved by Archi version 5.0.3 the model elements are organized based on folders representing each layer defined in ArchiMate, with each folder containing nodes that are of a type specific to the ArchiMate layer, e.g., Business layer containing nodes that have xsi:type equal to "archimate:BusinessFunction", "archimate:BusinessEvent", "archimate:BusinessProcess", etc. The xsi:type values of the nodes within the.archimate file can be used to define which ArchiMate Entity Types have been utilized in the EAMs contained in the XML file. Additionally, there is also a single folder dedicated to representing the relations between model entities, which are also assigned an xsi:type based on the relations that are included in the ArchiMate metamodel, e.g., AssociationRelationship. The proposed solution can utilize the xsi:type combined with the folder structure of XML to identify all the entities and relations that have been utilized to create the ArchiMate, thereby providing a schema that can guide the retrieval of model elements that can be relevant to answering a user's query.

With regards to user queries, at a high level of abstraction, there are four types of queries that can be defined:

1. Entity only query: Query that requires a response based only on model entities and not their relations, e.g., "What are the business processes that are represented in the model?".
2. Relation only query: Queries that do not specify any entities of interest and only their relations, therefore requiring a response based only on relations that are of a specific type. While the results will be entity-relation-entity pairs, retrieval is done only based on relations, e.g., "What associations relations have been defined in the model?".

3. Entity and Relation query: Queries that specify a response based on both entities and relations; e.g., "What association relationships does the Customer have?".
4. Out of scope queries: Where the query does not relate to the ArchiMate model, therefore cannot be answered.

Any solution that seeks to leverage EAMs must be capable of handling all four types of queries since there is the possibility for a user to define a query that can belong to any of these types. In the solution that is proposed in this paper (Fig. 1), entity retrieval and relations retrieval are preformed sequentially, where first, based on the user's query and the entity types that have been used in the ArchiMate model, an LLM is prompted to select the entity types that are relevant to the user's query. If no relevant entity types are identified, relations retrieval begins (in order to ensure that responses are generated for relations only queries); else, a subset of all the entities that have been defined in the model that are of the entity type(s) selected by the LLM are retrieved. A list is created based only on the names and the types that are associated with these entities, given that their IDs are not relevant to the LLM. This list is used in a subsequent prompt to further filter out the entities that are not relevant to the user's query, thereby resulting in a smaller subset of relevant entities that are of the relevant entity types. Finally, the LLM is prompted to generate a response based on the entities and, if that is not possible, the LLM does not generate a response and starts relation retrieval. This is followed by LLM specifying relation types that relate to the user's query, which is then used to inform the relation extraction, with the knowledge gained (if any) from the entity extraction (specifically the relevant entity names) being used to restrict the relations that are retrieved. This is done to ensure that the relations retrieved are not extensive, thereby preventing the likelihood of selecting irrelevant relations, and to also reduce the number of input tokens that are utilized since relations contain three times the number of string elements (to represent two entities and a single relation compared to just one). If a query is relation-only, the selection of the relation types reduces the risk of retrieving too many relations. If a response still cannot be defined based on the retrieved relations, the system makes the search less restricted by retrieving all the relationships where the selected entities are present. Doing so allows the LLM to analyze a submodel that is not restricted in the relationships it considers.

Additionally, it should be noted that a new LLM instance is created for each step in the process, thereby resetting the context windows of the LLM to prevent data leakage and increase context utilization.

A representation of how the proposed solution is meant to function is shown in Fig. 1.

The actual implementation of the solution was done using Python 3, hence why, in Fig. 1, the processes that are carried out without using LLMs have been labeled with the Python logo, and the tasks that are executed with the support of an LLM, are represented using an OpenAI logo, since in this work GPT-based models are used.

4 Evaluation of the Multi-step Schema-Aware RAG

In order to evaluate the proposed approach, the ArchiSurance case study was used, through an example solution for the case that is publicly available on GitHub under an open-source license [25]. This case study relates to a fictional insurance company

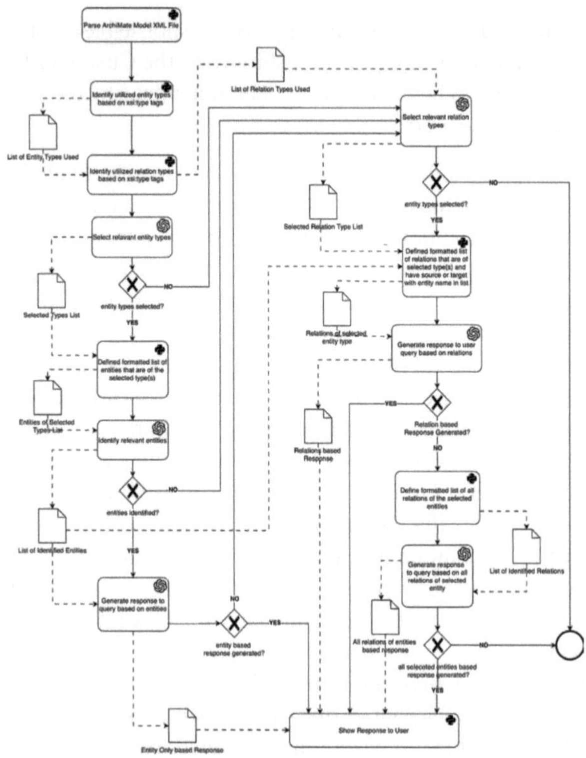

Fig. 1. Process model representing Multi-step Schema-Aware RAG

with the resulting EAM representing the strategy, business, application, technology, and physical, motivation, implementation, and migration aspects of the organization, which uses most of ArchiMate's entity and relation types, resulting in a total of 297 unique entities and 402 relationships. By organizing the model through views, the users are able to represent how different aspects of the organization relate to one another, an example of which is shown in Fig. 2 where the view on the left specifies that ArchiSurance Back Office Suite realizes Integrated Back Office Automation, and the view on the right shows the components of the ArchiSurance Back Office Suite and the flows of data to and from them.

The solution is implemented in a Python script that parses the XML data contained in a single ArchiMate file using the xml.tree.ElementTree module, and uses the OpenAI library for interacting with the selected LLM. The script reads the user's natural language query(s) from a JSON file and also outputs the associated response alongside the model elements, on which the response was based, and all the model elements that were included in the final prompt. This JSON file also contains the manually defined evaluation data, in the form of the expected response, the elements from the model that are expected to be used by the LLM to respond, Faithfulness Context, which consists of statements that represent the information from the model as natural language instead of as formatted data; finally Classification is used to specify the type of query (in terms of the aforementioned

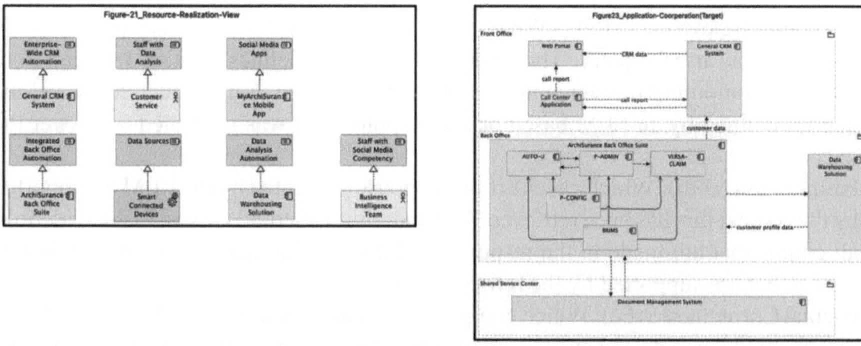

Fig. 2. Two views from the ArchiSurance ArchiMate model representing how resources are realized (left) and how applications cooperate (right).

four query types). An example response alongside the associated JSON data is presented in Fig. 3 for the question "What are the software components needed by the software that implements Integrated Back Office Automation?",


```
{
  "Question": "What are the software components needed by the software that implements Integrated Back Office Automation?",
  "Response": "The software that implements Integrated Back Office Automation (type: Resource) is ArchiSurance Back Office Suite (type: ApplicationComponent), and the software components needed by ArchiSurance Back Office Suite (type: ApplicationComponent) are AUTO-U (type: ApplicationComponent), BRIMS (type: ApplicationComponent), P-ADMIN (type: ApplicationComponent), P-CONFIG (type: ApplicationComponent), and VERSA-CLAIM (type: ApplicationComponent).",
  "Expected Answer": "The ArchiSurance Back Office Suite (type: ApplicationComponent) implements Integrated Back Office Automation (type: Resource) and is composed of AUTO-U (type: ApplicationComponent), BRIMS (type: ApplicationComponent), P-ADMIN (type: ApplicationComponent), P-CONFIG (type: ApplicationComponent), VERSA-CLAIM (type: ApplicationComponent).",
  "Elements Used": [
    "ArchiSurance Back Office Suite (type: ApplicationComponent) RealizationRelationship Integrated Back Office Automation (type: Resource)",
    "ArchiSurance Back Office Suite (type: ApplicationComponent) CompositionRelationship AUTO-U (type: ApplicationComponent)",
    "ArchiSurance Back Office Suite (type: ApplicationComponent) CompositionRelationship BRIMS (type: ApplicationComponent)",
    "ArchiSurance Back Office Suite (type: ApplicationComponent) CompositionRelationship P-ADMIN (type: ApplicationComponent)",
    "ArchiSurance Back Office Suite (type: ApplicationComponent) CompositionRelationship P-CONFIG (type: ApplicationComponent)",
    "ArchiSurance Back Office Suite (type: ApplicationComponent) CompositionRelationship VERSA-CLAIM (type: ApplicationComponent)"
  ],
  "Elements Included In Prompt": [
    "ArchiSurance Back Office Suite (type: ApplicationComponent) CompositionRelationship AUTO-U (type: ApplicationComponent)",
    "ArchiSurance Back Office Suite (type: ApplicationComponent) CompositionRelationship BRIMS (type: ApplicationComponent)",
    "ArchiSurance Back Office Suite (type: ApplicationComponent) CompositionRelationship P-ADMIN (type: ApplicationComponent)",
    "ArchiSurance Back Office Suite (type: ApplicationComponent) CompositionRelationship P-CONFIG (type: ApplicationComponent)",
    "ArchiSurance Back Office Suite (type: ApplicationComponent) CompositionRelationship VERSA-CLAIM (type: ApplicationComponent)",
    ... (other elements from the model that were included in the prompt)
  ],
  "Expected Elements": [
    "ArchiSurance Back Office Suite (type: ApplicationComponent) RealizationRelationship Integrated Back Office Automation (type: Resource)",
    "AUTO-U (type: ApplicationComponent) CompositionRelationship ArchiSurance Back Office Suite (type: ApplicationComponent)",
    "BRIMS (type: ApplicationComponent) CompositionRelationship ArchiSurance Back Office Suite (type: ApplicationComponent)",
    "P-ADMIN (type: ApplicationComponent) CompositionRelationship ArchiSurance Back Office Suite (type: ApplicationComponent)",
    "P-CONFIG (type: ApplicationComponent) CompositionRelationship ArchiSurance Back Office Suite (type: ApplicationComponent)",
    "VERSA-CLAIM (type: ApplicationComponent) CompositionRelationship ArchiSurance Back Office Suite (type: ApplicationComponent)"
  ],
  "Faithfulness Contexts": [
    "ArchiSurance Back Office Suite realizes Integrated Back Office Automation.",
    "ArchiSurance Back Office Suite is composed of AUTO-U, BRIMS, P-ADMIN, P-CONFIG, and VERSA-CLAIM."
  ],
  "Classification": "Entity and Relation"
}
```


Fig. 3. Example JSON data used to represent LLM response and the manually defined evaluation data for the query "What are the software components needed by the software that implements Integrated Back Office Automation?".

To evaluate the Multi-step Schema-Aware RAG, 29 queries were defined by the authors to represent the first three types of queries (8 queries for Entity Only, 6 queries for Relation Only, 15 Entity and Relation Queries (an example query and response is shown in Fig. 3), and 6 Out of Scope queries (with the full list being publicly available through a GitHub Repository [26]).

The results of these queries were evaluated based on the RAGAs framework [10] implemented through the RAGAs Python library [27], with the response-generation-related metrics used being:

1. Response Relevance (rRel): Which answers whether the response to the query addresses the user's query. The underlying method defines a value ranging from 0 to 1 by computing the semantic similarity between the user's actual query and the queries defined by an LLM based on the response that was generated to answer the query.
2. Faithfulness (rFth): Which checks if the response generated by the LLM is supported by the context that has been retrieved. The underlying method uses an LLM to identify all claims that are made in the response and divides that number by the number of claims that are supported by the retrieved context.
3. Factual Correctness (rFc): Which compares the claims made by the LLM to the claims that are made in expected answers to quantify the overlap between the two as a value between 0 and 1. The underlying method uses an LLM to identify the claims made by the LLM-generated response and the claims made in the grounded truth ("Expected Answer" defined by the authors).
4. Semantic Similarity (rSs): Computes the semantic (cosine) similarity between the LLM-generated response and the expected answer based on their vector embeddings. The underlying method uses an embedding model to generate vector embeddings to represent the two responses and then computes their cosine similarity based on the generated embeddings.

Four additional metrics are calculated to evaluate the model elements that are retrieved by the retrieval mechanism (element retrieval-based metrics), and the model elements that are used to define a response (based on the retrieval-related metrics defined in RAGAs but adapted for the content of EAM model element retrieval), namely:

1. Percentage of Elements Used (Elmnt_Pct): Calculates how many of the retrieved EAM model elements were utilized to define a response to the user's query. This is calculated by dividing the total number of elements used to define the response ("Elements Used") by the total number of elements included in the final prompt ("Elements included in Prompt").
2. Elements Precision (Elmnt_P): This calculates the precision between the elements used and the expected elements by comparing the elements used ("Elements Used") with the number of elements expected ("Expected Elements"). This is calculated by dividing the number of elements that overlap between Elements Used and the Expected Elements by the total number of Elements Used.
3. Elements Recall (Elmt_R): This calculates the recall between the elements used and the expected elements by comparing the elements expected ("Expected Elements") with the elements used ("Elements Used"). This is calculated by dividing the number of elements that overlap between Elements Used and the Expected Elements by the total number of Expected elements.
4. Element F1 Score (Elmnt_F1): This is a metric that provides a combined representation based on the element recall and element precision.

In addition to the response-related and model-element-related evaluation metrics, the number of input tokens used to enter the prompt(s) was also recorded. This number can be used to compare whether and to what extent Multi-step Schema-Aware RAG has an influence, compared to using a single prompt with all the data. This is recorded by parsing the response received from the OpenAI API, which included data on token usage.

The experimentation is done to see how the Multi-step Schema-Aware RAG compares to a baseline that utilizes a single prompt to respond to users' queries. The Python scripts used to evaluate both Multi-step Schema-Aware RAG and the Single Prompt baseline that includes the formatted versions of the XML data contained in the.archimate file, and the evaluation results are publicly available on a GitHub Repository [26]. Additionally, the experiments were conducted using GPT-5.2 (Reasoning.effort = none, and temperature = 0.2) and GPT-4.1 (temperature = 0.2) to compare the progression of the LLMs in generating responses to user queries based on EAMs. The RAGAs implementation utilized GPT-4.1 (temperature = 0.2, top_p = 1) and OpenAI's text-embedding-3-large to generate embeddings.

For each implementation, Table 1 reports the mean per query evaluation scores across the 29 answerable queries (with more detailed evaluation results available on GitHub [26]). The results show a clear trend of favoring Multi-step Schema-Aware RAG for all retrieval-related evaluation metrics with the exception of Elements Recall, where there is an increase of 2% (0.02) in the case of GPT-5.2 and 10% (0.10) in the case of GPT-4.1. This indicates that an LLM is capable of selecting more of the right model elements to respond to a query, but this comes at the cost of a very significant reduction in the percentage of elements included in the prompt that are used to respond to a query (which in turn reduces the input tokens used as shown in Table 2), in addition to the model including irrelevant or unnecessary model elements.

Table 1. Mean per-query evaluation results across 29 answerable queries for Percentage Elements Used (Elmnt_Pct), Elements Precision (Elmnt_P), Elements Recall (Elmt_R), Element F1 Score (Elmnt_F1)

Model + Prompting Approach	Elmnt_Pct	Elmnt_P	Elmnt_R	Elmnt_F1
GPT-5.2 + Multi-Step Schema-Aware RAG	0.32	**0.72**	0.70	**0.68**
GPT-5.2 + Single Prompt	0.01	0.44	0.72	0.47
GPT-4.1 + Multi-Step Schema-Aware RAG	**0.60**	0.69	0.64	0.65
GPT-4.1 + Single Prompt	0.01	0.54	**0.74**	0.59

The mean of the per query evaluation scores for all 35 responses and the total number of input tokens used to generate these responses using each implementation are shown in Table 2.

The results of the evaluation of the responses generated show a variability in the performance across metrics, with the GPT-4.1 + Single Prompt combination achieving the best relevance. This indicates that the responses generated through a single prompt using GPT-4.1 were more relevant to user queries. With the next two metrics (Factual Correctness and Semantic Similarity) GPT-5.2 + Multi-step Schema-Aware RAG achieves better results than using a Single Prompt (as well as both GPT-4.1) based response generation with a 2–4% improvement in performance. Overall, the results indicate that the

Table 2. Mean of evaluation results on Relevance (rRel), Factual Correctness (rFc), Semantic Similarity (rSs), Faithfulness (rFth), and across responses for 35 User Queries and the Total Token Usage per approach

Model + Prompting Approach	rRel	rFc	rSs	rFth	Token Usage
GPT-5.2 + Multi-Step Schema-Aware RAG	0.71	**0.79**	**0.85**	0.68	102365
GPT-5.2 + Single Prompt	0.64	0.75	0.80	0.68	463090
GPT-4.1 + Multi-Step Schema-Aware RAG	0.72	0.67	0.83	**0.73**	**75682**
GPT-4.1 + Single Prompt	**0.76**	0.73	0.83	0.61	463160

responses generated by Multi-step Schema-Aware RAG should be of a better quality in terms of factual correctness, semantic similarity to the expected answer, and faithfulness to the ideas represented in an EAM. Overall, when comparing Multi-step and Single prompt performance the differences range from + 0.00 to +0.07 for GPT-5.2 and from −0.06 to + 0.12 for GPT-4.1.

However, the most notable difference is in the token usage, where the token usage, when comparing Multi-step Schema-Aware RAG and Single Prompt that includes all model elements, is approximately 4.5 times and 6.1 times lower for GPT-5.2 and GPT-4.1, respectively. A reduction of such a scale implies a subsequent reduction in the cost of generating EAM-based responses to users' queries.

5 Conclusion and Future Work

This research explores LLM-based generation of responses to natural language queries based on an XML-serialized ArchiMate model, by proposing a Multi-step Schema-Aware RAG approach. The approach consists of several steps that narrow down the number of model elements considered when responding to a user's queries. The identification of relevant entities and relationships is informed by the ArchiMate entity and relationship types that have been instantiated in the model. Doing so allows the retrieval process to first narrow down the number of entity and relation types that must be considered before selecting the actual model elements needed to respond to a given query.

The approach was implemented in Python and evaluated on the business case of ArchiSurance using RAGAs metrics, retrieved model-element-related metrics, and on token usage. The experimentation was done using GPT-4.1 and GPT-5.2, with the Multi-step Schema-Aware approach being compared with a baseline that uses a single prompt consisting of formatted data representing all the entities and relationships within the ArchiMate model. The results of responding to 35 queries defined by the authors indicate that there is no significant difference (less than 10%) between the approaches in terms of the quality of the response generated and the selection of ArchiMate model elements that were used to respond to the query. A significant difference, however, is the approximately 4.5 (in the case of GPT-4.1) to 6.1(in the case of GPT 5.2) fold reduction in the number of input tokens used. Overall, it can be concluded that such a Multi-step Schema-Aware retrieval approach can perform as well as a baseline where no filtering of

1 Introduction

The exponential growth of biomedical publications and structured scientific data has transformed the process of scientific discovery. Automated systems are now capable of generating large numbers of candidate hypotheses by identifying potential relationships among genes, proteins and chemical compounds. Approaches based on literature mining, embedding techniques and large scale graph analytics have demonstrated their ability to discover non-trivial associations applicable in scientific discovery [4,14].

However, the increasing effectiveness of automated hypothesis generation has shifted the primary bottleneck of scientific discovery. The challenge is no longer limited to generating hypotheses, but rather to evaluate, interpret and prioritize them. Domain experts are often confronted with hundreds or thousands of candidate relations, with partial or heterogeneous evidence.

Recent advances in Large Language Models (LLMs) have further expanded the capabilities of automated scientific reasoning. LLMs have been applied to idea generation, summarization and domain-specific problem solving, showing promising results across multiple scientific disciplines [21]. Nevertheless, their outputs may lack explicit grounding in structured knowledge, raising concerns regarding transparency and reliability in expert-driven evaluation workflows.

At the same time, Knowledge Graphs (KGs) have gained importance for representing structured biomedical knowledge, enabling explicit modeling of entities, relations and multi-hop paths. While KGs provide traceability and structured evidence, graph-based systems often expose complex representations that require technical expertise to interpret effectively [12,16,18].

Recent Hybrid AI approaches aim to integrate symbolic and sub-symbolic models to balance structured reasoning and natural language interpretation in support of domain experts [3,9].

This paper addresses this challenge by designing an evaluation support artifact that integrates evidence from a large-scale Knowledge Graph with grounded LLM-based explanation mechanisms to enable transparent and trustworthy biomedical hypothesis evaluation. The proposed architecture uses the Dimensions Knowledge Graph (DKG) [12] as a large-scale semantic representation, interlinking publications, entities and metadata across the research lifecycle. By combining the traceability and contextualization capabilities of the DKG with the interpretative and summarization abilities of LLMs, the framework supports transparent and trustworthy biomedical hypothesis evaluation.

The effectiveness of the proposed hybrid architecture was evaluated using a proof-of-concept implementation in a practical use case involving experts in the biomedical field. Participants interacted with the system prototype to analyze and prioritize automatically generated hypotheses within their area of expertise. The evaluation combined qualitative and quantitative feedback to assess usability, perceived transparency, and the trustworthiness of the integrated symbolic and sub-symbolic components. The results indicate that the proposed approach provides meaningful support to domain experts during hypothesis evaluation and prioritization tasks.

model elements takes place. Additionally, the mean semantic similarity, relevance, faithfulness, and factual correctness of the responses generated by the GPT-5.2 being over 70% for the 35 queries indicates that XML-serialized ArchiMate models are a viable knowledge source that can be utilized by LLMs.

This research presents findings of using only 29 author-defined queries related to a single ArchiMate model. Future research can consider expanding the evaluation by defining additional queries through experts relating to more than one ArchiMate model, potentially leading to the creation of a benchmarking dataset. Additionally, the generalizability of the results to other enterprise modelling languages (e.g., 4EM) can be explored.

References

1. Arslan, M., Ghanem, H., Munawar, S., Cruz, C.: A Survey on RAG with LLMs. Procedia Comput. Sci. **246**, 3781–3790 (2024)
2. Edge, D., et al.: From Local to Global: A Graph RAG Approach to Query-Focused Summarization. arXiv preprint arXiv:2404.16130 (2024)
3. Trivedi, H., Balasubramanian, N., Khot, T., Sabharwal, A.: Interleaving Retrieval with Chain-of-Thought Reasoning for Knowledge-Intensive Multi-Step Questions. arXiv preprint arXiv: 2212.10509 (2022)
4. Dolha, D.N., Buchmann, R.A.: Experimental assessments of retrieval-augmented conversational agents interpreting RDF-serialized BPMN models. In: Perspectives in Business Informatics Research. BIR 2025. LNBIP, vol. 562, pp. 286–304. Springer, Cham (2025)
5. Dolha, D.N., Buchmann, R.A.: Experiments with natural language queries on RDF vs XML-serialized BPMN diagrams. Procedia Comput. Sci. **246**, 3246–3255 (2024)
6. Perez-Castillo, R., Ruiz, F., Piattini, M., Ebert, C.: Enterprise Architecture. IEEE Softw. **36**(4) (2019)
7. Pérez-Castillo, R., Delgado, A., Ruiz, F., Bacigalupe, V., Piattini, M.: A method for transforming knowledge discovery metamodel to ArchiMate models. Softw. Syst. Model. **21**, 311–336 (2022)
8. Malakhov, K.: From Archimate to Computer Ontologies: Advancing Semantic Enterprise Architecture With RAG/RIG AI Services in RDF/OWL (2025) https://doi.org/10.31274/isudp.2025.197.02
9. Archi Homepage. https://www.archimatetool.com/. Accessed 10 Mar 2026
10. Es, S., James, J., Espinosa-Anke, L., Schockaert, S.: RAGAS: automated evaluation of retrieval augmented generation. In: Proceedings of the 18th Conference of the European Chapter of the Association for Computational Linguistics: System Demonstrations, pp. 150–158. Association for Computational Linguistics (2024)
11. Barn, B.S., Barat, S., Sandkuhl, K.: Adaptation of enterprise modeling methods for large language models. In: The Practice of Enterprise Modeling (PoEM 2023), pp. 3–18. Springer (2023)
12. Müller, E., Nast, B., Sandkuhl, K.: LLM support for domain experts in enterprise modeling: experiences and implications. In: International Conference on Business Informatics Research, pp. 124–141. Cham: Springer Nature Switzerland (2025)
13. Reitemeyer, B., Fill, H.-G.: Applying Large Language Models in Knowledge Graph-based Enterprise Modeling: Challenges and Opportunities. arXiv:2501.03566 (2025)
14. Herron, D., Jiménez-Ruiz, E., Weyde, T.: On the benefits of OWL-based knowledge graphs for neural-symbolic systems. In: 17th International Workshop on Neural-Symbolic Learning and Reasoning, CEUR Workshop Proceedings, vol. 3432, pp. 327–335 (2023)

The remainder of the paper is organized as follows. Section 2 reviews related work and formulates the research question. Section 3 presents the adopted Design Science Research methodology. Section 4 introduces the evaluation scenario and the derived requirements. Section 5 describes the proposed hybrid AI architecture. Section 6 presents the implementation and evaluation results. Section 7 discusses the limitations of the solution. Finally, Sect. 8 concludes the paper.

2 Related Work

Automated scientific discovery has increasingly shifted from hypotheses generation to hypotheses evaluation, where domain experts must assess plausibility, novelty and relevance across sets of candidate hypotheses [1,19]. The literature reflects hypotheses generation models, knowledge graph for scientific evidence representation, LLMs for scientific reasoning and explanation and hybrid KG-LLM architectures.

The generation of biomedical hypothesis has been explored with different paradigms, such as literature mining [2] and predictive modeling. A recurring theme is that generation methods can enumerate candidate links, but do not provide a universally accepted method for validation of candidates. Widely used approaches rely on co-occurrence patterns mined from the scientific literature. For example, paper [4] uses semantic similarity methods (e.g., Word2Vec-based representations) to predict protein-protein interactions. Such techniques scale well, but their output often lacks contextualization. More recent works investigate predictive modeling for scientific discovery, including genome-scale approaches and structured classifiers [8]. These methods may achieve strong performance but they lack evidence to support experts reasoning. In this work, the input hypotheses are derived from [2], a predictive model that generates candidate protein-gene interactions ranked by a confidence score, a numerical value reflecting the predicted likelihood of a biological interaction between two entities based on the model's learned associations.

In parallel, KGs shows how structured knowledge can be used to extract and show meaningful paths and text helping researchers to speed up the process of learning. For example Dimensions Knowledge Graph [12] provides a platform that link publications, citations, grants and patents to support the search and contextualization of biomedical entities and links. Another example, such CS-KG 2.0 and domain-specific biomedical KGs (e.g. KGen) [6,16] can offer structured knowledge to highlight connection between entities. These works expose key limitations: KGs can be incomplete and evolving, they are not capable to summarize concepts for human consumption without additional layers.

LLMs have been adopted for summarization and explanation in scientific discovery [7,21], though their outputs can be non-verifiable or affected by hallucinations [5]. These constraints motivate RAG-based architectures where LLMs operate in synergy with structured knowledge to reduce hallucinations and improve consistency.

Apart from retrieval, other approaches use graph structure to help reasoning. Reinforcement-learning approaches such as REx [13] adopt this idea by rewarding explanations that balance predictive utility with interpretability, using explanatory paths as optimization targets. Hybrid methods have been explored for hypothesis assessment, including LLM-as-a-judge setups where models score hypotheses against criteria such as novelty. The main limitation of judge only approaches us that the evaluation can inherit LLM biases. This emphasize the need of use them integrating structured knowledge, such as graph paths and linked publications [20].

There is a growing interest in defining evaluation metrics to assess the quality of a hypothesis. Prior research [15,17] proposes quantitative metrics for hypothesis assessment. However, existing solutions typically focus either on hypothesis generation without integrated evaluation support, or on isolated scoring and explanation components that are not embedded within a structured, expert-centered evaluation workflow. As a result, domain experts still lack an integrated framework that combines structured graph-based evidence, multi-criteria prioritization, and interpretable reasoning support.

This gap motivates the following research question: *How can a hybrid symbolic–subsymbolic system integrating KG and LLMs effectively support transparent and trustworthy evaluation of automatically generated biomedical hypotheses?*

3 Methodology

The methodology followed to answer the research question of this work is the Design Science Research (DSR), which proposes five main phases [11]: problem awareness, suggestion, development, evaluation and conclusion.

In the *problem awareness phase*, a systematic literature review was conducted to identify existing approaches to biomedical hypothesis generation and evaluation, highlighting the lack of integrated support for transparent and trustworthy assessment. In parallel, structured exploratory discussions were conducted with biomedical domain experts who regularly engage with automatically generated hypotheses. The aim of these interactions was to understand how experts currently evaluate hypotheses in practice, the types of contextual information they rely on and the limitations they encounter when navigating large sets of hypotheses.

In the *suggestion phase*, we proposed a new conceptual hybrid architecture (Sect. 5), which addresses key requirements emerged during the previous phase. The artifact was conceived as an evaluation support tool enabling users to search, inspect, and prioritize hypotheses through structured graph evidence, publication context, and grounded natural language explanations.

The *development phase* focused on implementing the proposed architecture as an interactive dashboard, integrating search, filtering, contextual panels, and LLM-supported explanations within a unified interface.

Finally, the *evaluation phase* assessed whether the proposed hybrid AI approach effectively supports transparent hypothesis evaluation. The artifact was tested through a real use case involving biomedical domain experts. Participants interacted with the system within their area of expertise and analyzed automatically generated hypotheses using the integrated graph-based evidence and LLM-supported explanations. The evaluation collected both qualitative and quantitative feedback, focusing on usability, perceived transparency, trustworthiness of individual components, and their contribution to assessing novelty, significance, and verifiability.

4 Scenario

This section introduces a representative scenario that illustrates a representative expert-driven biomedical hypothesis evaluation scenario.

A biomedical researcher is investigating potential therapeutic targets for a specific disease, focusing on molecular interactions involving proteins and genes. To accelerate the discovery process, the researcher consults a set of automatically generated hypotheses linking biological entities through predicted relationships. Faced with a large number of candidates, the researcher needs to quickly identify hypotheses relevant to their use case. Assessing whether a hypothesis is worth investigating traditionally requires consulting heterogeneous sources of evidence, understanding why a connection was proposed, and verifying whether an indirect biological pathway exists between the two entities. Figure 1 illustrates a simple possible manual workflow for biomedical hypothesis evaluation, representing the traditional approach followed by a scientist in the absence of automated tool support.

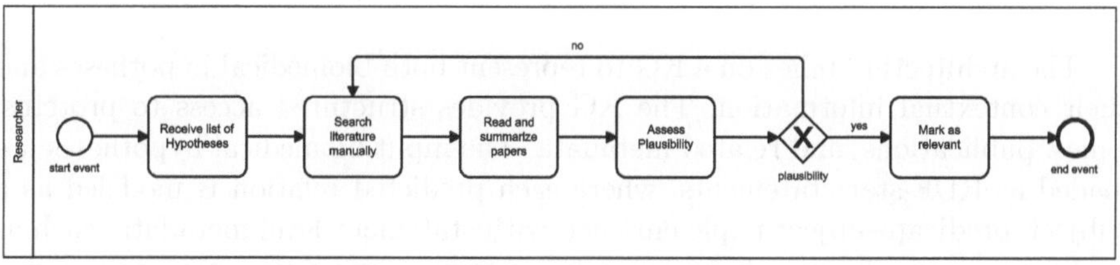

Fig. 1. An example of the biomedical hypothesis evaluation process.

Findings from the domain analysis led to a set of functional and non-functional requirements. The functional requirements capture the core capabilities the system must provide: Knowledge Graph contextualization (DR1), score transparency (DR2), evidence-grounded LLM explanations (DR3) and multi-source evidence integration (DR4). The non-functional requirements address system-level properties such as performance, usability, scalability, reliability, and maintainability.

5 The Hybrid AI Architecture

The Hybrid AI Architecture that we propose is designed to address the key requirements introduced in the previous section. Specifically, the KG backbone provides contextualization and structured exploration of evidence, and scoring mechanisms support transparent prioritization. The LLM component offers grounded, interpretative explanations that translate graph-derived evidence into biologically meaningful explanations for domain experts. The resulting architecture is reported in Fig. 2.

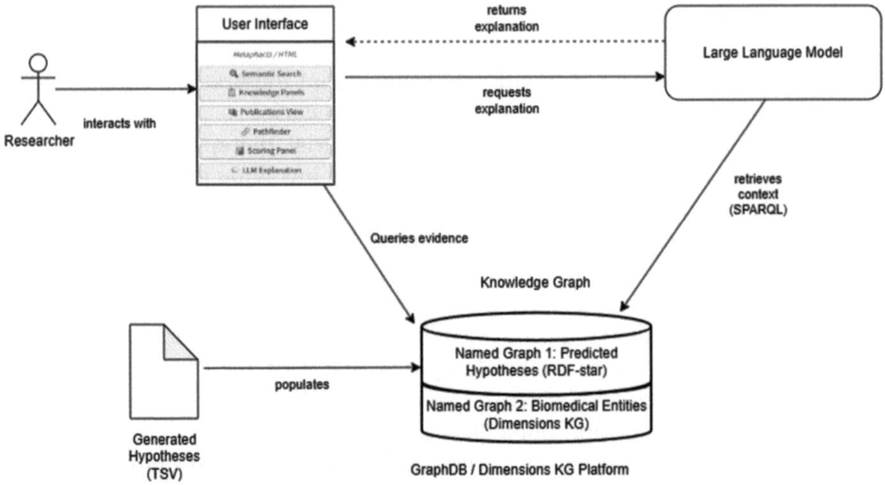

Fig. 2. Overview Hybrid AI Solution.

The architecture relies on a KG to represent both biomedical hypotheses and their contextual information. The KG provides structured access to proteins, genes, publications, and related metadata. The input biomedical hypotheses are loaded as RDF-star statements, where each predicted relation is modeled as a subject–predicate–object triple enriched with statement-level metadata, such as confidence score. From a Knowledge Engineering perspective, this design separates the hypothesis layer, stored as a named graph of RDF-star statements, from the background biomedical knowledge provided by the Dimensions KG, preserving traceability and enabling targeted querying.

The KG is accessed through SPARQL queries executed within the Dimensions KG environment. From an infrastructural perspective, the Dimensions platform relies on a GraphDB repository to store the triples. GraphDB acts as the triple store responsible for persisting entities, relations, publications, while the Dimensions App framework provides the application layer that exposes these data to end users through configurable components. A LLM is integrated as an explanation component responsible for generating humanreadable interpretations of hypotheses. The model operates in conjunction with the KG, retrieving contextual information such as entity descriptions, semantic paths, and publication summaries to generate explanations grounded in explicit graph-derived evidence. This retrieval-augmented interaction mitigates known limitations of language models, including hallucinations and lack of transparency.

6 Proof of Concept

This Section presents the proof of concept of the proposed Hybrid AI architecture. It is structured in two part. First, we described the development of the artifact. Second, we evaluate its effectiveness respect to the design requirements. It should be noted that the prototype was developed in collaboration with industry partners and implementation details are not publicly available.

6.1 Artifact Development

The proposed architecture has been implemented as a prototype within the Dimensions KG platform. The system uses GraphDB as the underlying repository responsible for storing and managing semantic triples of hypotheses. The Dimensions KG is a large-scale, externally maintained knowledge graph integrating publications, grants, patents, and clinical trials, and is used in this work as the underlying semantic infrastructure. It should be noted that the prototype was developed in collaboration with industry partners, and implementation details are not publicly available. However, the proposed architecture is based on widely adopted technologies (e.g., knowledge graphs, SPARQL querying, and LLM-based explanation components) and can be reproduced using alternative open datasets and tools. While results may vary depending on data coverage and quality, the overall design and interaction between components remain transferable across different settings.

The input of the system consists of automatically generated biomedical hypotheses provided in tabular (TSV) format. The alignment between the hypothesis dataset and the KG schema was facilitated by the shared use of OntoChem Identifiers (OCIDs) across both systems, a result of prior collaboration between the data providers. Before ingestion, identifiers for source and target were updated to the current version through a mapping process. The same was done with the name of relationships between source and target. The dataset comprises 1,524,046 automatically generated hypotheses involving 1,097 distinct biological entities (proteins and genes), organized into 711,568 unique entity pairs connected through 17 types of predicted biological relations. It was provided by an external industry partner and represents a subset of a larger collection of automatically generated hypotheses. A transformation pipeline implemented in Python converts each hypothesis into a RDF-star triple with associated metadata (e.g. confidence score). The use of RDF-star permits to associate the metadata directly with the relationships while remaining compatible with the Dimensions KG platform and GraphDB repository. Once transformed, hypotheses are integrated into the KG as a separate named-graph [10]. In the next part of the paragraph, we will detail the functionalities of the prototype, considering them as components.

The interface provides a Semantic Search component[1] for querying the KG through SPARQL patterns, returning hypotheses with prediction scores and evi-

[1] Metaphactory Semantic Search - https://help.metaphacts.com/resource/Help:SemanticSearchComponent.

dence indicators. Knowledge Panels[2] support entity disambiguation by displaying identifiers, synonyms and classifications, and aggregate literature references between entity pairs. The Publications component retrieves linked scientific literature and visualizes its temporal distribution, allowing users to assess whether a relationship is established or emerging.

Pathfinder discovers direct and indirect semantic paths between source and target entities in the KG. By exposing intermediate nodes and relations, it enables inspection of potential biological mechanisms and supports explainability[3].

Scoring mechanisms combine prediction confidence and literature-based metrics to support hypothesis prioritization. Scores are displayed alongside hypotheses to facilitate navigation of large candidate sets while remaining complementary to expert judgment.

Hypothesis evaluation produces multiple complementary outputs. The prediction confidence score, provided by the upstream generative model, is a numerical value between 0 and 1 indicating the likelihood of a biological interaction. The Mutual Information score quantifies the strength of association between two entities based on shared publications, while the Disruption Score is computed at the publication level to capture the impact of supporting evidence. In parallel, graph-based exploration through Pathfinder provides a visual representation of semantic paths connecting the source and target entities. Finally, the LLM generates a structured natural language explanation that synthesizes graph-derived evidence and concludes with an estimated probability score.

These outputs are designed to be complementary rather than conclusive, supporting expert judgment by providing multiple evidence perspectives instead of a single definitive evaluation.

From an implementation perspective, the LLM component is realised by integrating a GPT-4o model via the GraphDB extension (GPT Queries in GraphDB: https://graphdb.ontotext.com/documentation/11.0/gpt-queries.html). This involves using a predicate to invoke the model within SPARQL queries. These queries construct prompts based on graph-derived data, including entity descriptions, relation labels, and relevant publication abstracts. The LLM then generates step-by-step biological explanations and classifies the predicted relationship type. Grounding the explanations in explicit KG evidence mitigates the risk of hallucinations and improves transparency, thus partially compensating for the limited configuration imposed by the connector.

The user interface integrates search, contextual panels, path exploration and explanations within a unified dashboard. Results are presented in tabular form with filtering and grouping controls to support transparent and user-driven evaluation.

Figure 3 illustrates the evaluation flow supported by the prototype.

---

[2] Metaphactory Knowledge panel - https://help.metaphacts.com/resource/Help:KnowledgePanel.

[3] Metaphactory Pathfinding - https://help.metaphacts.com/resource/Help:Pathfinder.

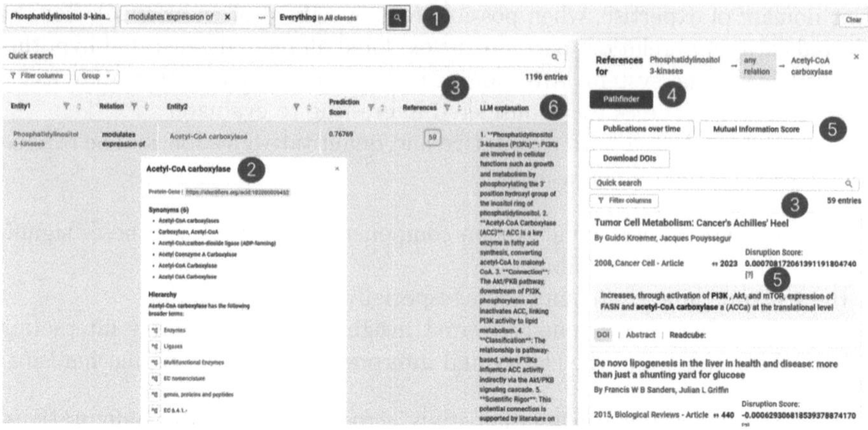

Fig. 3. Overview of the prototype.

Starting from the hypothesis search (1), the user accesses the entity Knowledge Panel to verify identifiers, synonyms and hierarchical classifications (2). Co-occurrence references and linked publications are then inspected to assess literature support (3). The Pathfinder enables exploration of graph paths between the two entities (4). Scoring indicators, including Mutual Information, Disruption scores and publications over time support hypothesis prioritization (5). Finally, the LLM-generated explanation synthesizes graph-derived evidence into a structured summary (6).

For instance, given the hypothesis *Phosphatidylinositol 3-kinases (PI3K) modulates expression of Acetyl-CoA carboxylase (ACC)* (confidence: 0.77, 59 supporting publications), the system retrieves semantic paths via the AKT/PKB pathway, identifies co-occurring publications, and generates an LLM explanation classifying the relationship as pathway-based with a high-potential probability score. This example highlights how heterogeneous evidence is integrated to support expert-driven hypothesis evaluation.

6.2 Artifact Evaluation

To evaluate the prototype, we conducted guided asynchronous user study involving 9 participants with a biomedical background and a specific interest in hypothesis evaluation. Participants were recruited based on explicit inclusion criteria: background in biology or related life sciences, experience in biomedical research or hypothesis evaluation workflows, and ability to interpret biological entities such as genes, proteins, and pathways. Participants with exclusively technical or computer science backgrounds and no domain knowledge in biology were excluded. The study was conducted asynchronously: participants received via email credentials to access the prototype, written instructions describing the evaluation task and a link to the evaluation questionnaire. Each participant was granted access to the prototype and assigned with a research question around

their domain of expertise, when possible (e.g. specific protein or gene). For the selected entity and relation, participants explored all related generated hypotheses available in the system. After an initial exploration phase, they were asked to select five hypotheses they considered interesting to evaluate.

The study collected both qualitative and quantitative feedback. The evaluation focused on these main aspects:

- the usefulness of individual system components assessing hypotheses significance, novelty and verifiability.
- the trustworthiness of components, especially LLM explanation.
- user confidence in machine-generated insights before and after interacting with the system, and the clarity and interpretability of scoring mechanisms.

While a fully systematic ablation study across different LLM configurations, knowledge graphs, and data sources is beyond the scope of this proof-of-concept, the user study provides a component-level evaluation that offers initial insights into the contribution of individual system elements.

Results indicate that publications were considered the most helpful component (41.7%), following by the LLM explanations. A relevant proportion of participants also highlighted the combined use of LLM explanations and publications. The most trustworthy component was the combination of publications and LLM explanations (45.5%). These results confirm the relevance of the functional requirements defined in the awareness phase. However, score transparency (DR2) proved less impactful than expected, as participants found quantitative metrics difficult to interpret without additional guidance or too small to be considered. Overall, the system was perceived as a useful exploratory support tool, but not yet sufficient to autonomously support hypothesis validation.

7 Discussion and Limitation

The proposed hybrid AI approach demonstrated that integrating KGs and LLMs is a viable approach to support the exploration and evaluation of automatically generated biomedical hypotheses. However, several limitations must be considered.

First, the implementation relies on a single LLM model integrated through the GraphDB connector. Although grounding responses in Knowledge Graph evidence helps reduce hallucinations, variations in model capabilities may affect system performance. Second, the system depends on the completeness and quality of the underlying knowledge base; missing entities or inconsistent identifiers may limit the reliability of the evaluation. Third, the current scoring mechanisms are constrained by the use of SPARQL queries, which limits the expressiveness and flexibility of evaluation metrics.

These limitations open several directions for future work. Scoring mechanisms could be extended with multidimensional criteria to better capture novelty and scientific impact. KG coverage could be expanded and further leveraged

to explain the reasoning of upstream hypothesis generation models. Additionally, future work should explore alternative LLMs to assess the impact of model selection on explanation quality and trustworthiness. Finally, further strategies may include fine-tuning LLMs on domain-specific biomedical data to improve the accuracy and specificity of generated explanations.

8 Conclusion

In this paper, we investigated how a hybrid AI architecture integrating Knowledge Graphs (KGs) and Large Language Models (LLMs) can support transparent and trustworthy evaluation of automatically generated biomedical hypotheses. By combining structured knowledge representation based on the KGs with grounded natural language explanations, the proposed architecture enables contextualization, multi-criteria prioritization, and interpretative support within an expert-centered evaluation workflow.

Following the Design Science Research methodology, we designed, developed, and evaluated a prototype aimed at supporting expert-driven hypothesis assessment. The evaluation shows that the system supports contextual exploration. However, it does not provide enough information to validate or reject hypotheses. The constraints are the dependence on the data completeness and coverage. The results support the combination of KGs and LLMs as a promising direction for augmenting biomedical hypotheses evaluation.

References

1. Akujuobi, U., Kumari, P., Choi, J., et al.: Link prediction for hypothesis generation: an active curriculum learning infused temporal graph-based approach. Artif. Intell. Rev. **57**, 244 (2024). https://doi.org/10.1007/s10462-024-10885-1
2. Besold, T.R., et al.: Literature-based hypothesis generation: predicting the evolution of scientific literature to support scientists. In: AI4X 2025 International Conference (2025)
3. Buchmann, R., et al.: Large language models: expectations for semantics-driven systems engineering. Data Knowl. Eng. **152**, 102324 (2024). https://doi.org/10.1016/j.datak.2024.102324
4. Cox, S., et al.: A semantic similarity based methodology for predicting protein-protein interactions. J. Biomed. Inform. (2020). https://doi.org/10.1016/j.jbi.2020.103579
5. Daoudi, M.: Ethical limits and suggestions for improving the use of AI in scientific research. Discov. Educ. (2025). https://doi.org/10.1007/s44217-025-00696-z
6. Dessí, D., Osborne, F., Buscaldi, D., Reforgiato Recupero, D., Motta, E.: Cs-kg 2.0: a large-scale knowledge graph of computer science. Sci. Data (2025). https://doi.org/10.1038/s41597-025-05200-8
7. Feng, Y., Wang, J., He, R., Zhou, L., Li, Y.: A retrieval-augmented knowledge mining method with deep thinking LLMs for biomedical research. GigaScience (2025). https://doi.org/10.1093/gigascience/giaf109

8. Fourquet, O., Krejca, M.S., Doerr, C., Schwikowski, B.: Towards the genome-scale discovery of bivariate monotonic classifiers. BMC Bioinform. **26**, 228 (2025). https://doi.org/10.1186/s12859-025-06253-7
9. d'Avila Garcez, A., Lamb, L.C.: Neurosymbolic AI: the 3rd wave. Artif. Intell. Rev. **56**(11), 12387–12406 (2023)
10. Hartig, O.: Foundations of rdf* and sparql*âĂŕ: (an alternative approach to statement-level metadata in rdf). In: Proceedings of the 11th Alberto Mendelzon International Workshop on Foundations of Data Management and the Web 2017âĂŕ: CEUR Workshop Proceedings, vol. 1912, Juan Reutter, Divesh Srivastava (2017)
11. Helms, R., Giovacchini, E., Teigland, R., Kohler, T.: A design research approach to developing user innovation workshops in second life. J. Virtual Worlds Res. **3** (2010). https://doi.org/10.4101/jvwr.v3i1.819
12. Hook, D.W., Porter, S.J., Herzog, C.: Dimensions: building context for search and evaluation. Front. Res. Metrics Anal. **3**, 23 (2018). https://doi.org/10.3389/frma.2018.00023
13. Nunes, S., Badreddine, S., Pesquita, C.: Rewarding explainability in drug repurposing with knowledge graphs. arXiv preprint (2024). https://github.com/liseda-lab/REx
14. Pio-Lopez, L., Levin, M.: Universal multilayer network embedding reveals a causal link between gaba neurotransmitter and cancer. BMC Bioinform. **26**, 149 (2025). https://doi.org/10.1186/s12859-025-06158-5
15. Preiss, J.: A hybrid approach to literature-based discovery: combining traditional methods with LLMs. Appl. Sci. (2025). https://doi.org/10.3390/app15168785
16. Rossanez, A., et al.: Kgen: a knowledge graph generator from biomedical scientific literature. BMC Med. Inform. Decis. Mak. (2020). https://doi.org/10.1186/s12911-020-01341-5
17. Sikirzhytskaya, A., Tyagin, I., Sutton, S.S., Wyatt, M.D., Safro, I., Shtutman, M.: Ai-based mining of biomedical literature: Applications for drug repurposing for the treatment of dementia. Artif. Intell. Med. (2025). https://doi.org/10.1016/j.artmed.2025.103218
18. Soman, K.: Biomedical knowledge graph-optimized prompt generation for large language models. arXiv preprint (2024)
19. Zamprogno, G., Tiddi, I., Verheij, B.: Hypothesis updating by combining knowledge graphs and argumentation. In: Proceedings of the 3rd International Conference on Hybrid Human-Artificial Intelligence. Frontiers in Artificial Intelligence and Applications, vol. 386, pp. 441–448. IOS Press (2024). https://doi.org/10.3233/FAIA240219
20. Zhu, L., Wang, X., Wang, X.: Judgelm: fine-tuned large language models are scalable judges. arXiv preprint arXiv:2310.17631 (2023)
21. Zimmermann, Y., et al.: 32 examples of LLM applications in materials science and chemistry. Mach. Learn. Sci. Technol. (2025). https://doi.org/10.1088/2632-2153/ae011a

Agentic Consensus for Evidence-Grounded Information Extraction

Adam Aron Rynkiewicz[1,2(✉)], Paulina Poniatowska-Rynkiewicz[1,3], Raul Palma[1], and Piotr Formanowicz[2]

[1] Data Analytics and Semantics Department, Poznan Supercomputing and Networking Center, Jana Pawla II 10, 61-139 Poznan, Poland
[2] Institute of Computing Science, Poznan University of Technology, Piotrowo 2, 60-965 Poznan, Poland
arynkiewicz@man.poznan.pl
[3] Department of Plant Genomics, Institute of Bioorganic Chemistry PAS, Noskowskiego 12/14, 61-704 Poznan, Poland

Abstract. Constructing Petri net models from biomedical literature is labor-intensive. We extend `Watson`, a semi-automatic platform, by introducing *Iterative Information Extraction* (IIE) and an *Extractor-Critic-Consensus* (ECC) architecture. IIE treats documents as persistent states to maintain context, while ECC uses a multi-agent "council of judges" to verify extractions. Evaluating on 100 PubMed articles, we show that while these methods reduce total yield, they significantly improve the reliability and traceability of candidate relations for expert-in-the-loop curation.

Keywords: Petri nets · iterative information extraction · agentic self-correction

1 Introduction

Biomedical knowledge is largely trapped in unstructured text. Petri nets (PNs) offer a systems-level formalism to represent these processes with a structure of bipartite graphs where *places* (P) represent entities and *transitions* (T) represent interactions [6]. Despite their utility, the manual extraction of PN components from literature is the primary bottleneck in systems biology.

Our previous work, `Watson` [11][1], automated this by chunking text and extracting relations. However, it suffered from context fragmentation and high false-positive rates. This paper proposes two procedural shifts: (1) **IIE**, which replaces chunking with a stateful annotation loop, and (2) **ECC**, which applies deliberative multi-agent verification to ensure every transition is grounded in explicit textual evidence.

[1] The name "Watson" relates to software "Holmes" for PN modeling developed by our lab and does not have any connection to IBM products.

R. Posenato and I. Vanderfeesten (Eds.): CAiSE 2026 Workshops, LNBIP 586, pp. 371–376, 2026.
https://doi.org/10.1007/978-3-032-28160-9_33

2 Related Work

Evidence-Grounded IE: Attaching textual spans to model predictions improves reliability. LLMs act as effective annotators when tasked with identifying evidence, with reasoning-oriented models outperforming standard instruction-tuned variants [3,5].

Iterative Verification: Reasoning loops, such as SELF - REFINE [9], CRITIC [4] and REFLEXION [12], employ feedback cycles where a model evaluates its own predictions and improves them over successive iterations.

Complementary work investigates multi-agent reasoning, where specialised agents generate diverse interpretations, debate their validity, and converge on a consensus. Frameworks such as MAD [8] and MADISSE [7] employ this approach, which enhances robustness and mitigates systematic biases.

3 Methods

We define a biological relation as a Petri Net fragment $R = (I, t, O, E)$, where I is a set of input places (substrates), t is the transition (interaction type), O is a set of output places (products), and E is the evidence span.

3.1 Iterative Information Extraction

To solve context fragmentation, IIE treats the full document as a persistent state. Instead of one-pass extraction, the system follows a loop:

1. **Propose:** The extractor reads the document and proposes exactly *one* relation R and its supporting evidence span E.
2. **Annotate:** The span E is wrapped in `<extracted>` tags within the document text.
3. **Reiterate:** The modified document is fed back to the model, while the model's context is reset. The visible tags signal the model to find *new* interactions, preventing duplicates.

3.2 Extractor-Critic-Consensus (ECC)

ECC adds a verification layer to the IIE loop. Each proposed (R, E) pair is evaluated by n independent "judge" models.

- **Majority Accept:** If majority of judges approve, the document state is updated.
- **Reject/Refine:** If rejected, the extractor receives critiques and attempts one revision. If it fails again, the iteration is discarded.

Each judge is implemented as an independent instance of the same base model with the same system prompt and no shared context. Independence arises from stochastic decoding.

ECC increases inference cost due to additional judge evaluations and potential revision cycles. In the reported experiments, judges were distributed across separate GPU devices and requests were in parallel scheduled in a round-robin manner to reduce wall-clock latency. Nevertheless, ECC intrinsically increases total compute consumption.

3.3 Evaluation Protocol

We first assessed the performance of the models using the HDL corpus underlying the established PN model [2], consisting of 19 reference publications. Both `Kimi-K2.5` [13] and `DeepSeek-V3.2-Speciale` [1] were applied to this corpus, and we manually evaluated the extracted relations against the reference pathway representation.

For each reference relation, the five most similar extracted relations were selected and assessed for agreement, taking into account the biological plausibility of the interaction as well as the correctness of identified substrates and products. This evaluation yielded comparable precision estimates of 48% for `DeepSeek-V3.2-Speciale` and 50% for `Kimi-K2.5`.

Given their similar performance, both models were retained as independent pseudo-gold standards. These were subsequently used to generate reference relation sets from a larger sample of 100 PubMed articles on HDL metabolism.

We tested two scenarios: *Scenario 1* (global set comparison) and *Scenario 2* (retrieval-oriented, evaluating the top-5 candidates per reference relation to simulate expert curation). All agreement judgments in both scenarios were produced by `gpt-oss-120b` [10] acting as the evaluation judge.

4 Results

Tables 1 and 2 summarize the performance.

Table 1. Mean Agreement Scores (95% CI) across 100 documents.

	Scenario 1 (Global)		Scenario 2 (Top-5)	
Model/Procedure	vs Kimi PGS	vs DS PGS	vs Kimi PGS	vs DS PGS
IIE (Single Model)	45.08 (±4.3)	42.53 (±4.7)	49.26 (±1.8)	48.81 (±2.2)
ECC (3 Judges)	**53.00** (±4.4)	46.34 (±4.8)	57.62 (±1.6)	54.65 (±2.1)
ECC (7 Judges)	52.98 (±4.0)	46.61 (±4.7)	59.89 (±1.5)	55.81 (±2.0)
`cannary-v2` (Baseline)	51.71 (±4.5)	**49.56** (±4.6)	**62.87** (±1.2)	**58.27** (±1.7)

The domain-specialized `cannary-reasoning-v2` model achieves strong agreement despite being substantially smaller than large general-purpose models and not relying on RL-based post-training. In the global comparison (Scenario 1), its mean scores are comparable to the proposed procedures, while in the retrieval-oriented setting (Scenario 2) it attains the highest mean agreement under both references. These results suggest that task- and domain-specific supervision can partially offset scale advantages for structured biomedical relation extraction. Although mean differences are consistent, overlapping confidence intervals in Scenario 1 indicate that not all improvements are statistically significant, with the clearest gains observed in Scenario 2.

Across all configurations, ECC surpasses single-model IIE. Under the `Kimi-K2.5` reference, ECC with three judges achieves the strongest Scenario 1 agreement among the proposed methods, while in Scenario 2 performance improves with the number of judges, with the seven-judge council performing best. This suggests that independent verification primarily removes weakly supported candidates and stabilizes acceptance decisions.

The number of judges yields a clearer monotonic improvement in Scenario 2 than in Scenario 1. Because Scenario 2 evaluates a small shortlist of candidates per reference relation, it better reflects the interactive curation pattern in `Watson`, indicating that ECC mainly improves the reliability of inspected candidates rather than global coverage.

Both IIE and ECC reduce output volume relative to baseline extractors, reflecting a shift from high-recall enumeration to precision-oriented acceptance.

Table 2. Extraction yield on the 100-document benchmark: total number of distinct relations produced by each system under the respective extraction procedure. The table highlights the contrast between conservative, verification-oriented pipelines (IIE/ECC) and high-recall extraction (**`cannary-reasoning-v2`**).

Model	Number of retrieved relations
IIE	1295
DeepSeek-V3.2-Speciale	785
Kimi-K2.5	1146
ECC - 1 judge	1753
ECC - 3 judges	1862
ECC - 5 judges	1936
ECC - 7 judges	2081
cannary-reasoning-v2	5943

Compared to **`cannary-reasoning-v2`**, the largest ECC configuration produces roughly one third of the relations (Table 2). This difference is consistent with the intent of IIE/ECC: rather than producing maximal candidate sets, the redesigned pipelines filter aggressively to retain relations with clearer textual support and explicit evidence attribution, thereby reducing downstream curation load.

5 Conclusions

This paper revisits semi-automatic Petri net construction from biomedical literature by addressing limitations of the original `Watson` pipeline through procedural redesign. The proposed approach targets three bottlenecks: loss of global context due to segmentation, over-generation of unsupported relations, and limited traceability between predictions and evidence. Importantly, the proposed methods are model-agnostic and do not rely on any specific underlying modeling paradigm, making them applicable across a wide range of extraction and structured modeling approaches.

IIE reformulates extraction as a monotonic annotation process over the full document, ensuring that each accepted relation is explicitly grounded in a visible evidence span. This mitigates chunking artifacts and promotes conservative, evidence-based outputs. Building on this, ECC introduces verification through independent model judgments, improving reliability across both evaluation scenarios, with the strongest gains in the retrieval-oriented setting. Increasing the number of judges further enhances shortlist quality, at the cost of higher computational demand.

Relation yield analysis shows that IIE/ECC shift the system toward a precision-oriented regime, producing fewer but better-supported and more traceable candidates. In expert-in-the-loop settings, this trade-off can reduce overall curation effort despite lower recall.

Overall, the results demonstrate that procedural changes - persistent document state, integrated evidence attribution, and multi-model verification - can substantially improve the usability of text-to-PN extraction pipelines. At the same time, disagreement between pseudo gold standards highlights limitations of current evaluation practices.

Future work will explore evaluation protocols aligned with incremental model-building workflows, investigate heterogeneous and prompt-diversified judge ensembles, and assess generalization beyond the biomedical domain on broader extraction and structured modeling tasks.

Acknowledgments. During the preparation of this work the authors used Writefull for Overleaf in order to improve language and stylistics of the manuscript. After using this tool, the authors reviewed and edited the content as needed and takes full responsibility for the content of the publication.

This work was supported by FAIR2Adapt (grant agreement No. 101188256) and SAGE (grant agreement No. 101195471). This work was partially supported by statutory funds of Poznan University of Technology.

We gratefully acknowledge Poznan Supercomputing and Networking Center for providing computing and hosting GPU capabilities.

Disclosure of Interests. The authors have no competing interests to declare that are relevant to the content of this article.

References

1. DeepSeek-AI: Deepseek-v3.2: pushing the frontier of open large language models (2025)
2. Formanowicz, D., Radom, M., Rybarczyk, A., Tanaś, K., Formanowicz, P.: Control of cholesterol metabolism using a systems approach. Biology **11**(3), 430 (2022)
3. Gero, Z., et al.: Self-verification improves few-shot clinical information extraction (2023). https://arxiv.org/abs/2306.00024
4. Gou, Z., et al.: Critic: large language models can self-correct with tool-interactive critiquing (2024). https://arxiv.org/abs/2305.11738
5. Kasner, Z., et al.: LLMs as span annotators: a comparative study of LLMs and humans (2026). https://arxiv.org/abs/2504.08697
6. Koch, I., Reisig, W., Schreiber, F. (eds.): Modeling in systems biology. The Petri Net Approach. Springer, London, England (Oct (2010)
7. Koupaee, M., et al.: Faithful, unfaithful or ambiguous? multi-agent debate with initial stance for summary evaluation (2025). https://arxiv.org/abs/2502.08514
8. Liang, T., et al.: Encouraging divergent thinking in large language models through multi-agent debate (2024). https://arxiv.org/abs/2305.19118
9. Madaan, A., et al.: Self-refine: iterative refinement with self-feedback (2023). https://arxiv.org/abs/2303.17651
10. OpenAI: GPT-OSS-120b & GPT-OSS-20b model card (2025). https://arxiv.org/abs/2508.10925
11. Rynkiewicz, A.A., Poniatowska-Rynkiewicz, P., Palma, R., Formanowicz, P.: Watson: accelerating biomedical petri net construction through literature mining (2026)
12. Shinn, N., Cassano, F., Berman, E., Gopinath, A., Narasimhan, K., Yao, S.: Reflexion: language agents with verbal reinforcement learning (2023). https://arxiv.org/abs/2303.11366
13. Team, K.: Kimi k2.5: visual agentic intelligence (2026). https://arxiv.org/abs/2602.02276

Author Index

R. Posenato and I. Vanderfeesten (Eds.): CAiSE 2026 Workshops, LNBIP 586, pp. 377–378, 2026.
https://doi.org/10.1007/978-3-032-28160-9

MIX
Papier aus verantwortungsvollen Quellen
Paper from responsible sources
FSC® C105338

If you have any concerns about our products,
you can contact us on
ProductSafety@springernature.com

In case Publisher is established outside the EU,
the EU authorized representative is:
Springer Nature Customer Service Center GmbH
Europaplatz 3, 69115 Heidelberg, Germany

Printed by Libri Plureos GmbH
in Hamburg, Germany

Lecture Notes in Business Information Processing 586

Series Editors

Wil van der Aalst, *RWTH Aachen University, Aachen, Germany*
Sudha Ram, *University of Arizona, Tucson, USA*
Michael Rosemann, *Queensland University of Technology, Brisbane, Australia*
Clemens Szyperski, *Oracle Cloud, Austin, TX, USA*
Giancarlo Guizzardi, *University of Twente, Enschede, The Netherlands*

LNBIP reports state-of-the-art results in areas related to business information systems and industrial application software development – timely, at a high level, and in both printed and electronic form.

The type of material published includes

- Proceedings (published in time for the respective event)
- Postproceedings (consisting of thoroughly revised and/or extended final papers)
- Other edited monographs (such as, for example, project reports or invited volumes)
- Tutorials (coherently integrated collections of lectures given at advanced courses, seminars, schools, etc.)
- Award-winning or exceptional theses

LNBIP is abstracted/indexed in DBLP, EI and Scopus. LNBIP volumes are also submitted for the inclusion in ISI Proceedings.